A History
of the Navajos

The publication of this book was made possible by
generous support from the Brown Foundation.

A History of the Navajos

The Reservation Years

Garrick Bailey
and Roberta Glenn Bailey

SCHOOL OF AMERICAN RESEARCH PRESS : SANTA FE, NEW MEXICO

SCHOOL OF AMERICAN RESEARCH PRESS
Post Office Box 2188
Santa Fe, New Mexico 87504
505 984-0741

DIRECTOR OF PUBLICATIONS: Jane Kepp
EDITOR: Tom Ireland
DESIGNER: Deborah Flynn
TYPOGRAPHER: Casa Sin Nombre
PRINTER:Bookcrafters

DISTRIBUTED BY UNIVERSITY OF WASHINGTON PRESS

Library of Congress Cataloging in Publication Data

Bailey, Garrick Alan.
  A history of the Navajos.

  Bibliography: p.
  Includes index.
  1. Navajo Tribe—History. 2. Navajo Tribe—Social life and customs. 3. Indians of
North America—Social life and customs. 4. Indians of North America—Government
relations. I. Bailey, Robert Glenn. II. Title.
E99.N3B177   1986   973'.0497   86-6641
ISBN 0-933452-14-4

Cover: Juanita (wife of Manuelito) and Governor Arny, 1874. Courtesy of the Smithsonian Institution.

Contents

List of Illustrations

List of Tables

List of Photographs

Preface

In the summer of 1977, I was contacted by an old friend at New Mexico State University, which had a contract from the Bureau of Indian Affairs to excavate historic sites in connection with the Navajo Indian Irrigation Project (NIIP) south of Farmington, New Mexico. Many of the sites scheduled for excavation were Navajo camps, and research was needed on the history of Navajo occupation in that area to help place the sites in their historical context.

At the time, I had little research interest in the Navajos. As a native of Oklahoma, my primary interest was in the Oklahoma tribes and in urban Indians; most of my work had been with the Osages and other Central Siouan tribes. My only contact with or knowledge of the Navajos came from having been a research assistant one year to David Aberle, a leading scholar on the Navajos; from having roomed with two Navajo students for a year and a half at the University of Oklahoma; and from having taken several vacation trips across the Navajo reservation. I was not what one would call a Navajo specialist, but I was an ethnohistorian, and that was what New Mexico State University wanted to hire.

My wife, Roberta's, knowledge of the Navajos was about as sketchy as mine. As a graduate student in history, she had written her thesis on the Canadian Blackfeet, a subject that reflected her broader interest in the history of the British Empire. She had grown up in Arizona, however, and so in a general sense was more familiar with the region than I.

My motive for accepting New Mexico State's offer of a one-month position as consultant ethnohistorian was partly that my research on the Osages was coming to a close; most of my original, elderly informants had died, and the data left to collect were extremely limited. Still, I think the real reason was simply that Oklahoma is unbearably hot in August, and anyone with the opportunity heads for the high country.

After we arrived in Farmington, Roberta volunteered to undertake the research into historical materials for the region, while I concentrated on fieldwork with local Navajos. Roberta was especially interested in a collection of old San Juan County newspapers at the San Juan campus of NMSU. I began the field work with some anxiety, not knowing exactly what I was going to do; and ended it the same way, feeling unsure about what I actually had done. The Navajos were even more of a mystery than they had seemed when we first arrived.

Much of our time during the fall of 1977 and spring of 1978 was devoted to reviewing the Navajo literature and preparing a written report (Bailey and Bailey 1980). Though studying the literature did not restore our confidence, it did relieve some of our anxiety because, as Aberle (1963:1) once noted, there is a "fuzzy" quality to Navajo culture as it has been recorded.

In the summer of 1978, we returned to Farmington and the Navajo Indian Irrigation Project, this time both employed as consultant ethnohistorians by the Navajo Nation Cultural Resource Management Program, which had received the contract to perform the next phase of excavation of historic sites. Roberta went back to her archival work, while I resumed my fieldwork.

It soon became obvious that we needed a well-defined research strategy. We had already written one report for New Mexico State University, covering, at least superficially, the more readily obtainable data on Navajo occupation of the region. With this preliminary report finished, we had to decide what questions to research in depth in order to write a report that did not merely repeat what we had already said. Moreover, our work threatened to become more difficult for administrative reasons. The Navajo Indian Irrigation Project was being developed in blocks of approximately ten thousand acres each. Our work during the summers of 1977 and 1978 covered blocks 2 and 3, and nine additional blocks remained to be studied. Archaeological contracts were being awarded competitively on a block-by-block basis, and it could not be predicted which institution, tribal agency, or private company might receive the contract for each block. If the ethnohistoric research remained tied to the archaeological contracts, there could be as many as eleven different ethnohistoric reports either repeating one another or focusing so narrowly on separate blocks as to have little cultural-historical value.

The Bureau of Indian Affairs and the consultant National Park Service decided that the most logical and economically efficient solution to this problem was to separate the ethnohistoric research from the archaeological and to award a single contract for all the ethnohistoric research required for the project. The ethnohistorians would thus be able to look at a relatively large area: virtually all of the northern portion of the Chaco Plateau. In January 1979, this separate ethnohistoric research contract was awarded to the University of Tulsa, with Roberta and me serving as co-principal investigators.

With this change in contracting, research would not be limited to the blocks per se, but could instead be focused on the extended families who had historically occupied portions of these blocks. By defining the ethnographic study area in terms of family use areas, its boundaries were expanded to encompass almost the entire northern portion of the Chaco Plateau. For the ethnohistoric research, even these boundaries need not apply. Because there has been significant regional variability in Navajo cultural change, historical materials would be collected not only for the plateau but also for other Navajo regions. Only by understanding the range of regional variations in culture change could the unique character of the northern Chaco Plateau be defined.

The new contract also made it possible to better integrate ethnographic field research and ethnohistoric findings. There were to be eleven months of ethnographic fieldwork spread over three seasons: the summer of 1979, the summer and fall of 1980, and the summer of 1981. When fieldwork conducted in the summers of 1977 and 1978 is included, the total comes to fourteen months, scattered over a period of forty-eight months. This approach proved ideal for the development of rapport with the local Navajos, because our time of acquaintance was lengthened. Between field seasons I tried to stay in contact with both of my interpreters and with some of the other Navajos with whom I worked.

Meanwhile, Roberta was involved in full-time research on primary historical materials. By the end of the summer of 1978, she had exhausted most of the collections of local newspapers and began work on government archival materials and other, more scattered primary sources. During the relatively long intervals between periods of field work, we had time to integrate and analyze the ethnographic and ethnohistoric materials and to define gaps in our data and formulate questions which we could focus upon during the next field season. The required contract report was finished in the summer of 1982 (Bailey and Bailey 1982).

Our final report for the Bureau of Indian Affairs focused heavily upon Navajo occupation of the northern Chaco Plateau; it drew on only a small portion of the comparative data collected for other Navajo regions. In the course of our research, we came to realize that Navajo culture change in general had never been adequately examined. Anthropologists had, at best, only skimmed the surface of the vast store of cultural-historical materials available for study. We decided that a deeper and more detailed analysis of these materials was critical to our understanding and interpretation of ethnographic data. During the academic year 1982–83, I was able to combine a sabbatical leave from the University of Tulsa with a position as a Weatherhead resident scholar at the School of American Research in Santa Fe, New Mexico. The first draft of this book was written at that time.

Acknowledgements

Writing a book is no simple task, but it is a joy to remember the many people who have helped, challenged, and inspired us along the way. The basic research for the book was conducted under contract to the Bureau of Indian Affairs, monitored by the National Park Service. Later, with a 1982–83 Weatherhead resident scholar fellowship, the School of American Research made the writing possible.

The year in Santa Fe was unforgettable. To the staff of the School we say thank you, again and again. Special thanks go to Doug Schwartz, Inge Powers, Jeton Brown, Cecile Stein, Betty Kingman, and Joe Sweeney and his sons. To the other scholars that year—Bob Canfield, Flora Clancy, Christine Rudicoff, and Scott Whiteford—thanks for the freewheeling discussions, which clarified ideas and suggested new paths to be followed.

Much of the book came from conversations with Navajos of the Fruitland, Burnham, and Huerfano chapters, and we thank them for their courtesy and patience. The Hemstreet family was particularly helpful and generous. Elouise Hemstreet served as our interpreter during the summers of 1977, 1978, and 1979, and Minnie Hemstreet Howard during the summer and fall of 1980. Tom Harwood recounted the past and explained the present with extraordinary insight and humor, for which we will be forever grateful. Fannie Scott transcribed Navajo terms into written Navajo.

Thanks are due to Ted Birkedal, Barbara Holmes, Fran Levine, and the late George West of the National Park Service, who monitored the original research. The cooperation of Bureau of Indian Affairs staff members in the Farmington, Shiprock, Window Rock, and Crownpoint offices—particularly Albert Keller and Bill Smith—is also gratefully acknowledged.

Many traders shared their considerable knowledge of Navajo history with us. We give particular thanks to Sam Drolet and the late Jo Drolet of Carson Trading Post for welcoming us as friends into their home on countless occasions and offering their insights into Navajo trade. Sherill Brimhall loaned family photographs and helped locate the sites of early trading posts. Stewart Hatch of Hatch Brothers Trading Post shed considerable light on the economic history of the reservation. John and Jackie Foutz (The 550 Store) outlined the complex workings of a modern Indian store, and Jack Beasley (Beasley-Manning) explained pawn operations. Mr. Ira Hatch and the late Mrs. Hatch spoke from years of experience at Simpson's and other posts. Walter Scribner, who had worked at Carson, Huerfano, Oljeto, and the Indian Room in Farmington, clarified many points. Thanks also to Ken Washburn, Mrs. Kenneth Wynn, Barbara and Larry Busey (Fruitland Trading Company), and Tom Howard (Navajo Curio) for their assistance.

Andrew Hunter Whiteford and Fred Eggan read and commented on portions of the first draft. Dave Brugge of the National Park Service generously read the manuscript and made many helpful comments. We would also like to thank Stan Bussey, Bill Naylor, David Kirkpatrick, Richard Goddard, C. Timothy McKeown, and Larry Vogler.

Scott Sandlin, formerly of the *Farmington Daily Times*, was never too busy to help us understand the political and economic history of the San Juan region. We also wish to thank the *Times* for the use of their archives, Drew Harrington and the staff of the Farmington Public Library, and the Farmington Historical Museum.

For their help in the research, we thank Laura Holt of the Laboratory of Anthropology; Robert Delaney, director of the Center of Southwest Studies; Richard Gobble, library director at Fort Lewis College; Donald Worcester of Texas Christian University; Steve Nobles of the University of Tulsa library; and David Farmer, former director of special collections at the University of Tulsa. Dolores Glass and Ella Suttle performed the difficult task of transcribing tapes.

Jane Kepp and Tom Ireland of the School of American Research have been unfailingly professional, supportive, and patient, and we acknowledge our debt to them for helping transform a manuscript into a book. Thanks also to Anne Peacocke, who did the typing, and Georgia Bayliss, who drew illustrations.

It is our hope that the book does justice to the knowledge and generosity of these people. Any mistakes in form or content are the responsibility of the authors.

A History
of the Navajos

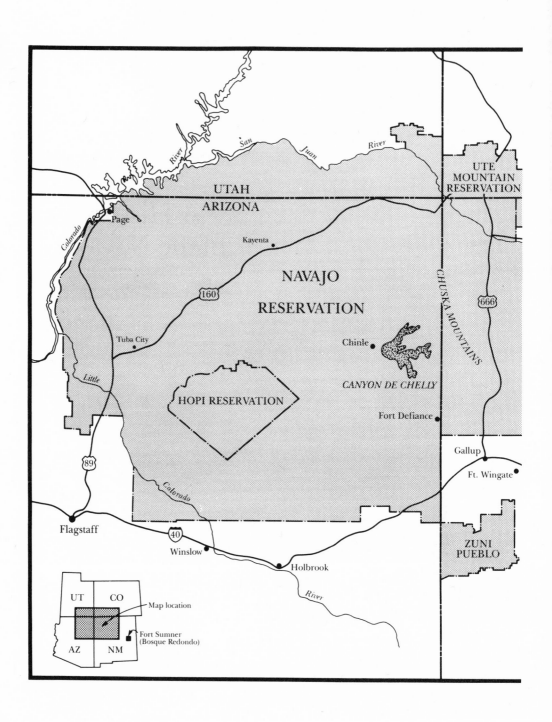

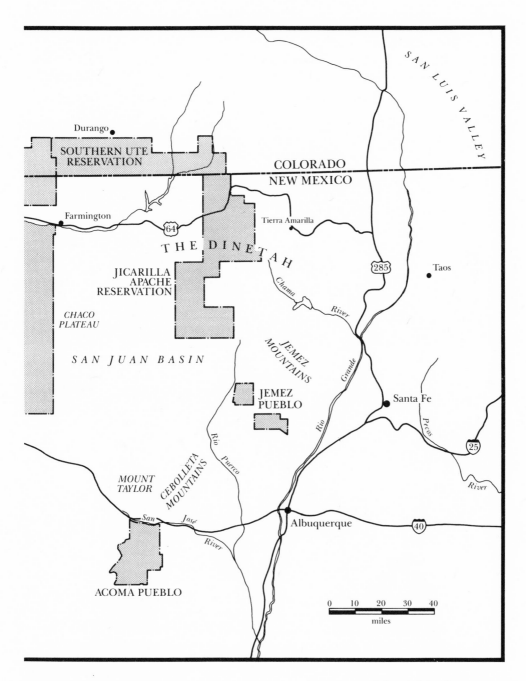

Map 1. Navajo country.

Introduction

"Navajos are different: they're not like other Indians." We can't recall how many times we have heard this comment or similar ones from members of other tribes. Indians outside the Southwest had little contact with the Navajos until the 1950s, when a shortage of schools on the reservation caused the Bureau of Indian Affairs to inundate boarding schools throughout the western states with Navajo students. In many of these schools, Navajos soon outnumbered "locals," as the non-Navajo students came to be called. Locals often considered the Navajos to be clannish and unfriendly; they didn't mix well, and sometimes there were clashes between students from the two groups.

Soon after arriving in Farmington, New Mexico, in the summer of 1977, we realized that our friends had been right: the Navajos weren't like other Indians. One immediately apparent difference was that although Navajos and Anglo-Americans had lived side by side in the San Juan Valley for a hundred years, there had been little social mixing of the populations. The boundaries separating the two communities were anything but ambiguous. One was either a Navajo or an Anglo-American, and only a few people of mixed ancestry were subject to confusions of allegiance. Equally striking, all Navajos except children and an occasional young adult spoke Navajo. We were also surprised to find that they showed little interest in or even curiosity about other tribes or Anglo-Americans.

Getting acquainted with the Navajos near Farmington, we remembered a story once told by an Osage woman. As a girl in a government boarding school, she tried to make friends with a Navajo girl by telling her that "we're all Indians." The Navajo girl replied, "You're an Indian, I'm a Navajo." By the 1950s many native Americans were subordinating their tribal identity to their identity as Indians. While acknowledging the cultural and historical differences between tribes, they saw a commonality in their experience that overrode what by that time had become superficial tribal distinctions. The Navajos, on the other hand, did not think of themselves as members of a larger Indian community. They considered their history to be unique and their culture, unlike that of many tribes, to be very much alive.

The Navajos have maintained their tribal identity because of a unique set of cultural-historical circumstances. To define these circumstances, we approached Navajo culture history as the interaction of external events (those involving other peoples, such as war, domination, and trade; and those involving environmental conditions, such as climate and the availability of natural resources) with internal responses (the changes in technology, social organization, and belief that allow a society to adapt to outside influences). External events and internal responses are constantly changing and often difficult to distinguish, especially when viewed at a single point in time, out of the broader context of cultural evolution. To establish the causal relationships between them, we examined the cultural adaptations of Navajo society over the more than a century that Navajos have lived on their reservation.

Attempting to define the major changes within Navajo society during this period, we created a chronological outline from primary sources—archival collections, newspapers, journals, government surveys, diaries, and other firsthand reports—and graphed quantitative data such as population and livestock estimates, weaving income, and school enrollment. Cultural data that could not be expressed in numbers, such as statements concerning the nature of economic activities and religious movements, were summarized and grouped chronologically.

We relied heavily on secondary sources to answer questions about external forces in Navajo history. Quantitative data on rainfall, trading posts, missions and missionaries, non-Indian population and livestock ownership in Arizona and New Mexico, and other such variables were graphed. Other external factors that might be important in understanding Navajo culture change—such as government programs, changes in program implementation, and incidents of conflict—were summarized and indexed chronologically.

But how did all these facts fit together? If, for example, livestock herds dwindled while railroad wage labor flourished, were these two changes significantly related or merely coincidental? If income from crafts sales increased or decreased before or after a particular historical event, did that imply a causal relationship? Searching the data for patterns and trying to explain their relationship constituted the most challenging and fascinating aspect of the study. Obviously, there were periods of rapid change and periods of relative stability, but far more complex, unanticipated patterns also began to emerge. Certain cultural traits might change concurrently during one period, but not in another; or a particular trait might fluctuate independently over time.

Sometimes the relationship between external events and internal changes was clear. There could be little doubt, for example, that the 1890s drought caused a sharp decline in Navajo livestock. But other events and changes could be explained only in part, or not at all. The relative composition of Navajos herds (that is, the percentage of the total number of livestock represented by sheep, goats, cattle, and horses) fluctuated significantly over time with little apparent direction. Explainable fluctuations such as a decline in relative numbers of goats in the 1930s and 1940s, when goats were the primary target of the government's stock reduction program, proved the exception rather than the rule.

As the study progressed, it became apparent that internal changes in Navajo society needed to be interpreted within their own cultural context. Marshall Sahlins (1981:67) wrote, "People act upon circumstances according to their own cultural presupposition." Given that all cultures are logically integrated systems, the problem became one of understanding the presuppositions on which the changes in Navajo history were formulated. Anglo-Americans view events differently from Navajos, and the logic of Navajo behavior sometimes even escapes the notice of anthropologists. For example, referring to the Navajo response to stock reduction, Clyde Kluckhohn and Dorothea Leighton (1974:26) remarked, "Government technicians developed a stock reduction program which was probably, at the purely rational level, in the best interest of the Navahos. But the Navahos did not see it in rational terms; they saw it in emotional terms." Our interviews with Navajos and the statements collected by Ruth Roessel and Broderick Johnson (1974) show that while the Navajo response to stock reduction was at times expressed emotionally, it was not at all irrational from a Navajo cultural perspective. To the Navajos, it simply did not make any sense to destroy thousands of useful animals, and in so doing, it was only the officials of the United States government who were acting irrationally.

Hoping to further our understanding of the relationship between external events (Sahlins's "circumstances") and internal adaptation from the Navajo point of view, we turned to ethnographic studies and Navajo informants. Some anthropologists had studied a particular subject or event (stock reduction, World War II, the peyote church) and its relation to changes in Navajo culture, but in most cases the ethnographies did not address our questions or answered them inadequately. Navajo informants, however, proved invaluable in filling in gaps in the ethnographic literature and providing answers on some of the more obscure points. We were extremely fortunate in being able to work with a number of Navajos who had been born about the turn of the century and who spoke good English, unusual for Navajos of their generation. They were all stock raisers and had never been absent from their communities for any significant length of time. Two excellent interpreters assisted in the work with non-English-speaking Navajos. From these informants, we began to gain a clearer understanding of internal changes in Navajo culture; for example, we learned that herding had been an extremely complex and constantly changing element of their economy, and that the composition of the herds was highly sensitive to the economic role of livestock and to the relationship between herding and other aspects of Navajo culture.

While ethnographic studies and informants could not satisfactorily answer all of our questions, the major periods in Navajo culture history could now be defined and at least partially explained. More important, it could be shown that Navajo culture has maintained its continuity in a logically consistent manner. It is this continuity that sets Navajos apart from other American Indians, allowing them to maintain a strong tribal identity and cultural distinctiveness.

The most striking changes in Navajo society have taken place since 1868, the year in which the Navajos were released from a four-year imprisonment near Fort Sumner on the plains of eastern New Mexico and allowed to return to a reservation located in their former homeland—the high, dry plateaus and mountains of northwestern New Mexico and northeastern Arizona (map 1). Heralded by some writers as a "new beginning," their return and the events leading up to it make a logical point at which to begin this book.

CHAPTER ONE

The Early Navajos

In the summer of 1863, while armies in the eastern states fought a bloody civil war, General James H. Carleton, commander of federal troops in the territory of New Mexico, launched his own military campaign against the Navajos. Though short, the Navajo War of 1863–64 proved to be one of the most violent and decisive military campaigns ever waged against a major North American Indian tribe.

Over 700 New Mexico volunteers under the command of Colonel Kit Carson invaded Navajo country. Fort Defiance, abandoned at the start of the Civil War, was reoccupied and renamed Fort Canby. From there, troops fanned out in all directions, attacking the scattered Navajo camps, killing or capturing their inhabitants, burning their hogans, destroying their crops, and seizing their herds. General Carleton declared an "open season" on the Navajos and their property (Trafzer 1982; Kelly 1970). Ute and Pueblo Indians, as well as Spanish-American and Anglo-American civilians, were actively encouraged to join in the hostilities.

By winter, the war was all but over. Official estimates of casualties at the end of 1863 listed 301 Navajos killed out of a total population of slightly more than 10,000 (Keleher 1952:315).[1] However, the estimates did not take into account many of the killings carried out by Utes, Pueblos, and white civilians, nor the Navajos who died from exposure that winter. In addition, hundreds of women and children were taken captive and sold into slavery. Thus, while it is impossible to say precisely how many Navajos died as a result of the war, losses were undoubtedly severe.

The winter of 1863–64 found the surviving Navajos on the verge of starvation. Their corn and wheat fields had been destroyed before harvest, and most of their livestock had been killed or stolen. Many families were reduced to eating roots and nuts; some even ate their dogs.[2] Carson had succeeded where his Spanish, Mexican, and Anglo predecessors had failed: he had totally defeated the Navajos. Impoverished, hungry, and fearing for their lives, thousands trekked to Fort Canby that winter to surrender to the army and seek safety from the parties of Indian and white auxiliaries who were scouring the country for slaves and stock.[3]

The war was only the first stage of a plan General Carleton had devised for ending the territory's "Navajo problem." The second stage called for relocating the Navajos on a reservation along the Pecos River on the plains of eastern New Mexico, where it was thought they could be easily controlled and readily converted into peaceful farmers. In August 1863, the first party of Navajo prisoners began the long walk to Bosque Redondo.[4] Eventually, almost 8,500 Navajos were imprisoned on this reservation, under the close guard of troops stationed at nearby Fort Sumner.

The plan to establish the Navajos as self-sufficient farmers failed because of poor planning, abuses in the supply system, and the unsuitability of the location. For four years the once wealthy Navajos lived in disease-ridden squalor, subsisting on rations issued by the government. Finally, late in the spring of 1868, peace commissioners William T. Sherman and Samuel Tappan decided that Carleton's plan was unworkable and negotiated a treaty that was signed by the leading Navajo headmen on the day of its presentation (Thompson 1976:155). The Treaty of 1868 established a reservation for the Navajos in northwestern New Mexico and northeastern Arizona and allowed them to return to their homeland.

The effects of the war and subsequent imprisonment certainly have not gone unnoticed by scholars. James Downs (1964:97) stated that the internment at Bosque Redondo "profoundly changed Navajo culture."[5] Ruth Underhill (1956:144) called the return to their homeland a "beginning," comparing its cultural impact to that of their original entrance into the Southwest. Clyde Kluckhohn and Dorothea Leighton (1974:41) eloquently described the effects of Bosque Redondo on the Navajos:

Probably no folk has ever had a greater shock. Proud, they saw their properties destroyed and knew what it was to be dependent upon the largess of strangers. Not understanding group activity and accustomed to move freely over great spaces, they knew the misery of confinement within a limited area. Taken far from the rugged and vivid landscape which they prized so highly, they lived in a flat and colorless region, eating alien foods and drinking bitter water which made them ill. . . .

Fort Sumner [Bosque Redondo] was a major calamity to The People; its full effects upon their imagination can hardly be conveyed to white readers. . . .

One can no more understand Navaho attitudes . . . without knowing of Fort Sumner than he can comprehend Southern attitudes without knowing of the Civil War.

Kluckhohn and Leighton went on to say that the Navajos faced further "privations and hardships" when they went home in 1868, having "to start all over again in their struggle to make a living." Before examining the effects of these events on Navajo culture, however, it is necessary to survey Navajo culture history before the war.

THE NAVAJOS BEFORE 1696

Together with the various Apachean tribes of the Southwest, the Navajos are Athabaskan speakers, and the languages of these tribes are still similar enough to be mutually intelligible. While scholars agree that the Navajos and their kinsmen, the Apaches, originally lived in western Canada with other Athabaskan speaking tribes, there is widespread disagreement on when and how they arrived in the Southwest. Because they were nomadic hunting and gathering people who lived in small, scattered bands, these early Athabaskans left meager and sometimes ambiguous archaeological remains. As a result, archaeologists have postulated four different migration routes: an intermountain route through western Colorado and eastern Utah; a Rocky Mountain route through central Colorado; a High Plains route through eastern Colorado; and a Plains border route through Kansas. They differ widely on the date of this migration, placing it between A.D. 800 and 1000; 1200 and 1400; and sometime after 1541, when the Spaniards first arrived in the Southwest.[6] There is no doubt, however, that by the late sixteenth and early seventeenth centuries, Athabaskan speakers occupied much of what is now Arizona and New Mexico. Spanish accounts from this period often mention "Querechos" and "Apaches," many if not most of whom were Athabaskan speakers.

The major problem confronting historians and anthropologists in studying the Navajos of the sixteenth and seventeenth centuries is determining which of the various "Querechos" and "Apaches" they were. The term "Navajo" did not appear in the Spanish records until 1626, when Fray de Zárate Salmerón noted the presence of the "Apache Indians of Nabajú," a group occupying the Chama Valley and a portion of the San Juan Basin in northwestern New Mexico (Milich 1966:94). Today the Navajos speak of this region as their original homeland, the Dinetah (Underhill 1953:15–16). The Navajos may not, however, have been restricted to the Dinetah during the late sixteenth and early seventeenth centuries. The word "Nabajú" is simply a place name, not the name of a group of people. The concept of a Dinetah homeland itself may not have developed until the eighteenth century, and may have been the result of Puebloan influence (Reed 1945:54). Another difficulty with the theory that the Navajos were restricted to the Dinetah region is that "Querechos" and "Apaches" occupied other parts of northwestern New Mexico and northeastern Arizona during this period. As early as 1583, the Espejo expedition encountered "Querechos" living near Mount Taylor and the Hopi villages (Hammond and Rey 1966:189, 200–201; Correll 1979, 1:24–25). Jack Forbes (1960:57) and George Hammond and Agapito Rey (1966:182 n. 61) argued that at least the Querechos living in the vicinity of Mount Taylor were "Navajos," and it is possible that the Querechos near Hopi were also Athabaskan speakers. By the late sixteenth century, Athabaskan peoples were probably scattered throughout northwestern New Mexico (Brugge 1983:490–91).

The major obstacle to identifying the Navajos during this period is that they did not emerge as a distinct cultural or political entity—at least not as we think of them today—until the early eighteenth century. Before then, there were no Navajos as such, but numerous small bands of Athabaskan speakers scattered in and around the San Juan Basin, having only the generic identity of *diné* (people) to tie them loosely together. Because the San Juan bands practiced agriculture, the Spaniards distinguished them from Athabaskans living elsewhere. We continue to refer to them as "Navajos" even though as a distinct sociocultural group, the Navajos became readily distinguishable from other Athabaskans only after these bands were joined by Puebloan peoples fleeing Spanish persecution.

Navajo history during the Spanish period has been painstakingly researched by Frank Reeve (1957, 1958, 1959, 1960), Donald Worcester

(1947), and Jack Forbes (1960). The Spaniards began establishing settlements in New Mexico in 1598. They quickly subdued the Pueblo Indians and set about establishing Catholic missions at the Rio Grande pueblos and at Acoma, Zuni, and Hopi. Attempts to establish missions among the Athabaskan bands in northwestern New Mexico failed, and these groups remained outside the sphere of Spanish domination. The Navajos frequently raided Spanish settlements and the pueblos for livestock and other booty, and in turn, Spaniards and Pueblo Indians raided the Navajos for slaves to be sold into the mines of central Mexico. During periods of peace, the three groups traded with each other. In 1680 the Pueblos secretly organized and successfully carried out a revolt against the Spaniards, driving soldiers, settlers, and missionaries from New Mexico. The role of the Navajos in this revolt is unclear, if in fact there was any. Late in the summer of 1692, the Spaniards began their reconquest of New Mexico, and despite fierce resistance from some of the Pueblos, full Spanish control had been restored by 1696.

The Navajo economy at this time probably centered around hunting, farming, and the gathering of wild plants, although most sources refer only to farming. In 1583 Diego Pérez de Luxán of the Espejo expedition reported that the Querechos living near Mount Taylor were growing crops (Hammond and Rey 1966:201), as were the Navajo-Apaches mentioned by Fray Alonso de Benavides in 1630 (Correll 1979, 1:31). In 1678 a military campaign against the Apaches destroyed 2,500 *fanegas* of corn (a *fanega* is equivalent to an English bushel or hundredweight), and it is probable that these Apaches were Navajos (Reeve 1957:50). Corn is the only crop mentioned in the Spanish documents (Reeve 1957:49–50), but beans and squash may also have been cultivated, as they were by the Pueblo Indians. It has yet to be determined if the Athabaskans learned agriculture from the Pueblos after entering the Southwest or if they acquired it from farming people on the Great Plains during their migration southward (Ellis 1974:41).

Though references to hunting are rare in the Spanish accounts, it was almost certainly important to the economy of the Navajos. In 1583, Antonio de Espejo noted that the "Querechos" traded deerskins at Acoma Pueblo for cotton mantles (Correll 1979, 1:24). More enlightening is Fray Benavides's statement in 1630 that it was dangerous for the Pueblo Indians to gather alum in Navajo country except when the Navajos had gone hunting (Worcester 1947:56). This probably means that the Navajos went on communal hunts at some distance from their normal range—most likely antelope hunts on the Chaco Plateau. The Dinetah abounded in deer, elk, mountain sheep, and smaller game such as rabbits and squirrels. Even today, the Athabaskan peoples have a strong hunting tradition.

Another unanswered question is whether the Navajos began herding live-stock prior to the Pueblo Revolt. Frank Reeve (1957:49) thought it was "quite possible that the well-known livestock (especially sheep) holdings of the Navaho Apaches in the eighteenth century had their origins in these years immediately preceding the pueblo uprising" (see also Downs 1964:99). Apacheans raided Spanish settlements for horses and cattle as early as 1608 (Worcester 1947:49), and sheep and goats were also taken during the early seventeenth century. Many of the stolen horses were eaten, but the Athabaskans soon found that they were more valuable for transportation than for food, and readily adopted them during the seventeenth century. The same was not true for cattle, sheep, and goats, whose maintenance requires a more extensive knowledge of animal husbandry and a well-developed butchering strategy to prevent depletion of the herds. We are not even certain if the Navajos of this period successfully bred and maintained their horse herds, or if they relied on raiding. The herding aspect of their economy probably did not develop until the last decade of the seventeenth century, after the Pueblos, with their knowledge of Spanish animal husbandry, became resident among them.

THE DEVELOPMENTAL HERDING PERIOD: 1696 TO ABOUT 1800

The Spanish reconquest of New Mexico, which began in 1692 and ended in 1696, was a protracted and at times bloody conflict. Fearing Spanish reprisals, thousands of Pueblo Indians fled their villages along the Rio Grande. Some joined the Hopis, but most took refuge with the Athabaskans living in the Dinetah region along the upper San Juan River.

These refugees brought with them Puebloan ideas and technology, along with technology learned from the Spaniards before the revolt. The years of the reconquest were

> probably the time when the Navahos not only learned more about Pueblo technology (agriculture, animal husbandry, weaving, pottery), but also absorbed more Pueblo religious and social concepts and procedures: ceremonial masks, altars, prayer sticks, use of corn meal, sand paintings, the origin myth, and perhaps even selected aspects of the Pueblo matrilineal clan system. A number of contemporary Navaho clans had their origins in groups of Pueblo refugees

who stayed with Navahos—for example, the Jemez clan, the Zia clan, the "Black Sheep People" reportedly derived from San Felipe. (Vogt 1961:301)

Archaeological research has disclosed still other changes. James Hester (1962a:67) and Roy Carlson (1965:57) noted the appearance of Pueblo-style pottery at Navajo sites of the period and the development of a new, indigenous Navajo style of painted pottery, Gobernador Polychrome. Stone masonry also appeared at Navajo sites for the first time. This kind of construction was initially limited to *pueblitos*, small, multiroom structures, many of which appear to have been defensive in purpose. Masonry hogans soon appeared, but most Navajos still preferred the old forked-stick hogans (Brugge 1983:493).

Some anthropologists have argued that small Navajo villages developed during the eighteenth century. A member of a Spanish expedition into the Dinetah in 1743 reported that because of the ferocity of the Utes, Navajos were living on the tops of mesas in stone, log, or clay houses (W. Hill 1940a:407–8). Kluckhohn and Leighton (1974:35) construed the report to mean that the Navajos lived "in small, compact communities located away from the fields." Vogt (1961:294) doubted that the Navajos had "ever lived in compact communities." He based his hypothesis on an eighteenth century account (see W. Hill 1940a:408 and Reeve 1958:217–20) of a Spanish expedition attacking a party of Navajo farmers along the San Juan River in 1705. After fleeing south for several days, the Navajos took refuge on a fortified mesa top. On the other hand, Hester (1962a:24–25) hypothesized that the "pueblitos" were intermittently occupied.

Whether they lived in villages or not, the Navajos consisted of two culturally distinct populations in the first decade or so after 1700—Athabaskans and Puebloans—that were rapidly fusing. Although scholars have tended to view the Navajos as Athabaskans whose culture had absorbed Puebloan cultural traits, we prefer to see them as biological and cultural hybrids, neither Athabaskan nor Puebloan, but a product of both. As a culturally distinct population, the Navajos developed in the Dinetah during the first decades of the eighteenth century.

For some twenty years after the reconquest, Navajo raiders warred against Spanish settlements. A number of Spanish military expeditions ventured into the rugged canyon and mesa country of the Dinetah to punish them. From 1720 until about 1770, these adversaries maintained relatively peaceful relations (Reeve 1958, 1959), but the Utes and Comanches began raiding both Navajos and Spaniards with increasing intensity (Brugge 1968:31, 144). Albert Schroeder (1965:59) and Frank Reeve (1960:202–4) contend that Ute raids had forced the Navajos to abandon the densely populated Dinetah region by 1754. From there, the Navajos fled south to the Cebolleta Mountains and west to the Chuskas, disseminating their hybridized culture to the Athabaskan bands already occupying these areas. At the same time, Spanish settlers also began moving west toward the Cebolleta Mountains and the adjacent valley of the Rio Puerco of the East, perhaps also to escape the destructive raids of the Comanches. A number of Spanish settlers requested and received land grants in the Rio Puerco Valley and to the west between 1753 and 1772 (Jenkins and Minge 1974:4–7). With Navajos and Spaniards moving into the same region, the peace disintegrated, and intermittent conflicts broke out between the two groups (Reeve 1960; Brugge 1963:fig. 2).

The Pueblo refugees who joined the Navajos brought with them their knowledge of sheep and goat herding, and probably some animals as well.[7] Many of them had worked on Spanish ranches as herders, and others had kept sheep and goats of their own. Still, there is evidence that herding remained only marginally important during the first half of the eighteenth century. Spanish expeditions as late as 1743 reported only small herds of sheep, the largest estimated at just 700 head (W. Hill 1940a:407). As long as they lived in the Dinetah region, the Navajos may not have developed sheep and goat herding because, as John Loring Haskell (1975:178) noted, the "Dinetah does not lend itself to pastoral activities as it is characterized by deep canyons and lofty mesas." Contemporary Navajo stockmen tend to concur, describing the terrain as acceptable for goats but too broken for herding sheep. Archaeological studies of Navajo settlement patterns during this period indicate that residence sites in the Dinetah were chosen for proximity to arable land (Dittert, Hester, and Eddy 1971:242). In contrast, for twentieth-century Navajos, "the location of cornfields seldom influences the site of the homestead. . . . The demands of the herd are more immediate, [and therefore] fields may in fact be several miles from the homestead" (Downs 1972:45). In the era before fencing, large herds could not be kept near the fields because they might damage the crops.

In view of these factors, we believe that the Navajos tended only small herds of sheep and goats during the first half of the eighteenth century. In 1786 Pedro Garrido y Duran (quoted in A. Thomas 1932:350) wrote the following description of the Navajos:

> Their possessions consist of five hundred tame horses; six hundred mares with their corresponding stallions and young; about seven hundred black ewes, forty cows also with their bulls and calves, all looked after with the greatest care and diligence for their increase.

His estimates correspond closely to depositions made in the 1740s. As sources of milk and meat, goats probably contributed more to subsistence, while sheep provided wool for use in the evolving blanket trade (see W. Hill 1940a).

By the 1790s, the Navajos were becoming increasingly oriented toward herding, though the shift to real dependence upon livestock did not come until early in the next century. In 1794 Colonel Don Fernando de la Concha, the outgoing governor of New Mexico, wrote his successor that the Navajos "possess much cattle and sheep" (quoted in Correll 1976:70). The next year Governor Don Fernando Chacon wrote that the Navajos "do not want for sheep, for those that they possess are innumerable" (quoted in Correll 1976:71).

Precisely why the Navajo economy began to change is not clear. Haskell (1975:178) believed it was a result of population pressures and an increasing dependence on livestock: abandonment of the Dinetah was a response to the need for better forage for the increasing herds. Brugge (1963:23–24) thought that the growing importance of herding resulted from warfare, as well as population pressures. Farmers, dependent upon their fields for subsistence, would have been considerably more vulnerable to Ute and Comanche raiders than would herders, who could quickly move their stock to places of safety and concealment. On the basis of the rather skimpy evidence available, we would argue that the cause was probably warfare. While we have reliable evidence for Ute and Comanche raiding, there is no evidence that a significant herding economy developed prior to the Navajos' abandonment of the Dinetah, nor that the Navajo population was expanding.

THE HERDING AND RAIDING PERIOD: 1800–1863

By 1800 Navajo raids on Spanish settlements had become so frequent and costly that Governor Chacon led a force of 500 men into Navajo country and negotiated what proved to be another temporary peace (Wilson 1967:7–8). Raiding resumed in 1804, and the governor sent out three major military expeditions. One of them, penetrating Canyon de Chelly in January 1805, fought with the Navajos who had taken cover behind a fortified position, killing 25 Navajo women and children and 93 men. There followed still another negotiated peace that lasted until about 1817 (Wilson 1967:9–10; Correll 1979, 1:98–100; Reeve 1971:116–17). In that year, Navajos raided Spanish herds in the Rio Grande Valley, and the following spring, a combined Ute and Navajo raiding party ran off some horses near

Jemez Pueblo (Reeve 1971:225). Raids and reprisals by both sides continued, and the assumption of control by the newly independent Mexican government in 1821 had little appreciable effect on relations between Navajos and whites. During the almost quarter century of Mexican rule, the Navajo and "Mexican" populations waged almost constant warfare (McNitt 1972:59–91).

The United States government inherited this war when it seized control of New Mexico in 1846. General Stephen Watts Kearny considered the Navajo situation to be so critical that shortly after leaving Santa Fe for California he sent orders to Colonel Alexander Doniphan to reach some agreement with the Navajos before proceeding with the planned invasion of Chihuahua. Doniphan met with Navajo leaders near present-day Fort Wingate and persuaded them to sign the Treaty of Ojo del Oso (Underhill 1956:91–92; McNitt 1972:95–123). Despite this treaty, Navajo raids scarcely diminished. The tribe had no central government to bind it together under the treaty, and many Navajos considered themselves superior in military strength to the Americans. Between 1846 and 1850, Navajos and Apaches took an estimated 450,000 sheep from Spanish-American settlements (Van Valkenburgh 1938:11). Several punitive expeditions were dispatched between 1847 and 1851 in a futile attempt to stop the Navajo depredations. Eventually, Colonel Edwin Sumner, commander of the Ninth Military Department, decided that the only way to control the raiders was to establish a fort in the very heart of Navajo country, and Fort Defiance was built in 1851 (McNitt 1972:195).

The fort's presence did not altogether stop the raiding, but no major conflicts broke out between Indians and military until July 1858, when a Navajo who was visiting Fort Defiance killed the slave of the post commander. The Navajos refused to surrender the murderer, and a series of expeditions marched against them in the late summer and fall. On Christmas day 1858, the army imposed a new treaty on fifteen Navajo headmen who gathered at Fort Defiance. The treaty blamed the Navajos for the conflict and exacted a number of concessions from them, but neither side was prepared to honor it, and relations continued to deteriorate. In the spring of 1860, a large party of Navajos attacked Fort Defiance but was repulsed (McNitt 1972:325–84).

Fort Defiance was abandoned in 1861, at the outset of the Civil War. As Ruth Underhill put it, New Mexico became a "madhouse" (1956:109). Navajos, Utes, Zunis, Apaches, Spanish-Americans, and Anglo-Americans all seized the opportunity for vengeance and looting, a time of disruption that ended only with the army's return in 1863.

In spite of frequent warfare with Spanish-Americans, the Navajos appear to have prospered during the early nineteenth century, and their numbers began to increase. From a population of 3,000 to 4,000 in the seventeenth and eighteenth centuries (Benavides 1916:44, 59; W. Hill 1940a; A. Thomas 1932:350), the Navajos were expanding with a speed that soon attracted the attention of surrounding peoples. In 1846 Charles Bent, the recently appointed governor of New Mexico, wrote, "The Navajoes so far as I am informed are the only Indians on the continent having intercourse with white men, that are increasing in numbers" (Correll 1979, 1:210). In 1850, Colonel George McCall noted that "for some years past [the Navajos] are believed to have steadily increased in numbers" (McCall 1968:99). Twenty-four different estimates of Navajo population for 1846 to 1860 ranged from a low of 5,000 to a high of 15,000, with most falling between 8,000 and 12,000. The average of these figures came to slightly more than 10,000 (table 1). Given that about 8,500 Navajos were imprisoned at Bosque Redondo in the mid-1860s (some had never been captured; others were killed or enslaved, or died of other causes), it seems reasonable that the population of the 1850s exceeded 10,000. During the first half of the nineteenth century, then, Navajo population must have doubled and possibly even tripled.

Spanish accounts from the middle and late 1700s described Navajo sheep herds as comprising hundreds of animals (W. Hill 1940a; A. Thomas 1932:350). However, between 1846 and 1860, Anglo-American observers counted the animals in the hundreds of thousands. Their estimates ranged from 200,000 to 500,000, with an average of slightly more than 300,000 (table 2). Others objected that these estimates were too high. In 1850, Colonel McCall contended that the numbers of stock owned by the Navajos had been "extravagantly represented" (McCall 1968:99). A few years later Major Henry Kendrick echoed this sentiment when he reported that "the number of sheep which these people own has been vastly overrated" (Kendrick to Messervy, May 13, 1854, RBIA RNMS). In 1859, Major J. S. Simonson stated that the size of Navajo herds was "very greatly exaggerated" (RSW 1859, 2:311). Though the estimates may be open to question, there is no doubt that the Navajos' herds increased dramatically during the first half of the nineteenth century and that the increase coincided with a rapid growth in population.

Although the Navajos were shifting their economic dependence from farming and hunting to herding in the late 1700s and early 1800s, the role of livestock in their subsistence economy at mid-nineteenth century must not be overemphasized. Even if the estimates just given are accepted, we

TABLE 1.   *Navajo Population: 1846–1860*

Year	Population Estimate	Source
1846	12,000	Hughes 1914:103
	7,000–14,000	Able 1915:7 (Charles Bent estimate)
	13,500	RCIA 1867:135
1849	5,000	RSW 1850, 2:999
	8,000–10,000	McNitt 1964:98
	12,000	Bell 1869, 1:179
	7,000–12,000	RSW 1850, 1:179
1850	10,000	RSW 1851:16
	10,800	McCall 1968:99
1853	10,000	Meriwether to Manypenny, Sept. 19, 1853, RBIA LR NMS
	8,000	*Santa Fe Gazette*, Dec. 31, 1853
	10,000[a]	U.S. Congress 1854, 1:73 (Hacha estimate)
	5,000	U.S. Congress 1854, 1:73 (Leroux estimate)
	8,000	U.S. Congress 1854, 3:83 (Whipple estimate)
1854	8,000	RCIA 1854:173
1855	8,000–10,000	Meriwether to Manypenny, July 27, 1855, RBIA LR NMS
	7,500	RCIA 1855:188
	12,000	Davis 1938:235
1856	12,500–15,000[b]	Letherman 1856:283
1857	12,000	Kendrick to Meriwether, Jan. 23, 1857, RBIA RNMS
	9,000–12,000	RCIA 1857:275
1859	12,000–15,000	RCIA 1859:350
	12,000	*Santa Fe Gazette*, Jan. 8, 1859
1860	15,000	Domenech 1860, 2:7

[a]José Hacha estimated the Navajo population as five times that of Zuni, which had an estimated population of 2,000.
[b]Letherman estimated that the Navajos had between 2,500 and 3,000 warriors. We multiplied these numbers by five for an estimate of the total Navajo population.

calculate a human-to-sheep ratio of only about 1:30.[8] Since it is estimated that a human-to-sheep ratio of between 1:40 and 1:50 is necessary for subsistence level support, the Navajo herds in the 1840s and 1850s could not by themselves have filled that need.[9] Herding may have become the most

TABLE 2. *Sheep Owned by the Navajos: 1846–1860*

Year	Number	Source
1846	500,000	Able 1915:6 (Charles Bent estimate)
1853	250,000	Meriwether to Manypenny, Sept. 19, 1853, RBIA LR NMS
	250,000	*Santa Fe Gazette*, Dec. 31, 1853
1855	200,000	Davis 1938:235
1856	200,000	Letherman 1856:291
1859	250,000	*Santa Fe Gazette*, Jan. 8, 1859
1860	500,000	Domenech 1860, 2:7

important component of Navajo economy, but it still had to be supplemented by intensive farming, hunting, and gathering.[10]

As the economic orientation shifted toward herding, settlement patterns changed dramatically. Instead of living in a single, relatively permanent camp near their fields, people began using separate summer and winter camps where forage and water were available for their stock. They became less sedentary and more mobile. David Brugge (1963:24) has suggested, moreover, that the evolution of a pastoral economy led to a decline in pottery making. Gobernador Polychrome, the Navajo style of painted pottery, disappeared about 1785 (Brugge 1963:fig. 2), and its extinction may be the first indication of this shift in economic activities.

Herding and raiding had become inextricably linked by the mid-1800s. The reliance on livestock, which may have begun as an adaptation to raids by Utes and Comanches, became increasingly pronounced as conflict with Euro-Americans increased. Greater dependence upon sheep and goats prompted more raiding of Spanish-American herds, which heightened the hostilities. Eventually there had to be a showdown between the Navajos and the expanding Euro-American settlers in the Southwest. The Navajo War of 1863–64 and the subsequent imprisonment of the Navajos were, in a sense, inevitable consequences of the economic system that had evolved. The link between raiding and herding had to be broken, and it was— through a decisive military defeat.

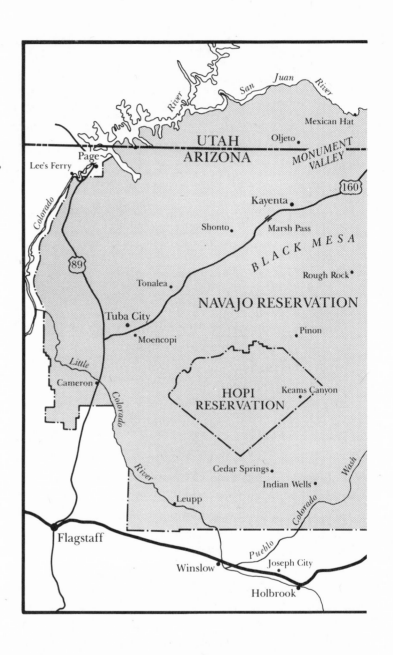

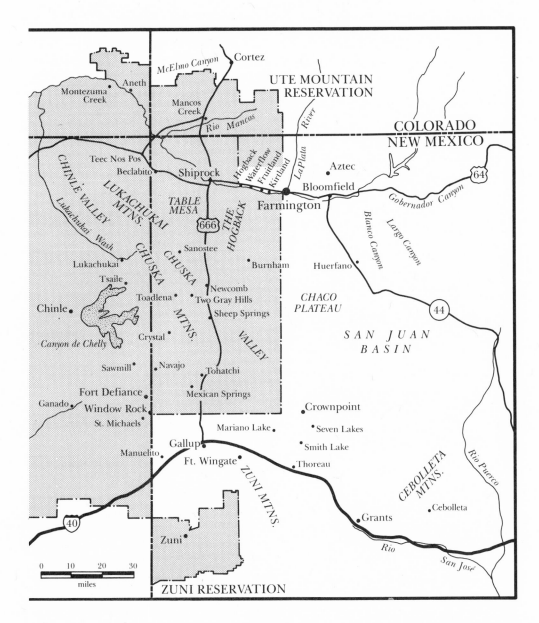

Map 2. *The Navajo reservation. General reference, 1863–1975.*

CHAPTER TWO

The Early Reservation Years: 1868–1900

By the spring of 1868, federal officials had judged the Bosque Redondo experiment a disaster that had to be quickly rectified. In May of that year the Indian Peace Commission, created by President Grant and headed by General William Tecumseh Sherman, arrived at Fort Sumner to negotiate a new treaty establishing a reservation for the Navajos and ending their imprisonment. The commissioners first suggested a location in the Indian Territory, but the Navajos wanted to go back to their homeland. The commission agreed. On June 1, 1868, a new treaty was signed by General Sherman and Colonel S. F. Tappan, representing the United States government, and the Navajo leaders. It created a reservation in northwestern New Mexico and northeastern Arizona and provided for the government to help the Navajos rebuild their shattered economy (Underhill 1953:176–81).

The government's motives in negotiating this treaty were more practical than altruistic. Those who had conceived of resettling the Navajos at Bosque Redondo in 1863 thought that the Navajos would quickly become self-sufficient farmers. Soon after their arrival, an irrigation ditch had been dug by the Navajos and the Mescaleros, who were also being held at Bosque Redondo, to divert water from the Pecos River to the fields. The harvests were ruined by insects, however, and the government was forced to issue rations (Thompson 1976:39–126).

From the outset, critics had charged that the forced captivity of the Navajos was not economically feasible. Including expenditures for troops and facilities, the annual cost of maintaining the Navajos at Bosque Redondo exceeded $1,000,000 (Thompson 1976:165). Within four years, it became obvious to all parties that the Navajos would never become self-sufficient farmers at Bosque Redondo and that the government would be forced to issue rations indefinitely.

For a nation recovering from an expensive and destructive civil war, these costs were prohibitive. Many government officials argued that the expense was unnecessary: the Navajos had been self-supporting before 1863 and could be again if they were given the opportunity. Theodore Dodd, the Navajo agent, declared in 1867 that "if the Navajoes were furnished liberally with sheep and goats they would in a short time be enabled to furnish themselves with meat for their subsistence, milk for their families, and wool to make a good share of their clothing" (RCIA 1867:200–201). Fiscal reality soon forced others to concede the issue, and as Gerald Thompson (1976:165) noted, "the Navajos were returned to their homeland because the program had been so costly, not due to the military's humanitarian desires."

As defined by the treaty, the Navajo reservation included only 3.5 million acres, a small fraction of their former domain. Located along the New Mexico-Arizona border, the rectangular reservation measured approximately eighty miles from north to south and sixty-five miles from east to west. It encompassed the Chuska Valley on the east, Lukachukai Wash and Canyon de Chelly on the west, and a small portion of the San Juan Valley (see map 3). Several areas of critical economic importance to the Navajos were left out: the farmlands of the Chinle Valley and around Pueblo Colorado (Ganado) and Ojo del Oso; and the rich grazing lands of the Chaco Plateau, the Cebolleta and Zuni mountains, Black Mesa, and the valley of the Little Colorado River.

Even as the treaty was being discussed, officials in New Mexico recognized the inadequacies of the reservation it created. If the Navajos were to rebuild their herds and reestablish their farms, they would need far more land than it provided. General Sherman recognized the problem and told Navajo leaders that their people would not be confined to the treaty reservation but would be allowed to use any off-reservation areas not occupied by white settlers (Brugge 1980:49). Since there were virtually no white settlers in northwestern New Mexico or northeastern Arizona in the 1860s, Sherman's statement meant that most Navajo families could return to their former homes (Bennett to Clinton, Dec. 30, 1869, RBIA LR NMS).

There was considerable apprehension that the Navajos would soon resort to raiding if they did not receive economic support from the government. Several provisions of the treaty were meant to provide such assistance. Because the Navajos would be getting home too late in the summer of 1868 to plant crops, the treaty set aside money for rations until the 1869 harvest. The government planned to distribute 15,000 sheep and goats, along with various seeds and farming implements. Annuity goods, not to exceed a value of five dollars per capita per year, were also to be issued for a period of ten years (Underhill 1953:176–81; Link 1968:18–25).

After the treaty was signed, some small groups left for home almost immediately. But because the route passed through the still hostile Spanish-American settlements along the Rio Grande, the majority of the Navajos—slightly more than 7,000—waited and returned as a group under military protection. They arrived at Fort Wingate on July 23, 1868 (Underhill 1956:147; Dodd to Davis, Aug. 5, 1868, RBIA LR NMS).

The late summer of 1868 marked the low point in Navajo economic history. War and neglect had rendered the land desolate. The old cornfields were overgrown with weeds, the ditches were filled with sand, and what had been orchards were now fields of tree stumps. Most families had no livestock at all. Because they lacked any individual means of support, large numbers of the returnees camped near Fort Wingate to receive rations. When the agency was established at the site of old Fort Defiance, most families moved there, but some drifted back to their old camps and attempted to survive on whatever food they could find. Of these families, some had cached corn and other farm produce during the Navajo War; others joined relatives who had escaped Bosque Redondo and who still had herds. Most eked out a bare existence by hunting and gathering.

The economic strides made by the Navajos in the subsequent quarter century are unique in the history of Anglo-American and Indian relations. Scholars have noted how Bosque Redondo affected Navajo attitudes toward the government (Underhill 1956:144–63), but they have tended to overlook its effects on government policy toward the Navajos. Neither the Navajos nor the government wanted another war, and neither side felt that it could afford another Bosque Redondo. Their common and primary objective was to rebuild the Navajo economy at least to the level of self-sufficiency. Civilian and military officials alike were extraordinarily supportive of tribal interests in matters that pertained to Navajo economic development, even when such support collided with the interests of local Anglo-American and Spanish-American settlers. Conflicts between Navajos and white settlers were downplayed or ignored. When forced to intervene, the military usually responded with a restraint and objectivity that were rare for the army in the western territories. The Navajos prospered under the favorable combination of peace in the region and strong support from officialdom. By the late 1880s and very early 1890s, they had attained a level of prosperity which they had never known before, and which they have never known since.

ADMINISTRATION AND CONTROL OF THE NAVAJOS

Fort Defiance was reoccupied and established as the Navajo Agency, but conditions in the region were volatile, and the Navajos were still considered a military threat. Consequently, a new Fort Wingate was established off the reservation at Ojo del Oso, about forty-five miles southeast of Fort Defiance.[1] By stationing troops at the new fort, the army could at once protect and intimidate the Navajos.

Probably no other Indian agents during the late nineteenth century faced problems comparable to those confronting the Navajo Agency. The Navajos were one of the largest American tribes during this period, and the only one with a rapidly growing population. In the twenty-five years between 1868 and 1892, they increased approximately from 9,000 to 18,000 (Johnston 1966a:362). To further complicate the administration of the tribe, this relatively large population lived in small family groups dispersed over a rugged, roadless, and unmapped area of between 20,000 and 30,000 square miles. The site chosen for the agency was far from ideal: Fort Defiance lay only a few miles south of the original reservation boundary, hardly a central location. Navajo family camps were scattered almost one hundred miles to the north, east, and west.

Transportation and communication problems made effective management of the Navajos impossible from a single administrative center, regardless of its location. As early as 1870, William F. M. Arny reported that "the agent of the Navajoes has too many Indians under his charge for one agent to control," and suggested that four subagencies be established (Arny to Parker, July 19, 1870, RBIA LR NMS). However, nothing came of such plans until the late 1880s, when Indian Service personnel were stationed outside Fort Defiance.

The problem of administering the Navajos from a single center was compounded by inadequate staffing and the lack of knowledge of agency employees. Few of the agents or acting agents who served between 1868 and 1900 had any previous contact with or knowledge of the Navajos. In most cases their tenure was so brief that they had little time to learn, even if they were so inclined. Only a handful of Navajos spoke English at the time, and only one agent, F. T. Bennett, spoke any Navajo (Notes of Council, 1880, RBIA LR NMS). Until the early 1880s, no one at the agency could translate directly from one language to the other: translations were made from English to Spanish to Navajo, or the other way around (Young 1968:46). Travel conditions and time restraints prevented most agents from traveling any distance from Fort Defiance. At any one time, usually fewer than a dozen clerks, teachers, or other employees were available to assist the agent in administration.

Having no other means at their disposal, the agents came to rely on Navajo leaders to keep the people under control. The Navajos had never developed a centralized political system. Men known as *naat'anii* (a term usually translated as "chief," but more accurately defined as "big man" leaders), rather than occupying formal political positions, attracted and retained groups of followers because of their charismatic and leadership qualities. They held no real authority; their power rested only on their persuasive ability. A few major *naat'anii* counted a large number of lesser ones among their followers.[2]

Anglo-American political custom dictated that some form of centralized authority—an individual or group of individuals—be legally responsible for the Navajos as a whole. At Bosque Redondo the military organized the tribe into twelve bands and appointed a chief for each one (Kelly 1968:14). These leaders—Armijo, Delgado, Manuelito, Largo, Herrero, Chiqueto, Muerto de Hombre, Hombre, Narbono, Ganado Mucho, Narbono Segundo, and the "principal" chief, Barboncito (Link 1968:24–25; Underhill 1953:274)—signed the 1868 treaty on behalf of the Navajos. They formed the core of what soon evolved into a "chiefs' council," the group recognized as the legal representatives of the Navajos.[3]

When plans were being made for the distribution of annuity goods, it was suggested that the goods be given to the chiefs, who could then redistribute them to their bands. Agent Theodore H. Dodd protested to the commissioner of Indian affairs:

> It will be impossible to make an equal distribution to the Navajo Indians if the said goods are turned over to the chiefs. . . . Each head of a family is its own master, and governs his household according to his will. There are some persons among these Indians who we call chiefs, and who do exercise considerable authority among them, but this submission is voluntary. . . . If the goods are

turned over to the so called chiefs for them to distribute to the tribe,
. . . the result would be that two thirds of the Navajos would not
receive any of said goods, as the chiefs would distribute only to their
friends & relatives. (Dodd to Taylor, Sept. 19, 1868, RBIA LR NMS)

Dodd's immediate successors appear to have heeded his warning: rations,
annuity goods, and livestock were given directly to the people. The chiefs
played a limited role as legal representatives, signing receipts for specified
amounts of goods (Certificate of Issues for the Fourth Quarter 1869, RBIA
RNMS).

Some Navajos resumed raiding immediately after their release from
Bosque Redondo, placing their agents and the military in a serious quan-
dary. Any involvement of the army might cause the Navajos to panic and
escalate the conflict into a major war, so a policy of working through the
chiefs' council evolved. In December 1869, Agent Bennett convened the
twelve chiefs to discuss the problem, expressing his

> views on the subject [of raiding] in very strong terms. [The chiefs]
> then promised . . . faithfully that upon hearing of any raid or cam-
> paign they would immediately organise [sic] and go to the place and
> stop it, using force if necessary. [He] told them that was what was
> wanted and would be required of them. (Bennett to Clinton, Dec.
> 23, 1869, RBIA LR NMS)

Naat'anii had no authority to prohibit raiding, and there was no precedent
for the use of force to stop raiding parties or to seize stock taken by raiders.
Nevertheless, after the meeting the chiefs attempted to persuade raiders to
surrender livestock that had already been taken, and succeeded in turning
over several herds of stolen animals to the agent (Bennett to Clinton, July
1, 1870, RBIA RNMS).

In August of 1870, Manuelito and Narbono resorted to force to recap-
ture a herd of sheep from a raiding party (Bennett to Clinton, Sept. 2, 1870
and Nov. 1, 1870, RBIA RNMS). This event marked a major change in the
Navajo political system: for the first time, the chiefs were attempting to
assume control over raiding. The following summer they went even further
in their assumption of power, killing one raider and bringing two others to
the agency to be placed under arrest (Miller to Pope, June 30, 1871, RBIA
RNMS). In terms of the *naat'anii* system, the failure of the chiefs to stop the
raiders by means of persuasion, along with their subsequent use of force,
indicates that they had limited influence or authority.

In August 1872, Acting Agent Thomas V. Keam recruited a tribal police force known as the Navajo Cavalry to patrol the reservation and return stolen property—usually livestock. Manuelito, considered the most aggressive chief, was placed in command of a force variously reported as 100 (Hall to Dudley, Dec. 16, 1872, RBIA LR NMS) and 130 (RCIA 1872:302) men, including "nearly all of the principal chiefs" (RCIA 1872:686). Described as "very enerjetic [sic] and determined in the discharge of their duties" (Arny to Smith, Sept. 5, 1873, RBIA LR NMS), Manuelito and his men returned several herds of stock to their owners, and warned known raiders to stop their forays. The Navajo Cavalry proved so effective that in the summer of 1873 Agent W. F. Hall reported, "No stock has been stolen by this tribe to my knowledge since I have been Agent" (Hall to Dudley, June 7, 1873, RBIA RNMS). At his suggestion the force was disbanded (Hall to Dudley, July 19, 1873, RBIA LR NMS).

After this campaign, the Navajos did not resume raiding. In December 1874, Major William Price wrote, "I cannot hear of a single depredation, even of the most trifling character having been committed by [the Navajos] during the past year" (Price to Willard, Dec. 13, 1874, RBIA LR NMS). Nevertheless, a new voluntary Navajo police force of 200 men under the command of the chiefs was organized in May of 1874 (RCIA 1874:307).

During the 1870s, the chiefs began taking control over the distribution of annuity goods. As early as 1874, the agency issued flour directly to the chiefs (Certified Voucher to H. Reed for period Oct. 1, 1873, to Mar. 27, 1874, RBIA LR NMS; Estimate of Indian Supplies for Fourth Quarter 1876, RBIA LR NMS; Irvine to Smith, Apr. 21, 1877, RBIA LR NMS). In 1877 they received annuity goods for between 1,300 and 1,400 "absent" Navajos (Blair to AAA, May 2, 1877, RBIA LR NMS), claiming they would distribute the goods to the absent members of their bands. This assumption of control had become so pronounced by 1877 that Agent Alexander G. Irvine complained, "[The chiefs] consider every pound of supplies and all the annuities as under their control and for their personal benefit. I have done much during the two years to do away with that idea, but they are very tenacious and still hold out" (RCIA 1877:159).

By the mid-1870s, the council of chiefs had become powerful enough to successfully challenge the power of their agent. In 1874 Agent William F. M. Arny attempted to take a census of the Navajo tribe in spite of opposition from the council. He also tried to force the Navajo chiefs into giving up the San Juan area of the reservation in exchange for a southern extension. The chiefs signed the agreement, but Congress turned down the exchange because the extension was within the Atlantic and Pacific Railroad grant (McNitt 1962:149–55). In May 1875, the chiefs asked that Arny be replaced because he had used "threats and coercion to make us sign numerous papers of which we have no knowledge whatever" (Petition to CIA, May 28, 1875, RBIA LR NMS). In July the chiefs went to Fort Wingate and drew up another petition requesting Arny's removal (Petition of Navajo Chiefs, July 15, 1875, RBIA LR NMS). Arny submitted his resignation in late August, but the situation continued to deteriorate. In September the chiefs told Arny's family and several white employees to leave the agency. They also "forbade the Navajo laborers to work any more at the agency; and when the laborers resisted, a portion of the chiefs drove them away and tied and whipped some of the Indian laborers" (RCIA 1875:300).

The reasons for this conflict cannot be clearly ascertained from Arny's reports or other statements made at the time.[4] However, it seems likely from a later report that the trouble was in part related to the distribution of annuity goods. In 1877 Agent Irvine also attempted to take a census, reporting that

> the only unpleasantness or difficulty during the past year was on account of the change in the manner of issue of supplies, commenced January 1, 1877, when all refused to give their names, number of families, etc., when I stopped the issue to all who refused to comply, obtained a guard of ten men from Fort Wingate, and placed them over the Government stores. When they saw that I was determined, all the Navajoes, with the exception of a few chiefs, submitted. I am having the same difficulty at the present time, enrolling for census required under act of March 3, 1877. A correct census has never been made; the nearest attempt was made by the agent in 1874, when he succeeded in enrolling 1,600 families, when the Navajoes drove the agent [Arny], his family, and nearly all the employees from the reservation. The opposition comes from the council or chiefs, not from the Navajoes. They are under the lead of Mannelito [sic], who has been a disturber ever since the Navajoes were placed upon the present reservation. . . . I can very truly say that the . . . chiefs have given me all the trouble I have had at this agency, and they will do the same with any other agent. (RCIA 1877:159; RCIA in RSI 1877:555)

Irvine doubted that the chiefs held much influence with their own people: "I do not think that one [Navajo] in ten acknowledes [sic] any allegince [sic] to any chief or Head-man recognised [sic] as such at the agency" (Irvine to Smith, July 26, 1877, RBIA LR NMS).

As the conflict escalated, thefts of agency property became more frequent. Irvine reported that "the Head Chief has refused to either assist in preventing the depredations or to recover the property stolen." A military guard from Fort Wingate (Irvine to CIA, Nov. 12, 1877, RBIA LR NMS) was requested to thwart the chiefs' attempt to seize control of the distribution of annuity goods. However, the continued distribution of flour to the chiefs (Irvine to Smith, Apr. 21, 1877, RBIA LR NMS) indicates that they had not lost all their bargaining power.

In the decade following the return of the Navajos from Bosque Redondo, a more centralized Navajo political system began to evolve. Such a change benefited both the agent and the chiefs. Given the agent's limited resources, the chiefs offered the most effective way to manage the reservation. Rewarded with annuity goods and special rations, the chiefs could in turn control their followers. The early agents probably did not anticipate the growth in the power of the chiefs, nor the coming challenge to their authority.

In addition to conflicts between the agency and the tribe, early records refer to a growing problem on the reservation—witchcraft. In May 1878, Ganado Mucho, a member of the chiefs' council, accused two medicine men in the Ganado area of being witches and had them killed by his followers (Pyle to CIA, Aug. 17, 1878, RBIA LR NMS). A few days later, Manuelito told Lieutenant Colonel P. T. Swaine, the commander of Fort Wingate, that he had been "witched" and that his men were holding six witches captive (Manuelito's statement, June 10, 1878, RBIA LR NMS). A small group of soldiers freed the accused men after they promised they would never practice witchcraft again (Mitchell to Post Adjutant, Fort Wingate, June 18, 1878, RBIA LR NMS). Although the official correspondence makes no further reference to witchcraft on the reservation at this time, the trouble continued at least into the fall of 1878, and in the Navajo version of these events, more than forty "witches and thieves" were killed by Manuelito and Ganado Mucho (Young 1968:48; Hoffman 1974:101, 148).[5]

Most scholars agree that the killings had some relation to the chiefs' campaign against raiders. Virginia Hoffman (1974:148) wrote that the raiders and the witches may have been the same people. Robert Young (1968:48) thought that Manuelito and Ganado Mucho accused known raiders of being witches to have an excuse for killing them, and Clyde Kluckhohn (1962:112) made a similar interpretation. But documents from the period indicate that Manuelito and other chiefs genuinely feared these men, and that the accusations of witchcraft were legitimate.[6] J. L. Hubbell communicated Manuelito's statement to Swaine:

"One of his cousins was killed the other day, . . . he saw them do it. He says that they are afraid of the medicine. . . . He says they have threatened to kill him . . . by your interfering it will prevent them from killing more people. . . . They have threatened that they will kill him sometime during the summer, that the men that they have tied up said that they put a stone in Manuelito's head, and that is why he had the swelling in his throat, that they have said so themselves." (Manuelito's statement, June 10, 1878, RBIA LR NMS)

As Kluckhohn and Leighton (1960:178) have written, witchcraft is a "check upon the power and authority of 'political' leaders, who dare not act the autocrat lest they either be accused as witches or have witchcraft directed against them" (see also Kluckhohn 1962:112–21). Because of the well documented abuses of traditional power by the leading *naat'anii* just prior to 1878, it would have been only natural for the victims of that abuse to direct witchcraft against them.[7]

In 1880 the system which had evolved for the management of Navajo internal affairs broke down completely. Conflict developed between the agent and the chiefs, and the chiefs in turn lost control over the majority of younger Navajos. Although the chiefs no longer exerted any significant influence on the reservation, councils continued to be called after this date, and agents still tried to use them to influence the tribe.

Two major events led to the collapse of the council. First, in October of 1879, the last distribution of annuity goods under the Treaty of 1868 took place—a severe economic blow to the chiefs. Agent Galen Eastman became very sparing in his distribution of the few goods still at his disposal, mainly rations. One of his supporters, the agency interpreter John Navajo, reported that "the chiefs found fault some because Mr. Eastman would not give them more—Mr. Eastman in justice to the Navajos gave more liberally to the poor Navajos than to rich chiefs" (John Navajo to the Great Father, July 5, 1880, RBIA LR NMS). Eastman further aggravated the chiefs by cutting off rations to those who failed to enroll children in the agency school (Bennett to AAA, Apr. 24, 1880, RBIA LR NMS). Enraged by these actions, the chiefs held an open council at Fort Wingate in April to call for his removal and solicit the support of the officers (*New Mexican*, Apr. 28, 1880).

Second, the White River Utes in Colorado rebelled, killing their agent and several agency employees. As fear of a more general Indian war spread throughout the Rocky Mountain region, tension and paranoia became rampant among the Navajos and their white neighbors. During the spring and summer of 1880, Navajos made a series of attacks on both Hispanics and Anglo-Americans. The chiefs were not able to prevent these attacks or arrest the murderers.

It is difficult to say with any certainty if the chiefs' council lost its power during this period of unrest or if events only served to illustrate their lack of power. In either case, after the summer of 1880 their influence with and use by the agents declined rapidly. In June, Eastman was temporarily relieved by F. T. Bennett, now a captain in the army. Bennett found the Navajos in a very "unsettled condition," but not on the verge of war (Bennett to CIA, Aug. 5, 1880, RBIA LR NMS). The influence of the chiefs had diminished greatly since 1869, when Bennett first used them to control raiders. Thomas Keam, a longtime resident and trader on the reservation, reported that the "chiefs have no confidence in each other and fear to arrest [the] murderers" (Keam to Townsend, July 1, 1880, RBIA LR NMS). When the chiefs failed him, Bennett tried to create a Navajo police force, but was unable to recruit policemen for the salaries offered (Bennett to CIA, Sept. 12, 1880, RBIA LR NMS; RCIA 1880:133). As Agent Dennis Riordan observed in 1883, "A Navajo who has character and intelligence enough to be a good policeman will not work for $5.00 a month and rations. They can earn five and six times that amount" (Riordan to CIA, Jan. 15, 1883, RBIA GR).

Inadequate police funding also plagued Bennett's successors. With no other means of controlling the Navajos, agents attempted to revive the old technique of using the chiefs. Agent Riordan threatened to replace Manuelito in the eastern area if he could not control the younger Navajos (Riordan to Price, Feb. 14, 1883, RBIA GR), and soon extended the ultimatum to all the chiefs (Riordan to Price, Feb. 21, 1883, RBIA GR). Riordan must have known such threats were meaningless: even if they had wanted to, the chiefs were virtually powerless to act. In 1884 the agency finally received enough money to organize a police force, and hired fifteen tribal policemen. Unlike earlier police forces, this one was not comprised of chiefs. The new policemen proved "very efficient" (RCIA 1884:134), and from then on agents did not have to depend on the chiefs to police the tribe. Consequently, the creation of the new tribal police force further weakened the *naat'anii* system.

Since they had little interaction with the Navajos as a whole, agents still held meetings with the chiefs periodically. In 1880 Bennett noted that "about one-third of [the tribe] . . . seldom or never visit the agency" (RCIA 1880:131), and a few years later it was reported that some of the families in the northern portion of the reservation "have never seen an Agent"

(Riordan to CIA, Sept. 3, 1883, RBIA GR). The council of chiefs degenerated into little more than the agent's advisory committee and a convenient means of communicating with the widely scattered camps. Writing in 1889, Agent Charles Vandever remarked,

> The influence of the chiefs is rapidly waning. . . . It is very seldom their advice is sought, . . . and when offered it is very rarely accepted. When disputes occur which cannot be settled among themselves, the matter is generally laid before the agent, whose decision and advice are accepted in good faith by the interested parties (RCIA 1889:257).

The chiefs' health waned along with their influence. In 1889 Ganado Mucho was about eighty years old and sickly (RCIA 1889:257). Manuelito, only a few years younger, had developed a severe drinking problem (Hoffman 1974:102; RCIA 1884:134). As early as 1884, the agent wrote that the Navajos needed "younger, more progressive and vigorous" leaders (RCIA 1884:134). However, as we will discuss in the last part of this chapter, conditions on the reservation during this period were not conducive to the rise of new, younger *naat'anii* in the traditional manner. Manuelito died in 1893; Ganado Mucho shortly thereafter (Hoffman 1974:152–53). Although the power and influence of both men had already greatly diminished, their passing marked the end of an era: the link between the *naat'anii* system as it existed before and after the creation of the reservation had been broken.

RECOVERY OF THE SUBSISTENCE ECONOMY

Herding, farming, hunting, and gathering formed the basis of the Navajo subsistence economy. While farming was important, harvests fluctuated greatly, and production estimates do not give a reliable measure of the economy's general health. Though critical at times, hunting and gathering played only minor roles. Since herding made the greatest contribution, changes in the size of the herds provide the best indication of the tribe's overall economic situation.

The four categories of animals owned by the Navajos—goats, sheep, horses, and cattle—differed significantly in terms of economic function and relative importance. Goats surpassed sheep in subsistence value because they supplied milk and cheese as well as meat, and because they gave birth to twins more frequently (Bailey field notes). Goat meat (chevon), a dietary staple (F. Bailey 1940:272), was "more generally used for food than that of the sheep" (Hollister 1972:44–45). Goat milk and goat cheese also constituted an important part of the Navajo diet (Bailey field notes; Beadle 1873:547). Speaking of life in the 1880s, Frank Mitchell (Frisbie and McAllester 1978:32) recalled, "That is about all the food we ever ate in those early days: we lived on milk." As a result of this versatility, goats were the mainstay of Navajo subsistence. Not every family owned sheep, but they all kept goats for milk and cheese. A poor family might own nothing but goats, and inversely, calling a man a "goatherder" implied that he was poor (Bailey field notes; Counselor and Counselor 1954:307; Chabot c. 1941:608, 617).

One could have "too many" goats, but there was no such thing as having "too many" sheep (Bailey field notes). Although sheep ranked second to goats in subsistence value, they were considerably more important in the total economy because they supplied the raw material for trade items. Wool was used to make dresses for women and blankets for both sexes. Besides their domestic uses, blankets were the Navajos' major trade item until the 1880s, when the trade in raw wool outstripped the market for blankets.

Horses—a category including mules and burros—ranked third in terms of economic importance. Besides providing transportation, they were commonly butchered for meat (C. Mindeleff 1898:483) during the winter, but also during food shortages to preserve the sheep and goat herds. Wealthy Navajos kept large herds of horses and mules, which, unlike burros, enhanced the prestige of their owners (Bailey field notes).

Cattle had little economic importance for the Navajos, who were not fond of beef. Most cattle were raised for trade, and only by wealthy families (Bailey field notes; Downs 1964:38, 41).[8] The advantage of cattle over sheep and goats was that they required little care (Downs 1972:65–66).

In view of the relative economic importance of these categories, the rebuilding of Navajo herds should have occurred in four distinct stages during the last thirty years of the nineteenth century: (1) a major increase in goats, (2) increases in sheep almost immediately thereafter, (3) a rapid increase in horses after the numbers of goats and sheep leveled off, and (4) an increase in the relative number of cattle.

Rebuilding the Herds

The Navajos depended on livestock to survive, and in 1868 they began rebuilding their herds of sheep, goats, and horses. Official reports list 940 sheep, 1,025 goats, 1,550 horses, and 20 mules owned by Navajos immediately after their return from Bosque Redondo (RCIA 1868:165). Since the number of animals at Bosque Redondo in 1867 was given as 940 sheep,

1,025 goats, 550 horses, and 20 mules (RCIA 1867:203), we can assume that Agent Dodd used the previous year's figures in his 1868 report, added 1,000 horses, and resubmitted the figures—a common practice during the nineteenth and early twentieth centuries. Santiago Hubbell made the only actual count in 1868 when the main party of Navajos crossed his toll bridge on the Rio Puerco on the way to Fort Wingate. Hubbell charged the government for 7,136 Navajos, 564 horses, and 4,190 sheep; Lieutenant Colonel Charles Whiting, in charge of the party, verified the count (Affidavit from Charles Whiting, Dec. 29, 1870, RBIA LR NMS). Goats must have been counted as sheep, and accordingly, the main party of returning Navajos had twice as many sheep and goats as Dodd estimated in 1868.

It is difficult to say how many Navajos returned on their own from Bosque Redondo or had never been imprisoned, let alone how many animals they owned. During the internment, the number of Navajos "at large" was variously estimated at 8,000 (RCIA 1864:183), 480 (U.S. Congress 1867:222), and between 700 and 1,000 (RCIA 1868:164). In 1869 it was estimated that 2,000 Navajos were still living with other tribes or "roaming" (RCIA 1869:22). No estimates were made of the number of stock owned by these families. From these data, we can only conclude that in 1868 the Navajos owned more than 4,000 sheep and goats, and possibly in excess of the 1,570 horses and mules officially estimated.

In accordance with the 1868 treaty, 14,000 sheep (300 rams and 13,700 ewes), 100 billy goats, and 900 nanny goats were distributed in November 1869 (Contracts and Vouchers, Agreement with V. Romero, Oct. 5, 1869, RBIA RNMS; RCIA in RSI 1870:609). Although they were impoverished and often hungry, most people refrained from butchering the few animals they owned, and relied on hunting and gathering of wild plants (L SR 1931; Bailey field notes). In 1870 Bennett wrote, "They are not killing any [lambs or kids], but have large additions of young in their flocks in all parts of the reservation" (RCIA in RSI 1870:612). Rations of corn, flour, and beef between 1868 and 1878 also helped them keep their herds intact.

Official annual estimates of the number of sheep and goats owned by the Navajos show dramatic increases in the early 1870s. Aberle (1966:30) states that "this rate of increase is impossible," which would be true if the herds had grown by reproduction alone. To expand their herds more rapidly, the Navajos quickly returned to two of their traditional methods of acquiring livestock: raiding and trading.

Many families resorted to raiding immediately after their release from Bosque Redondo, stealing whatever was available—sheep, goats, horses, mules, burros, oxen, and cattle. Nobody was spared. They raided the Utes,[9] Jicarillas,[10] Mescaleros,[11] Pueblos,[12] Spanish-Americans,[13] Anglo-Americans,[14] and Mormons.[15] From the fall of 1868 until the summer of 1872, Navajo raiders ranged widely over the Southwest, raiding as far west and north as the Mormon settlements in southern Utah, and as far east and south as the Mescalero reservation in southern New Mexico. For the most part they took only small numbers of animals, and rarely fought for livestock. However, in June 1869, raiders took 3,000 to 4,000 sheep from along the Rio Puerco, and killed 3 Spanish-Americans (A. W. Evans to AAA Gen'l, Dist. of N.M., Oct. 20, 1869, RBIA RNMS; J. Francisco Chavez to William Clinton, Aug. 4, 1869, RBIA RNMS; J. C. French to J. M. Gallegos, July 10, 1869, RBIA LR NMS).

Military officials chose to downplay the numerous reports of raids and claims for depredations: the army had no desire to be drawn into another war with the Navajos. A letter of February 15, 1870, from Major Charles McClure to Major William Kobbe, acting assistant adjutant general for the District of New Mexico, illustrates the prevailing attitude of the time:

> The Navajoes have behaved exceedingly well, and have observed strictly their part of the agreement [the Treaty of 1868]. Only one or two cases of murder and theft have occurred which can be traced to them, and in these instances the Indians committing the outrages have been small bands of ladrones [thieves] whose conduct has been disapproved of and condemned by the tribe. (RBIA LR NMS)

McClure was probably correct in attributing these incidents to a few members of the tribe, but considering the frequent reports of Navajo depredations, it seems unlikely that there were only "one or two cases."

The military seldom got involved in resolving claims for depredations. The responsibility for recovering stolen animals fell to the agent, who in turn pressured the council of chiefs. Believing that the Navajos had turned to raiding out of dire need, the agents asked for rations, not soldiers, to put an end to the trouble (Bennett to Clinton, Feb. 20, 1870, RBIA LR NMS; Arny to Parker, Jan. 5, 1871, RBIA LR NMS; Miller to Pope, Apr. 16, 1872, RBIA LR NMS).

Enemy raiders—Utes,[16] Pueblos,[17] Spanish-Americans, and even Mormons[18]—also took livestock from the Navajos. Ute raiding parties in particular harassed the Navajos from virtually the moment they returned, taking livestock and captives. In a single raid in 1869, Utes stole three herds of sheep and goats and seven horses, killing two Navajos in the process (RCIA 1870:151). Since Navajo herds were increasing rapidly during this period, the Navajos must have been staying well ahead in the exchange.

Trading was another important means of rebuilding the herds, but immediately following their imprisonment, Navajos had little to trade with. They could not weave blankets (the mainstay of trade prior to Bosque Redondo) because the drastic reduction of the sheep herds had deprived them of wool. The only expendable items were annuity goods, which soon became a major trade item. Agent James H. Miller wrote in 1871 that "the Indians as a general thing attach but little value to most of the goods they get and in nine cases out of ten trade them for sheep at less than half their value" (Miller to Pope, July 20, 1871, RBIA LR NMS). Miller outlawed the trade in annuity goods, but admitted the futility of his action (Miller to Pope, Nov. 30, 1871, RBIA LR NMS). To rectify the situation, the government reduced spending for annuity goods in 1872, and used the "freed" funds to purchase livestock. About 10,000 ewes were delivered late that summer (Voucher for 7,414 ewes, Aug. 31, 1872; Voucher for 2,030 ewes, Sept. 6, 1872, RBIA LR NMS). Trading in annuities continued as late as 1877 (Irvine to Smith, Mar. 1, 1877, RBIA LR NMS).

The Navajos also traded wild horses. Herds of these animals, probably including many that had been lost during the war, had grown in number during their absence. Captured and broken, they could be traded for other stock (Newcomb 1964:80).

Animosity between Navajos and Spanish-Americans sometimes made trading for goats and sheep a dangerous undertaking. In August 1869, a Spanish-American offered to trade two Navajos some sheep for two mules and a horse. On the pretense of buying some sheep to satisfy his part of the bargain, he led the Navajos away, murdered them, and stole their animals. Between July 1868 and September 1869, whites murdered at least twelve Navajos, and most if not all of the murders were committed by Spanish-Americans (Bennett to Clinton, Sept. 9, 1869, RBIA RNMS). Because of such incidents, most Navajos refused to travel any further east than Jemez, and in the summer of 1870 soldiers began to accompany all Navajo trading parties (Bennett to Clinton, July 29, 1870, RBIA RNMS). Instead of sending out trading parties, in 1869 the chiefs took the precaution of inviting a Spanish-American rancher to come to the reservation to trade his sheep (Bennett to Clinton, Feb. 1, 1870, RBIA RNMS).

After the creation of the Navajo police in 1872 and the resulting decline in raiding, the herds increased mainly by reproduction and trade. In 1878 the last distribution of sheep took place when the government bought 7,500 sheep with money that had been budgeted for annuity goods (Schurz to CIA, May 3, 1878, RBIA LR NMS). Some Navajos periodically resumed raiding, however, and in 1878 F. M. T. Pahies, a mining and civil engineer in New Mexico, complained, "Navajos still give frequent cause for complaint on account of their depredation on stock as far east and south as the eastern slope of Manzanas mountains" (Pahies to Schurz, Aug. 18, 1878, RBIA LR NMS). Raiding persisted as late as 1883, when Agent Riordan recovered 46 horses and more than 500 sheep (RCIA 1883:121–22). Economic conditions had improved so dramatically by that time, however, that only the poorest families had to resort to it.

Between 1868 and 1890, the Navajo agency submitted livestock estimates almost every year. While unreliable in terms of absolute numbers, they do reflect trends consistent with contemporary narrative reports. Sometimes the reports gave separate estimates for sheep and goats, and sometimes they combined these figures. Where they estimated numbers of "sheep" alone, they may or may not have been including goats. In spite of this ambiguity, the figures show an unmistakable trend (fig. 1).

As noted earlier, the Navajos owned about 4,000 sheep and goats in 1868. After the initial government distribution, it was estimated in 1870 that they owned 15,000 sheep and 2,300 goats ("'D' wild tribe of Indians of New Mexico as enumerated by W. F. M. Arny, Agent for Indians and Census Service in New Mexico, 1870; Navajoes as enumerated by Lieutenant F. T. Bennett, RBIA LR NMS). Estimates in 1871 ranged from 30,000 sheep (RCIA 1871:378) to 40,000 sheep and goats (Pope to Parker, July 6, 1871, RBIA LR NMS); in 1872, from 100,000 (RCIA 1872:792–93) to 125,000 (RCIA 1872:304) and 130,000 (RCIA 1872:53); in 1873, from 175,000 sheep and goats to 250,000 "sheep" (RCIA 1873:272, 266). In 1874, when a hard winter resulted in heavy stock losses, the estimate declined to 130,000 (RCIA 1874:62, 307). From 1874 to 1880 the herds increased almost without interruption, and by 1880 the Navajos owned an estimated 1,000,000 sheep and goats (RCIA 1880:131). The numbers leveled off in the 1880s: with the exception of 1885, when 1,500,000 sheep were reported, the numbers stayed in the 900,000 to 1,200,000 range. The reports estimated 1,583,754 sheep and goats in 1891 (RCIA 1891:309), and 1,715,984 in 1892 (RCIA 1892:803).

There is no way to verify these estimates. Still, the rapid growth trend of the 1870s and the leveling off of the 1880s agree with other data and independent narrative statements made during this period. Aberle (1966:32) felt that the Navajos may have had as many as 1,000,000 sheep by 1890, but considered the peak estimates of 1885 and 1892 "extraordinarily high." However, given that the Navajos owned over 1,800,000 sheep and goats in 1915 (RCIA 1915:189, 191; appendix A)—a figure based at least in part on

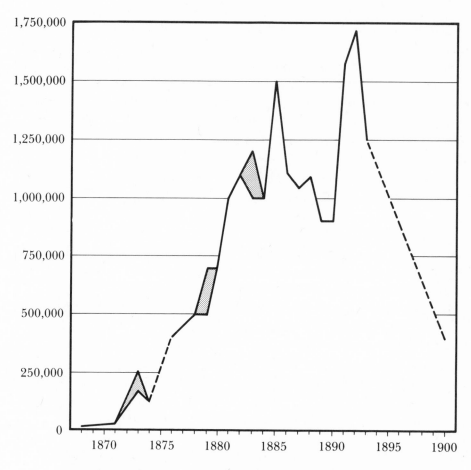

Figure 1. Estimated number of sheep and goats owned by the Navajos, 1868–1900. Shaded areas indicate range of estimates. Broken line indicates missing data.

actual counts—and given that they occupied approximately the same rangelands in 1915 as they did in the early 1890s, it is conceivable that they owned as many as 1,700,000 animals in 1892.

Since the government did not distribute horses to the Navajos, they had to acquire them by their own means. Only 564 horses crossed Hubbell's toll bridge with the returning party of Navajos in 1868 (affidavit from Charles Whiting, Dec. 29, 1870, RBIA LR NMS), and Agent Dodd estimated only 1,550 horses and 20 mules in his 1868 report (RCIA 1868:165)—undoubtedly a low estimate. Horses increased gradually from an estimated 8,000 in 1870 ("D" wild tribe of Indians of New Mexico as enumerated by W. F. M. Arny for Indian and Census Service in New Mexico 1870, Navajoes as

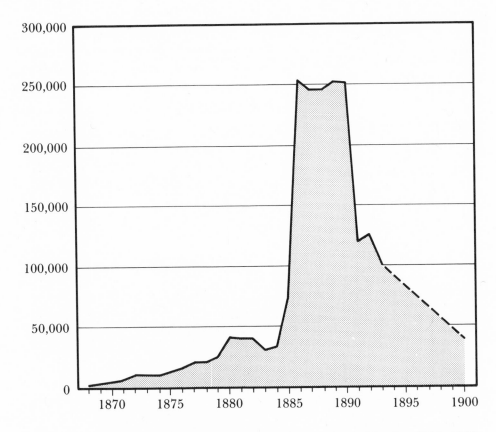

Figure 2. Estimated number of horses owned by the Navajos, 1868–1900. Broken line indicates missing data.

enumerated by Lieutenant F. T. Bennett, RBIA LR NMS) to 22,500 horses and 500 mules in 1879 (RCIA 1879:115); jumped to 41,500 in 1880 (RCIA 1880:132); and in the mid-1880s rose dramatically to 250,000 horses, 3,000 mules, and 500 burros (RCIA 1886:203). The number remained at approximately 250,000 from 1886 to 1890, only to drop sharply in 1891 and 1892 (fig. 2).[19]

The government purchased cattle to butcher and distribute as rations, but made no distribution of live cattle. As early as 1873, Agent Arny suggested that annuity goods be paid at least partly in cattle (Arny to Smith, Sept. 15, 1873, RBIA LR NMS), but apparently the government did not follow his recommendation. The reports listed negligible numbers of cattle during the 1870s and 1880s, and only one cow in 1874 (RCIA 1874:437). Beginning in 1887 the number increased rapidly, reaching 9,876 head in 1892 (RCIA 1892:803) (fig. 3).

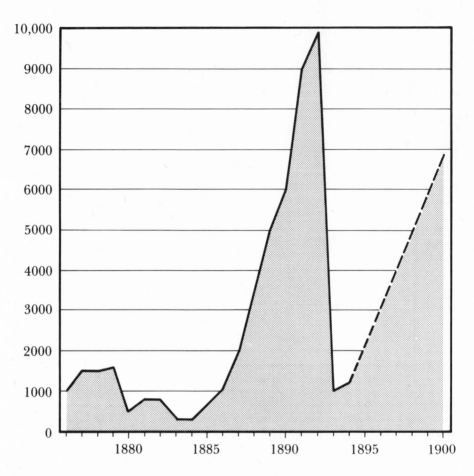

Figure 3. Estimated number of cattle owned by the Navajos, 1876–1900. Broken line indicates missing data.

Clear trends can be derived from these data. In the 1870s the number of sheep and goats increased rapidly, while the number of horses increased slowly. Although the Navajos raided for horses and traded blankets for them with other tribes during this decade, the horse stock was used largely as currency for acquiring sheep from Spanish-Americans (McClure to Nichols, Nov. 14, 1868, RBIA LR NMS; Bennett to Clinton, Sept. 9, 1869, RBIA RNMS; Bennett to Clinton, Feb. 1, 1870, RBIA RNMS). While horses were traded or butchered, the sheep and goat herds increased in size (Beadle 1873:528; Claim of Balthazar Marfin, 1870, RBIA LR NMS; Miller to Pope, Mar. 19, 1872, RBIA LR NMS; Newcomb 1964:80).

By the late 1870s, the Navajos had enough sheep and goats to meet their subsistence needs, and in 1878 they began trading sheep for horses (Pyle to CIA, Sept. 30, 1878, RBIA LR NMS; Phillips to Schurz, Dec. 28, 1878, RBIA LR NMS; Bennett to CIA, Nov. 22, 1880, RBIA LR NMS). Although the numbers of sheep and goats remained relatively constant during the 1880s, horses increased rapidly until the late 1880s when their numbers leveled off, and the number of cattle started to rise. By the late 1880s the Navajos were beginning to sell or trade their surplus horses, "manifesting a desire to deal more largely in cattle with a view of that being a more profitable investment" (RCIA 1887:171). Thus, while each of the estimates in themselves may be subject to question, the broad pattern of herd growth follows a sequence which is logically consistent with the relative economic values and uses of the various categories of herd animals.

Farming

As early as 1865, it was suggested that the Navajos be resettled in agricultural "pueblos" in Canyon de Chelly, the San Juan Valley, and along the eastern slope of the Chuska Mountains (U.S. Congress 1867:337). Government officials favored agriculture because an economy based on farming rather than herding would allow the tribe to be accommodated on a considerably smaller land base; also, concentrating them in villages would facilitate the control and administration of the tribe. Officials were extremely optimistic about such a major remodeling of Navajo culture and economy: the Indians already knew how to farm, and were "in all other respects far in advance of all other tribes within the Territory" (RCIA 1863:136).

The Treaty of 1868 allocated far more money for seed and farm implements than for livestock. The agency provided these goods at every annuity distribution from the spring of 1869 until 1879, when the original program expired. After 1879 seeds and equipment continued to be supplied, but they were purchased with other funds.

In 1869 the agent's immediate concern was to supply the Navajos with seeds and tools so they could plant their fields in time for a good harvest. But before long, the agency became involved in "improving" Navajo farming practices by introducing new crops and farm tools.

The government supplied mainly seed corn and wheat. The Navajos had probably planted wheat since the early eighteenth century, but in 1870 F. T. Bennett noted that the Navajos "don't rely on their wheat crop and . . . only planted small proportions of wheat" (Bennett to Clinton, Aug. 10,

1870, RBIA LR NMS). Agency officials chose to ignore the Navajo preference for corn and persisted in issuing corn and wheat in almost equal quantities (Pope to Walker, Apr. 16, 1872, RBIA LR NMS; Estimate of Seed Wheat and Corn for 1873, RBIA LR NMS; Arny to Dudley, June 4, 1874, RBIA LR NMS).

The agency handed out smaller quantities of bean, watermelon, muskmelon, squash, and pumpkin seeds—crops the Navajos were already familiar with. It also tried to introduce unfamiliar varieties: turnips, beets, cabbage, peas, sweet potatoes, carrots, parsnips, cucumbers, tomatoes, sugar beets, spinach, cauliflower, parsley, asparagus, rutabaga, and potatoes (Voucher for purchase of seeds, Seligman and Bros., 1870, RBIA LR NMS; Estimate for Seeds for Navajos for 1871, RBIA LR NMS; Arny to Dudley, June 4, 1874, RBIA LR NMS; RCIA 1889:257). During the 1870s and 1880s, the Navajos were introduced to almost every major garden crop grown by Euro-Americans.

Seed distributions had little significant impact on Navajo farming. Except for the potato, which eventually became an important crop in some areas of the reservation, most of the "exotic" crops introduced during this period had little lasting effect on the Navajo diet. Corn remained the most important crop in spite of official efforts to encourage the planting of wheat.

Until 1879 farming tools were purchased annually with funds provided by the treaty. In 1870 the superintendent of Indian affairs for New Mexico advised the agency to distribute tools "of the simplest kind, such as Hoes, Spades, Sickles, Mattocks, and Axes, as the Navajoes are not acquainted with the use of any other kind" (Clinton to Parker, Jan. 26, 1870, RBIA LR NMS). Shovels and pickaxes were also issued during the 1870s (Clinton to Parker, May 18, 1870, RBIA LR NMS; Irvine to Smith, Aug. 20, 1877, RBIA LR NMS), but plows were not distributed until the 1880s (Gardner to Secretary of the Interior, Oct. 15, 1883, RBIA LR GR), when the chiefs expressed a desire for them (Notes of a talk with the Navajoe Chiefs, Dec. 1880, RBIA LR NMS).

Tools issued by the government had as little effect on Navajo farming practices as seed distribution. Many tools distributed during the late 1860s and early 1870s were probably traded for livestock, and in the 1880s, Navajos left many corn cultivators at Ft. Defiance (RCIA 1886:203). Although some Navajos began to use plows in the 1880s, their use was limited. The vast majority of Navajo farmers continued to use traditional methods, and the digging stick remained their main tool.[20]

Thompson (1976:162) has remarked that "with regard to farming, the Navajos returned to their homeland with a mature knowledge of irrigation.

Navajos now farmed with hoes, shovels, plows, and rakes; they had learned farming techniques that caused greater crop production." The Navajos did learn something of Anglo-American farming technology during their captivity at Bosque Redondo, but the long-term effect was limited. As late as 1887, they were planting their wheat in small, separate mounds, and agency employees were trying to teach them how to use plows, cultivators, and sickles (RCIA 1887:172).

Agents periodically estimated the number of acres planted and the size of harvests, but since most fields were small and scattered, these estimates are not very reliable. At best, they tell us only part of the story of Navajo farming during this period. Navajo farmers irrigated with floodwater, depending on spring runoff from the nearby mountains. If the snowpack in the mountains were deep, they planted extensively, expecting a heavy spring runoff to irrigate their crops. If the snow were light, they planted very little (Bailey field notes). Consequently, farming intensity was determined more by climatic than economic conditions.[21]

The plan to increase Navajo dependence on farming did not succeed. On the contrary, as we will argue later in this chapter, Navajo farming may actually have declined as the herds increased.

Hunting and Gathering

In 1868 and for most of the following decade, their herds remained too small to provide the Navajos with enough meat for their diet. As much as possible, they abstained from butchering productive animals, and relied on hunting. In 1931 older Navajos from the Leupp area told their superintendent that during this period "their own flocks provided [only] a part of their meat," and that most of it had been supplied by "the great antelope herds" along the Little Colorado River (L SR 1931:1). A similar situation existed on the northern Chaco Plateau (Bailey field notes). The Chaco Plateau was ideal antelope country (Russell 1964:9), and Navajos constructed antelope corrals in the grasslands to capture them (Bailey field notes). Heavy reliance on hunting was probably characteristic of the Navajos in general in the decade after 1868.

Intensive hunting rapidly brought game animals to the point of extinction in most areas. In 1874 it was reported that "the game has been nearly all hunted out of the country" (Dudley to Smith, Jan. 15, 1874, RBIA LR NMS). By 1876 Navajo and Ute hunters had exterminated most of the game in the San Juan Valley (RCIA 1876:45), and in the early 1880s, the agent estimated that only five percent of Navajo sustenance was obtained from hunting (RCIA 1881:139; RCIA 1882:398). Referring to New Mexico, Vernon Bailey (1931:22) wrote:

> The largest area from which they [antelope] have entirely disappeared lies in the northwestern corner of the state, within the range of the Navajo Indians. In the early days of bows and arrows, antelope were abundant over these great arid plains, and as late as 1883 they were still found in the San Juan Valley. . . . [There have been] no antelope in that valley since 1883. In 1908 no recent record of antelope could be obtained in the Navajo region. The Navajo Indians are excellent hunters, and with their abundance of good horses and rifles have extirpated the antelope from their country.

The other big game animals, deer and elk, suffered a similar fate. Intensive exploitation destroyed the game animals in Navajo country by the mid-1880s, if not earlier, and Navajo hunters had to range farther and farther from home. In the fall of 1882, forty-six Navajos were given passes to hunt deer in the Upper San Juan Valley (Bean to AAA Gen'l, Dist. of N.M., Oct. 29, 1882, RBIA LR GR). In 1885 citizens of Socorro, New Mexico, complained that Navajo hunters had been coming into their area "for several years past" (Memorial from citizens of Socorro to Ross, Sept. 3, 1885, RBIA LR GR). Two or three hundred Utes and Navajos were reported hunting in the Blue Mountains of Utah in the fall of 1889 (Williams to Post Adjutant, Fort Lewis, Dec. 11, 1889, WD RUSAC LR FL).

These reports indicate that the Navajos continued to hunt intensively after their herds had been rebuilt. Even when the need for game animals as a food source had been eliminated, they still needed hides. Navajos made moccasins from buckskins (usually deerskins, although the term can also refer to the skin of an elk or antelope). Sheep and goat hides were not suitable. Complaints from white settlers in southern Utah during the 1880s suggest that by that time, Navajos were hunting primarily for hides. The settlers reported that hunters in the Blue Mountains left "the carcass and killed for the hides alone" (Williams to Post Adjutant, Dec. 11, 1889, WD RUSAC LR FL).

With the extermination of game animals in their country, the Navajos faced a leather crisis. When they first started selling wool, they traded much of it for leather (RCIA in RSI 1876:513), and in the early 1870s, the distribution of hides from butchered beef-ration cows helped to relieve the scarcity. In 1877, however, the government did not follow this practice. Agent Irvine wrote, "the Navajoes are in need of all hides for Moccasins and unless they receive them will suffer much in consequence," requesting that all hides of cows killed at the agency be given to them (Irvine to CIA, Oct. 19, 1877, RBIA LR NMS).

The leather shortage made buckskins a major trade item. Navajos traded for them with Utes, who were skilled in the preparation of hides (Bailey field notes). George Chittenden noted in 1875 that the Navajos "are especially fond of leather. . . . They refused $5 for a sheep, and finally traded it for a couple of pounds of flour and a saddle-leather readily replaced for 75 cents" (Chittenden 1877:358).

Speaking of his boyhood during the 1880s, Frank Mitchell (Frisbie and McAllester 1978:36) recalled, "Buckskin was scarce. I wore moccasins, but mine were made just any old way; all that mattered was that they covered my feet. Mine were made from moccasins that had been used before and had worn out; the materials were just handed down from my mother or others in the family."

In addition to hunting, Navajos survived by gathering the roots, nuts, fruits, bulbs, seeds, and leaves of a wide variety of wild plants (Elmore 1943:104–105). In 1869 Agent Bennett wrote, "Last year there were large quantities of pinon nuts, but this winter there are none" (Bennett to Clinton, Dec. 16, 1869, RBIA LR NMS). A few years later, Thomas Keam reported that a late frost had ruined "nearly all the wild fruits and seeds, which they depended and partially lived on, when their crops failed" (Keam to Pope, June 25, 1872, RBIA LR NMS). These reports substantiate statements of living informants who said that their families survived on wild plants immediately after their return from Bosque Redondo (Bailey field notes). Shortages of such food resulted in major hardships. As the herds grew in size and the farms were reestablished, dependence upon wild plant foods lessened significantly, but did not end. In 1881 Captain Bourke wrote that the Navajo diet included piñons, acorns, grass seeds, sunflowers, wild potatoes, and the inner layers of the pine tree (Bloom 1936:88).[22]

Economic Recovery

In 1868 government officials planned to issue rations only until the fall of 1869, when it was expected that the Navajos' first harvest would make them self-sustaining. The harvest fell far short of expectations, however, and rationing had to be continued throughout the 1870s. From 1869 through the early 1870s, small herds, disappointing harvests, and inadequate game plagued the Navajos, but at no time did Indian Service officials blame them for their economic difficulties. Instead, they regularly praised them for efforts on their own behalf.

In the late 1870s, the economy of the Navajos started to show signs of self-sufficiency. In 1877 Lieutenant Thomas Blair reported that the Navajos discarded goods on the agency grounds, including "nearly rotten" calico and "poor quality" knives and hatchets (Blair to AAA Gen'l, N.M., May 2, 1877, RBIA LR NMS). Fewer than 500 Navajos attended a rations distribution in the winter of 1878 (Earle to Kingsley, Dec. 30, 1878, RBIA LR NMS). Often, they only came to get tobacco (Irvine to Smith, Mar. 19, 1877, RBIA LR NMS). From 1868 to 1879 the agency paid its Indian laborers in commodities such as sugar and flour (Eastman to CIA, Nov. 15, 1879, RBIA LR NMS), but by 1880 workers wanted "silver" money—preferably malleable Mexican coins for making jewelry—instead of food (Eastman to CIA, Jan. 26, 1880, RBIA LR NMS).

Officers, agents, and Navajo leaders confirmed the economic recovery. Navajos came "well fed and well clad" to the annuity goods distribution in 1877 (Blair to AAA Gen'l, N.M., May 2, 1877, RBIA LR NMS). The following year Agent John E. Pyle stated, "They have by the cultivation of the soil and by judicious management of their flocks and herds of domestic animals, now attained to a condition virtually independent of government aid" (Pyle to CIA, Nov. 8, 1878, RBIA LR NMS). Later that year, another official remarked that "they are wealthy and rapidly becoming more so" (Earle to Kingsley, Dec. 30, 1878, RBIA LR NMS). The Navajo leader Ganado Mucho told a visiting official in 1880 that his people had "stock enough," and that they only needed some flour, sugar, and coffee for the poor and elderly (Notes of a talk with the Navajoe Chiefs, Dec. 1880, RBIA LR NMS).

Between 1878 and 1880, numerous narrative statements indicate that the Navajo economy had recovered to at least its pre-1863 level of self-sufficiency. Also, we have seen that the basis of their economy, the herds, continued to expand after 1880. The economic changes of the 1880s and early 1890s and the level of prosperity attained will be examined later in this chapter.

CRAFT PRODUCTION

For several centuries the Navajos had depended on trade with the Spaniards, the Pueblos, and other tribes in the region for some material goods. In some cases, as with the Spaniards, they traded for metal items—silver jewelry, iron bits, knives, axes—that could be obtained in no other way. They also traded for items of high quality that they could not make themselves, for example, painted Pueblo pottery and Ute buckskins. As the Navajos were the premier weavers in the region, they found a market for their textiles with neighboring tribes and Spanish-Americans, and a complex trade network evolved among the various groups in the region.

The Navajos practiced five major kinds of craft production: weaving, pottery, basketry, ironsmithing, and silversmithing. Although significant changes took place in these crafts during the late nineteenth century, they did not follow a common trend. During this period weaving remained the most important craft, ironsmithing and silversmithing came into their own, and pottery and basketry declined.

Stylistic changes in Navajo weaving during this period have received the attention of numerous scholars, in particular Charles Amsden (1975).[23] Our concern is solely with economic, technological, and functional changes. The record indicates three major changes of this nature: first, commercial yarn increased in availability and use; second, commercial dyes became available for the first time and made significant inroads because of their lower cost; and third, Anglo-American wool cards (used to prepare wool for spinning) became popular, although high cost and an inadequate supply limited their use.

Before Bosque Redondo an extensive trade had existed in Navajo textiles, particularly blankets, and Indian Service officials realized the potential of these products for economic recovery. Besides blankets, Navajo weavers produced saddle blankets, sash belts, garters, saddle cinches, women's dresses, and knitted socks and leggings (Amsden 1975; Kluckhohn, Hill, and Kluckhohn 1971)—items woven for domestic use as well as for trade. To increase the quantity as well as the quality of work, Colonel Dodd purchased weaving looms and spinning wheels for the Navajos while they were still incarcerated at Bosque Redondo. After 1868 the remaining equipment was shipped to Fort Defiance (Labadi to French, Mar. 29, 1869, RBIA LR NMS). The government purchased additional looms in 1871 and 1875, and weavers were hired to teach Navajo women how to use them. Both attempts failed because the Navajos were "very much opposed to any other than their old plan of spinning and making blankets" (Bennett to Pope, Feb. 15, 1871, RBIA LR NMS; Pope to Parker, Feb. 22, 1871, RBIA LR NMS; Irvine to Smith, Nov. 10, 1876 RBIA LR NMS), and in 1879 the looms were sent to Laguna Pueblo (Thomas to Hoyt, July 25, 1879, RBIA LR NMS).

Efforts to encourage Navajo weaving were not limited to the ill-fated loom experiments. The government distributed bayeta (scarlet) blankets, yarn, dyes, and wool cards as annuity goods, and Navajo weavers readily accepted them. The list of annuity goods for 1869 included 38 pairs of indigo blankets, 35 pairs of bayeta blankets to be unraveled and used in weaving, 2 boxes of indigo, 2,245 pounds of scarlet yarn, 700 pounds of assorted yarn, and 148 pounds of red and white thread skeins (Contracts and Vouchers Certificate of Annuity Goods Issued . . . Oct. 1869, RBIA LR NMS). By 1874, the yarn issue had increased to 6,100 pounds (List of Annuity Goods Issued . . . May 6, 1874, RBIA LR NMS). Agent Irvine noted a constant demand for scarlet yarn in 1877 (Irvine to Smith, Mar. 19, 1877, RBIA LR NMS), and in the same year, an invoice from Martinez's trading post at Fort Defiance listed yarn and bayeta among the major trade items (Invoice of Merchandise purchased by "Trader" Romulo Martinez, Mar. 31, 1877, RBIA LR NMS). By 1880 the Navajos needed a red yarn to use in place of bayeta because the price of this "Mexican cloth" had risen from $3 to $4 a yard (McNeil to Schurz, Dec. 23, 1880, RBIA LR NMS). The high price of bayeta may have led to the increased use of cheaper Germantown yarns in the early 1880s. In 1884 Washington Matthews (1884:376) noted that bayeta was "still largely used," but that Germantown yarn "has lately become very popular among the Navajos, and many fine blankets are now made wholly, or in part, of Germantown wool."

Navajo weavers considered the fiber-bristled and steel-toothed wool cards distributed by the agency far superior to their own. The Navajo cards were made of thistles mounted on a wooden board with a handle—probably an invention of Mexican origin (Amsden 1975:35). The government issued 250 dozen wool cards in 1871 (Parker to Pope, June 15, 1871, RBIA LR NMS), but they were not distributed regularly during the early 1870s. In 1876 Agent Irvine asked the commissioner of Indian affairs for permission to add wool cards to the estimated annuity list, pointing out that "wool cards . . . are used by all the wimen [sic] in the tribe and are essential" (Irvine to Smith, Mar. 11, 1876, RBIA LR NMS). Romulo Martinez listed only 2 dozen wool cards on his invoice of trade goods in 1877 (Invoice of Merchandise purchased by "Trader" Romulo Martinez, Mar. 31, 1877, RBIA LR NMS), which suggests that many Navajo weavers were still using homemade wool cards.

It is difficult to determine whether the role of weaving in the Navajo economy changed significantly during this period. The Navajos continued to weave blankets for their own use and for trade to surrounding groups, as they had for well over a century before Bosque Redondo. The completion of the Atlantic and Pacific Railroad across much of the southern Navajo country in the early 1880s created still another market among Anglo-American tourists (RCIA 1882:129). Even with the development of this new market, the Navajos kept a sizeable proportion of their blankets for domestic use. In 1887 Agent S. S. Patterson estimated that two-thirds of Navajo blankets were either sold or traded (RCIA 1887:172), and in 1890 Agent Vandever reported that they produced $39,000 worth of blankets, and kept $15,000 worth (RCIA 1890:162). Since similar data are not available for the pre-Bosque Redondo period, it is impossible to establish a comparable trend in the early history of the blanket trade.

Navajo silverwork has also been the subject of substantial scholarly research. Readers interested in the various forms and stylistic changes of Navajo jewelry are referred to the excellent studies by Margery Bedinger (1973), John Adair (1944), and Arthur Woodward (1971). Our present study is concerned with the economic implications of and technological changes in Navajo silversmithing.

The Navajos were wearing silver jewelry obtained from the Spaniards by the late eighteenth century, and learned silversmithing from them in about the mid-nineteenth century. Although many scholars have contended that the Navajos did not begin working in silver until after Bosque Redondo (Adair 1944:193; Mera 1960:1), it seems likely that they were learning the rudiments of the trade in the previous decade (Bedinger 1973:13–15). However, the evolution of silversmithing as an economically important craft did not take place until after 1868.

In 1869, Edward Palmer, who led several expeditions from the Peabody Museum to the Southwest during the 1870s (Palmer n.d.; Bedinger 1973:13–14), wrote that the Navajos were making silver buttons from Spanish and Mexican one *real* coins. According to Palmer, the buttons were used as money. A one *real* coin was worth 12½¢, or eight to the dollar, and the buttons had the same value.

Lack of proper tools limited the quality and variety of items produced by early Navajo silversmiths. In 1871 the agency requested and presumably issued a small number of anvils, vises, hammers, files, file saws, and bellows to help Navajo blacksmiths (Clum to Pope, Nov. 2, 1871, RBIA LR NMS), who usually worked as silversmiths as well.

During the 1870s, the quality of Navajo silverwork improved as smiths acquired a wider variety of tools from traders and learned to make tools themselves. Matthews (1883:171–75) noted in the early 1880s that Navajo smiths purchased scissors, iron pliers, hammers, awls, emery paper, fine files, and borax for soldering from local traders. They had also learned to make goatskin bellows, anvils, dies and bolts, sandstone molds for casting, tongs, and brass blowpipes.

As their equipment improved, the silversmiths could produce a greater variety of items. By the early 1880s, they were making buttons, rosettes, bracelets, bridle ornaments, and concha belts. Three or four of the smiths were fashioning canteen-shaped tobacco cases (Matthews 1883:171–72). About 1880, some of the smiths in the Ganado area started to make jewelry with turquoise sets (Bedinger 1973:48).

Silversmithing flourished during the 1880s, when the Navajos prospered and began investing their wealth in silver jewelry. In 1880, when Navajo employees of the agency were asking for their pay in Mexican coins, Manuelito decided to make bridles out of silver money (Hubbell to Eastman, May 10, 1880, RBIA LR NMS). Navajo silversmiths were finding a ready market for their work among their own tribesmen, and a profitable trade in silver jewelry was evolving with local whites and members of other tribes (McNeil to Schurz, Dec. 23, 1880, RBIA LR NMS).

The development of the pawn system during the 1880s further encouraged silversmithing. Silver ornaments, no matter what kind, could be pawned to traders in exchange for other goods (Vandever to CIA, Aug. 9, 1889, RBIA LR GR; RCIA 1889:256). The pawn system expanded the function of silver jewelry from personal adornment to "savings" which could be used during times of economic crisis.

Bedinger (1973:22) thought that silversmithing probably started in the Ganado area, and noted that most of the "pioneer" Navajo silversmiths lived within twenty-five to forty miles of Ganado. The number of smiths rapidly increased during this period, and by 1900 silversmiths lived throughout Navajo country. Nevertheless, in terms of technique, design, and skill, the Ganado smiths continued to excel (Bedinger 1973:48).

Unlike their silverwork, Navajo ironwork was so closely patterned after its Spanish prototypes that it is virtually impossible to tell one from the other (Simmons and Turley 1980:98–105). The Navajos first acquired iron and steel items through trade with the Spanish. Trained by Hispanic blacksmiths, they began forging iron tools of their own in the mid-nineteenth century.

The Navajos learned the art of ironworking before Bosque Redondo, but few had become proficient (Bedinger 1973:13–14). Following their return, a number of Navajo blacksmiths approached Agent Miller and asked for tools and anvils (Miller to Pope, Sept. 3, 1871, RBIA LR NMS). Miller requested 6 small (35 pound) anvils, 6 small vises, 6 blacksmith hammers, 36 files, 36 three-cornered handsaw files, and 6 small bellows (Estimate of Blacksmith Tools required for Navajo Indians . . . 1871, RBIA LR NMS). The commissioner of Indian affairs approved the request (Clum to Pope, Nov. 2, 1871, RBIA RNMS). Several years later Agent Irvine reported that "all articles containing iron are eagerly sought after by the Navajos in order to make bridle bitts [sic] and other articles" (Irvine to Smith, Nov. 10, 1876, RBIA LR NMS).

By the early 1880s, a sizeable number of Navajos were working as blacksmiths. "We have plenty of Indian blacksmiths," said Ganado Mucho in 1880, asking for files, hammers, and anvils (Notes of a talk with the Navajoe Chiefs, Dec. 1880, RBIA LR NMS). Two years later Major J. C. McKee remarked, "Among the men, skillful workers in iron are quite common" (McKee to CIA, May 5, 1882, RBIA LR GR). About the same time, Washington Matthews (1883:171) wrote, "There are many smiths, who sometimes forge iron and brass, but who work chiefly in silver," qualifying the previous statements. Even smiths who knew how to work with iron usually worked with silver: not only was it softer and easier to work, but it was also more profitable.

Iron bridle bits, the major product of Navajo blacksmiths, were made from old horseshoes and scrap iron, and styled after Spanish bits obtained earlier through trade (Franciscan Fathers 1968:150; Kluckhohn, Hill, and Kluckhohn 1971:82–83; Simmons and Turley 1980:102–104). While most ironwork was manufactured for domestic use, the Navajos traded bits to the Utes for buckskins and hides (Adair 1944:6–7).

Pottery and basketry did not have the commercial potential of other Navajo crafts, and their manufacture declined as they came into competition with and were replaced by items of Anglo-American manufacture. In 1868 pots and baskets still made up the majority of Navajo household utensils. Clay vessels of various shapes were used for cooking or holding liquids, flat coiled baskets for serving food, and pitch covered baskets for holding water.

Annuity goods often duplicated the function of pots and baskets. At the first annuity distribution in October 1869, the agency distributed 15 boxes of camp kettles (Certificate of Annuity Goods Issued . . . Oct. 1869, RBIA LR NMS). Brass kettles and frying pans were listed among the "most necessary articles" to be distributed in 1870 to the Navajos living at Cebolleta (Bibo to Clinton, May 11, 1870, RBIA LR NMS). The following year the government gave the Navajos 300 dozen pans, 600 kettles, and 50 dozen dippers (Parker to Pope, June 15, 1871, RBIA RNMS). From 1873 to 1878 every list of estimated annuity goods named items such as pans, pails, plates, cups, kettles, and dippers (Estimates of Annuity Goods, RBIA LR NMS). After the agency stopped distributing such goods on a massive scale, traders began to fill the increasingly keen demand.

As early as 1890, Agent Vandever reported that older women still made pottery cooking vessels, but not the younger women (RCIA 1890:161, 164).

Writing a few years later, A. M. Stephen (1893:359) noted that "the iron camp-kettles and tin cups and coffee pots brought in by the trader are rapidly displacing the primitive gourd ladles and earthen jars." Families who could not afford to buy tin cups and other tin items from the traders used discarded food cans (Bailey field notes). In 1890 Vandever (RCIA 1890:161, 164) wrote that the Navajos still produced "many beautiful specimens of basketry," but that "the ordinary utensils of civilization are forcing . . . basketry into disuse." Washington Matthews (1894:202) observed baskets in use only during religious ceremonies, and reported that Navajos were buying most of theirs from other tribes, "having generally let the art of basketry fall into disuse."

TRADE

Long before Bosque Redondo, a well established trade network linked the Navajos with neighboring tribes and Spanish-American communities. After 1868 the old network was quickly reestablished, but with a higher volume of trade and greater overall economic importance. At the same time, a new trade network evolved with the rise of trading posts and a market for Navajo wool. Since the two networks handled different goods, they were complementary, rather than competitive.

As early as December 1869, Bennett reported that "the Navajos express themselves at peace with all, and trade, and visit with all the adjoining tribes" (Bennett to Clinton, Dec. 30, 1869, RBIA RNMS)—something of an exaggeration. The hostility which had prevailed during the war did not evaporate with the signing of the treaty. Periodically, conflicts broke out between the Navajos and some of their neighbors, particularly the Utes (Bailey and Bailey 1982:71–79). The Navajos also remained extremely wary of Spanish-Americans, and several years passed before conditions returned to normal.

By the close of this period, the trade network encompassed most of the Southwest and much of the Intermountain West. Navajos traded mainly with Spanish-Americans, Utes, and Pueblos, but also with Comanches (Pope to Walker, Aug. 27, 1872, RBIA LR NMS), Mescalero Apaches (Coleman to AAA Gen'l, Oct. 18, 1872, RBIA LR NMS), Chiricahua Apaches (Hatch to AA Gen'l, Dec. 27, 1876, RBIA LR NMS), Paiutes (Arny to Dudley, Feb. 16, 1874, RBIA LR NMS), White Mountain Apaches, San Carlos Apaches, Jicarilla Apaches, Walapais, Yavapais, and Havasupais (W. Hill 1948:377). The establishment of Lee's Ferry on the

Colorado in 1872 and the subsequent expansion of Mormon settlements into northern Arizona quickly brought the Mormons into the network.[24] Navajos traded with Mormons along the Little Colorado, at Moencopie, and in southern Utah (Measeles 1981:7, 29). By the 1880s and 1890s, Navajo traders were reported as far north as Snake Creek, Wyoming (Hollister 1972:49).

Trading customs varied from group to group. The Navajos formed a system of trade partnerships with the Utes in which the partners were called *hak'is* ("sibling") and trade usually took the form of gift exchanges (W. Hill 1948:388–89; Bailey field notes). A similar system may have existed with the Chiricahua Apaches (Opler 1941:398). With the Pueblos, however, whom the Navajos considered greedy, all exchanges "were on a hard and fast commercial basis" (W. Hill 1948:389).[25]

The Navajos marketed deerskins, livestock, and blankets through this network. Prior to 1863, deerskins were a major trade item, but poor hunting put them in short supply after 1868. Horses became the standard of exchange in the early 1870s. Navajos were trading blankets to the Utes for horses (Arny to Dudley, Feb. 16, 1874, RBIA LR NMS; Hanson to Pope, Sept. 1, 1871, RBIA LR NMS) at about the same time they were trading horses to Spanish-Americans for sheep and goats (Bennett to Clinton, Feb. 1, 1870, RBIA RNMS). Blankets remained a major trade item, as they had been since the eighteenth century. Surrounding Indian and white populations showed a strong preference for Navajo blankets over the cheaper but more loosely woven Mexican product. The Pueblos, who according to the governor of Santo Domingo Pueblo could weave "better and finer blankets than those of the Navajo" (Lange and Riley 1966:103), were not weaving much. Navajos were weaving mostly for the Indian trade by the late 1870s. The majority of these blankets were coarsely woven and worth only a few dollars each, but about a fourth were "fancy blankets" costing as much as $100 (RCIA 1885:156; RCIA 1887:172).

Through this system the Navajos also bartered annuity goods; silverwork to other tribes and local whites (McNeil to Schurz, Dec. 23, 1880, RBIA LR NMS); ironwork, particularly bridle bits, to the Utes and possibly other tribes (Adair 1944:6–7; Bailey field notes); and woven items such as sash belts and legging ties (Amsden 1975:plate 21), as well as goat meat and mutton to the Pueblos (Dyk 1967:49–51, 137; Cushing 1920:529; Frisbie and McAllester 1978:38–39). On a limited scale, Navajos acted as brokers of Euro-American goods. According to Grenville Goodwin (1969:72–73), they supplied guns, lead, gunpowder, percussion caps, and cloth to the Western Apaches, in addition to buffalo robes obtained from eastern tribes.

In exchange for their products and possessions, the Navajos received live-stock, agricultural produce, and material items. Livestock continued to be exchanged via the trade network even after the rebuilding of the herds. They prized Ute horses for their strength and endurance, and always considered them prime trade items (Bailey field notes). They also began to build their cattle herds through this network, notably from the Mormon settlement at Moencopie (Dyk 1967:155–58).

Various Puebloan groups supplied the Navajos with agricultural produce during this period. Corn, peaches, and baked bread were in demand from the Hopis, Zunis, and other Pueblos (Dyk 1967:49–51, 137; Cushing 1920:530; Frisbie and McAllester 1978:38–39). Cosmos Mindeleff (1898:485) noted, "Until ten years ago more grain was obtained in trade from the Pueblos than was grown in the Navaho country." In 1893 Alexander Stephen (Parsons 1936:955) reported that the Hopis had traded 650,000 pounds of corn to the Navajos. Farmers themselves, the Navajos were coming to rely on the Pueblos for a large portion of their produce.

They also traded for a wide variety of material items: buckskins, buffalo robes and hides, mountain lion pelts, elk hides, beaded bags, beaded clothing, and baskets from the Utes; buckskins, basketry trays, pitched water bottles, unfinished bow staves, and bows and arrows from the Western Apaches; turquoise, beads, and painted pottery from the Pueblos; buckskins, basketry bowls, and pitched water bottles from the Paiutes; beaded buckskins from the Shoshones; buckskins from the Havasupais, Yavapais, and Walapais; and a wide range of ritual items not available in their own country from all of these tribes (W. Hill 1948:377).

Trading posts and the new trade network they belonged to did not evolve until after Bosque Redondo. Parties of itinerant Spanish-American and Anglo-American traders frequented Navajo country before 1863 (McNitt 1962:45–46), but did not establish permanent posts until later. Not much is known about the early trading posts because many were off the reservation, and therefore unlicensed.

The government issued the first license for a trading post to Lehman Spiegelberg in August 1868, allowing him to open a post at Fort Defiance or wherever he chose on the reservation (McNitt 1962:46). A few months later C. F. Ludlove was licensed (Taylor to Davis, Oct. 20, 1868, RBIA RNMS; Gallegos to Dodd, Nov. 3, 1868, RBIA RNMS). In addition to these officially sanctioned on-reservation traders, off-reservation traders began to operate. About 1870 "the almost mythical Berrando" opened a "kind of trading post" at Horse Head Crossing, Arizona, later renamed

Holbrook (McNitt 1962:69). McNitt did not explain what he meant by a "kind of trading post."

Before trading posts could succeed on the reservation, they would have to answer a real economic need. In the early 1870s, licensed traders frequently came and went, partly because the low level of trade did not sustain them. The Navajos had more interest in rebuilding their herds than in acquiring Euro-American manufactured goods, and the early trading posts did not deal in livestock. The government supplied an abundance of manufactured goods at annuity distributions, and most of these were traded for livestock within the old trade network. Even if the traders had stocked necessary goods, the Navajos would have had little to exchange for them.

The wool market added a new dimension to Navajo trade and allowed the trading post to develop into an essential economic institution. Ruth Underhill (1956:181) credits Agent Arny with encouraging some Navajos to take their surplus wool to the sutler (civilian provisioner) at Fort Defiance in 1871 and trade it for goods. The year was 1875, and the man involved was actually Arny's son, but we agree with Underhill that trading posts and the wool trade evolved together.

The price of wool rose during the Civil War, and continued to go up after 1865. With good prices and high demand, it is not surprising that an enterprising individual thought of exploiting the untapped commercial possibilities of the rapidly expanding Navajo herds. In August 1875, an official of the Wisconsin Woolen Mills wrote the commissioner of Indian affairs about buying the annual Navajo wool clip for either cash or trade (Jones to Smith, Aug. 14, 1875, RBIA LR NMS). He was not the only one with an eye to profit. With the assistance of Mr. Owens, the storekeeper at Fort Defiance, Agent Arny's son had already purchased more than 60,000 pounds of Navajo wool the previous spring (Price to Mahnken, Oct. 9, 1875, RBIA LR NMS).

Two business strategies were employed in the early years: shipping the wool to textile mills and markets in the east, and establishing mills in the region. With the idea of acquiring and processing Navajo wool, Lot Smith supervised the establishment of a mill at the Mormon settlement of Sunset, Arizona, in 1876. Crude, handmade machinery and an equally crude product soon led to its abandonment. In 1879 John W. Young, a son of Brigham Young, repeated the experiment at Moencopie, but with no better luck (Barnes 1935:430; McClintock 1921:159; Haskett 1936:22–23; V. Mindeleff 1891:78).[26]

The failure of local mills necessitated shipments of Navajo wool to eastern markets. Wool brokers needed a way to gather large quantities of a relatively inexpensive item and ship it long distances for processing. Since the old trade network could not accommodate the market, trading posts evolved to fill this need.

As the herds increased, the wool trade developed, and a network of trading posts developed along with it. Officials reported 60,000 pounds of Navajo wool sold in 1875, 200,000 pounds in 1876 (RCIA 1876:513), 800,000 pounds in 1880 and 1881 (RCIA 1880:131; RCIA 1881:261), more than 1,000,000 pounds in 1882 (Gardner to Secretary of the Interior, Oct. 15, 1883, RBIA LR GR), 1,050,000 pounds in 1886 (RCIA 1886:203), 750,000 pounds in 1887 (RCIA 1887:172), and 1,370,000 pounds in 1890 (RCIA 1890:162).

The traders soon discovered other marketable items. By the late 1880s, between 240,000 and 300,000 sheep pelts and 80,000 to 100,000 goat skins were traded annually. Since sheep pelts sold for 10¢ each, and goat skins from 15¢ to 50¢ each (RCIA 1886:203; 1887:172; 1888:190), the trade in them was fairly lucrative. They also bought and sold large quantities of corn and piñon nuts (RCIA 1890:162).

The trading posts did not enter the blanket trade to any significant degree until the end of this period. Within the old trade network, a lively blanket trade continued between the Navajos and surrounding tribes until the late 1880s. In 1887 it was reported that 75 percent of Navajo blankets were of the coarser variety, and that large numbers of these blankets were being sold or traded to the Apaches and Utes (RCIA 1887:172). As late as 1889, Navajos sold only $24,000 in blankets to traders (RCIA 1890:162)—a small fraction of the total trade, and insignificant compared to the rug trade in the early part of the twentieth century.

Dollar estimates of trade can be calculated for some years. Based on reported figures, the Navajos sold $63,000 worth of wool, $24,000 worth of sheep pelts, and $12,000 worth of goat skins in 1886. A decrease in wool sold during 1887 and 1888 did not result in a decline in income because the price of wool rose from 6¢ per pound in 1886 to between 8¢ and 10¢ per pound in 1887 and 1888. Goat skins rose in price from 15¢ in 1886 to between 25¢ and 50¢ in 1887 and 1888. Based on these figures, the Navajos traded approximately $135,000 in products in 1887, $140,000 in 1888 (RCIA 1886:203; 1887:172; 1888:190), and $180,000 in 1890 (RCIA 1891, 2:93).

From 1868 to 1878, probably no more than one trading post was operating on the reservation at a time, and there may have been periods when the sutler's store at Fort Wingate was the closest place of business. Romulo Martinez, who received his trading license in 1873, managed to survive into the period of the wool trade. Still the only on-reservation trader in 1877, Martinez opened a second store at Washington Pass by 1878 (McNitt 1962:253). Agent Pyle reported that there were "eight or ten" traders doing business with the Navajos in 1878 (Pyle to CIA, May 20, 1878, RBIA LR NMS). He may or may not have included the Mormon traders in southern Utah and the merchants along the San Juan. Regarding the prices charged by Martinez that year, Agent Irvine wrote, "I would recommend no prices to be placed upon his goods for the reason that there is sufficient competition to keep him within bounds" (Irvine to Smith, Mar. 31, 1877, RBIA LR NMS).

Martinez's invoice of goods purchased in 1877 indicates the nature and volume of the Navajo trade at that time. His purchases included two coffee mills, two wash bowls, twelve Mexican bits, eleven pocket knives, ten ebony handled hunting knives, twelve butcher knives, six bridles, twelve black leather belts, twenty-four wool cards, a large number of beads, six pairs of overalls, four dozen blue military caps, a large amount of yarn and cloth goods, flour, sugar, coffee, hams, lard, crackers, candy, ginger snaps, black pepper, allspice, honey, peaches, oysters, deviled ham, apples, matches, indigo, and borax (Furnished invoice of merchandise purchased by "Trader" Romulo Martinez, Mar. 31, 1877, RBIA LR NMS). The small size of Martinez's stock probably reflected the minor extent of his trade. As late as 1880, however, he was still the only trader operating on the reservation, besides six or seven off-reservation traders (Eastman to CIA, Jan. 5, 1880, RBIA LR NMS).

The railroad reached western New Mexico in 1881, and Gallup was established. White settlers saw an opportunity to tap the potentially lucrative Navajo trade, and their numbers increased in the vicinity of the reservation. Trading posts developed rapidly, and stores, selling mainly whiskey, sprang up along the railroad.

In 1881 another trading post opened at Fort Defiance (Gardner to Secretary of the Interior, Oct. 15, 1883, RBIA LR GR), and by 1886 the number of on-reservation posts had risen to nine. Except for one in the Chinle Valley and another at Washington Pass, these posts were in the southern portion of the reservation near Fort Defiance (Weidemeyer to West, June 20, 1886, RBIA LR GR). The estimated Navajo wool sale in 1886 surpassed the 1880 figure by only 250,000 pounds (RCIA 1886:203; RCIA 1880:131), but in 1886, large numbers of sheep pelts and goat skins were reported sold for the first time. Increased competition from new trading posts may have forced traders to deal in commodities other than wool, and some traders could not survive. By 1889 the number of on-reservation posts had declined to seven. In the same year, "thirty odd" off-reservation posts were in business and had purchased most of the 1889 wool clip of 2,100,000 pounds (Vandever to CIA, Aug. 9, 1889, RBIA LR GR).

Trade was rapidly being diverted to off-reservation posts, and by the end of this period the Navajos were literally surrounded by such stores. The heaviest concentrations occurred along the Atlantic and Pacific Railroad, which skirted the southern edge of the reservation, and in the San Juan Valley, in the northeast. In the northwestern portion of the range, the Navajos were trading with Mormons in southern Utah and northern Arizona in the early 1870s. Sometime before 1880 a trading post was established at The Gap, and another in 1881 at Tonalea or Red Lake (McNitt 1962:265). By the mid-1880s, every major population of Navajos had the opportunity for regular trade with Anglo-Americans.

"CIVILIZING" THE NAVAJOS

In the last third of the nineteenth century, federal Indian policy underwent a major reorientation. Before the Civil War, the government had isolated the tribes on reservations outside areas of white settlement, and except for military surveillance, basically ignored them. Following the Civil War, white settlers moved westward, occupying virtually all of the vacant lands in the western states and territories. Indian Affairs officials realized that physical and social isolation of native American populations was no longer feasible. As traditional means of livelihood deteriorated, the tribes became increasingly dependent on rations. Although food distribution burdened the government economically, it was preferable to warfare and genocide. With these problems in mind, officials shifted federal Indian policy from one of isolation to one of assimilation, hoping that the tribes would become economically self-sufficient and socially integrated into the surrounding non-Indian communities.

The government's assimilation or "civilization" program concentrated on education, missionary activities, housing, and dress. Schools were established to teach the Indians at least to speak English, if not to read and write it as well. Government policy encouraged missionary work in order to convert the Indians to Christianity and impose Christian values and norms of behavior on them. Overt signs of "Indianness" were to be eliminated: the men would have their hair cut short and wear Euro-American clothing. Indians were to stop living in traditional dwellings and move into permanent houses. To emphasize the importance of the program, in his annual report every agent was required to note the number of Indians under his supervision who could speak, read, and write English, those who were Christians, those who wore "citizen's clothes," and those who lived in houses. The enforcement of this policy varied from reservation to reservation and from agent to agent. Indian religious ceremonies were prohibited on some reservations. Physical and economic harassment forced people to enroll their children in school, or otherwise to comply with official policy. It was fortunate for the Navajos that in their case, the civilization program was only weakly implemented during the late nineteenth century.

Schools and Education

"To insure the civilization of the Indians," Article 6 of the Treaty of 1868 called for their education. By the terms of the treaty, the government agreed to furnish a schoolhouse and a teacher for every thirty students, while the Navajos "pledged" to send their children between the ages of six and sixteen. Of all of the provisions of the treaty, this was the slowest to be fulfilled. Even if the Navajos had wanted to send their children to school in 1868, the government could not have afforded such a system.

During the late nineteenth century, the government contracted with various missionary societies to provide schooling on the reservations. In 1869 the Board of Foreign Missions of the Presbyterian Church sent Reverend James Roberts and his wife to Fort Defiance as missionaries to establish the first school for the Navajos (Parker to Clinton, July 23, 1869, RBIA RNMS). The school opened in December (RCIA 1870:614, 617), and Reverend Roberts and Miss Charity Gaston, the major teacher, soon enrolled about thirty students. In a glowing report, Agent Bennett remarked, "The children are learning very fast, and take great interest in the school, most of them attend daily. . . . The chiefs often visit the school and are very much pleased with it" (Bennett to Clinton, Dec. 23, 1869, RBIA LR NMS).

Bennett's optimism was not long-lived. In the spring of 1870, Reverend Roberts performed a mixed marriage without the agent's knowledge or approval. Angered, Bennett requested Roberts's removal from the reservation (Roberts to Parker, Mar. 18, 1870, RBIA LR NMS; Bennett to Clinton, Mar. 9, 1870, RBIA LR NMS). Whether because of pressure from the agency or by his own choice, the minister resigned. Reverend J. A. Menaul replaced him in the spring of 1871 (Bennett to Pope, Feb. 15, 1871, RBIA LR NMS), but when Charity Gaston married Menaul and moved to Laguna Pueblo (Warner 1970:213), the school was left without teachers.

The school was facing more serious problems than quarrels between teachers and agents. In 1869 large numbers of Navajos had been living in the vicinity of Fort Defiance and subsisting on agency rations, and a teacher could easily recruit day students. But as Navajo herds increased in size, families moved away in search of pasture and took their children with them.

During the 1870s, agency and tribal leaders discussed the possibility of opening additional schools in more accessible locations. Agent Miller recommended establishing a school along the San Juan River (Miller to Pope, Feb. 14, 1871, RBIA LR NMS). In 1876 some Navajo leaders asked for a school in the Chuska Valley so their children could attend school without leaving home. Irvine thought that it was "the best location for a school to accomplish the most good to the Indians," but the agents were having enough problems keeping the Fort Defiance school open without worrying about new ones (Irvine to Smith, Feb. 12, 1876, RBIA LR NMS).

For one thing, it was hard to find teachers who were willing to live in an isolated area and work under extremely primitive conditions. Underhill (1956:199–200) summarized the problems of the school during the middle and late 1870s:

> From that time [1872] the reports for the treaty period proceed in zigzag pattern, with high hopes one year and utter discouragement the next. Or there may be discreet silence which tells more than words. In 1873, Agent Arny thought that in four years he could turn out two hundred native teachers who would educate the whole reservation. The next year, Arny was driven away, with his three teachers. . . . Teachers . . . came and went, taking vacations, complained one agent, whenever they chose and without consulting anyone. Once they quarreled and all left together. Pupils went, but very few came. In 1879, the average attendance was eleven.

Under these conditions, Navajo leaders naturally developed a poor opinion of education, telling Agent Pyle "that they could not aid [him] in maintaining schools at the agency and further that they could see no use in having their children educated" (Pyle to CIA, Nov. 8, 1878, RBIA LR NMS).

By the late 1870s, officials concluded that the attempt to educate the Navajos had failed. In 1879, ten years after the school opened, Agent Eastman wrote that only three Navajos could read McGuffey's first reader, and only ten could sign their names (RCIA 1879:222–23). He did not give the number of Navajos who could speak English, but four years later, it was estimated there were only five (RCIA 1883:276).

Clearly, something had to be done. Soon after arriving at Fort Defiance,

Agent Eastman recommended building a boarding school to alleviate the chronic shortage of students (Eastman to CIA, May 23, 1879, RBIA LR NMS). Construction began in the fall (Hammond to Eastman, Oct. 3, 1879, RBIA LR NMS), and was completed in May 1882 (Perkins to CIA, May 1, 1882, RBIA LR GR).

Troubles beset the new school. To keep children from running away, iron shutters were placed over the windows (RCIA 1892:577). "Drunkenness and disorderliness of Indians" (Perkins to Jackson, Mar. 12, 1882, RBIA LR GR) temporarily suspended classes in March of 1882. Conflict between the teachers and Agent Eastman (Perkins to CIA, May 1, 1882, RBIA LR GR) caused him to request their dismissal, and he asked that the school be closed until the Board of Foreign Missions could hire able teachers (Eastman to CIA, Dec. 9, 1882, RBIA LR GR). As it turned out, Eastman was fired—not the teachers.

The Fort Defiance boarding school did not have its anticipated impact. Forty-nine Navajos were attending in the fall of 1881 (Perkins to Haworth, Nov. 12, 1881, RBIA LR GR), but enrollment declined to three by July of 1884 (Parsons to Atkins, Mar. 13, 1886, RBIA LR GR). In 1887 Navajo spokesmen requested schools at Chinle and Pueblo Colorado because "the Agency School will never do much for them, for they are prejudiced against Fort Defiance and *will not send* their children there" (Ladd to CIA, Nov. 18, 1887, RBIA LR GR).

In 1883 a group of Navajo students was sent to Carlisle Indian School in Pennsylvania—an alternative to the Fort Defiance boarding school. Three Navajo students died there in the fall, two of whom were apparently Manuelito's sons (Riordan to CIA, Jan. 22, 1883, RBIA LR GR; Riordan to CIA, Nov. 5, 1883, RBIA LR GR; RCIA 1889:259). Nevertheless, Navajos continued to attend. In 1885 six boys were enrolled in schools in the "east" (RCIA 1885:154), but Navajos increasingly opposed sending their children away to school, and by 1889 Navajo students were no longer attending Carlisle (RCIA 1889:259).

Out of a population of almost 18,000 Navajos (Johnston 1966a:362), fewer than 100 children were enrolled in school in 1892: 75 at Fort Defiance and 20 at off-reservation schools (RCIA in RSI 1892, 2:578). In 1886 a boarding school was opened at Grand Junction, Colorado, but almost half of the Navajo children sent there in 1890 ran away (RCIA 1892, 2:210).

Besides lack of facilities and conflicts between school officials and agents, throughout this period the schools had to deal with the strong resistance of parents to formal education. According to Frank Mitchell (Frisbie and McAllester 1978:55–56),

One of the main objections to enrolling the children was that white people are not Navajos. They are foreign people, people of another race. The People were suspicious; they thought that if they put their children in school, the white people would take the children away from them and either kill them or do something so they would never be seen again. Even if they remained alive, the children would just go further and further from their homes and before the People knew it, they would never come back. That's what they used to say.

Given these problems, it is not surprising that between 1882 and 1891 the estimated number of English-speaking Navajos ranged from a low of 5 to a high of only 65. Most agents reported about 50 English speakers during this period, and between 26 to 45 who could read or write (RCIA in RSI 1882:398; RCIA 1891:72). It is evident from such figures that the attempt to educate the Navajos during the 1870s and 1880s failed.

Missionary Activities

Early missionary activity on the reservation was associated with the school. Reverend James Roberts and his successor, Reverend J. A. Menaul, doubled as missionaries and part-time teachers. Charity Gaston Menaul, the main teacher, was hired by the Presbyterian Home Mission Board as a "missionary teacher" (Parker to Clinton, July 23, 1869, RBIA LR NMS; Underhill 1956:198–99; RCIA 1870:150; Bennett to Pope, Feb. 15, 1871, RBIA LR NMS).

Official reports contain little information about missionary activity during the middle and late 1870s. The agent reported eight Navajo church members in 1874 (RCIA in RSI 1874:419) and seven in 1875 (RCIA 1875:115), indicating at least some proselytizing, but no missionaries were working on the reservation the following year (RCIA 1876:513). Primitive facilities and language barriers may have discouraged religious zeal. Missionary work made slow headway, and in 1878 Agent Pyle could claim no "professed Christians among the Navajos" (Pyle to CIA, Nov. 8, 1878, RBIA LR NMS).

The failure of the Presbyterians to make converts caused the agents some concern. According to Mormon beliefs, "the Mormon calling was to bring them [Indians] to a knowledge of their Fathers . . . [and to] remove the 'scales of darkness' from their eyes" (Flake 1965:2). By the time Agent Irvine expressed his fear that the Mormons would step in and convert the Navajos (RCIA in RSI 1876:513), they were already doing so.[27] Mormons had first undertaken Navajo missionary work in the 1850s, but with little success. Missionaries took up residence among the western Navajos at Moencopie in 1871, and proselytizing began in earnest. In the spring of 1875, the first Navajos were baptized and became members of the Mormon church (Flake 1965:3, 10, 38).

Besides the Mormons, few missionaries worked among the Navajos during the 1880s, and except for some Mormon converts in the western and northern portions of the reservation, few Navajos had converted to Christianity by the early 1890s. In 1890 non-Mormon missionary activity resumed (RCIA 1890:457) and was reported annually from that year on.

Dwellings

In 1872 Agent Miller suggested the government build houses for the major Navajo chiefs, hoping that the rest of the tribe would follow their example and move into houses (Miller to Pope, Apr. 30, 1872, RBIA LR NMS). Nothing came of the idea, but by 1874 six houses were occupied by Navajos, four of them built that year (RCIA in RSI 1874:437). Thus, only two houses had been built by or for Navajos prior to 1874.

Lack of milled lumber hindered the construction of houses. Agent Irvine thought that "the most important step to be taken for the Navajoes is to induce them to build permanent houses," something that could be accomplished only with a ready supply of lumber. Accordingly, he suggested buying a steam sawmill, boiler, and engine (Irvine to Smith, Mar. 9, 1877, RBIA LR NMS). Although the sawmill was scheduled for delivery in September 1877 (Irvine to Smith, Sept. 3, 1877, RBIA LR NMS), the first evidence of its operation comes in July 1880 (Report of Irregular Employees at Navajo Indian Agency . . . for the month ending July, 1880, RBIA LR NMS).

The annual report for 1882 listed twenty occupied houses, five of which were new (RCIA in RSI 1882:399), but when John Bowman was appointed agent in 1884, he observed that "there was not on this entire reservation one single house or cabin built or occupied by any member of this tribe" (RCIA 1884:135). Bowman may have chosen to ignore the true situation (agents often deprecated their predecessors' accomplishments to enhance their own), or perhaps he could not bring himself to classify the crude dwellings built before 1884 as "houses." At the time of his report, twenty-five houses were under construction, and he estimated that "at least fifty good snug little houses" would be built and occupied that year (RCIA in RSI 1884:135).

The official record indicates a Navajo housing boom during Bowman's term as agent. His 1885 report stated "I believe there are between 100 and 200 of such [small houses] already built and occupied" (RCIA 1885:156), but his successor noted only thirty occupied houses in 1886, twelve of which had been built during that year (RCIA 1886:403). In June 1886, the agency distributed lumber and hardware to Navajos who wanted to build houses, and during the summer construction began on twenty-two stone houses of two to three rooms each. According to Agent Patterson, "the erection of these houses has caused many others to ask for materials to enable them to construct buildings of like character, and to abandon their hogans of sticks and mud" (RCIA 1886:204). Reportedly, forty houses were built during 1887, but the agency could not supply doors and windows for them (RCIA 1887:375, 175). The shortage of building materials may explain why only seventy-five houses were occupied in 1888 (RCIA 1888:420).

The newly appointed agent, C. E. Vandever, vouched for only thirty occupied houses in 1889, five of which had been constructed during the year (RCIA in RSI 1889:506, 259). The sawmill was running that year, and the Navajos were "incessant in their requests for building material." In his annual report to the commissioner of Indian affairs, Vandever described "the increasing demand" for building materials, and noted that almost one hundred sets of carpenter's tools had been distributed to Navajos during a twelve-month period. Two hundred houses were reported under construction in the spring of 1890 (RCIA 1890:164; Dorchester to the Secretary of the Interior, May 12, 1890, RBIA LR GR).

During this period, Navajo dwellings were passing through a transitional stage. The Navajos had been exposed to various Anglo-American and Spanish-American construction techniques, some of which began to appear in their own dwellings. In 1898 Mindeleff wrote that the old forked-stick hogans (earth-covered tripod frames with dug-out floors and often, elongated doorways) were "rapidly disappearing, and the examples left today are more or less influenced by ideas derived from the whites. Among the Navaho such contact has been very slight, but it has been sufficient to introduce new methods of construction and in fact new structures" (C. Mindeleff 1898:487).

About this time Navajos started to build octagonal log hogans modeled in construction technique after Anglo-American log cabins. Unlike other early hogans, these buildings had doors and possibly windows. While we classify these structures as hogans, early agents may have identified them as "houses." R. W. Shufeldt (1892:280–81) noted an interesting hybridization in "house" building by some Navajo families in the vicinity of Fort Wingate between 1886 and 1888. Combining Navajo and Euro-American building techniques and forms, the results defied classification.[28] One can imagine the dilemma of an agent attempting to classify such structures as hogans or houses, and discrepancies in the number of reported "houses" may reflect this ambiguity.

For several reasons, very few Navajo families lived in Anglo-American style houses in 1890. The form of a hogan had been given to the Navajo people "by the gods themselves," and had religious significance (C. Mindeleff 1898:488). Religious curing ceremonies had to be held in circular structures—a requirement satisfied by hogans, but not by rectangular "house" structures (Tremblay, Collier, and Sasaki 1954:216). In the late nineteenth century, since each family needed a hogan for curing ceremonies, only wealthy Navajos could afford the additional expense of a house (C. Mindeleff 1898:495). Even in the first half of the twentieth century, people built houses more as prestige symbols than for living. Families affluent enough to own a house usually lived in a nearby hogan and used the house for storage (Lockett 1952:137; Bailey field notes). The necessity of abandoning a structure in which an individual had died also discouraged the construction of houses. Few families could justify the expense and effort of building an Anglo-American style house if they might have to abandon it within a few years (Ostermann 1917:27). If these factors influenced the Navajos in the twentieth century, they undoubtedly exerted an even stronger influence in the 1800s.

Clothing

The Office of Indian Affairs required the agent to estimate in his annual report the number of Indians under his supervision who were wearing "citizen's" or Euro-American style clothing. Since Indians often mixed traditional and white styles of dress, some agents broke the figures down into those "wholly" dressed in citizen's clothes, and those who "partially" met the requirements.

The agency distributed little in the way of finished clothing. The Treaty of 1868 stipulated that the Navajos were "to manufacture their own clothing, blankets, etc.; [and] to be furnished with no article which they can manufacture themselves." In 1869 the agency issued coats and pants to 94 subcaptains (men chosen by the chiefs on the basis of their local influence), and in 1871 handed out 400 beaver coats (RCIA 1869:238; Parker to Pope, June 15, 1871, RBIA RNMS). Such distributions represented the exception, not the rule. Varying amounts and types of yard goods were given away, as well as needles, thread, and thimbles. For example, in 1874 the annuity goods included 30,000 yards of calico prints, 10,006 yards of satinet, 30,025 yards of sheeting, 2,000 yards of linsey, 100 "M" needles, and 75 pounds of linen thread (List of Annuity Goods Issued, May 6, 1874, RBIA LR NMS).

In 1876 the agent reported that the Navajos had traded part of their wool for calico (RCIA 1876:513). The demand for cloth was so high that Romulo Martinez stocked an extensive inventory of yard goods at Fort Defiance in 1877 (Invoice of merchandise purchased by "Trader" Romulo Martinez, Mar. 31, 1877, RBIA LR NMS).

Galen Eastman wrote the following description of Navajo clothing in 1879:

> Most of the males wear pants and shirts made of woolen cloth and cotton goods, and the women are for the most part dressed in skirts and waists [blouses] of calico and woolen cloth, the latter of their own manufacture; also, both men and women knit stockings which they wear with moccasins on their feet. . . . On dress-up occasions the men wear leggins or pants elaborately trimmed with buckskin fringe and silver buttons, and the women wrap their ankles in thick and even folds of nicely tanned goat and buckskin reaching from below their ankles to the knee. . . . They all wear blankets and mantles used as shawls. (RCIA 1879:117)

This account suggests that the Navajos observed by Eastman were rapidly incorporating calico and other cloth goods into their standard costume, and saving traditional styles of dress for special occasions. Five years later Agent John H. Bowman reported that "both sexes [are] wearing calico suits the year round. The men wear calico pants and shirts (no underclothing) in the summer, and the same costume with the addition of a blanket, in the winter" (RCIA in RSI 1884:178).

Descriptions of mid-1890s clothing do not differ markedly except to emphasize jewelry. Stephen (1893:355–56) wrote:

> Their typical dress has been almost obliterated since the advent of the trader among them, but as the Navajo now appears he may thus be sketched: Hair all drawn smoothly to the back of the head and done up into a compact club or cue of hour-glass shape; a red silk sash worn as a turban and decorated with feathers and silver ornaments; large silver ear-rings and heavy necklaces of coral, thin discs of white shell and turquoise, and strings of globular silver beads and other ornaments of their own manufacture; a loose sack or short

shirt of bright-colored calico, and loose breeches of the same material; belts consisting of large heavy discs or oval plates of silver strung upon a strip of leather are worn both by men and women; low moccasins of buckskin, soled with rawhide, surmounted with leggings of dyed deerskin, which are secured with garters woven of thread in fanciful designs. There is little or no difference between their summer and winter dress, and they constantly wear a heavy woolen blanket as a mantle. . . .

Like the men, most of the women wear calico; their dresses made in the simple fashion, of a loose jacket and short petticoats; but, differing from the men, each of them possesses the typical Navajo woman's costume, which she wears on all ceremonial occasions. . . . The typical dress is a heavy woolen tunic of dark blue, with wide designs in scarlet along the borders; it reaches just below the knee and is confined round the waist with a woven girdle. . . . the young women now generally wear a calico dress under this rough tunic. The moccasin is shaped just like the men's, but fastened to the back part of the upper is the half of a large buckskin, which is wrapped around the leg in regular folds from ankle to knee, and on the outside of the leg with a row of silver buttons.

The women also wear a blanket as a mantle.

Eickemeyer's description of the Navajos in 1896 is similar in many respects:

Their apparel consists generally of a shirt open down the front, leaving the chest exposed; a breechcloth, leggins, and moccasins. Over these thin garments a blanket carelessly is thrown. . . . Their heads are usually encircled by a handkerchief, in which is rolled up a little money, tobacco, buttons, sinew, or other small possessions. . . .

The women, who the night before had appeared barefooted, and clad in a single cotton garment, were decked in their holiday costumes, with ornaments galore. Moccasins and black squaw dresses, which Navajo women wear only on state occasions, such as going to the trader's, were donned in our honor. . . . The moccasin of the Navajo women is similar to that of the Pueblo, the upper part having a long strip of buckskin, which is wrapped spirally around the limb as far up as the knee.

Instead of cheap calico garments, they wore the black native-woven squaw dresses, with bright-colored borders reaching nearly to the knee. On their necks were many strings of beads: both of shell, which they had obtained by frequent trading of horses and blankets with the Pueblos; and of silver, that had been made from coin by some of the Navajo silver-men. Bracelets, necklaces, and rings of silver adorned the arms and necks of both men and women; and belts made of oval silver disks encircled many a waist. . . .

Belts made of oval silver disks, strung on a narrow leather thong, are worn by both men and women on special occasions; while armlets of leather, mounted with silver plates, are the exclusive property of the more prominent men of the tribe. (Eickemeyer 1900:73, 175–76, 223)

According to these descriptions, calico dresses had replaced woolen dresses for daily use by the mid-1890s, but women still kept woolen dresses for special occasions. Stephen and Eickemeyer visited only Fort Defiance and the Chuska Mountain area, and we can assume some stylistic variation in other areas of the reservation. Richard Simpson, a trader near the San Juan river, told Charles Amsden (1975:97) that the Navajos were "going calico" about 1895, and that there were so many native dresses in pawn that they sold "for as little as five dollars each." Nevertheless, Navajo women may have dressed more conservatively in some regions than in others.

Observers gave varying accounts of men's dress, probably reflecting regional differences. Stephen wrote that the men wore calico pants and shirts. An 1894 memorandum written by E. C. Vincent, who was supervising irrigation work on the reservation, described a "blanket, cotton trousers made wide, and slit open to the knee, and a calico shirt" (Pocket Memorandum, May 5–13, 1894, RBIA LR GR), while Eickemeyer noted breechcloths and leggings.

None of the reports from these years mentioned shoes or boots—only moccasins—and with the exception of coats, which were distributed as annuity goods, they did not refer to factory-made American clothing. Styles were changing, particularly as Navajo women shifted from woolen to calico dresses, but Navajos continued to make their own clothing until the mid-1890s. This resistance to change can be addressed as a function of economics and style, but also as a broader cultural question. Frank Mitchell (Frisbie and McAllester 1978:35–36) stated:

The People were suspicious of those things [shoes] at first; whenever they came across a white man in shoes, they were too shy even to touch those shoes. They said those were made by white men and they were not supposed to wear them or even touch them. There were times when they would find clothing, like pants, shirts, coats and even hats, and they were scared to wear those things. The old people said you were not supposed to wear anything made by a white man or belonging to a white man. . . . We were told not to wear white men's clothes because those people were our enemies and we would get sick from the effects of using their clothing. If the People were given some clothes, they would just throw them out.

An examination of agency reports shows that the government program to "civilize" the Navajos failed during these decades. In terms of formal education, Christianity, dwelling, and dress, the Navajos were at best only slightly influenced by Anglo-Americans, and adopted only those items which they considered advantageous.

THE NAVAJOS AND THEIR NEIGHBORS: 1868–1892

Between 1868 and 1892, the Navajo population grew approximately from 9,000 to 18,000 (Johnston 1966a:362). Their herds grew even more dramatically, leading to more intensive use of traditional rangeland and expansion into new areas.

Other populations in the Southwest were also expanding rapidly. In 1860 the Territory of New Mexico, which at that time included Arizona, had a non-Indian population of approximately 83,000, and by 1890 the non-Indian population of the territories of Arizona and New Mexico exceeded 200,000 (U.S. Bureau of the Census 1975:24, 32). This growth coincided with the development of sheep and cattle ranching, economic activities that brought non-Indians into direct competition with Navajos for rangeland. However, changes in the geographical distribution of non-Indians, resulting from the development of transportation networks in the Southwest, had far greater consequences for the Navajos than the growth in numbers of the newcomers and their livestock.

Before Anglo-American occupation of the Southwest, the non-Indian population was concentrated in two main areas: southern Arizona and the Rio Grande Valley. Hispanic settlements extended north from Sonora to southern Arizona, and were not linked by trade or transportation networks with the other Hispanic settlements in the Rio Grande Valley. The Rio Grande settlements, which stretched from Taos on the north to El Paso del Norte on the south, were located along a major north-south trade corridor linking manufacturing centers in the eastern United States with markets in central Mexico. Since the Navajos lived well outside the Rio Grande corridor and the southern Arizona settlements, they were isolated in terms of trade and contact (Meinig 1971:17–24).

After the Mexican War, Anglo-American penetration of California resulted in a shift from north-south trade corridors to east-west corridors, linking eastern industrial centers with the west coast. The earliest of these new corridors connected El Paso to California via Tucson, and for the first time, linked Hispanic communities in southern Arizona to Rio Grande Valley settlements. Immigrants, freight, herds, and mail traveled along this route, but because it passed well south of their range, it had no direct impact on the Navajos (Meinig 1971:22–24).

A more northern east-west corridor did not develop until 1857, when Edward Beale opened a wagon road between Fort Defiance and the Mohave villages on the Colorado River. A road already existed from Fort Defiance to Albuquerque and the Rio Grande settlements. Beale's Road never attracted much in the way of trade or immigrant traffic, not even after the creation of Arizona Territory in 1863 (Bancroft 1962:494–95, 500, 521). Consequently, the Navajos remained relatively isolated from the centers of Southwestern development when the Navajo War started.

Isolation from major transportation routes prior to 1863 benefited the Navajos in the long run. The lack of such a network limited white intrusions into their homeland during the imprisonment at Bosque Redondo, and when they returned in 1868, they found their country much as they had left it. With the exception of some Hispanic settlements in the Rio Puerco Valley and the Rio San José Valley, there were no white settlements in the vast region bounded on the east by the Jemez Mountains, on the west by the San Francisco Peaks, on the north by the Colorado River and La Plata Mountains, and on the south by the White Mountains and Black Range. Except in the extreme southeastern and southern areas of Spanish-American encroachment, the Navajos quickly reoccupied most of their former range.

During the 1870s, the Navajos came under increasing pressure from white settlers in their frontier areas. This encroachment fell into three main areas: Mormons in the Little Colorado Valley, Anglo-Americans in the San Juan Valley, and Spanish-Americans along the southern and eastern borders.

Mormon religious beliefs caused their relationship with Indians to differ considerably from those of typical Anglo-American frontier populations. The Mormons also differed culturally and socially from other white settlers, with whom they were frequently antagonistic (Kluckhohn and Leighton 1960:129; Vogt and Albert 1970).

The Mormons arrived in Utah in 1847, and from the main settlements in the vicinity of Salt Lake, soon began moving into the southern part of the state. By the 1850s, Mormon missionaries were already attempting to convert the Navajos. Led by Jacob Hamblin, they resumed their proselytizing efforts soon after Bosque Redondo, and as early as 1871 a few Mormon missionaries were stationed at Moencopie (McClintock 1921:157; Flake 1965:10, 38).

The Colorado River effectively prevented large-scale Mormon migration and settlement in northern Arizona. The situation changed in 1871 when John D. Lee, a Mormon, settled at Lonely Dell on the Colorado, and began to ferry passengers across the river the following year. Lee's Ferry, which the Mormon church later helped to maintain (Measeles 1981:7, 25), opened northern Arizona to Mormon settlement. In 1875 Mormon families joined the missionaries at Moencopie, and in 1876 four companies (a company consisting of fifty men and their dependents) set out to colonize the Little Colorado Valley. Of their early settlements, only St. Joseph—later renamed Joseph City—survived (Granger 1960:242–43, 246). Instead of moving back to Utah from abandoned settlements, the Mormons established other communities in the Little Colorado Valley (McClintock 1921:138, 148, 157; Bancroft 1962:531). The population of these settlements grew from an estimated 564 in 1877 to 2,507 in 1884 (Bancroft 1962:531).

Of the various groups that intruded on the Navajos in the 1870s and early 1880s, the Mormons were the least disruptive. Mainly farmers, they occupied areas that the Navajos had not been using, and so did not compete with them for land. Instead of actively attempting to displace the Navajos, the Mormons came to trade, as well as to convert them to Mormonism (Kluckhohn and Leighton 1974:129–30).

The first major contact point between Navajos and Anglo-American settlers was in the San Juan Valley during the 1870s. The Utes occupied the area while the Navajos were at Bosque Redondo, and fearing Ute raids, the Navajos avoided it for a few years after 1868. Relations between the two tribes improved, and by the mid-1870s, the Navajos had reoccupied most of the valley (Bailey and Bailey 1982:71–79).

In 1874 an executive order incorporated part of the San Juan Valley to the east of the Navajo reservation into the Jicarilla reservation. Few, if any, Jicarillas actually lived in the valley, and on July 18, 1876, another executive order returned the area to the public domain (Kappler 1904:874–75), opening it to white settlement.

The situation in the valley changed radically within a few years. The government confined the Utes to reservations in southern Colorado and New Mexico, and established Fort Lewis on the La Plata River. Anglo-American settlers came south from the mining camps and valleys of southern

Colorado to claim the rich farmlands and rangelands along the San Juan, just east of the reservation line. The towns of Farmington, Aztec, Bloomfield, Waterflow, Jewett, Fruitland, and Olio (later named Kirtland) were established, and by 1881 between 1,000 and 1,200 whites lived in the valley (Bailey and Bailey 1982:79–80).

Conflict accompanied the movement of Anglo-Americans into the area. A small group homesteaded near the mouth of McElmo Canyon in southern Utah in 1878, just to the north of the reservation. Led by "Captain" H. L. Mitchell, this small settlement, which was not Mormon, became a center of conflict between Anglo-Americans and Navajos (Affidavit of H. L. Mitchell, Dec. 24, 1879, RBIA LR NMS). The San Juan Valley was an important Navajo winter range, as well as a productive farming area. When Anglo-American farmers moved into the San Juan Valley, they attempted to drive Navajos from their fields and deny their herds access to the river (Bailey and Bailey 1982:80–82). At the same time, Anglo-American ranchers were expanding their herds. By 1881 an estimated 20,000 cattle and 50,000 sheep were grazing in the valley and surrounding areas (Reeve 1946:4). When the Navajos tried to hold their range, farms, and water rights in the off-reservation areas against the Anglo-American invasion, the San Juan became the site of the bitterest conflict of the period.

Spanish-Americans moved into the valleys of the lower Rio Puerco and the lower Rio San José during the late eighteenth century, but their control of the area remained extremely tenuous. Many settlers left during the Navajo wars of the early and mid-nineteenth century (Rittenhouse 1965:19–20). Bosque Redondo and the relative peace which followed allowed them to reoccupy the region (Rittenhouse 1965:20; Calkins 1937b:7–12). Between 1865 and 1870 (Calkins 1937b:7–8), ranchers moved large herds into the Rio Puerco Valley—rangeland undoubtedly used by the Navajos before 1863.

Such encroachments were not limited to ranchers. After 1864 large numbers of Spanish-American farmers emigrated from the overcrowded Rio Grande Valley and established communities along the Rio Puerco (Calkins 1937b:9–10). During the same period, Spanish-American farmers and ranchers were moving west from the Chama Valley across the mountains into the upper San Juan Valley to settle in Blanco, Gobernador, and Largo canyons (Brugge field notes). It seems likely that a similar movement took place in the Rio San José Valley, and by 1866 Spanish-American ranchers lived as far west as Concho in the Little Colorado Valley of eastern Arizona (Haskett 1936:19).

White settlers reached the boundaries of Navajo country within a decade after Bosque Redondo, and their settlements virtually surrounded the Navajos by the late 1870s. Because the majority of Navajo families lived off-reservation on public domain lands and depended on public range for grazing their stock, competition for these lands had a profound effect on the tribe. Although the settlements were small and scattered, the boundary separating the Navajos from them remained changeable and undefined. The struggle for control of public grazing lands had begun.

Land and Sheep

Outsiders moved into Navajo country for a variety of reasons. Mormons settled in the Little Colorado Valley because their leaders wanted to maintain an escape route south to Mexico in case of difficulties with the United States (Measeles 1981:25), and Mormon farmers mistakenly thought the valley had major agricultural potential. The San Juan settlers—farmers, cattlemen, and sheepmen—saw an opportunity to supply food to the mining camps of western Colorado. Spanish-Americans moved into the region to take advantage of an expanding sheep industry, and before long, Mormons and Anglo-Americans joined them.

Before the Civil War, New Mexican sheep ranchers marketed their animals as mutton in mining camps throughout the western states. Between 1852 and 1860, more than 550,000 sheep were driven to markets in the California gold camps. Other herds were taken to Utah, Nevada, Colorado, Wyoming—even as far east as Kansas, Missouri, and Nebraska (A. Carlson 1969:28–29).

But no market existed for New Mexican wool. Writing in 1844, Josiah Gregg stated,

> A large quantity of wool is of course produced, but of an inferior quality. . . . They formerly sheared their flocks for their health and rarely preserved the fleeces, as their domestic manufactures consumed but a comparatively small quantity. The sheep of New Mexico are . . . scarcely fit for anything else than mutton. (Gregg 1954:123)

He went on to say that wool sold in New Mexico brought only 3¢ to 4¢ per pound, and wool shipped to Missouri only 15¢ per pound. Gregg assessed New Mexican sheep correctly: in the 1840s most of them were churros, hardy animals that produced excellent mutton and a low commercial grade of wool (A. Carlson 1969:27–33).

The demand for wool increased sharply during the Civil War and stayed high during the postwar period. Wool prices rose, peaking at 31¢ per pound for average grade wool in 1872 (appendix B). Although the railroads had not reached New Mexico and Arizona by the early 1870s, their rapid expansion improved access to eastern markets. Because wool commanded such high prices, even the most isolated ranchers in southern Arizona could afford to have their wool hauled by oxcart to the railroad terminal in Trinidad, Colorado, or to ship their wool by boat from the mouth of the Colorado River to Boston (Haskett 1936:23). High prices and improved transportation soon induced sheep ranchers to shift from mutton to wool production. Only 33,000 pounds of New Mexican wool were shipped to eastern markets in 1850, but by 1880 the figure exceeded 4,000,000 pounds a year. High prices also made it worthwhile for ranchers to improve the quality of their stock, thereby increasing wool yields. Stockmen introduced Merino sheep, renowned for wool production, and "improved" an estimated 40 percent of the sheep in New Mexico by 1880 (A. Carlson 1969:32–34).

At first, the development of the wool market and the resulting growth of trading posts benefited the Navajos, but its harmful effects soon became apparent. New Mexico's rangeland supported approximately 1,667,000 sheep in 1870, 4,547,000 in 1880, and 5,230,000 by 1883 (see table 3, fig. 4)—a 300 percent increase in slightly over a decade. Some New Mexican ranchers moved into east-central and southern Arizona in the late 1860s, but the major impetus for the growth of the Arizona sheep industry came from California, where sheep ranching had also developed on a large scale. In 1870 and 1871, southern California suffered a major drought, and owners moved thousands of sheep into Arizona to find water and pasture (Haskett 1936:19–21). The migration continued through the 1870s. Between 1870 and 1880, the number of sheep in Arizona increased from 17,000 to 560,000, and peaked at 660,000 in 1883 (see table 4, fig. 5). Anglo-Americans, Spanish-Americans, and Navajos—all of whom depended on the public domain to graze their sheep—came into direct competition for rangeland.

The reservation alone could not support Navajo herds, and agents considered access to public domain lands a necessity. In 1876 Agent Irvine, speaking on behalf of the chiefs, asked that the reservation be enlarged:

> The present reservation does not contain sufficient grass to subsist their horses, cattle and sheep for one day . . . [and] it is impossible for them all to live or subsist themselves within the present limits.

. . . The tribe is increasing in numbers, their children are growing up, their flocks of sheep are increasing and more land is needed, than was given them eight years ago.

The chiefs wanted to extend their holdings to the San Maria (San Mateo?) Mountains on the east, the salt lakes south of Zuni on the south, the Little Colorado on the west, and the Rio Mancos on the north (Irvine to Smith, Apr. 13, 1876, RBIA LR NMS). Irvine claimed that Navajo rangelands were being taken over by Spanish-Americans, whom he characterized as "inferior to . . . [the Navajos] in both intelligence and industry" (Irvine to Smith, Mar. 1, 1876, RBIA LR NMS).

Officials in Washington did not accept the plan, and the first extension of the reservation was postponed until 1878. General Sherman wanted to include the rich Navajo farmland in the Chinle Valley, arguing that the Treaty of 1868 had inadvertently omitted it. Because only Navajos lived there at the time (Pyle to CIA, Sept. 9, 1878, RBIA LR NMS), President Hayes included the area in his executive order of October 29, 1878, which moved the reservation boundary twenty miles west (map 3; Kappler 1904:875–76).

On December 10, 1878, a council was held with Navajo leaders to explain the extension. Far from satisfied, the chiefs complained that white settlers were crowding them on all sides, and asked for a similar extension to the east. Manuelito wanted more land in that direction for winter range and hunting. Making no effort to cloak his resentment, Mariano said, "The Navajoes who live around here and East furnish such soldiers [scouts] and do all the Government wants them to do, so they get nothing, while the Navajoes who live west and who do nothing get it all, more land" (Swaine to AA Gen'l, Dept. of N.M., Dec. 20, 1878, RBIA LR NMS).

The following spring Agent Eastman forwarded the request of a Navajo council that the reservation boundary be extended between fifteen and twenty miles on the east and south sides of the reservation. Eastman noted that not more than half a dozen white settlers and two traders occupied land in the suggested extension (Memorandum of the Minutes . . . May 21, 1879, RBIA LR NMS). The request was favorably received in Washington. Acting on the advice of the commissioner of Indian affairs, President Hayes signed the executive order of January 6, 1880, extending the reservation boundary fifteen miles east from mid-current of the San Juan River to the southern boundary (map 3). The southern boundary was also extended and more land was added on the southwest (Kappler 1904:876), but because the change still did not provide sufficient range,

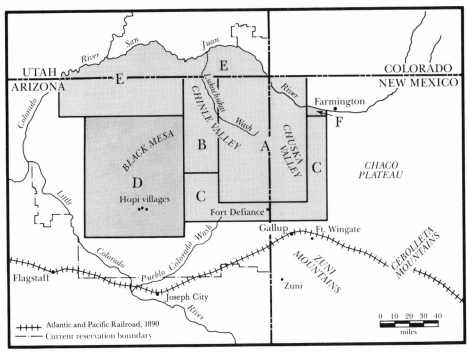

Map 3. *Growth of Navajo land base, 1868–1886. A, Treaty of June 1868. B, Executive order of Oct. 29, 1878. C, Executive order of Jan. 6, 1880. D, Executive order of Dec. 16, 1882, the "Moqui Reservation," partially occupied by Navajos. E, Executive order of May 17, 1884. F, Executive order of Apr. 24, 1886. Adapted from Williams (1970).*

most Navajo families continued to use public domain lands for much of the year. Instead of alleviating tension between Navajos and white settlers in the San Juan Valley, the executive order of January 1880 forced white farmers to vacate farms along the south bank of the river, further heightening resentments (Ebert to Schurz, Apr. 15, 1880, RBIA LR NMS; Kimble to U.S. Land Agent, Apr. 19, 1880, RBIA LR NMS).

Vacillating government policy toward the Utes and Agent N. C. Meeker's determination to impose the program of forced culture change (no gambling, no horse racing) led to trouble at the White River Ute Agency in northern Colorado in 1879. Utes killed Meeker, seven agency employees, and twelve cavalrymen; thirty-seven Utes died in the ensuing military "confrontation" (Jorgensen 1972:45–46). The so-called "Meeker Massacre" terrified white settlers and Indian agency personnel throughout the Southwest and contributed to an already volatile situation in Navajo country.

In February 1880, the murder of two white prospectors in Monument Valley was attributed to Navajos (Carpenter to Schurz, Feb. 28, 1880,

RBIA LR NMS).[29] The March 17 edition of the *Denver Tribune* sensation-alized the incident, stating that Mormons had supplied the murderers (a renegade band of Utes, Paiutes, and Navajos) with arms and that they were "interested in these depredations."[30] To broaden the conspiracy theory, the article capitalized on the Meeker Massacre furor by reporting "suspicious" meetings between well-armed bands of southern Utes and the Navajos, sug-gesting an imminent alliance between the two tribes.[31] An investigation of the Monument Valley murders revealing that the two men had been killed by Utes or Paiutes instead of Navajos (Bennett to AA Gen'l, Dist. of N.M., Mar. 22, 1880, RBIA LR NMS) did not set fears to rest.

The paranoia of white employees at the Navajo Agency turned to panic. Reporting that some of his employees had already fled and others were preparing to leave, Agent Eastman asked permission to purchase ten Win-chesters and one double-barreled shotgun. As a final note, he added that "since the Meeker murders most white men and women prefer to earn their living inside" (Eastman to CIA, Apr. 6, 1880, RBIA LR NMS).

Real problems soon developed. In April and May, Navajos killed seven Spanish-American herders in the Gallina Mountains west of Socorro. Offi-cials minimized the significance of the murders, claiming that the Navajos were retaliating for the murder of two of their people (Taylor to AAA Gen'l, Dist. of N.M., July 25, 1880, RBIA LR NMS; Bradley to AA Gen'l, Dist. of N.M., Aug. 22, 1880, RBIA LR NMS). The coolness of official response to the crime can also be explained by unspoken prejudice against Spanish-Americans.

Conflicts between Navajos and whites continued to escalate. In early May, Navajos killed two Anglo-Americans about fifty miles northeast of Fort Defiance, taking two mules, one horse, weapons, saddles, and about $200 in cash (Bennett to CIA, Aug. 5, 1880, RBIA LR NMS). A few days later, a group of five or six drunk Navajos attacked a mail carrier on the road near Bluewater, New Mexico. He was not seriously injured, and besides cutting the mail sacks, the Navajos did not damage the mail (Hop-kins to Chief Sp'l Agt., Post Office Dept., May 18, 1880, RBIA LR NMS). Another major incident occurred in late May. Navajos ambushed two more Anglo-American travelers some forty-five miles north of the agency. One was killed, but the other, seriously wounded, escaped and rode to Fort Defi-ance (Bennett to CIA, Aug. 5, 1880, RBIA LR NMS).

Private citizens and newspapermen fueled the hostilities by spreading rumors of "suspicious" happenings among the Navajos. Newspaper accounts of an alleged meeting between Navajo and Ute leaders at Tierra Amarilla suggested they were planning a joint war against the whites (Pope to Whipple, June 4, 1880, RBIA LR NMS). Two white ranchers reported that friendly Navajos warned them to leave with their families because others were planning to attack the ranches south of Fort Defiance (Affidavit of Daniel DuBois, June 6, 1880, RBIA LR NMS; Affidavit of Joseph Thacker, June 6, 1880, RBIA LR NMS). L. W. Le Noin reported that on May 27, while traveling between Fort Wingate and Joseph City, he saw a "good many Indians on the road," including an unarmed Navajo riding west. The next day he saw the same man riding east, but armed with a new Winchester and Colt. On May 29, he observed three or four Mormons showing guns to Navajos in Joseph City (Affidavit of L. W. Le Noin, June 8, 1880, RBIA LR NMS). Le Noin's affidavit illustrates the habitual distrust of Mormons by Anglo-Americans, and the prevailing fear of an Indian uprising.

The military stayed calm. Since Agent Eastman had already lost the Navajos' confidence, he was temporarily replaced by former agent F. T. Bennett, whom the Navajos trusted. Bennett quickly defused the situation, and in late June, General Pope telegraphed General Sheridan that "all apprehensions about the Navajoes can be safely dismissed and the best reports about the southern Utes are of the same favorable character" (Pope to Sheridan, June 25, 1880, RBIA LR NMS). Another Navajo war had possibly been averted, but the problems that led to the crisis in the first place remained unsolved.

The Development of the Cattle Industry

In 1866 Congress granted the Atlantic and Pacific Railroad permission to build a line from Springfield, Missouri, to the Pacific along the 35th Parallel. Construction started west from Albuquerque in 1880, and by February 1881 the track had reached Fort Wingate, about 150 miles west of Albuquerque at the edge of the Navajo country. Construction progressed slowly. The rails did not get to the Colorado River in Arizona until August 1883. In California, interference from competing railroads temporarily prevented the Atlantic and Pacific from reaching the coast. As a result, several years passed before the route developed into a major artery of commerce (Greever 1957:152–55, 164–67).

The federal government subsidized the railroad with a grant of alternate sections of public domain land for a distance of fifty miles on either side of the track. Because the track skirted the southern edge of Navajo country, this grant blocked any extensions of the reservation in that direction, and many off-reservation Navajos found themselves occupying railroad land.

Even though transcontinental use of the Atlantic and Pacific developed slowly, the railroad quickly transformed the economy of northeastern Arizona and northwestern New Mexico. Railroad towns like Winslow and Gallup grew rapidly along the newly completed track; Holbrook expanded as a trade center for a burgeoning ranching industry; and Flagstaff developed as one of the first major lumber towns in the Southwest, utilizing the rich timber resources of the central Arizona mountains (Meinig 1971:42).

The cattle industry developed as the most important and immediate result of the railroad's completion. Cattle had been a part of New Mexican ranching since the Spanish colonial period, but had never rivaled sheep in importance. In the late 1870s, ranchers were raising cattle on a small scale in the Little Colorado Valley, and approximately 20,000 head were reported in the San Juan Valley in 1880 (Morrisey 1950:153; Reeve 1946:4). However, the lack of markets imposed major limitations on the industry. San Juan Valley cattlemen found a ready, albeit limited, outlet in the mining camps of western Colorado, and ranchers in other parts of Arizona and New Mexico had to depend on small local sales to mining camps, forts, or Indian agencies where cattle were butchered for rations.

Railroads effectively eliminated the problem. For the first time, ranchers gained access to the eastern markets and their almost insatiable demand for cattle. Meinig (1971:39–41) stated that rail service to New Mexico and the Southwest "was effectively opened when the rails reached Las Vegas [New Mexico] on January 1, 1879," and that by 1885 railroads had penetrated most of the region.

Added to the almost immediate impact of the railroad, wool prices were falling, and beef prices were on the rise. Wool declined gradually from a high of 31.7¢ per pound in 1872 to an average of 14.5¢ in 1884 and 1885 (appendix B), and cattle peaked in 1884 at $20.20 per head (Baydo 1970:225). Suddenly, cattle ranching had become more profitable than raising sheep. Texas cattlemen started moving herds into New Mexico and Arizona after the completion of the rail lines, and many local sheep ranchers decided to switch to cattle (A. Carlson 1969:37; Morrisey 1950:153).

The number of sheep in New Mexico and Arizona began to decline in 1884. Between 1883 and 1887, the number of sheep in Arizona dropped from 660,000 to 550,000. The industry began to recover in the late 1880s, and by 1892, Arizona rangelands supported an estimated 675,000 sheep. In New Mexico, the numbers decreased more abruptly, falling from 5,230,000 to 3,196,000 between 1883 and 1890. The decline in New Mexican herds continued unabated until the late 1890s. The sheep industry recovered in Arizona because new rangeland was still available, while in New

Mexico, the resources had been fully exploited (Haskett 1936:31–32, 35).

Cattle ranching expanded rapidly in both territories. The number of cattle in New Mexico increased from an estimated 711,000 head in 1883 to a high of 1,340,000 in 1890. Similarly, the number of cattle in Arizona increased from 570,000 in 1883 to a high of 984,000 in 1891 (tables 3, 4). However, because of fluctuations in the relative numbers of sheep and cattle in the two territories, and because cattle require significantly more forage per head than sheep, these statistics reveal little about changes in the intensity of range use. A measure known as a "sheep unit" (the forage requirement of one sheep) reduces these differences to a common measure. Developed by the Soil Conservation Service for the Indian Service to use on the Navajo reservation in the 1930s, this method converts numbers of livestock to sheep units according to the following ratios: one sheep or goat equals one unit, and one cow equals four units (U.S. Soil Conservation Service 1938:table XIV; Aberle 1966:66–67).

These ratios allow cattle and sheep estimates to be combined in a single figure, giving us a fairly accurate picture of changes in range utilization over time. In 1870 New Mexico supported 2,295,000 units; Arizona, 1,017,000. By 1880 these numbers had increased to 6,727,000 in New Mexico and 2,280,000 in Arizona. The intensity of range use in New Mexico reached its maximum in 1888, at 8,907,000; while Arizona herds continued to grow throughout the 1880s, and did not peak until 1891, at 4,586,000 (tables 3, 4; figs. 4, 5).

Southwestern cattle ranchers prospered throughout the 1880s. Even the disastrous winters of 1885–86 and 1886–87, along with a decrease in beef prices that bankrupted most ranchers in the Plains area, did not seriously affect them (Baydo 1970:79, 212, 218, 225). While the number of sheep in the region declined or stabilized in the 1880s, the number of cattle continued to increase until 1890 in New Mexico, and until 1891 in Arizona (tables 3, 4; figs. 4, 5).

As the cattle industry developed, cattlemen replaced sheepmen in the competition with Navajos for public domain grazing lands, partly because they were more aggressive. In the early 1880s, the Kansas-New Mexico Land and Cattle Company took over a large portion of the Chaco range, just east of the reservation boundary (Bailey and Bailey 1982:89–91; Brugge 1980:105–6; Judd 1968:112–13; H. Clark 1963:54–55). The Carlisles, as they were known locally, did not hesitate to forcibly evict Spanish-American sheepherders from the range (H. Clark 1963:54–55). Although most of the cattle ranchers were small local operators, a syndicate composed of Santa Fe Railroad officers, financiers, and Texas ranchers formed the Aztec Land

TABLE 3. *Cattle and Sheep on New Mexico Range: 1870–1900*

Year	Cattle (thousands)	Cattle (sheep units)	Sheep (thousands)	Total sheep units (thousands)
1870	157	628	1,667	2,295
1871	185	740	1,667	2,407
1872	213	852	1,817	2,669
1873	250	1,000	1,908	2,908
1874	281	1,124	2,061	3,185
1875	306	1,224	2,226	3,450
1876	339	1,356	2,560	3,916
1877	386	1,544	2,944	4,488
1878	436	1,744	3,238	4,982
1879	487	1,948	3,886	5,834
1880	545	2,180	4,547	6,727
1881	567	2,268	4,981	7,249
1882	606	2,424	5,230[a]	7,654
1883	711	2,844	5,230[a]	8,074
1884	812	3,248	4,968	8,216
1885	949	3,796	4,471	8,267
1886	1,065	4,260	4,471	8,731
1887	1,149	4,596	4,247	8,843
1888	1,218	4,872	4,035	8,907[a]
1889	1,303	5,212	3,632	8,844
1890	1,340[a]	5,360	3,196	8,556
1891	1,266	5,064	3,226	8,290
1892	1,227	4,908	3,065	7,973
1893	1,142	4,568	2,820	7,388
1894	1,051	4,204	2,961	7,165
1895	916	3,664	2,961	6,625
1896	817	3,268	2,813	6,081
1897	847	3,388	2,757	6,145
1898	821	3,284	2,922	6,206
1899	795	3,180	3,214	6,394
1900	843	3,372	3,535	6,907

Source: Adapted from U.S. Department of Agriculture 1937:125.
[a]Peak years.

TABLE 4. *Cattle and Sheep on Arizona Range: 1870–1900*

Year	Cattle (thousands)	Cattle (sheep units)	Sheep (thousands)	Total sheep units (thousands)
1870	250	1,000	17	1,017
1871	250	1,000	26	1,026
1872	265	1,060	36	1,096
1873	290	1,160	54	1,214
1874	300	1,200	76	1,276
1875	320	1,280	114	1,394
1876	340	1,360	160	1,520
1877	350	1,400	240	1,640
1878	375	1,500	326	1,826
1879	390	1,560	437	1,997
1880	430	1,720	560	2,280
1881	475	1,900	600	2,500
1882	520	2,080	648	2,728
1883	570	2,280	660[a]	2,940
1884	625	2,500	650	3,150
1885	690	2,760	600	3,350
1886	750	3,000	565	3,565
1887	800	3,200	550	3,750
1888	875	3,500	575	4,075
1889	925	3,700	600	4,300
1890	980	3,920	625	4,545
1891	984[a]	3,936	650	4,586[a]
1892	963	3,852	675[a]	4,527
1893	943	3,772	675[a]	4,447
1894	940	3,760	660	4,442
1895	900	3,600	650	4,250
1896	880	3,520	625	4,145
1897	865	3,460	670	4,130
1898	850	3,400	720	4,120
1899	850	3,400	775	4,175
1900	850	3,400	850[a]	4,250

Source: Adapted from U.S. Department of Agriculture 1937:127.
[a]Peak years.

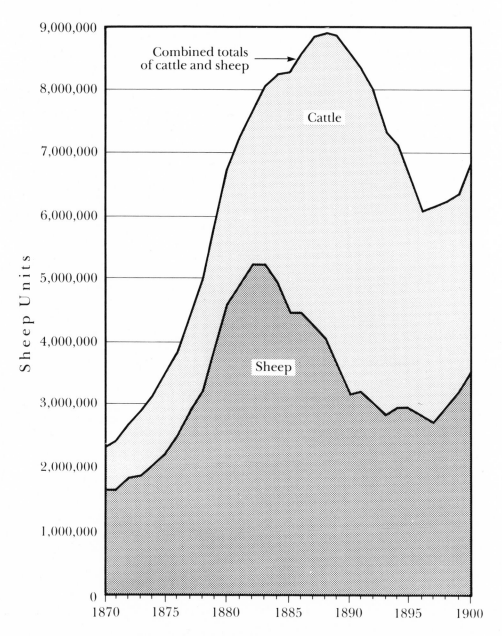

Figure 4. Number of cattle and sheep on New Mexico rangelands, 1870–1900. Top line represents combined totals of cattle and sheep.

and Cattle Company in the early 1880s. Also known as the "Hashknife Outfit," this company bought a million acres of right-of-way from the Atlantic and Pacific Railroad in the Little Colorado Valley. Measuring approximately ninety miles from east to west and forty miles from north to

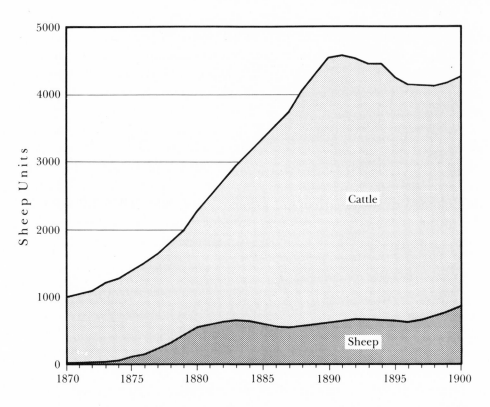

Figure 5. Number of cattle and sheep on Arizona rangelands, 1870–1900. Top line represents combined totals of cattle and sheep.

south, this ranch included large tracts of rangeland occupied by Navajos. Initially, the Hashknife Outfit stocked the range with 40,000 head of cattle transported from Pecos, Texas, to Holbrook, Arizona, and by 1888 they were grazing 60,000 head (Meinig 1971:44–45; Morrisey 1950:153). Thus, an organization of tremendous economic power and political influence, as well as aggressive local cowboys and sheepmen, was challenging Navajo range rights in the 1880s.

The Navajos and the Public Domain

Navajo agents did not fail to notice the challenge to Navajo range rights from the expanding cattle industry. Although the tribe prospered as never before during the 1880s, the agents realized that if white ranchers forced the Navajo herds off the public domain and onto the confines of the reservation, the self-sufficient Navajo economy would collapse. At best, the tribe would have to be supported by rations, like many other tribes; at worst, the

ranchers' actions would lead to a bloody war. To prevent either consequence, agents tried to strengthen the Navajo economic position by enlarg-
ing their reservation land base and improving productivity on the reservation. In these endeavors, local officials apparently received limited support
from Washington.

White settlers blocked extension of the reservation to the east, as did the
Atlantic and Pacific right-of-way to the south. Any northward extension
would have to enter Utah, which presented political problems, so the reservation could only expand west toward the junction of the Colorado and Little Colorado rivers (Sherman to Lincoln, Oct. 7, 1881, RBIA LR GR). In
the spring of 1882, Secretary of the Interior Teller expressed the opinion
that expansion was not "advisable" at that time (Teller to CIA, May 26,
1882, RBIA LR GR).

Shortly thereafter, the executive order of December 16, 1882, created the
Hopi reservation adjacent to the Navajo reservation on the west. This measure, which provided that "other Indians" could settle there, in part
alleviated the Navajo land problem. At the time, Navajos occupied much
if not most of this tract, and the new provision protected their grazing from
white intruders (Kappler 1904:805).

Opposed to further extensions of the reservation, settlers tried to evict
Navajos from the public domain, and lobbied to return choice portions of
the reservation to public status. On May 17, 1884, an executive order
restored the south bank of the San Juan to the public domain and opened
it to homesteading (Kappler 1904:876). Frank Reeve (1946:10–11) wrote of
this action, "No specific explanation can be found in official documents
and [it] must be judged the result of influences working through the routine political channels." Chaos resulted as white settlers quickly occupied
portions of the area and evicted Navajo farmers from their lands. Fearing
open conflict in the valley, Indian Office officials intervened, and on April
24, 1886, the area was returned to the Navajos by executive order (Bailey
and Bailey 1982:92–95; Kappler 1904:877).

A second executive order of May 17, 1884, extended the reservation
north into Utah, adding a strip of land between the Arizona border and the
San Juan River; and west to the Colorado River, adding a long, east-west
tract (Kappler 1904:876). Along with the restoration of the south bank of
the San Juan, these were the last extensions of the reservation during the
nineteenth century.

Even the expanded reservation could not support the tribe's vast herds.
During the late 1880s and early 1890s, it was variously estimated that between
one-third and one-half of the Navajos lived off the reservation on public

domain and railroad lands for at least part of the year, usually during the winter months (Atkins to Sec. of the Int., Dec. 19, 1885, RBIA LR GR; Welton to CIA, July 8, 1888, RBIA LR GR; Vandever to CIA, Mar. 4, 1890, RBIA LR GR; Tinker to Sec. of the Int., June 16, 1892 RBIA LR GR).

In retrospect, it is evident that Navajos had as much legal right as anyone to settle on public lands. The Act of March 3, 1875, clearly stated that non-reservation Indians had a right to settle on the public domain and file for homesteads (Strickland 1982:130). Indians also qualified for homesteads under the Act of May 14, 1880, and as early as 1881, Agent Eastman informed off-reservation Navajos of their eligibility (RCIA 1881:196). In 1882 C. H. Howard, an inspector for the Department of the Interior, recommended that the Indian Service help Navajos acquire and improve homesteads on the public domain (Howard to Sec. of the Int., Oct. 25, 1882, RBIA LR GR). Two years later, when white settlers began evicting Navajos from the south bank of the San Juan, Indian homesteading rights were recognized once again (Bowman to CIA, Sept. 27, 1884, RBIA LR GR). If any doubt remained about the legal status of off-reservation Navajos, the General Allotment Act of 1887 stated that any non-reservation Indian could receive an allotment on the public domain (Strickland 1982:131). In spite of this legislation, Navajos living on the public domain were periodically ordered back to the reservation, and soldiers escorted the more reluctant (Bailey and Bailey 1982:182–89).

The Navajo Agency failed to act on suggestions that off-reservation families file for homesteads because it lacked sufficient personnel to undertake such an extensive and time-consuming project. In addition, the Atlantic and Pacific Railroad opposed any such action. Navajos were occupying railroad land in some areas (Greever 1954:39), and railroad officials looked upon off-reservation Navajos as a hindrance to the economic development of the region. Undoubtedly, the railroad applied political pressure to have them returned to the reservation, and the inaction of agency officials only exacerbated the conflict.

While working to expand the reservation, agency officials also tried to increase the productivity of the existing reservation in order to support a higher percentage of the population. Accordingly, they initiated projects to develop wells and reservoirs in dry range areas, increase acreage under irrigation, and improve the quality of Navajo sheep.

Insufficient sources of water for stock left much rangeland on the reservation unused, or used below its grazing potential. For this reason, in 1879 the government authorized Agent Eastman to spend $500 for windmills (Eastman to CIA, Sept. 26, 1879, RBIA LR NMS). Eastman thought that a program to develop permanent water sources would gradually bring off-reservation families back to the reservation (Eastman to CIA, Jan. 26, 1880, RBIA LR NMS), and in the spring of 1880, he was authorized to spend not more than $3,000 "to furnish . . . Indians with a supply of water for their stock and for irrigating purposes" (Eastman to Trowbridge, March 30, 1880, RBIA LR NMS). The agency purchased three windmills and planned to place them at Pueblo Colorado, as requested by Ganado Mucho; Manuelito's camp; and Fort Defiance (Eastman to CIA, Apr. 26, 1880, RBIA LR NMS; Contract with Stover and Co., 1880, RBIA LR NMS). Eastman was temporarily replaced before the windmills were installed (Townsend to Trowbridge, June 15, 1880, RBIA LR NMS), and by 1883 at least two of them had yet to be erected (Riordan to CIA, Jan. 20, 1883, RBIA LR GR).

Development of water resources accelerated in the 1880s and 1890s as the land shortage became more severe. Investigating the reservation, Special Indian Agent William Parsons thought it imperative to bring Navajos back to the reservation to alleviate the increasing conflict between them and whites. Parsons named the lack of water on the reservation as the major obstacle to their return, and recommended

(1) That the sum of $50,000 be expended as soon as practicable in constructing dams, reservoirs, irrigating ditches, and sinking wells upon the Navajo reservation, with a view to store a sufficient supply of water for the necessities of the whole tribe.

(2) That when this has been done, or when sufficiently near completion to remove all doubt, the non-reservation Navajos be required upon reasonable notice . . . to return and remain upon the reservation. (U.S. Congress 1886:12)

In November 1886, Congress appropriated $7,500 for the development of water resources on the reservation. The following year, 14 reservoirs, 5 dams, 15 springs, and 9 irrigation ditches from 50 feet to 1.25 miles in length were developed—all within a fifty-mile radius of Fort Defiance (RCIA 1887:174; Dorchester to CIA, May 13, 1892, RBIA LR GR).

The effectiveness of these projects is open to question. Construction had been done carelessly, and some of the dams washed out. Work began on three irrigation ditches on Whiskey and Chusen creeks, respectively, thirty and thirty-five miles north of the agency, but the commissioner of Indian affairs halted construction in April 1888 (RCIA 1888:190). As for the irrigation projects, "the ditches were evidently built without any regard to utility, durability, or knowledge of the subject" (RCIA 1889:258).

Officials called for better planning to prevent such problems. In 1889 Lt. J. M. Stotsenburg surveyed portions of the reservation for the development of irrigation projects (RCIA 1889:258), and in 1892, three parties of army engineers made a large-scale survey to plan for worthwhile irrigation projects and to develop a dependable supply of water for livestock (U.S. Congress 1893:5–16). Funds for water development became available in the early 1890s, when some of the money appropriated for the support and civilization of the Navajos was diverted to irrigation projects (U.S. Congress 1891:3).

Officials first proposed the upgrading of Navajo herds in 1875, suggesting that Leicester or Cotswold rams be introduced (Goodale to Smith, May 10, 1875, RBIA LR NMS). W. B. Truax, the agency farmer, supported the proposal "as meeting a long neglected want, & introducing a much needed improvement" (Truax to Smith, May 11, 1875, RBIA LR NMS).

No action was taken until 1884, when the agency tried to improve the quality of the herd with Merino rams (Blunn 1940:104; Wentworth 1948:547). In 1883 Agent Riordan characterized the existing Navajo sheep as "scrubs" that sheared only "a scant pound" per fleece. Riordan believed that the wool yield could be increased to between six and ten pounds per fleece and that the herds could be reduced by two-thirds if the quality of the stock were improved (RCIA 1883:122). He resigned before specifying the details of his plan, and when the agency bought seventy-five Merino rams in 1884 (Bowman to Teller, Sept. 16, 1884, RBIA LR GR), his successor found himself wondering what to do with them. Agent Bowman planned to construct a building and corrals near Washington Pass to start an agency sheep ranch, but high elevation, cold winters, and the difficulty of securing adequate feed for the stock made the location unsuitable (Keam to Teller, June 5, 1884, RBIA LR GR). In September the rams were still at Fort Defiance "doing no good," so Bowman suggested buying some Merino ewes (Bowman to Teller, Sept. 16, 1884, RBIA LR GR). Secretary Teller rejected the proposal and told Bowman to distribute the rams to Navajos who would "take care of and properly use them" (Teller to Bowman, Oct. 1, 1884, RBIA LR GR). Since these rams were not referred to again in the correspondence, we can assume that was what happened.

Even with the best of planning, the programs to upgrade Navajo herds and establish permanent water systems probably would have failed. The Navajo herders were still thinking in terms of the subsistence value of stock (food for home consumption), rather than the market value of animal products (wool for the traders). The existing herds of churros—good foragers and meat producers, even if they did not grow the heaviest fleeces—probably suited the Navajos' needs better than Merinos. As for the water development projects, even if they had been well engineered and constructed, they were not far-reaching enough, and came too late to help off-reservation Navajos.

By the late 1880s, ranchers had overstocked the rangelands of New Mexico and Arizona with sheep and cattle, and competition for water and grazing rights intensified. As cattle replaced sheep, Anglo-American cowboys replaced Spanish-American sheepherders as the major competitors for Navajo range. As Colonel Buell noted in 1882, "the cattle-man and cowboy is the Indian's avowed enemy considering no rights of the Indian that he shall respect" (Buell to AA Gen'l, Mar. 13, 1882, RBIA LR GR). Added to this, the famous antagonism between sheepmen and cattlemen, described here by Special Agent Parsons, only made matters worse:

> The Navajos are mainly engaged in sheep and goat raising. The interests of cattle and sheep raisers, whether white or Indian, are hostile. Cattle cannot range where sheep are in the habit of grazing, and cattle men will drive off the sheep herders by force. (U.S. Congress 1886:12)

As the more aggressive Anglo-American cattlemen took over the range from Spanish-American sheepherders, confrontations between whites and Navajos became more violent. Not surprisingly, the major areas of conflict during this period—the San Juan River and the Little Colorado Valley—centered in areas of strong cattle ranching interests (RCIA 1893:111).

By the winter of 1889–90, the conflict reached a climax. A band of thirty cowboys decided to evict some Navajo families from the "Chaco country," east of the reservation and south of the San Juan, and in the process, reportedly stole horses and blankets (Mitchell to Commandant Post, Fort Lewis, Jan. 9, 1890, RBIA LR GR). Things went from bad to worse in December when a cowboy named John Cox shot and killed Chis-chilli, a Navajo, in an incident north of Aztec. Reports of the killing varied in particulars, but agreed in substance. The cowboys were harassing a Navajo hunting party, shooting broke out, Chis-chilli was killed, and the other Navajos fled to the reservation (Bailey and Bailey 1982:185–86). Following the incident, cowboys organized to drive the Navajo families off the public domain and back to the reservation, and some had even driven herds of cattle onto the Navajo reservation (Adams to C.O., Fort Lewis, Jan. 13, 1890, RBIA LR GR).

Prompt action by federal officials averted a range war between the Navajos and the cowboys. Deputy U.S. Marshall Winfield Mitchell asked for troops, reporting that "hostile feeling is at such a fever-heat, that trouble is liable to commence at any moment" (Mitchell to Commandment Post, Fort Lewis, Jan. 9, 1890, RBIA LR GR). Terrified by the prospects of Navajo reprisals, white settlers offered to compensate Chis-chilli's family, and placed $200 in the Second National Bank of Santa Fe for that purpose. The Navajos and their agent rejected the offer (RSW 1890, 1:166; Vandever to CIA, Mar. 4, 1890, RBIA LR GR). San Juan County officials finally bowed to strong pressure from federal officials and arrested Cox and his companions (RSW 1890, 1:166), temporarily placating the Navajos and intimidating the local cowboys. Eventually, the grand jury dismissed the case (Shipley to CIA, Apr. 13, 1891, RBIA LR GR), and the men were released. Tensions remained high, but other than routine complaints that trespassing Navajos were killing and scattering stock (Prince to Morgan, Dec. 24, 1892, RBIA LR GR), no major incidents involving Navajos and Anglo-American cowboys took place in the San Juan region in 1891 and 1892.

DISCUSSION: THE NAVAJOS ABOUT 1890

Navajo culture changed significantly between 1868 and 1892, particularly the structure and emphasis of its economy. Government officials wanted to alter some aspects of Navajo culture, but their programs and policies played only minor and often indirect roles in the changes that actually occurred. Unlike the majority of Indian populations during the late nineteenth century, the Navajos did not succumb to external cultural influences, but were responding to major economic changes in the territories of Arizona and New Mexico.

Despite growing conflicts with their neighbors, the Navajos enjoyed greater prosperity in the late 1880s and early 1890s than at any previous time in their history. In 1892 Agent David Shipley wrote that with the exception of the Osage, the Navajos were the wealthiest tribe in the United States (RCIA 1892:576)—a significant comparison, considering that only a few years earlier the Osage had been called, on a per capita basis, the "wealthiest people in the world" (E. White 1965:203). However, the wealth of the Osage resulted from favorable treaties with the United States government, which allowed them to sell, not merely cede, their reservation in Kansas (G. Bailey 1973:80–81); while the Navajos prospered as a result of their own industry.

As previously noted, subsistence level support required a human-to-sheep ratio of between 1:40 and 1:50. At the most, the Navajos had thirty sheep to each person during the 1840s and 1850s, indicating that herding alone could not have supported them. By the late 1880s and early 1890s, the ratio of humans to animals had increased to between 1:70 and 1:95, far beyond subsistence needs. Although most families continued to plant small fields, farming also appears to have decreased as the herds surpassed subsistence level, and Navajos began to trade livestock and livestock by-products (wool and blankets) for farm produce. The decrease in wheat production appears to correspond to the development of trading posts. Flour was one of the principal commodities traded by the early posts, and the Navajos probably found it easier to trade wool for flour than to grow wheat for themselves.[32] Similarly, they were trading livestock to the Hopis and Zunis for corn, bread, peaches, and other farm products during the 1880s (Dyk 1967:49–51; Cushing 1920:530). In 1893 Stephen estimated that the Navajos had traded 5,000 sheep to the Hopis for 500,000 pounds of corn (Parsons 1936:955), an exchange that would have been impossible during the pre-Bosque Redondo period because of the relatively small size of the herds.

Among other factors, the depletion of game animals and wild food plants caused the Navajos to become increasingly dependent on herding. Heavy dependence upon hunting and the intensive exploitation of game animals in the years immediately following 1868 had virtually eliminated the country's wild game resources, and by the late 1870s, hunting no longer made a significant contribution to Navajo subsistence. The rapid expansion of the herds soon resulted in severe overgrazing, and by the 1880s, wild food plants, many of which were also forage for stock, underwent a marked decline. The expansion of the herds both compensated for and contributed to the decline of these resources.

Furthermore, the Navajos preferred herding to farming—probably the most important incentive for change. Although W. W. Hill believed that the Navajos were "emotionally identified with agriculture" (Robert Roessel 1951:73), they did not consider it as prestigious or lucrative as herding. Cosmos Mindeleff (1898:483) remarked, "The people who live here [Canyon de Chelly] are regarded by the other Navaho as poor, because they own but few sheep and horses and depend principally on horticulture for their subsistence." Evidently, Navajos considered farming a poor man's occupation, even in a prosperous farming area such as Canyon de Chelly (W. Hill 1938:51). Wealthy families had farms but did not plant as extensively as poor families, and frequently traded for farm produce. At best, farming provided a tenuous livelihood; herding, on the other hand, could lead to wealth (Bailey field notes). In view of these attitudes, it is not surprising that Navajos turned away from farming when their herds exceeded subsistence needs.

It was no coincidence that as herding increased, trade also grew in volume and importance. The new intensified herding economy required increased dependence on trade, and thus, the two had to evolve together. The Navajos sold mainly the by-products of herding: nonproductive livestock (surplus rams and old ewes); sheep pelts and goat skins from animals butchered for home consumption; wool that was not needed for weaving; and blankets, which brought a much higher price per pound than raw wool.

Two distinct trade networks marketed these goods, each dealing in different items. The older intertribal and Spanish-American network handled Navajo livestock and blankets. Trading posts provided the major outlet for wool, sheep pelts, and goat skins, but took only a small percentage of the blanket trade. Both networks used barter-market systems, and as late as 1888, Special Indian Agent H. Welton reported that "the entire Navajo wool clip is sold by them without getting One Dollar in money" (Welton to CIA, June 17, 1888, RBIA LR GR). Navajos sometimes accepted silver Mexican coins in payment for goods, but only because they could make silver jewelry out of them, not to use as money.

The trade networks supplied foodstuffs, which the Navajos no longer grew in sufficient quantities to meet their needs; Indian trade items; and Anglo-American manufactured goods. Again, the two networks handled different kinds of trade. Buckskins, baskets, pottery, and other items of Indian manufacture could be obtained through the intertribal network, while the trading posts supplied items of Anglo-American manufacture, principally metal goods. Both networks were of crucial importance to the Navajos.

The intensification of herding did not cause any appreciable changes in Navajo animal husbandry practices. By the end of this period, the Navajos owned between five and eight times as many sheep and goats as they had before 1863, and per capita, between three and four times as many. While larger herds produced surpluses of livestock and livestock products, herding techniques and the quality of animals remained virtually unchanged. The Navajos moved into marginal rangelands in search of forage, moving camp frequently and building larger corrals to help them handle the stock. These movements of large numbers of animals accelerated the depletion of forage resources.

Intensification of herding necessitated economizing, or cutting back, in other aspects of their economy, a change made possible only by the expansion of the trade networks. Changes in Navajo material culture did not reflect acculturation or acceptance of Anglo-American technology, however, because the Navajos traded for manufactured goods functionally equivalent to items they already used, and rejected items that forced them to adopt new methods of production. In the eighteenth century, and probably as early as the seventeenth, they were trading with the Spanish for metal axes and knives. The availability of such items increased after 1868, and at the same time, metal shovels, metal hoes, sheep shears, needles, and guns began to replace wooden scoops, digging sticks, awls, and bows and arrows. Navajos rejected new tools which required changes in their methods of production (corn cultivators), or accepted them to a limited degree towards the end of the period (plows, wagons, and carpentry tools).

Changes in clothing reveal a similar pattern. Navajos traded for a few Anglo-American items of clothing and for beaded buckskin clothing and hide robes from other tribes, but they also began to trade for materials from which clothing could be made. The intertribal trade network carried on a lively trade in buckskins, used to make moccasins, leggings, and other clothing items. The availability of buckskins through trade lessened the Navajos' dependence on hunting, and saved them the labor of tanning hides. In time, yard goods such as calico began to replace buckskin and wool, and women started wearing homemade calico skirts and blouses in place of homemade woolen dresses.

A series of changes occurred in weaving. Anglo-American wool cards were replacing the homemade variety. Many weavers shifted to commercial yarns, eliminating the time-consuming processes of carding, spinning, and dying. Navajo weavers quickly accepted items which saved time and increased productivity, but rejected technological innovations such as the Anglo-American loom which would have altered their methods of production.

The production of household items also declined when goods made by other groups became available through trade. The decline in Navajo basketry was compensated in part by bowl baskets and pitched water bottles from surrounding tribes, and in part by Anglo-American functional equivalents such as tin plates, buckets, pails, and canteens. Similarly, painted Pueblo pottery and Anglo-American metal kettles, pots, pans, and cups replaced domestic production of pottery. Tschopik (1938:261) suggested that "taboos" surrounding the manufacture of basketry and pottery were primarily responsible for their decline. While we agree that taboos increased the labor of making pots and baskets, they could not have caused such a decline by themselves. Pitched basketry water bottles had no taboos involved in their construction, yet declined along with styles of basketry that did (Tschopik 1940:459). Brugge (1963:21) suggested that the growth in

Navajo herding contributed to the reduction in Navajo pottery making during the late eighteenth century, and perhaps again in the late nineteenth century. It would be extremely awkward for a seminomadic population to transport heavy, breakable pots.

Unlike other aspects of Navajo material culture, the production of silverwork and ironwork increased sharply during this period. Silversmithing in particular seems an exception to the general economizing in the manufacture of material goods. However, the production and ownership of jewelry constituted a sort of insurance policy against the failure of the herding economy, and in that sense, was integral to it. Jewelry was more than a luxury ornament or symbol of wealth to the Navajos. Between 1868 and 1900, they were not yet participating in the cash economy, and only by accumulating "hard goods" such as silver and turquoise jewelry could they acquire permanent, storable wealth and economic security. The intensification of herding further increased the importance of jewelry. As Aberle (1963:4–5) pointed out, Navajo economic resources have long been subject to major fluctuations, and "virtually no feature of the Navaho subsistence base is stable annually." Historically, the Navajo economy has been based on a variety of resources, but the heavy reliance on herding during this period courted economic disaster, especially during years of harsh winters and dry summers. Navajos periodically converted surplus livestock and animal products into silver and turquoise jewelry. If herds were destroyed by deep snows or drought, the family jewelry could be pawned at the trading post for food, or traded to more fortunate stockmen for stock to rebuild the herds.

We have seen how increased dependence on herding resulted in economizing and a major restructuring of the Navajo economy. Changes of this magnitude undoubtedly had major effects on other aspects of Navajo culture, but primary ethnohistoric data on social organization, religion, and most other aspects of the culture are not available for this period.

What we know of pre-Bosque Redondo Navajo political organization is sketchy at best. In at least some areas, chiefs or *naat'anii* headed localized bands. Although the evidence is not clear, we agree with Esther Goldfrank's (1945:272–75) suggestion that early Navajo political leadership was probably based on the control of or access to farming areas. As we discussed earlier in this chapter, the agents attempted to use the *naat'anii* to help police and administer the reservation. This served to eventually undermine the influence and prestige of the *naat'anii* by repeatedly forcing them to take actions which were not supported by the people as a whole. At the same time, Navajo families were deemphasizing farming and searching for new rangeland for their stock. This scattering of families obliterated the geographical distinctions between the bands. Thus, the traditional band/*naat'anii* system declined in significance.

Toward the end of this period, a more localized, less formal arrangement, which we call the "outfit" system, replaced the old band/*naat'anii* system. These outfits, extended-family, cooperative herding units headed by the wealthiest family member, cared for herds too large to be supervised by a nuclear family. Prior to 1863, slaves herded livestock for families that were short of labor, but by the 1880s, the use of slaves was no longer permitted. Navajos who owned large herds had no alternative but to recruit poorer kinsmen—biological or nominal—to work as year-round or seasonal herders.

Federal officials played only minor roles in Navajo culture change, and their attempts to "civilize" the Navajos failed almost completely. Few Navajos attended the schools, and by the early 1890s only about fifty spoke English. Missionary attempts were sporadic and unsuccessful. With the exception of a few Mormon converts, few if any Navajos had become Christians by the early 1890s. Although the agency distributed free building materials, only a few wealthy families built houses as prestige symbols.

Paradoxically, the economic success of the Navajos prevented agents from "civilizing" them. On one hand, officials were extraordinarily pleased with such advances, for the Navajo Agency required little government funding for rations. Even when the government had to distribute rations to the Navajos, the number of destitute families remained small, and the cost of feeding them minimal. Rations distributed to Navajos averaged 11¢ per capita in 1882, compared to $25.28 per capita for the Southern Utes, $42.07 for the Mescalero Apaches, and $40.00 for the San Carlos Apaches (Robert Roessel 1980:69–70). On the other hand, such independence deprived agents of a means of controlling and manipulating the behavior of their charges. William Parsons, a special agent, summarized the government's predicament:

> Their very independence and industry makes them less susceptible than other tribes to civilizing influences. Other tribes which receive supplies of food and clothing, can be induced to cut their hair and wear the garb of white men, but every Navajo wears long hair, fastens it back with a red "banda" and clings to his blanket and Indian dress. None but the scouts and school boys will consent to wear anything but the Indian dress. (Parsons to Atkins, Apr. 26, 1886, RBIA LR GR)

Navajo prosperity not only weakened the agency's economic leverage, but also reduced contact with officials. Until the late 1880s, when the government established a school at Keams Canyon and stationed a farmer on the San Juan, all agency personnel stayed at Fort Defiance, severely limiting their influence. Self-sufficient Navajo families in the northern and western areas had no reason to visit the agency, and few did.

Most agents decided to leave well enough alone. Reluctant to meddle in what they considered the internal affairs of the tribe, they devoted themselves to keeping peace between Navajos and whites. As long as the Navajos refrained from raiding local white ranchers, the government usually let them do what they pleased. For example, Agent Shipley chose not to investigate a murder, preferring to let the families involved resolve the matter according to Navajo cultural practices (Shipley to CIA, July 19, 1892, RBIA LR GR).

Anglo-American military domination brought a period of peace and security to the Southwest, permitting the expansion of Navajo herds to levels that would not have been possible in the chaotic years before 1863. At the same time, the Anglo-American trade network integrated the Navajos, though only marginally, into the national economy. The intensified herding economy which evolved during this period depended on expanded trade with other Indians, Hispanics, and Anglo-Americans.

Unfortunately, the very circumstances that brought prosperity to the Navajos also attracted other populations to the region. Mormon farmers moved south to settle portions of the Little Colorado and lower San Juan valleys. Hispanic ranchers moved their growing herds west out of the Rio Puerco and Rio Grande valleys. Anglo-American farmers and ranchers settled the upper San Juan Valley, and following the construction of the Atlantic and Pacific Railroad, areas to the south of the reservation. By the late 1880s, the rangelands were overstocked with sheep and cattle, conflict between Navajos and their new neighbors continued to escalate, and the unprecedented prosperity brought on by the livestock boom was about to end.

ECONOMIC COLLAPSE: 1893–1900

In 1893 the luck of the Navajos and the white ranchers ran out. Drought destroyed most of the forage on the rangelands, and many water sources dried up. The Panic of 1893 caused the national economy to collapse, and drastically lowered prices of livestock and wool. In 1893 Acting Agent Edward H. Plummer wrote,

The condition of the Navajo Indians is worse than it has been for a number of years . . . partly, [due] to a succession of very dry seasons, which have caused a great scarcity of foliage, very poor crops, loss of many sheep and ponies from starvation during the winters, and a very poor yield of wool. Increasing poverty has led to the necessity of selling many sheep. . . . Many of the Navajos are in a condition bordering on starvation. When caught killing cattle which do not belong to them, their excuse is that their children are crying for food. Owing to the very poor yield and low price of wool this season, pawning of articles to traders commenced before the wool season was over . . . the conclusion is that when winter arrives many of them must steal or starve. Their sheep herds . . . have been decreasing for several years through necessity of selling and killing to obtain food, on account of continued inbreeding, and from starvation. (RCIA 1893:109)

The Navajo grazing strategy could not adapt to a drought of this severity. When droughts occurred in the past, Navajos had been known to move their herds one hundred miles or more to rangelands less seriously affected (Newcomb 1964:11–13). Overstocking of the range denied them that kind of flexibility in 1893 and led to long-term losses for both the Navajos and the ranching industry. As the drought persisted, herds crowded into the vicinity of the few remaining water sources, stripping rangeland near major wells and springs bare of forage. This crowding resulted in "permanent" deterioration of the range in these areas—damage not repaired by increases in rainfall in later years (Wooton 1908:21). Pollen studies of grasslands in the San Juan Basin of New Mexico reflect the severity of this deterioration during the 1890s (Hall 1977:1603).

The economic condition of the Navajos continued to worsen throughout 1893. In January of 1894, Agent Plummer reported,

The Navajos are now in a worse condition, financially, than they have been before, on account of the low price of wool, deterioration of sheep and other stock and exceedingly dry seasons succeeding each other for several years. They are therefore unable to provide for themselves. (Plummer to CIA, Jan. 31, 1894, RBIA LR GR)

In September 1894, the Navajo reservation as well as the entire Southwest continued to suffer from the drought, having received the lowest rainfall in years (Report of Supt. of Irr. and Specl. Disbg. Ag., Sept. 30, 1894, RBIA LR GR). Plummer's 1894 report noted that the Navajos "are poorer than at this season last year. More are starving . . . . Many of them have lost their entire crop of corn" (RCIA 1894:99). As if natural calamities were not enough, the price of wool fell from 16.3¢ per pound in 1892 to 11.1¢ per pound in 1894, when Congress removed the protective tariff on wool (appendix B; C. Mindeleff 1898:486).

The winter of 1894–95 added to the Navajos' misery. "An unprecedented spell of cold weather, accompanied with heavy snow-fall" (Murphy to CIA, Feb. 18, 1895, RBIA LR GR) caused further livestock losses. The situation became so desperate that Acting Agent Constant Williams took it upon himself to purchase and issue 10,000 pounds of flour to the Navajos, noting that "the destitute are now killing the ponies and sheep of other Indians on the reservation to an alarming extent, and quarrels upon this subject are frequent." From chiefs and headmen, Williams learned that throughout the reservation, between 4,000 and 5,000 Navajos were destitute—about one-fourth to one-fifth of the tribe. People had nothing left to trade, and with one exception, "all the trading-stores on the San Juan River" had closed. He requested an immediate shipment of an additional 100,000 pounds of flour to be issued as rations (Williams to CIA, Jan. 26, 1895, RBIA LR GR).

Mary Eldridge, a government field matron who dispensed food, medicine, clothing, seeds, and tools, described the misery of the San Juan Navajos during this period:

> For the past few years the range has been very poor, hundreds of sheep dying every spring, no sale for produce, and ponies now not worth taking to market . . . the people have been gradually growing poorer and poorer and the flocks decreasing in number, until last fall [1894] found our Indians in a pitiable condition. . . . The Navajoes had tided over the two preceding winters by living upon their sheep and goats, and the poorer of the Indians had eaten up their flocks, so at the beginning of winter they had nothing to eat except their horses and burros, which they began to kill for food in November. Some of the Navajoes lived entirely upon meat until the issue of flour in the spring. . . . Some of the Indians got work from the white settlers, receiving their pay in corn, vegetables, and some money. (RCIA 1895:120)

As conditions got worse, a group of Anglo-American residents in Farmington, New Mexico petitioned the secretary of the interior:

> Their destitution is VERY great, . . . they are in pressing need of immediate relief, . . . they are in that stage of want that they are

now eating their horses . . . unless prompt and effecient [sic] aid be rendered them at once large numbers of them will perish this spring. (Petition from Citizens of Farmington to the Sec. of the Int., Mar. 4, 1895, RBIA LR GR)

The plight of the San Juan Navajos probably typified conditions throughout the reservation, and in response to appeals from government officials as well as private citizens, rations were issued.

In the spring of 1895, the Navajos planted "more . . . than ever before" (RCIA 1895:118). Good summer rains improved pasture conditions, and that fall they had a successful harvest. The situation continued to improve through 1898, but in the winter of 1898–99, two feet of snow blanketed most of the northern part of the reservation from December 10 until spring (*Farmington Daily Times*, Nov. 21, 1951), and unusually heavy snows also fell on the south. At Fort Defiance, the mercury dropped to minus 24 degrees Fahrenheit. Once again, the herds sustained heavy losses, and it was "estimated that fully 20 percent of the sheep on the reservation either froze or starved" (RCIA 1899:157).

Normally, heavy winter snows produce a substantial spring runoff, creating ideal conditions for floodwater farming of the washes, and usually ensuring a good crop. Likewise, in an ordinary year heavy winter snows guarantee good spring and summer pasture, compensating at least in part for livestock losses. However, the 1898–99 snowpack "appeared to evaporate, going off without leaving much moisture in the ground" (RCIA in RSI 1900:191–92), resulting in a poor harvest in the fall of 1899.

The winter of 1899–1900 was uncommonly mild, and not much snow fell in Navajo country. Although the herds came through the winter well, spring brought a shortage of grass, and scant rainfall during the spring and summer left the land parched (RCIA in RSI 1900:192). Without any way to feed their animals, many Navajos began to sell them to traders and local ranchers. In midsummer, an official reported, "One man on the San Juan says 'There are Indians here who have been induced to part with their sheep and now have no wool to sell and no meat to eat' " (Peabody to CIA, July 18, 1900, RBIA LR GR). Those who did sell were lucky. By August, animals were starving to death and dying of thirst (RCIA in RSI 1900:192). Crops failed that fall, and the government had to issue more rations than usual during the winter of 1900–1901 and the following summer (RCIA 1901:180). The drought persisted in the northern portion of the reservation through the summer of 1902, and added to the already heavy livestock losses (RCIA 1902:63).

The Navajos suffered a severe decline in livestock between 1892 and 1902 (see figs. 1–3), but because the agency did not revise its annual estimates from 1893 through 1899, it is difficult to determine the magnitude of the loss. Between 1892 and 1900, the number of sheep and goats owned by the Navajos went from an estimated 1,715,984 to 401,882—a decline of over 75 percent. Judging from contemporary narrative statements, the herds reached their lowest numbers in 1895 or 1896, and recovered to some degree by 1900. The general livestock estimates for New Mexico indicate that 1896 marked the low point for white ranchers (table 3).

During the same period, the population of the tribe increased from an estimated 17,204 in 1890 (Johnston 1966a:367) to 21,009 in 1900. A figure of 18,000 in 1892 gives a human-to-sheep-and-goat ratio of 1:95, well above the 1:40 or 1:50 necessary for subsistence level support. By 1900, the ratio had dropped to 1:19, less than half of that level.

Herding intensification and the prosperity that followed had resulted from a unique set of circumstances. Rainfall was unusually heavy in the 1880s, producing more forage and water resources for livestock, and in turn allowing herds to expand to unprecedented numbers. On a national level, the prices paid for livestock and livestock products were extremely high throughout this period. Expansion of transportation facilities in the Southwest enabled Navajos to participate in the national economy for the first time, further stimulating their livestock industry. The Navajos joined regional and national markets without any qualitative changes in animal husbandry practices. Herding remained subsistence-oriented, and trade items merely the surpluses of expanded production.

This ideal situation did not last. What had led to the intensification of Navajo herding also brought on the rapid expansion of non-Navajo herds, until the range could no longer support the new demands being put on it. By the 1890s, the Navajo economy had become too specialized to adapt to the climatic and economic catastrophes that were to follow. The intensified herding economy collapsed, and with it, prosperity vanished.

CHAPTER THREE

The Reorientation of Navajo Culture: 1900–1930

The severe economic depression which beset the Navajos in 1893 persisted until the first decade of the twentieth century. Its tenacity arose from several factors. Navajos and Euro-Americans fully occupied the rangelands of the southwest, leaving no room for further expansion. During the 1890s, over-grazing caused major damage to the range, and it was slow to recover. In some areas, invasive juniper and sagebrush may have permanently lowered the grazing capacity of the range (Wooton 1908:21; Hall 1977:1603). However, these factors alone would have had little impact on the Navajos had it not been for their rapidly increasing population, estimated at 17,204 in 1890, 21,009 in 1900, and 38,787 in 1930 (Johnston 1966a:362). Such growth necessitated more than a reestablishment of the intensified herding economy. Before the tribe returned to prosperity, a new economic order would have to evolve.

The Navajo economy depended considerably more on the national economy during the early decades of the twentieth century than it had before 1892. Although wage labor became an important supplementary source of income, and farming increased in economic importance, a shift from subsistence-oriented herding to market-oriented herding constituted the major change.

At the same time, the relationship of Navajos to the dominant Anglo-American society was changing. Government controls tightened, and for the first time officials made genuine efforts to suppress "objectionable" aspects of Navajo culture. Schools and enrollment increased dramatically, and missionaries became more active. As the economy improved and trade expanded, the number of trading posts and traders increased. In general, the frequency and depth of Navajo contact with Anglo-Americans and their culture increased several times over, particularly between 1900 and 1920. The cumulative effects of these changes were staggering, and a new way of life evolved.

THE GOVERNMENT TAKES CONTROL (MORE OR LESS)

The change in federal policy from isolation to assimilation occurred gradually; it was not until the late 1880s that the change was explicitly formulated into policy. The General Allotment Act (Dawes Act) of 1887 set the tone of this shift. Indian reservations were to be broken up, lands allotted to tribal members, and the "surplus" unallotted lands opened to white homesteaders.[1] Two years later, Commissioner of Indian Affairs T. J. Morgan established a "new" Indian policy, which included six major points:

> (1) The reservation system . . . must soon cease to exist, (2) The logic of events demands the absorption of the Indians into our national life, not as Indians, but as American citizens, (3) The relations of the Indians to the Government must rest solely upon the full recognition of their individuality, (4) The Indians must "conform to the White man's ways," peaceably if they will, forcibly if they must, (5) A comprehensive system of education . . . compulsory in its demands . . . should be developed as rapidly as possible, (6) The tribal relations should be broken up, . . . and the autonomy of the individual substituted. (RCIA 1889:3–4)

Morgan subsequently summarized his position when he wrote, "The American Indian is to become the Indian American." To achieve these goals, Congress passed the Appropriations Act of July 13, 1892, which made Indian education compulsory (Strickland 1982:139–40).

These policies had little effect upon the Navajos until Agent David Shipley tried to enforce compulsory education by seizing Navajo children and sending them to boarding school. His actions culminated in the Round Rock incident, in which he was assaulted by a local Navajo leader named

Black Horse and had to be rescued by the Navajo police and cavalry (Underhill 1956:205–6).[2]

By resisting physically, the Navajos had succeeded in thwarting the first direct challenge to their internal autonomy. Although government officials continued to round up children for boarding school, it was done surreptitiously. Even if the Navajos had not resisted, Shipley's actions would have been futile. In the 1890s the government could not have afforded to enroll the entire school-age population, just as it lacked the means to enforce other aspects of Indian policy. It was simply a problem of too many Navajos, and not enough money. Consequently, the tribe did not begin to feel the effects of assimilationist policy until the early years of the twentieth century.

As early as 1870, it became apparent that such a large tribe could not be managed from a single center. The government took no action to correct the problem until 1899, when it began to create additional administrative districts. By 1909 six separate agencies shared responsibility for the reservation (Kelly 1968:27; E. Hill 1981:163), and regardless of geographical location, Navajos began to come into more frequent contact with government officials. The activities of each agency centered around at least one boarding school, and some had day schools as well. The government supplied each agency with at least one physician, medical facilities, and one or more farmers or stockmen to help develop farms and herds.

The first of the new agencies was created in 1899, when land set aside under the executive order of December 16, 1882, was removed from the jurisdiction of the Navajo Agency and organized as the Moqui reservation (its name was changed to the "Hopi Agency" in 1923), with Keams Canyon as its administrative center. Primarily concerned with the Hopis, the agency also supervised the affairs of large numbers of Navajos within its boundaries (E. Hill 1981:163; Young 1968:60). An executive order of January 8, 1900, set aside the tract of land between the Hopi reservation and the Colorado River. In 1901 this tract and the one covered by the executive order of May 17, 1884, were removed from the Navajo Agency and placed under the jurisdiction of a newly created Western Navajo Agency. At first the superintendent of Western Navajo lived at the Blue Canyon School, but in 1903, after the relocation of Mormon settlers, the agency moved to Tuba City (WN NR 1915:2; Kelly 1968:27). An executive order of November 14, 1901, gave the Navajos a checkerboard of public domain lands along the Little Colorado River (Kappler 1904:877) known as the Navajo Extension and administered by a resident farmer. The government built a school there in 1908, and established the Leupp Agency. In 1903 the northern portion

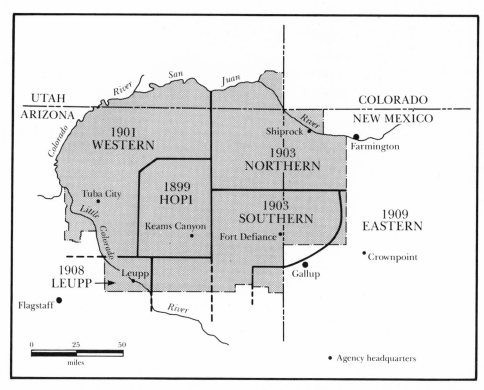

Map 4. Navajo jurisdictions, 1909–1935. Adapted from Williams (1970).

of the Navajo reservation was reorganized as the San Juan Agency, with offices at Shiprock (Kelly 1968:27). Authorized in 1907, the Pueblo Bonito Agency moved its offices to Crownpoint soon after it was established in 1909 (Stacher c. 1940:1; Kelly 1968:27).

On January 1, 1927, the names of three of the agencies were changed: San Juan became Northern Navajo, Pueblo Bonito was renamed Eastern Navajo, and the original Navajo Agency at Fort Defiance became Southern Navajo (map 4; Underhill 1953:275, 277). For the sake of clarity, we will refer to these agencies as Northern, Eastern, and Southern Navajo throughout this chapter.

The quality of government control also changed during this period. During the early 1900s, career civil servants began to fill positions in the Indian Service, instead of political appointees (Van Valkenburgh 1938:53). Tenure in office lengthened significantly, and as a result, superintendents and other workers became better acquainted with the Navajos and their problems than had their predecessors. However, there were drawbacks. Career civil servants could not exercise the same freedom of choice that political appointees could, and regardless of their personal opinions, were forced to conform more closely to policy decisions.

With a larger and stabler work force, the Indian Service prepared for an assault on Navajo autonomy. Performing the same administrative function as agents, the new superintendents and their staffs put regulations into effect on all the reservations concerning trade or aimed at eradicating "vices" such as child marriage, polygyny, and gambling. The Navajo Indian police and the Court of Indian Offenses (the primary regulatory body at each agency) were responsible for enforcing the regulations, although federal and state courts held jurisdiction over major offenses (L NR 1913:11).

In general, federal officials made little effort to establish any meaningful form of tribal government. The government continued to appoint leaders who would not oppose federal Indian policy (Williams 1970:16). The earliest business council appears to have been formed at Leupp (then the Navajo Extension) in about 1904. This council, composed of the two Navajo court judges and three "elected" Head Men, met between eight and ten times a year (L NR 1910:23), but informal meetings replaced it in 1911 (L NR 1911:18). At Southern Navajo, a business council met only once a year, and consisted of "all the most intelligent members of the tribe" (N NR 1911:14). Northern Navajo held its earliest informal council in 1921, consisting of all adult males from the agency who wished to attend (Kelly 1968:49).[3] Western Navajo did not report any such meetings until 1922, when monthly councils of "influential men" were being held (WN NR 1922:31). No evidence has been found of a council ever being held at Eastern Navajo during these years.

The councils did not function as a tribal government. In 1917 the superintendent at Leupp complained, "the Government took away the old tribal form of control and substituted nothing adequate in its place. Nothing that really governs . . ." (L NR 1917:1). However, many superintendents considered the absence of formal Navajo government an advantage. Superintendent Shelton of Northern Navajo wrote in 1910 that "we have no business councils with the Indians on this reservation for the reason that we do not consider them desirable from any point of view" (SJ NR 1910:24). Some superintendents preferred to deal directly with individual Navajos instead of working through a business council. Certainly this approach conformed to the policy of "individualizing" the Indians rather than dealing with them as a tribe. It also minimized the possibility of any widespread, organized resistance to government policies. Where councils did exist, they did not really govern or even advise, but merely served the interests of the superintendents. For example, the early Leupp business council met to "report violations" of policy and to "control" other Navajos (L NR

1910:23). Consequently, superintendents had a relatively free hand in implementing policies within their jurisdictions. Navajos resisted this usurpation of power only to a limited degree and on a local level. In some cases, they were forcibly suppressed when they did.

Superintendent Shelton tried to enforce the new order in Northern Navajo, and met resistance from Bai-a-lil-le and his followers, the most openly defiant group of Navajos in the district. Called a witch by some, Bai-a-lil-le was an influential medicine man who defied Shelton by refusing to have his sheep dipped for protection against scabies, selling his young ewes to traders instead of building up his flocks, having more than one wife, and opposing compulsory education for children. In the fall of 1907, a troop of cavalry was dispatched to Aneth at Shelton's request and attacked Bai-a-lil-le's camp. Soldiers killed two Navajos outright, seriously wounded another, and captured Bai-a-lil-le and nine of his men (Correll 1970:4–13, 26; U.S. Congress 1907:7–8).

In 1913 another major incident took place on Northern Navajo. After raiding Shiprock and freeing three women who were being held for violating Shelton's ban against polygyny, a local leader named Bi-joshii and his followers fled to Beautiful Mountain, a natural stronghold above Sanostee. When Bi-joshii refused to surrender and the Navajo police were unable to arrest him, the cavalry was summoned. The episode ended peacefully, however, when General Hugh Scott persuaded the Navajos to surrender. The harshest sentence handed out was thirty days in jail (McNitt 1962:347–58).

In Western Navajo, the superintendents struggled to maintain any semblance of control. During the teens, Tuba City officials complained that their police force was not as efficient as the Fort Defiance force (WN NR 1914:1); furthermore, that their force was made up in part of feeble old men who were too conservative for the job (WN NR 1915:6). Superintendents leveled similar allegations at the judges of the local Court of Indian Offenses. One complained that he lacked authority, and that "this system of government has resulted in placing absolute control of reservation affairs in the old medicine men who have always been supported by the criminal element" (WN NR 1916:2).

Navajos living in the vicinity of Navajo Mountain caused many of the difficulties in the Western Navajo Agency. In 1916 the superintendent ordered the Navajo police to arrest one of the leaders of this band, but they refused. Instead of granting the superintendent's subsequent request for military support, the Indian Service authorized hiring a truant officer. The new officer, an Anglo-American, confronted the Navajo leader, and killed him when he resisted (WN NR 1916:3–4). This show of force did not enhance the government's position in the west. The following year, the superintendent reported that Navajos in his district had "never learned to respect . . . governing authority," and that "they have absolute control of their own affairs and have done practically as they pleased" (WN NR 1917:3).

Although there can be little doubt that by their use of the Indian police, Indian judges, business councils, and the military, the superintendents increased their control over the lives of individual Navajos during the first two decades of the twentieth century, the degree of that control varied from region to region, and was tenuous at best.[4] The Bai-a-lil-le and Beautiful Mountain affairs showed Navajos that they could not openly defy the government. However, the number of Anglo-American officials on the reservation remained relatively small, and the superintendents had to rely on the Indian police, whose effectiveness they questioned. The tribe's increasing prosperity deprived officials of economic leverage, one of their most effective means of control. At least covertly, the Navajos continued their practices of plural marriage, child marriage, gambling, and other activities officially considered "vices."[5]

It was not until the 1920s that the Indian Service began to recognize a real need for some formalized governmental units among the Navajos. As we will discuss later, the discovery of oil in Northern Navajo and the difficulties that oil companies encountered in attempting to lease tracts of reservation land from informal councils resulted in the establishment of the Navajo Tribal Council in 1923. However, this elected, twelve-member council was established primarily to serve the interests of the oil companies and functioned only at the tribal level, failing to respond to the needs of the agency superintendents or the problems of local communities.

In 1927 the superintendent of Leupp decided that the Navajos needed some organization at the community level and proceeded to set up what he termed "chapters" within his jurisdiction (Williams 1970:33–34). Chapters were loosely defined Navajo communities, usually held together by kinship ties and centered around a trading post. Averaging about 500 people, chapters had elected officials and served as a means of communication between superintendents and the families of a particular region. The concept of chapter organization spread rapidly, and within a few years, superintendents had organized chapters in every jurisdiction. By the 1930s, about 80 chapters had been organized on and off the reservation (Williams 1970:38). The Indian Service, however, made no attempt to formally link the chapters and the Tribal Council, and at the end of this period, reservation political structure remained in an incipient stage of development.

THE NAVAJOS AND THE WHITE MAN

During the early decades of the twentieth century, the Navajos were affected by political and economic events in a white world of which they had little awareness and over which they exerted even less control. Competition between off-reservation families and white ranchers for public domain lands continued. New Mexico and Arizona became states in 1912, giving local white ranching interests congressional representation and making it more difficult to protect Indian land rights. The outbreak of World War I in Europe and the entrance of the United States into the war in 1917 had little direct effect on the Navajos, but tremendous indirect effects. Finally, the discovery of oil in the northern portion of the reservation in the early 1920s introduced the Navajo people to yet another element of the Anglo-American world—the oil companies—some of which were politically ruthless in their attempt to gain access to Navajo resources.

Land

The collapse of the livestock industry in the mid-1890s temporarily eased range competition and tension on the public domain. The white populations of New Mexico and Arizona were growing rapidly, however—from 200,000 in 1890 to 273,000 in 1900—and demand for land grew accordingly. Between 1900 and 1930, the white population in New Mexico and Arizona almost tripled in size, reaching approximately 770,000 (U.S. Bureau of the Census 1975:24, 32).

The challenge to Navajo holdings on the eastern margins of the reservation came primarily from a regenerated sheep industry. Starting about 1898 or 1899, large herds wintered just east of the reservation line on the Chaco Plateau in New Mexico, an area used mainly by Navajos in the past (Brugge 1980:156-58, 199-200). In the area adjoining the southeastern corner of the reservation, the discovery of artesian water and the development of artesian wells after 1900 led to increased conflict between Navajos and white ranchers. In the past, scarcity of water had kept white ranching operations out of the region (Kelly 1968:23), but once water became available,

> hordes of sheep were driven over this range during the winter by White sheep owners, who ranged over the Indian occupied lands without regard to the range rights of the Indians; and without any payment for the use of the range to the Indians or any Department of Government or the State. (Stacher c. 1940:1)

Doubting that more than half of the Navajo population lived on the reservation, in 1899 Agent Hayzlett wrote,

> Many complaints are coming in from parties who reside in the Territories of Arizona and New Mexico and the State of Utah, in regard to the Indians going there with their flocks. I am unable to find a remedy, for the reason that there is not vegetation nor tillable land enough on this reservation to support more than one-half of the tribe. (RCIA 1899:158)

Despite the acknowledged inadequacies of the Navajo land base, W. A. Jones, then commissioner of Indian affairs, opposed any extension of the reservation boundaries (Jones to Sec. of Int., July 15, 1899, RBIA LR GR). However, just five months later a shootout between Navajos and whites near Flagstaff, Arizona left five Navajos and one cowboy dead (*San Juan Times*, Nov. 17, 1899), and shook the government out of its complacency. Reverend W. R. Johnston had established a mission for the Navajos at Tolchaco, Arizona in 1897, and lobbied vigorously to protect the land rights of off-reservation Navajos in the Little Colorado Valley (L NR 1931:2; Kelly 1968:21). His efforts and the killings near Flagstaff resulted in a quick reversal of the government's position against extending the boundaries of the reservation in Arizona. On January 8, 1900, an executive order removed "from sale and allotment" 1,575,369 acres of land bounded on the east by the Navajo and Hopi reservations and on the west by the Colorado River (Kappler 1904:877; Kelly 1968:22). Although not specifically designated an extension to the Navajo reservation, the land came under the jurisdiction of the Western Navajo reservation when it was established the following year (Kelly 1968:22). On November 14, 1901, a second executive order withdrew 425,171 acres from the public domain along the Little Colorado River (map 5).

Although these actions secured portions of the Navajo land base and helped relieve tensions, they did not solve the problem. Many Navajo families in Arizona were still living on lands that had not been withdrawn from the public domain. Approximately one-third of the land specified in the 1900 order and all of the land in the 1901 order were scattered in a "checkerboard" among sections owned by the Santa Fe Railroad and leased to white ranchers (Kelly 1968:21–22; Kappler 1904:877).

While the government made progress toward resolving the land problem in Arizona, the situation was getting worse in New Mexico. In 1901 territorial representatives from San Juan County learned from their constituents that the Navajos were

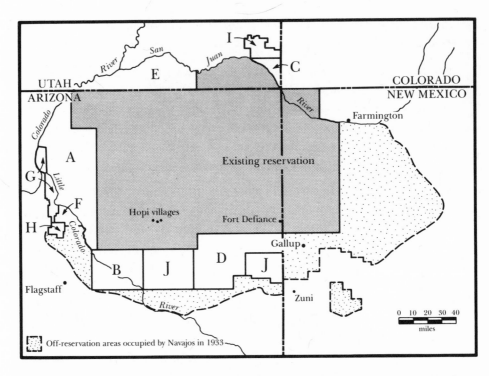

Off-reservation areas occupied by Navajos in 1933

Map 5. Growth of Navajo land base, 1900–1933. A, Executive order of Jan. 8, 1900. B, Executive order of Nov. 14, 1901. C, Executive order of May 15, 1905. D, Executive order of Nov. 7, 1907. E, The "Paiute Strip": returned to the public domain in 1892; Navajo 1908–1922; public domain 1922–1929; removed from homestead entry 1929–1933; Navajo 1933. F, Executive order of May 7, 1917. G, Act of May 23, 1930. H, Act of Feb. 21, 1931. I, Act of Mar. 1, 1933. J, Act of June 14, 1933. Adapted from Williams (1970).

acting in a very arbitrary manner toward the settlers in that region . . . Indians were allowed to leave the limits of the reservation and have wandered all over that section of territory . . . . They [have] practically taken possession of a strip of land some 50 miles wide and 200 miles long and are barring out of this strip, lying along the east side of the Navajo reservation, on public domain, all stock whose owners do not pay them for water privileges, and even when an excessive tax is paid the cattle and sheep are driven away from the watering places immediately after they have taken water, so that when they again require water another tax may be levied against the owners. This tax is generally in the nature of a demand by the Indians that they be given ten sheep for every 1000 head allowed to water. (*Farmington Times*, Mar. 1, 1901)

The conflict between Navajos and whites in the New Mexico off-reservation areas continued to escalate. During a disagreement over the watering of stock, the owner of Chico Trading Post, southeast of Farmington, shot and wounded a Navajo (*Farmington Times*, June 6, 1902). Navajos were suspected of murdering three traders between December 1902 and July 1903, and some Anglos claimed the killings were part of a conspiracy (*Farmington Times*, July 10, 1903).

The establishment of the Northern Navajo Agency in 1903 and the arrival of Superintendent Shelton temporarily contained the problem. Shelton did not mince words on the land controversy, telling a meeting of local whites who were unhappy about off-reservation Navajos that they "misunderstood the purpose of a reservation. Reservations were to keep the white men off, not the Indians on" (Bailey field notes).

In January 1905 a state livestock inspector declared that Navajo sheep herds were infected with scabies. Both Navajo agents in New Mexico—Perry (Southern Navajo) and Shelton (Northern Navajo)—had made plans for dipping Navajo sheep, but needed time to raise money and construct dipping vats. The delay gave white ranchers an opportunity to complain about the government's management of the problem and to demand that Navajo herds be put under quarantine on the reservation (Brugge 1980:198–213).

Perhaps angered by the scabies controversy, Indian Service officials pressed for protection of Navajo interests on the public domain in New Mexico. In the summer of 1905, superintendents Shelton and Perry jointly requested that a tract of public land measuring twenty-four miles east to west and seventy miles north to south be added to the eastern side of the reservation (Brugge 1980:199–200). Commissioner of Indian Affairs Francis Leupp visited the disputed area and recommended implementation of the plan. By this time, white ranchers had already occupied portions of the tract, and proved influential enough to force a compromise. Accordingly, on November 9, 1907, President Theodore Roosevelt temporarily withdrew most of the area from homestead eligibility.[6] Resident Navajo families would have time to file for allotments under section four of the General Allotment Act of 1887, and unallotted lands would be restored to the public domain (Kelly 1968:23–24; Kappler 1913:669).

In 1907 the government placed off-reservation Navajos under the jurisdiction of the newly authorized Eastern Navajo Agency. Samuel Stacher became the agency's first superintendent in 1909, when it actually began operations (Stacher c. 1940:1). In 1910 he reported 2,783 allotments in New Mexico and Arizona, saying that "the allotment work has been completed except to those Indians who live in three townships east of Seven Lakes" (PB NR 1910:18). By the fall, claimants had filed allotments on 319,363 acres in New Mexico and 54,880 acres in Arizona (RCIA 1911:95–96, 206). Surplus lands were returned to the public domain (Kelly 1968:25).

Indian Service officials knew that Congress would soon make Arizona and New Mexico states, thereby increasing the power of Anglo ranching interests. Consequently, while allotment progressed in New Mexico and Arizona, they moved quickly to consolidate Navajo landholdings in the "checkerboard" area of Arizona named in the executive orders of 1900 and 1901. Under a provision of the Indian appropriations bill of 1904, private lands within an executive-order reservation could be traded for public lands "of equal area and value . . . in the same State or Territory." In exchange for other land, on December 17, 1912, the Santa Fe and Pacific Railroad Company transferred its title to all of the odd section lands (327,000 acres) within the 1900 and 1901 tracts to the government as trustee for the Navajos. No solution to the checkerboarding of landholdings was reached, however, because the solicitor in the Interior Department wrote an unfavorable opinion on the legality of the exchange (Kelly 1968:22).

Before New Mexico became a state in 1912, many white occupants opposed Navajo allotments on the public domain. The most outspoken opposition came from communities bordering the reservation. The *Farmington Enterprise* (June 7, 1907) protested that the Navajos were

> being allotted all the government land which is worth having, south of the San Juan River, and east of the reservation. While all these matters will probably be adjusted in the course of time it will be a slow process, and it certainly seems to be a shame that it's necessary to hold the development of the greater part of the best and most resourceful section of the Western slope back for a generation in order to accommodate the Indians.

While vehemently opposed to Navajo allotments on the public domain, many Anglos assumed that the reservation would eventually be opened to white settlement. In 1908 the New Mexico Bureau of Immigration issued a pamphlet to encourage migration, stating, "It is the announced intention of the Government eventually to allot the lands within the Navajo reservation" (BINM 1908:5). In the spring of 1907, Major James McLaughlin, an Indian inspector, met with a group of Navajos in Shiprock to discuss leasing part of the reservation for oil and natural gas exploration. The *Farmington Times Hustler* (Mar. 14, 1907) strongly endorsed leases, but not because they might benefit the Navajos:

This step is the initial one that will ultimately lead to the allotment of all the lands and the throwing open of the entire reservation for settlement. Those who are interested in getting a portion of the best Indian reservation that yet remains unopened had better keep an eye on the movements here. Of the 6,400,000 acres included in this reservation, there are many mesas that are as beautiful as a garden.

While many whites cast covetous eyes towards the reservation, others continued to fight Navajo allotments on the public domain. In 1909 the Indian Rights Association discovered that white ranchers had successfully delayed allotment applications in local land offices for more than two years (ARIRA 1909; ARIRA 1910:15). Final approval of these allotments came under the jurisdiction of the General Land Office, not the Indian Office, and partly because of this opposition, it had not patented any of the Navajo allotments made on the public domain by the time New Mexico became a state. The General Land Office "was not as lenient toward the Navajos as was the Indian Bureau" (Kelly 1968:32) concerning residence and improvement requirements for patents.

The first New Mexico legislature asked Congress to allot the Navajo reservation and open any remaining lands to white homesteaders. Senator Albert Fall led the fight against expanding the reservation, consolidating off-reservation holdings, and granting allotments of public domain lands. A 1914 compromise limited allotments to Navajos who had lived on the public domain before June 30, 1913 (Kelly 1968:27–31), but political opposition continued to thwart Navajos in their attempt to acquire land. In 1916 a government field inspector found that the General Land Office had failed to approve about 2,900 allotment applications from Eastern Navajo, and they were in danger of being cancelled (Kelly 1968:32). Supposedly, the applicants did not meet improvement and residence requirements; in reality, the office was bending to local pressure, and withholding patents for no legitimate reason.

In 1918 Senator Marcus Smith of Arizona introduced legislation forbidding the creation or extension of any Indian reservation within the boundaries of a state without the consent of Congress. When it became law, it put an end to enlargements of the Navajo reservation by executive order (Kelly 1968:33–34). Fortunately for the Navajos, World War I was under way. High livestock prices induced white and Navajo stockmen to sell large numbers of animals, temporarily alleviating the demand for rangeland once again.

World War I

Navajos took very little part in World War I, which they considered a white man's problem. Like other reservation tribes, they were not citizens of the United States, so they could not be drafted; unlike members of other tribes, few Navajos volunteered. Most officials tolerated the Navajos' passive attitude towards the war. The superintendent at Leupp thought that "these Indians are not sufficiently advanced or educated to really understand much about the war. They are very much opposed to enlisting, but are not in any sense disloyal" (L NR 1918:1). At Eastern Navajo, some Navajos bought War Saving Stamps and Liberty Bonds and even contributed fleeces to the Red Cross, but very few volunteered (PB NR 1918:2). Only the superintendent of Northern Navajo suggested disloyalty, accusing the Navajos of being openly sympathetic to the Germans (SJ NR 1918:5).

Southern Navajo, Western Navajo, and Leupp reported no enlistments. Two Navajos from Eastern volunteered (PB NR 1918:2) in 1918; one from Northern served before the armistice (SJ NR 1919:7). Paul Jones, later tribal chairman, was working and attending high school in Grand Rapids, Michigan when he was drafted and sent to France (Johnson and Hoffman 1978:58–60).[7] Although other Navajos undoubtedly volunteered or were drafted, no more than a dozen served during the war.

The war, however, had a pronounced economic impact on the tribe, causing a major increase in the prices of wool, mutton, lambs, and cattle. Prices started to rise rapidly in 1914, after the war broke out in Europe. Between 1914 and 1918, when the prices of these commodities peaked, wool jumped from 16.6¢ to 57.7¢ per pound, sheep from $3.91 to $11.76 per head, and lambs from $6.36 to $13.96 per hundredweight (appendix B)—all prices paid in eastern markets. Although the trading posts paid below these figures, strong demand and competition between traders for Navajo products resulted in a narrowing of the price margin. In 1918 Navajos were getting about 50¢ per pound for their wool even though it was of poor quality (SJ NR 1918:5), and with prices higher than ever before, they sold off enormous numbers of stock (N NR 1918:12).

While Navajo goods commanded high prices, so did the products that Navajos bought. The consumer price index rose 50 percent between 1914 and 1918. Inflation continued after the war was over, and by 1920 consumer prices had almost doubled their 1914 mark (appendix B). Expenses increased along with income on the reservation,[8] particularly for heavy equipment such as wagons, plows, harrows, cultivators and mowing machines (N NR 1919:12). It is difficult to gauge the effects of inflation on the Navajos during this period, however, other than to note that they attempted to increase their income by more weaving and wage labor.

While the country was still at war, a flu epidemic struck the United States. When it reached the Navajos in October 1918, all public places in towns surrounding the reservation were closed to keep the disease from spreading (*Farmington Times Hustler*, Oct. 10, 1918, Oct. 31, 1918),[9] but these precautions failed to keep the flu from reaching isolated Navajo camps. That fall about 150 Navajos were employed in the construction gangs of the Durango-Silverton highway in southern Colorado when the flu infected their work camps. Many workers tried to take refuge on the reservation and carried the disease home with them (SJ NR 1919:9; *Farmington Times Hustler*, Oct. 24, 1918).

For a short-lived phenomenon, the influenza epidemic had devastating effects. According to Albert Reagan (1919:243, 245–46), no other population in the United States suffered comparable losses. In fear they "fled from the places where it appeared . . . they often abandoned everything, even their sheep in some cases. . . . Whole families were wiped out, leaving their flocks wandering over the hills at the mercy of the wolves." In Northern Navajo, the only member of one family to survive was a boy out herding sheep, and a family of eight on a piñon gathering trip all died near their wagon.

While deaths were reported in every district, the flu affected some areas much more severely than others. Approximately 200 people died in Western Navajo, about 3 percent of the population, but in Eastern Navajo an estimated 18 percent of the population perished (table 5). Although some new cases appeared as late as December 1918, the epidemic had already

TABLE 5. *Estimated Deaths from 1918 Influenza Epidemic*

Agency	1918 Population[a]	Deaths	Percentage
Leupp	1,411	144	10[b]
Southern Navajo	12,080	780[c]	6
Western Navajo	6,087	c. 200[d]	3
Eastern Navajo	2,724	c. 500[e]	18
Northern Navajo	6,500	?	?

[a]1918 population estimates are taken from RCIA 1918:88, 92.
[b]Only percentage given, L NR 1919:3.
[c]N NR 1919:4.
[d]WN NR 1918:13.
[e]PB NR 1919:2.

passed its peak in October of that year, and quarantines were lifted in the border towns (*Farmington Times Hustler*, Oct. 31, 1918).

The epidemic was also responsible for the destruction of Navajo livestock. As Reagan (1919) noted, herds belonging to stricken families were frequently left on their own. Even in Western Navajo, where the epidemic had the least effect, herds declined for lack of care (WN NR 1919:14; table 5).

Oil

Off-reservation oil exploration began in the San Juan Basin just before 1900 (H. Clark 1963:94), but the first successful well was not completed until 1918. Wartime equipment shortages delayed any further exploration until the early 1920s, when oil companies decided that the reservation itself held the best prospects.

The companies soon learned that getting leases on the reservation was no easy matter. Superintendent Evan Estep of Northern Navajo informed the commissioner of Indian affairs that he did not "want anything to happen that will deprive these Indians of their rights" (Kelly 1968:48) and that both he and the people of his jurisdiction opposed oil surveys. The lack of any formal tribal government to either approve or disapprove leases constituted the major deterrent to oil exploration. William Shelton, the first superintendent of Northern Navajo, had opposed the creation of a business council, and it appears that none had ever existed. However, on May 7, 1921, oil companies met with an informal Northern Navajo "council" consisting of any adult males from the jurisdiction who wished to attend. Representatives of four oil companies presented plans for leasing portions of the reservation, but the "council" unanimously rejected them (Kelly 1968:48–50). According to Estep, "the old men dominated the council and the young men did what they were told to do" (SJ NR 1921:40).

On August 13, 1921, a second council meeting of "probably" 150 Navajos approved a 4,800 acre lease in the Hogback area for Midwest Refining Company. Midwest was willing to hire Navajos for some of the work at relatively high wages, which probably influenced the decision (Kelly 1968:51; SJ NR 1922:50).

The discovery of natural gas on the adjacent Ute Mountain reservation in southern Colorado encouraged oil interests to pursue leases in other portions of Northern Navajo. The commissioner of Indian affairs brought pressure to bear on the still reluctant Superintendent Estep to call a third meeting. On March 25, 1922, Navajos rejected all leases. Estep wrote that the approximately 100 men in attendance "did not consume much time; they knew what they were going to do. . . . They were not going to do so [consent] until the Midwest had drilled the lease they gave them" (SJ NR 1922:50–51; Kelly 1968:53).

Late in the summer of 1922, Midwest stopped drilling at the Hogback and said it would not start again until some "friendly" companies (like Midwest, subsidiaries of Standard Oil) were granted leases on adjacent tracts. Deferring to his superiors, Estep called a fourth meeting on September 23, 1922, when the Navajos leased Tocito Dome to the Producers and Refiners Corporation—not one of Standard's "friendly" companies.[10] On September 24, apparently unable to delay any longer, Midwest announced that it had struck oil at the Hogback (Kelly 1968:53–55; SJ NR 1923:24).

The complex political maneuvering which led up to and followed the opening of the reservation to oil development goes beyond the scope of this study. Certainly, the appointment of Senator Albert Fall as secretary of the interior in March 1921 was a major contributing factor. As a senator from New Mexico, Fall had opposed any expansion of the reservation, and later on, his close association with certain oil companies would be exposed in the Teapot Dome scandal. After the Hogback strike, the oil companies and their advocates in the Department of the Interior successfully circumvented Estep and the local "council," stripping the superintendents of all five Navajo agencies and Hopi of their power over tribal mineral leases. Herbert J. Hagerman filled the newly created position of commissioner to the Navajo Indians, with general authority over the six reservations.[11] A new Navajo Tribal Council, to be composed of twelve elected delegates (four from Southern, three from Northern, two from Western, and one each from Leupp, Eastern, and Hopi), inherited jurisdiction over mineral leases from the Northern Navajo "council" (Kelly 1968:55–56, 61–64; Williams 1970:22).

Over the protests of Northern Navajo leaders, Superintendent Estep was dismissed (*Farmington Times Hustler*, July 6, 1923). On July 7, 1923, the Tribal Council held its first meeting in Toadlena, New Mexico, electing Chee Dodge chairman and unanimously passing "a resolution, drawn up in Washington, granting the Commissioner of the Navajo Tribe the authority to sign on 'behalf of the Navajo Indians' all oil and gas mining leases which might in the future be granted on the treaty portion of the reservation" (Kelly 1968:69).

The wholesale leasing of mineral resources began in October 1923, when 21,500 acres in the Northern jurisdiction were leased at auction. The Navajos received $87,600 in lease bonuses from this transaction (*Farmington Times Hustler*, Oct. 19, 1923). Oil companies made new strikes in the

Hogback in 1923 and 1924, and in the nearby Rattlesnake oilfield in February 1924 (*Farmington Times Hustler*, Aug. 10, 1923, Nov. 23, 1923, Oct. 24, 1924, Feb. 29, 1924). Continental Oil discovered oil at Table Mesa, about twelve miles south of Hogback (*Farmington Times Hustler*, Sept. 4, 1925), and by January 1926, these three fields were producing 12,173 barrels a day (*Farmington Times Hustler*, Jan. 22, 1926).

The discovery of oil caused an economic boom in northwestern New Mexico. Companies hired roustabouts, pipeline workers, and freighters (*Farmington Times Hustler*, Apr. 16, 1926). Continental built an off-reservation refinery near Farmington, creating additional jobs (*Farmington Times Hustler*, Dec. 5, 1924, Apr. 3, 1925). Although local Navajos found jobs in the industry, the most important economic gains took place at the tribal level. Between 1923 and 1929, the Navajos received more than $700,000 in oil bonuses and royalties (*Farmington Times Hustler*, May 3, 1929).

The Land Question Renewed

In 1916 it was reported that 2,900 applications had been received from Navajos for land allotments. From then until 1918, when the Indian Service sent A. W. Simington to investigate, 618 allotments were approved, and patents issued for 100 of them by the General Land Office. When he arrived, Simington found only 2,410 allotment applications and no explanation for the some 500 that were missing (Kelly 1968:32, 34–35).

To compound the Navajos' difficulties, in 1912 Congress reduced the residence requirement for homesteads from five to three years, and in 1916 the Stock Raising Homestead Act increased the homestead limit from 160 to 640 acres (Webb 1931:423). As a result of these measures, increasing numbers of Anglo-Americans filed for homesteads in the disputed areas surrounding the reservation—some legitimate settlers, but also cowboys or "ringers" who filed on behalf of local ranchers who intended to acquire the homesteads (Bailey and Bailey 1982:213–16).

Simington continued his efforts to file allotment applications for off-reservation families until his transfer in the summer of 1925. Appeals for his reinstatement went unheeded, leaving the position vacant until Charles Roblin's appointment in 1928. Roblin approached the job with great vigor, and in his first seventeen months helped Navajos file on 65,000 acres. Disturbed by such efficiency, the New Mexico Cattle Growers' Association led ranching interests in the fight to end Navajo allotments. They succeeded in the spring of 1930, leaving two decades of allotment work unfinished. By that time, only 3,700 Navajos had received allotments out of an estimated

8,000 living off the reservation in New Mexico (Kelly 1968:122–24).

Meanwhile, Indian Service officials went ahead with plans to buy privately owned land for the tribe. In 1919 Commissioner of Indian Affairs Cato Sells appealed to Congress for money to purchase land in the Crownpoint area. Of $100,000 received, $93,628.24 was used to buy 12,000 acres from the Chaco Land and Cattle Company. The Navajo tribe was required to repay the government for the appropriation (Kelly 1968:35).

With the discovery of oil in Northern Navajo, significant amounts of money became available to the tribe for the first time. Commissioner Hagerman realized that oil revenues could alleviate the tribe's pressing need for land. On the day after the first oil lease auction, he proposed buying certain off-reservation areas with lease income. Although the plan died in congressional committee, Hagerman was not a man to be easily discouraged. On the advice of the commissioner and the Indian Bureau, in 1926 the Navajo Tribal Council voted to set aside 20 percent of oil revenues to purchase land. Even before the plan received the necessary congressional approval, the council raised the figure to 25 percent in 1927 (Kelly 1968:115–17, 119–21).

In spite of opposition from the New Mexico delegation, in 1928 Congress appropriated $1,200,000 for Navajo land purchases. Hagerman left his position from December 1927 until March 1930, but when he returned, arrangements were made to purchase extensive tracts of land in Arizona and New Mexico from the Santa Fe Pacific Railroad Company, the New Mexico and Arizona Land Company, Babbitt Brothers, and several small ranchers, and to transfer land from Tusayan National Forest and the public domain. In May 1930, Congress agreed to transfer some of the forest land (Kelly 1968:124–26, 128–30); however, the purchase and exchange were not achieved until 1940.

An attempt to restore the Paiute Strip to the reservation made slow headway. The executive order of 1884 included this area of southern Utah in the reservation, but it was returned to the public domain in 1892 (see maps 3 and 5). The land went back to the Navajos from 1908 until 1922, when Secretary Fall, wrongly anticipating that oil might be discovered there, engineered its return to the public domain. The area was withdrawn from homestead entry in 1929, and in 1933 the state of Utah sanctioned its return to the reservation (Kelly 1968:126–27).

Executive orders, land purchases, and allotments had won large areas for Indian use between 1900 and 1932, but the land problems of many off-reservation Navajos remained unsolved. Out of a total population of more than 39,000, approximately 8,000 Navajos lived outside the reservation, and of that number, less than half had secured allotments. Even allotted Navajos could own no more than 160 acres—not enough to support anyone who depended on herding for a living. The tribe needed still more rangeland, and as a result, competition for the public domain continued.

THE REORIENTATION OF THE NAVAJO ECONOMY

As the Navajo economy began to recover in the early years of the twentieth century, a new way of life emerged. Herding remained the most important means of support (by the mid-teens, sheep, goats, cattle, and horses equaled or exceeded their highest pre-1892 levels), but commercial herding started to replace subsistence herding and the trading of surplus products. This change affected other aspects of the economy such as weaving and silversmithing, which became oriented toward the production of goods for market. Wage labor gained in significance, and by the 1920s, the Navajo economy was integrated into the national economy.

Livestock

Because sheep and goats constituted the most numerous category of livestock and the most vital aspect of the Navajo economy, trends in their numbers reflect the general economic health of the tribe. In 1900 Navajos owned an estimated 401,882 sheep and goats (RCIA in RSI 1900:659)—fewer than before 1893, but more than during the mid-1890 decline. This figure indicates that the herds were already recovering at the turn of the century. Navajos owned 754,500 animals in 1904 and 1,819,000 in 1915 (fig. 6), about the same as before the collapse.

Favorable climatic conditions, economic alternatives to subsistence herding such as wage labor and weaving, and government regulations prohibiting the sale of productive stock from the reservation contributed to the growth of the herds after 1900—especially the latter. The date of the earliest regulation is unknown. On November 15, 1907, the *Farmington Enterprise* reported that sales to traders had been prohibited in Northern Navajo for "several years." Just as vaguely, in 1910 the superintendent wrote, "The flocks and herds are increasing in number and quality from year to year. The Indians have not been permitted to sell their female stock for several years" (SJ NR 1910:2). The policy led to conflict with traders and Navajos in Northern Navajo, and probably other agencies as well. In large part, this restriction led to the Bai-a-lil-le "uprising" of 1907 (U.S. Congress 1907:7).

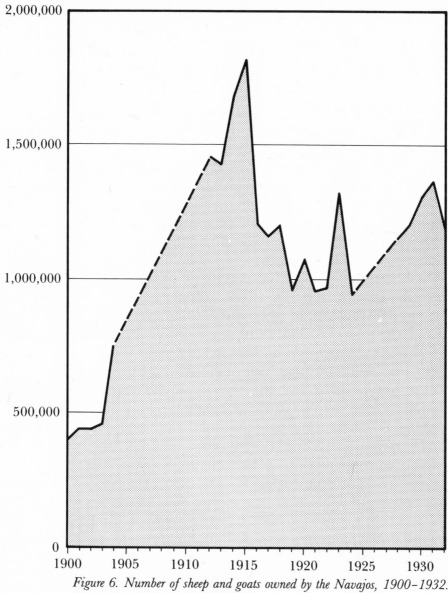

Figure 6. Number of sheep and goats owned by the Navajos, 1900-1932. Broken line indicates missing data.

It may have been lifted during World War I to take advantage of the rapid rise in wool and mutton prices. In 1918 the superintendent of Northern Navajo allowed stock sales in response to poor range conditions (SJ NR 1918:14).

Between 1915 and 1919, the number of sheep and goats dropped by almost half, from 1,819,000 to 956,012 (appendix A). The most important cause of this decline was a massive sell-off precipitated by high livestock prices. Faunce (1981:278) stated that "traders were telling them [the Navajos] that lambs and sheep would be worth much money and that they should sell all they could because never would white men pay as much again." In their haste to capitalize on high sheep prices, many families failed to keep a sufficient number of young rams for breeding stock, and the number of lambs declined (N NR 1918:12). The influenza epidemic also contributed to the decline because the disruption of normal family herding activities deprived the herds of proper care (WN NR 1919:14; Reagan 1919).

After 1919 the number of sheep and goats stabilized at about 1,000,000 until the late 1920s. This stability, uncharacteristic of previous periods, was caused by the switch to a commercially oriented herding economy and its emphasis on the marketing of feeder lambs. In the late 1920s and early 1930s, the demand for livestock fell off, and the numbers of sheep and goats began to increase again (fig. 6).

Cattle statistics during this period follow a slightly different trend from sheep and goat statistics. The herds increased rapidly from an estimated 6,858 in 1900 to 37,180 in 1914, went down to 29,310 in 1915, and held at about 30,000 head throughout the war years. In 1920 the number rose to 36,222, approximately the prewar level, where it remained at least until 1924. Records from the late 1920s yielded no complete estimates, but in 1930 it was reported that the Navajos owned about 25,000 head of "mature" cattle. Because earlier estimates included calves, the 1924 and 1930 figures can be taken as approximate equivalents, meaning that the number of cattle remained stable throughout the 1920s (fig. 7).

As in earlier discussions, the term "horse" includes mules and donkeys. Navajos owned an estimated 65,625 horses in 1904. By 1913 the number had risen to 324,931, significantly higher than any estimate before 1892, and probably a grossly inflated figure. Nevertheless, there can be little doubt that the herds had fully recovered by the mid-teens. Like sheep, goats, and cattle, horses underwent a sharp decline during World War I, and by 1919 the Navajos owned only 60,000. The reason for this decline, more pronounced than in the other categories of livestock, is not altogether clear. Certainly, the war increased the demand for horses, and some were sold, but the greatest part of the decrease can probably be attributed to the dourine eradication program on the reservation. During the war years, government agents killed large numbers of infected mares and castrated stallions to prevent the spread of this venereal disease (L NR 1919). Following this decline, the number of horses on the reservation remained fixed at about 60,000 during the 1920s (fig. 8).

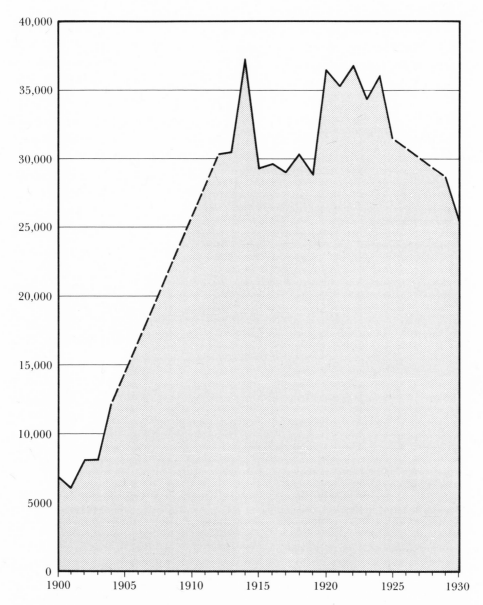

Figure 7. Number of cattle owned by the Navajos, 1900–1932. Broken line indicates missing data.

During this period, significant changes started to take place in herding techniques. The Navajos traditionally kept their rams with the herd throughout the year. Since sheep will breed in any season, lambs were born year round. This practice resulted in a high mortality rate for lambs, particularly those born during the winter. It also reduced the commercial value

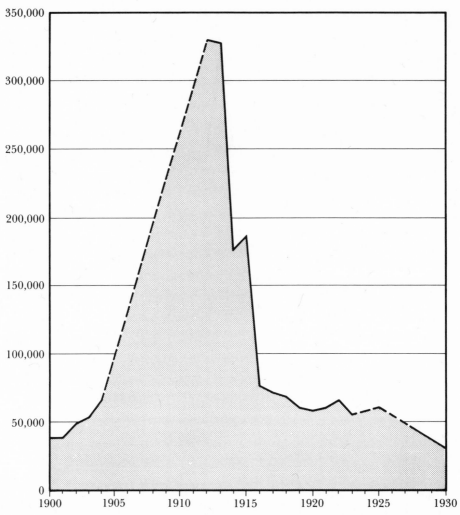

Figure 8. Number of horses owned by the Navajos, 1900–1932. Broken line indicates missing data.

of lambs, which varied greatly in age and weight when marketed in the fall: the underweight lambs sold for substantially less. Agency officials wanted to establish a single lambing season in the late spring in order to reduce losses caused by severe weather and to insure that all lambs would reach full weight for sale in the fall.

The Navajos developed two techniques for controlling the indiscriminate breeding of sheep. The ram apron, a rectangular section of canvas or other durable cloth, was tied around the belly of the ram to prevent the animal from breeding out of season (Kluckhohn, Hill, and Kluckhohn 1971:79; Downs 1964:35). Another and more effective technique was separating the rams from the rest of the herd, isolating them in ram herds during the summer. In some areas, poor people took care of rams belonging to several families until mid-October, then returned them to their respective herds. Owners compensated the ram herder with the wool from their animals (Bailey field notes).

In 1910 the superintendent of Western Navajo reported that rams were kept with the herds year round, and no "lambing season" existed on his reservation (WN NR 1910:2). In contrast, it was estimated that 60 percent of the people in Eastern Navajo separated the rams from the ewes (PB NR 1912:4). By the early 1920s, separation of rams had become standard among families living in the eastern portion of Northern Navajo (Bailey field notes). However, many Navajos were reluctant to accept the change. As late as 1931, the superintendent of Southern Navajo urged Navajos in his jurisdiction to form ram herds (SN NR 1931:13). Blunn (1940:105) reported in the late 1930s that "the Navajos rarely follow any breeding system and persist in allowing the rams to run with the ewes throughout the year." In the early 1960s, James Downs (1964:35) characterized ram separation in Western Navajo as "relatively new and . . . not universally practiced."

In the 1880s, the government's first attempt to upgrade Navajo sheep by introducing Merinos failed because of indifference on the part of the Navajos. As early as 1880 it was estimated that nearly 40 percent of the sheep in New Mexico had been crossed with Merinos (A. Carlson 1969:33), and some of this "improved" stock undoubtedly found its way into Navajo herds. At the turn of the century, however, the vast majority of Navajo sheep were still churros. Hardy, well suited to the range conditions of the region, and good meat producers, they adequately met subsistence needs. Their wool was ideal for weaving because it was long and relatively greaseless (Blunn 1940, 1943). From a commercial perspective, however, churros were less than satisfactory, shearing one to two pounds per head of low-quality, low-priced "carpet wool," and producing lambs that did not command high prices as feeders (Blunn 1943:144, 149–50).

Recognizing the commercial limitations of Navajo sheep, agency officials again attempted to upgrade the herds. In 1904 Agent Shelton initiated such a program in Northern Navajo, reporting,

> While the native Navaho sheep are of a hardy nature, and are good rustlers for feed, the long inbreeding has caused their wool to be of inferior quality, becoming mixed with kemp [short, wiry fibers] and straight hair. Last fall authority was secured to purchase and issue

400 blooded bucks, which will no doubt greatly improve the quality of the wool produced and make the sheep more valuable for
mutton. (RCIA in RSI 1904, 2:253)

Shelton did not name the breed of the rams.

The following year, the government purchased 635 Rambouillet rams,
which were loaned "at the proper time" to Navajo stockmen (RCIA in RSI
1906:183). Southern Navajo received 355 of them (RCIA 1905:167), but it
is not known if the rest were distributed among the other agencies. Eventually each agency set up its own program for upgrading sheep within its
jurisdiction. As early as 1910, it was reported that the Leupp herds had
"improved somewhat in quality" (L NR 1910:2). In contrast, the superintendent of Eastern noted in 1911 that the sheep in his jurisdiction showed
no improvement in quality (PB NR 1911), implying that a sheep improvement program was under way.

Sheep quality improved rapidly in some agencies, but lagged in others
because of indifference on the part of officials, Navajos, or both. In 1918 it
was estimated that 70 percent of the sheep in Southern Navajo were
improved (N NR 1918:10). Eastern Navajo reported steady progress
throughout the teens, and by 1919 traders in that jurisdiction provided
incentive to the program by paying more for improved Merino and Rambouillet wool (40¢ to 45¢ per pound) than for coarse wool (25¢ to 33¢ per
pound) (PB NR 1915:10; PB NR 1919:5). In Northern Navajo, traders
initiated the two-price system in the spring of 1922, when they paid from
5¢ to 8¢ per pound more for improved wool (SJ NR 1922:33–34). By the
spring of 1925, approximately 75 percent of the wool from Northern Navajo
was classified as "somewhat" improved. Traders went to a three-grade system, paying 35¢ per pound for improved wool, 30¢ for partially improved,
and 25¢ per pound for coarse (SJ NR 1925:35). The following year the
superintendent reported that "nearly every band of sheep has at least one
ram of this character [pure or mixed Rambouillet], and many bands have
no other class of sires with them." An estimated 75 percent were at least half
Rambouillet (SJ NR 1926:30, 34).

Leupp and Western Navajo trailed the other agencies in sheep improvement, introducing proportionately fewer purebred rams. In 1916 the superintendent of Leupp wrote that even though his office had issued rams to the
Navajos, they did not take care of them, and the quality of sheep in his
jurisdiction had not improved considerably (L NR 1916:12). In 1922 the
superintendent of Western Navajo characterized progress in his area as

"very slow" (WN NR 1922:6). In the early 1930s, families living in the western portion of the Navajo country still opposed "improving" their herds (Reichard 1973:9). Even in the early 1940s, "unimproved" sheep were found in isolated areas, although by that time their numbers were rapidly declining (Blunn 1943:141).

The successful programs improved both the quality of wool and the weight of individual fleeces. In addition, the crossing of Navajo ewes with purebred rams produced heavier, higher-priced lambs. As early as 1914, some startling results were being reported:

> The result of the first cross between native sheep and high-grade rams [was] . . . the production of an animal 20 to 25 per cent greater in weight and yielding 50 to 60 per cent more wool of a considerably better grade than that produced by the native Navajo sheep. (RCIA 1914:17–18)

The 1927 report from Northern Navajo emphasized the gains made by their program:

> The average price paid per lamb in 1924 was $4.46; the average price paid per lamb in 1926 was $6.05. This difference [was] . . . due to no cause other than that made by the introduction of good blood. The lambs weigh more per individual. (NN NR 1927:20)

Professional breeders who evaluated these early programs in the 1930s criticized them strongly. C. T. Blunn (1940:104) complained they had been carried out "without regard for the fundamentals of animal breeding . . . [and that] the multiplicity of sheep types introduced without any organized plan has resulted in a heterogeneous and very inferior sheep." Indeed, the sheep improvement programs were poorly planned and haphazardly implemented. Each new superintendent made at least minor changes in his predecessor's program. Genetic chaos resulted as officials introduced almost every major variety of sheep at one time or another.[12] Even though the early improvement programs were far from ideal, the "mongrelized" herds which evolved from 1910 to 1930 achieved commercial gains over native varieties, a fact that Navajos recognized and appreciated.

Throughout the nineteenth century, Navajos owned no other kind of goat than the common Spanish milk goat. Their most valuable herd animal in terms of subsistence, it had little commercial value besides leather for kidskin. In the early part of the twentieth century, they began to shift from milk goats to Angoras. Both varieties produced meat, but while Angoras were not milked, they produced mohair for sale to white traders. By shifting from milk goats to Angoras, the Navajos sacrificed subsistence value to commercial value.

Angoras first came to the United States in 1849, but failed to gain quick acceptance because of a low demand for mohair. When it was discovered that it made excellent plush, however, a new market became available. In 1882, it was estimated that 562,000 pounds of mohair were made into plush for railroad car seats (Black 1900:45, 131).

Lucien Maxwell of the Maxwell Land Grant first brought Angoras into New Mexico in 1872, the same year that Brigham Young established the first herd in Utah (Black 1900:45, 85, 92, 131). As early as 1882, herds had been introduced in the high country of northern New Mexico (Hayes 1882:71).

The early Angora ranchers built up their herds by crossing shorthaired Spanish goats with Angora bucks. After four or five generations of such crossings, the rancher would have a mohair-producing herd. There were approximately 30,000 Angoras in New Mexico by 1900, over half the total number of goats in the state. In the same year, Angoras numbered about 10,000 in Arizona, 6,000 in Colorado, and between 3,000 and 4,000 in Utah (Black 1900:85, 92, 104).

Government statistics failed to differentiate between milk goats and Angoras in the nineteenth century. The earliest specific reference did not come until 1899, when James McLaughlin, U.S. Indian Inspector, observed that Mormons near Tuba City had Angoras, and suggested crossing them with Navajo goats. The government took no action on his recommendation to buy and distribute 400 Angora bucks among the Navajos (McLaughlin to Secretary of the Interior, Sept. 29, 1899, RBIA LR GR).

About the turn of the century, Anglo-American ranchers in northwestern New Mexico began to raise Angoras along the eastern margin of the reservation, and by 1903 Angoras numbered between 3,000 and 5,000 in San Juan County (RGNM in RDI 1903:168). The Franciscan Fathers (1968:143, 258–59) at St. Michaels Mission near Fort Defiance published *An Ethnologic Dictionary of the Navajo Language* in 1910. The *Dictionary* includes the Navajo terms for Angora goat and mohair, indicating that Navajos had some knowledge of Angoras before that date. In 1932 it was noted that off-reservation Navajos in New Mexico had been raising Angora goats for about ten years (U. S. Congress 1932, 18:9590), which would date their introduction in the checkerboard area at about 1920. However, reports submitted by the superintendent of Northern Navajo in the early and mid-1920s indicate a much earlier date.

In 1922 Northern Navajo Agency bought ten Toggenberg bucks, but for no specified reason (SJ NR 1922:46). Two years later, the superintendent suggested crossing Toggenbergs (high quality milk goats) with the "Angora type" owned by the Navajos because "practically every family does milk goats and the milk forms a substantial portion of its diet" (SJ NR 1924:46–47). From these reports and one in 1925 stating that the Toggenberg herd at the Toadlena School could be used to upgrade the Navajo goats from Angoras to milk goats (SJ NR 1925:38), it seems evident that in Northern Navajo the goats were of mixed Angora and Spanish breeding by the early 1920s.

When the price of mohair rose in the mid-1920s, the policy towards Angoras changed. Northern Navajo bought fifty-one purebred Angora bucks, resolving "to do to the goat herds precisely what has been done to the herds of sheep and in this manner and through the goats provide the Navajo with another source of income, viz. Mohair" (NN NR 1927:15, 18, 21). With mohair bringing about 40¢ per pound in 1927, it appeared to be a sound economic move. In 1927 the Northern Navajos marketed 53,000 pounds of mohair, for which they received $20,000 (NN NR 1928:9). To further increase production, in the late 1920s the agency sold between 50 and 100 purebred Angora bucks a year to the Northern Navajos on the reimbursable plan, under which the Navajos were supposed to pay the agency for the animals they were using (NN NR 1929:10). Eastern Navajo followed suit in 1928 with 50 purebred Angoras, but even before they were distributed, some Navajos in the region owned "very well improved flocks of . . . goats" (EN NR 1929:3).

The market for mohair collapsed in the early 1930s. When the demand for new railroad cars fell off during the depression, manufacturers no longer needed the same quantities of mohair plush for making seatcovers. A change in women's fashions also contributed to this loss in popularity. Silk became the most fashionable material for dresses in the 1930s, causing static electricity when brushed against mohair seat covers. Brokers developed backlogs of mohair, and the price plummeted to 10¢ per pound (U.S. Congress 1932, 18:9590, 9665).

The low price of mohair led to another change in government policy. In 1931 the superintendent of Northern Navajo decided that "a campaign should be instituted immediately looking toward the reduction of . . . goats on the reservation." Convincing the Navajos to stop raising goats was no easy task, said the superintendent; even if they could be persuaded, the market was practically nonexistent (NN NR 1931:1).

Reports from Leupp, Western, and Southern did not mention Angoras.

In the case of Southern, the omission was probably an oversight; at the other two agencies, it probably reflects a lack of interest on the part of local Navajos. Mohair production figures for 1940 (U.S. Bureau of Indian Affairs 1941:table XII)—the earliest year for which such figures are available—reveal that while some mohair was being produced throughout Navajo country, most of it was being produced in the eastern half, which had been under the jurisdiction of Northern, Eastern, and Southern Navajo in the 1920s.

Although most superintendents recognized the need for cattle improvement programs, cattle rarely received the attention devoted to sheep. At the turn of the century, Navajos owned primarily "Mexican" or "Texas" longhorn cattle. As late as 1921 the superintendent of Northern Navajo described them as "sorry looking stuff—never fat and poor butcher stuff, seldom dressing over fifty per cent net beef and . . . never prime" (SJ NR 1921:33).

Most of the agencies were making some efforts to improve cattle by 1915. Southern Navajo received fifty Hereford bulls in 1913 (N NR 1913:9), and more were issued on the reimbursable plan before 1920 (N NR 1916:10; N NR 1918:10). By 1923 it was estimated that 50 percent of the cattle in the region had been improved (N NR 1922:10).

Western Navajo issued twelve "high grade" Hereford bulls in 1914 (WN NR 1914:6), and by 1917 an agency herd had been established to provide breeding stock (WN NR 1917:17). Cattle improvement progressed more rapidly at Western than sheep improvement (WN NR 1922:27), and bull distributions continued at least until 1929 (WN NR 1929, 4:5).

Little information is available on the cattle programs at Leupp and Eastern. At the latter, officials claimed some improvement as early as 1915, and some Navajos bought Hereford bulls without help from the agency (PB NR 1915:11).

At Northern Navajo, the superintendent reported that cattle were deteriorating because of inbreeding (SJ NR 1916:40, 45), but developed no program to correct the situation. "A few owners have some fairly good stuff," it was reported in 1921, "but most of it is of the Texas longhorn variety" (SJ NR 1921:33). The government did not make a significant effort to upgrade cattle at Northern until the late 1920s (NN NR 1927:19; NN NR 1929:10).

Although Navajos owned some burros, mules, donkeys, and "American" horses, most superintendents had a low opinion of the "ponies" that made up the vast majority of the stock, and which they considered unsuitable for pulling wagons or plows (NN NR 1929:11). When freighting goods, Navajo teamsters used four-horse teams, which one superintendent admitted did "a lot of work for their size" (SJ NR 1919:23).

The small market for Navajo horses limited their commercial value. In 1902 a herd of approximately ninety Navajo "ponies" was sold to be fattened and made into canned and dried meat (*Farmington Times*, Aug. 8, 1902). In about 1910, traders bought large numbers of Navajo ponies for sale to dealers in Kansas and Nebraska (Bailey field notes).

In view of the limited value of Navajo horses, most Indian Service officials thought that Navajos owned far too many of them and made only limited attempts at improving their quality. Southern, Western, and Leupp had a total of ten stallions in 1913 (L NR 1913:10; WN NR 1913, 4:5; N NR 1913:9), mostly or all Percherons (L NR 1913:10; WN NR 1913, 4:5). One superintendent claimed that the "ponies" Navajos already owned met their needs better than these heavy draft animals, and suggested using Morgans instead of Percherons to upgrade the stock (L NR 1915:10). In any case, the few stallions purchased by the government would have had little effect on the vast herds of Navajo horses. As late as 1926, an official noted that most Navajos used "Indian ponies" instead of "American horses" (N NR 1926:13). Most of the "American horses" had been acquired independently, not through any improvement program. Freighters who hauled goods for the trading posts and farmers along the San Juan River were the first Navajos to acquire "American horses" in any significant numbers (SJ NR 1921:35; SJ NR 1923:41). The number of such animals remained modest even along the San Juan, however, and in 1927 it was reported that only about one hundred families in Northern Navajo owned "good" teams (NN NR 1927:19).

Virtually every category of Navajo livestock increased during the early 1900s, but proportionally, some more than others. Conversion of livestock estimates into sheep units allows them to be expressed as a percentage, and makes changes in herd composition more readily discernible. In general, the combined category of sheep and goats increased steadily, until it accounted for 73 percent of the herds in 1930–1934; goats maintained an even percentage; horses declined steadily; and cattle showed the largest proportional increase (fig. 9).

Trends in Navajo livestock improvement programs and changes in the relative composition of the herds support other indications that Navajos were in the process of commercializing their herds. Agency officials designed improvement programs specifically to increase the commercial value of livestock. Navajo stockmen accepted the principle of upgrading

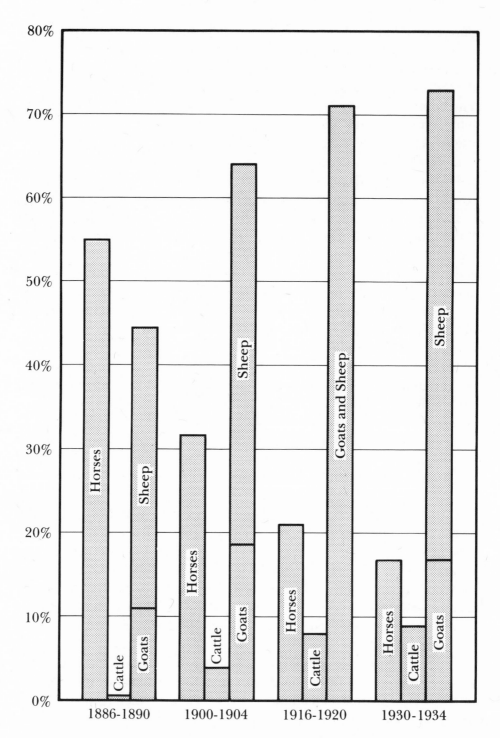

Figure 9. Relative composition of Navajo herds, 1886–1934.

more readily after 1900, to the extent that independent of agency programs, some purchased their own rams, bulls, and stallions. Even though commercialization at times reduced the subsistence value of animals, as in the case of the shift from milk goats to Angoras, more and more Navajos were developing their herds with an eye to commercial gain.

Significant regional variations marked these changes, however, especially in regard to sheep, and people in some areas showed decidedly less interest in 'improving' and marketing their livestock than in others. Of 226 rams placed on Northern Navajo in 1920, 216 were given to families living east of the Chuska Mountains, and only 10 to families on the west side (SJ NR 1921:26)—a pattern repeated in a 1921 distribution (SJ NR 1922:33). As a group, the families living west of the mountains saw little to gain from improving the commercial value of their sheep, an attitude that prevailed until the end of this period. Gladys Reichard (1973:9) commented that between 1930 and 1933, these people "quietly though firmly resisted the 'improving' of [their] flocks. On the eastern side of the Lukachukai Mountains, however, sheep have been highly bred for weight of flesh and wool, the aim being to sell in the world market."

Livestock sale and slaughter estimates also reflect these regional variations. From 1914 to 1923, each superintendent submitted annual estimates of the value of livestock sold to market or slaughtered for home consumption by the Navajos in his jurisdiction. Because the dollar figures in these reports were not much more than guesses, and because changing market values governed their fluctuations, they are useful mainly as a means of comparing the value of livestock sold to livestock slaughtered. In 1914 the superintendents of Northern, Western, and Leupp agreed that the subsistence value of the herds far outweighed their market value, a situation that continued until prices rose during World War I. At Northern Navajo, the relative amount of livestock sold climbed sharply during this period, while at Leupp, commercialization proceeded more slowly. In contrast, subsistence herding predominated at Western Navajo both before and after World War I (figs. 10, 11, 12).

Changes in the national economy made commercial herding possible for the Navajos. During the 1870s and 1880s, sheep ranching was oriented primarily toward the production of wool. Mutton was not a popular meat in the United States, which kept the market value of sheep low. This attitude persisted into the twentieth century, preventing sheep sales from playing a significant role in Navajo trade. Lamb became an increasingly popular American food with the influx of eastern and southern European immigrants in the 1890s and early 1900s, and while the price of mutton

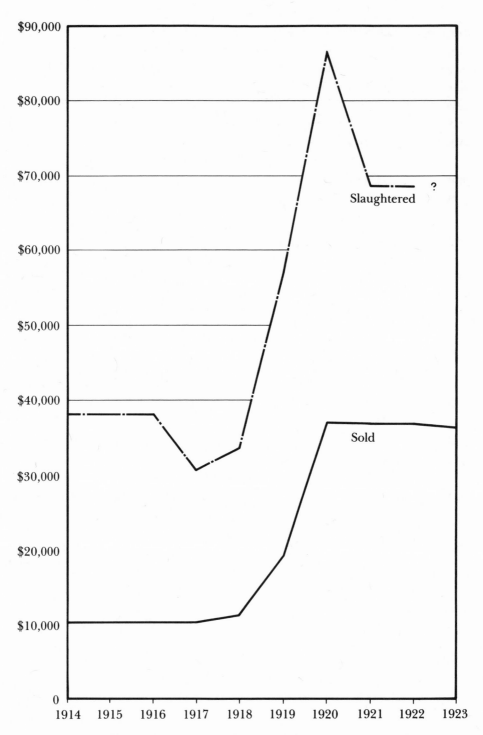

Figure 10. Dollar value of livestock sold and slaughtered, Western Navajo, 1914–1923.

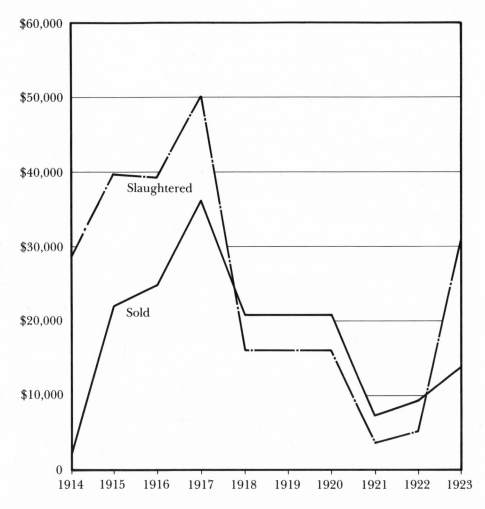

Figure 11. Dollar value of livestock sold and slaughtered, Leupp, 1914–1923.

remained relatively stable, the price of lamb began to rise. The margin of lamb sale prices over mutton went from 13.9 percent in 1885 to 57 percent in 1920, and jumped to 98.7 percent within another five years (Wentworth 1948:603). A significant market had evolved for feeder lambs, allowing Navajo sheepherders to produce two cash crops a year: wool in the spring, and lambs in the fall.

Farming

Indian Bureau officials believed that farming had the potential to support the Navajos on the reservation and solve their land problem. However, surveys conducted in 1889 and 1892 were discouraging: there simply was not

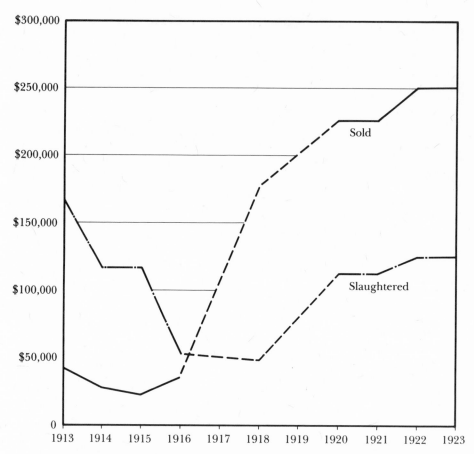

Figure 12. Dollar value of livestock sold and slaughtered, Northern Navajo, 1913–1923. Broken line indicates missing data.

enough water to shift the emphasis of the economy from herding to farming. Besides the San Juan Valley, surveyors found few areas suitable for government irrigation projects, and as a result, only a few relatively small projects were established outside the valley during the early twentieth century. Most superintendents devoted themselves to improving livestock, and gave little support to agricultural projects.

Before 1892 Navajos dug at least three and possibly as many as seven irrigation ditches along the San Juan (Bailey and Bailey 1982:242; Van Valkenburgh 1937:2–4). These early farms did not use Anglo-American technology. Open trenches carried water from the river to low spots in the bottomlands, where a series of diversion dams distributed the water in the fields. Such "high water" ditches, which carried water only during periods of normal or above normal runoff, were inefficient and difficult to maintain. If the spring runoff from the mountains were below average, the water might be too low to enter the ditch head, and families would have to carry water by hand from the river to water their crops. Because these ditches lacked headgates, farmers could not control the volume of water entering their ditch and fields, and an abnormally high runoff might wash out fields and dams (Bailey field notes).

Between 1886 and 1888, the Indian Service constructed a number of small irrigation projects in the vicinity of Fort Defiance (RCIA 1887:173–74; RCIA 1888:190). However, the irrigation surveys of 1889 and 1892 disclosed that the region with the greatest potential for irrigation bordered the San Juan. The Cambridge ditch, started under the sponsorship of the Cambridge, Massachusetts, branch of the Indian Relief Association in 1894, was the first San Juan irrigation project constructed for the Navajos under Anglo-American direction. Feeding out of the north side of the river just west of the reservation line, the ditch brought nearly 600 acres under irrigation (RCIA 1894:103; RCIA 1895:120).

By 1897 the number of "Navajo" ditches along the San Juan had increased to nine (RBIC 1897:40) without the direct involvement of the Indian Service. However, in 1899 S. E. Shoemaker, the head farmer for the Navajo reservation, was transferred to Fruitland (*San Juan Times*, Nov. 24, 1899). Under his leadership, the Navajos improved ditch heads, installed headgates, and lengthened ditches to bring water to more farmland. By 1905 almost 3,000 acres along the river had been brought under irrigation for Navajo farmers (RCIA in RSI 1900:192; Van Valkenburgh 1937:2–4).

In 1910–1911 the Indian Service lengthened the Cambridge ditch and renamed it the Hogback. Potential farmland in the project area increased from 768 acres to about 5,000 (Van Valkenburgh 1937:2; *Farmington Enterprise*, Feb. 3, 1911, Feb. 24, 1911; RCIA 1911:16). Between 1920 and 1923, construction on two other ditches increased irrigable land by another 625 acres (SJ NR 1922:5; SJ NR 1923:5). Thus, between 1899 and 1930, the number of irrigable acres along the San Juan increased from less than 1,000 to about 8,000. However, not all of this land was being farmed. In 1930, for example, farmers were planting only 3,500 acres of approximately 5,000 that could be irrigated from the Hogback (NN NR 1930:19).

After the establishment of Northern Navajo in 1903, the superintendents of that agency quickly recognized the potential for farming in their jurisdiction. Extremely isolated from the Fort Defiance agency, Navajos in the San Juan area had acquired few farming implements before 1890. In 1895 they still "had very few tools with which to work, and no money to buy [them] . . . with." One group dug an irrigation ditch with only an ax and a broken-handled shovel, while another used an ax and homemade wooden "mud spoons." In the spring of 1895 the government issued some farm tools (RCIA 1895:120), but they remained in short supply, and as late as 1908, Navajos in San Juan County still used digging sticks as their primary farming tool (BINM 1908:17).

Important changes in farming practices started to take place about this time. As Superintendent Shelton wrote in 1911, farmers in Northern Navajo were using plows, and irrigation by means of lateral ditches ("the rill system") had started to replace flooding:

> A few years ago, all of the farming was done by hand. Dikes were thrown up around small plots of ground and small holes were dug some six feet apart, in which corn was planted. Irrigation was applied by flooding the whole plot with water. Now, most of the Indians break up their land in the spring with turning plows, some of them laying off rows and planting corn and other crops like white people, using the rill system in irrigating. (SJ NR 1911:14–15)

The agency used several methods to modernize Navajo farm equipment. In the very early years, some equipment was given outright to individuals. Later, the agency paid Navajo laborers with tools (SJ NR 1920:37; SJ NR 1922:37). In the 1920s the government distributed equipment on the "reimbursable" plan, whereby Navajos used the equipment and paid the agency for it later (SJ NR 1923:10; NN NR 1928:17).

By the 1920s almost all Navajo farmers along the San Juan used plows (Bailey field notes), but still experienced shortages of proper equipment. In 1928 the superintendent wrote, "I have seen Indians plowing for corn when I believe fully one half the weight of the harness they were using was composed of wire. Given a few pieces of wire, string, and rope, and rawhide, and a Navajo will make a creditable harness" (NN NR 1928:17). Throughout the 1920s the agency continued to distribute plows and harness (SJ SR 1922:37; SJ NR 1922:40; NN NR 1930:19), and in smaller quantities, harrows, cultivators, mowers, hay rakes, hay forks, mattocks, shovels, hoes, and picks (SJ SR 1922:37; NN NR 1930:19).

The San Juan Navajos began to grow new kinds of crops as early as the mid-1890s. In 1892 a few families raised alfalfa (RCIA 1892:209); in 1895, some sorghum was planted; and in 1897, 150 concord grape vines were distributed (RBIC 1897:40). Programs at the Shiprock school and agency also accelerated the introduction of new crops. To train students in farming techniques and reduce the cost of feeding them, a school farm was established, and in addition, an experimental farm at the agency. Between 1913 and 1919, the agency issued seeds each spring (SJ NR 1915:25; SJ NR 1919:22).

Alfalfa, fed as hay to livestock in the winter, proved to be the most important crop introduced to the San Juan Navajos during the late nineteenth
century. In view of their isolation from Fort Defiance, they probably
learned how to grow it from Anglo-American farmers in the valley. In 1892
they cut an estimated thirty tons (RCIA 1892:209), not as much as it may
seem. In later periods they were harvesting two tons per acre, which would
mean that thirty tons could have been grown on as little as fifteen acres. In
1910 alfalfa was listed as one of the "principal" crops of Northern Navajo
(SJ NR 1910:1), and in the 1920s, the agency averaged between 1,000 and
1,500 acres planted in alfalfa (SJ SR 1920:26; SJ SR 1922:26; SJ SR
1923:26; NN SR AZ 1932:12; NN SR NM 1932:12).

The agency also encouraged the planting of fruit trees on farms along the
river. Except for a few peach trees, farmers in the area apparently did not
plant fruit trees before the establishment of the agency at Shiprock in 1903
(Lake Mohonk Conference 1910, 1:65). In 1905 a nursery was opened in
Shiprock (RCIA 1905:268), and by 1920, Northern Navajo farmers had
1,350 apple trees, 1,265 peach trees, 65 cherry trees, and 25 plum trees (SJ
SR 1920:38).

In spite of changes in farming methods along the San Juan, farms in that
region remained little more than oversized family gardens. Most covered
only a few acres, and very few exceeded ten. By Anglo-American standards, the equipment used by Navajo farmers was better suited to a family garden than a real farm. "The plowing done by them with their little
pony teams and ten-inch plows constitutes what a good white farmer would
term a mere hoeing," commented an official (NN NR 1927:18). These
farmers were not growing crops on a commercial scale, however, and light
plowing filled their immediate needs. Navajos sold surpluses to local traders
and flour mills (*Farmington Times Hustler*, May 12, 1904, June 9, 1905; SJ
NR 1910:1), but grew crops more for domestic use than for sale. As the
superintendent of Northern Navajo wrote in 1928, "They are not farmers
but rather sheep men and women and children. Their farming operations
consist of an effort to produce sufficient corn for home consumption, a few
melons, a little alfalfa, and in some instances a few peaches" (NN NR
1928:14).

Outside the San Juan Valley, changes in farming methods came slowly.
In most areas, limited water resources confined farming to washes, where
spring runoff saturated the ground, or to scattered areas where the soil
retained enough moisture to grow crops without irrigation. In 1894 construction began on three irrigation projects near Fort Defiance: the Wheatfields ditch, the Cottonwood ditch, and the Red Lake ditch (RCIA

1895:24–25).[13] Work was finished on Wheatfields and Cottonwood by 1898, but reportedly, the ditches had been poorly engineered and built (RSI 1898:123). In 1914 the reclamation branch of the Indian Service started an irrigation project at Ganado (N NR 1914:17) but did not finish the work until after 1920. Although the project brought 2,258 acres under irrigation, only a small fraction of the land was actually farmed (N SR 1920:42). Beginning in 1919, a project designed to irrigate 300 to 400 acres near Marsh Pass in Western Navajo (WN NR 1919:17) also ended in disuse. In 1924 Commissioner Hagerman complained that irrigation development on the reservation was an expensive failure, and that only about 2,000 acres near Shiprock and a few hundred acres near Ganado had been placed under cultivation (Hagerman 1924:19). Hagerman was basically correct in this appraisal, although he underestimated the number of acres being farmed along the San Juan.

Navajos living outside of Northern received little in the way of farming equipment. A Leupp superintendent thought that for farming their small, scattered plots, hoes and other hand tools suited them better than plows and other implements (L NR 1915:10), and in 1919 it was reported that all farming in the jurisdiction was being done with hoes (L NR 1919, 4:2). In 1927 Western Navajo distributed a carload of farm implements to replace the digging sticks and hoes still used by area farmers (WN NR 1928, 4:1), and as late as 1931 the superintendent of Southern Navajo reported "very little modern farming equipment" (SN NR 1931:12). It is not surprising that in his survey of Navajo farming in the late 1920s, Kirk Bryan (1929:453) found that many Navajos continued to rely on the digging stick for planting. Farmers would push away the caked surface soil, break up the damp earth underneath, push the digging stick down, plant seeds in a cluster above the tunnel, and tamp the earth down (W. Hill 1938:31–32).

New crops also came slowly to other regions, and superintendents did little to encourage their introduction. Although a nursery was established at Northern Navajo in 1905, a second one, at Southern Navajo, was not established until 1929 (SN NR 1931:11). Farmers in the other regions produced mainly traditional crops: corn, beans, melons, squash, and sometimes wheat. By 1920, however, alfalfa was being grown in small quantities at all of the agencies, and potatoes were becoming a major food crop, second only to corn in Southern Navajo (N SR 1920:26).[14]

Unlike Navajo herding, farming remained on a subsistence level. In most years, harvests did not even meet domestic needs, let alone produce surpluses for market. While Navajos in the west continued to trade with the Hopis for farm produce (WN NR 1918:24), in most areas they came to depend on the trading posts.

Hunting and Gathering

Hunting and gathering continued to decline in economic importance during the early twentieth century, partly because of the shifting focus of the Navajo economy, but primarily because of the exhaustion of most important plant and animal resources.

Large game animals—elk, deer, and antelope—had almost become extinct in the region before the economic collapse of the mid-1890s, and the few that managed to survive probably fell victim to Navajo hunters during this difficult time. Certainly by the turn of the century, large game had vanished from northwestern New Mexico. No antelope lived north of a line from Fort Wingate to Laguna Pueblo, although they were still plentiful on the Plains of San Augustine to the south. While elk were still common in southern Colorado, they were "almost gone" from the Jemez Mountains of New Mexico, and the few seen in northern New Mexico were probably seasonal residents that had migrated south to escape the hard winters of Colorado. Vernon Bailey (1931:22–24, 29, 40) held Navajo hunters responsible for the destruction of most of the game herds in northwestern New Mexico.

Drought, overgrazing, competition for range with domestic animals, and disease also contributed to the demise of game herds in the Southwest. Some diseases of domestic stock infected game animals as well. The 1896 outbreak of scabies may have played an important role in the destruction of the antelope herds (V. Bailey 1931:27). J. Stokley Ligon (1927:15) thought that these factors caused the game herds in New Mexico to decline further during the first two decades of the twentieth century and to fall to their lowest point in 1924. While data are lacking, we expect that a similar situation existed in northeastern Arizona.

The dearth of large game forced Navajos to hunt farther and farther from home. In 1908 Navajos were reported hunting antelope near the Plains of San Augustine in west-central New Mexico (V. Bailey 1931:24), and in the same year, the territorial governor complained that a group of eleven Navajos had killed 111 deer and 2 antelope on a hunt in southwestern New Mexico (RGNM in RSI 1908:428). In the fall of 1916, a party of five Navajo hunters was observed near the headwaters of the Gila River in southwestern New Mexico; they had four pack horses loaded with deer and antelope meat (V. Bailey 1931:25). Navajo hunters from the northern portion of the reservation frequented Colorado, where hunting was still good (Bailey field notes), and it is reasonable to assume that they also hunted off-reservation areas in Arizona and Utah during this period. The establishment of state game and wildlife departments and the imposition of game laws slowed Navajo hunting, but did not stop it. By the 1920s, hunting was evolving into more of a sport than a serious economic activity for most Navajos (Bailey field notes).[15]

On the reservation itself, people hunted small animals, mainly prairie dogs, cottontails, and jack rabbits (Carpenter and Steggerda 1939:303; Steggerda and Eckardt 1941:224). Although their overall importance was limited, prairie dogs constituted a seasonally important source of meat for some families during food shortages (Bailey field notes).

The literature makes few references to the economic importance of wild plant foods during this period. In the 1930s, Flora Bailey (1940) and Francis Elmore (1943) interviewed Navajos in the eastern and southern areas and compiled extensive lists of wild plants used in these areas. In general, although people still had a knowledge of wild plants, their use of them had declined:

> The younger generation pays little or no attention to plant names and uses . . . . The various grass seeds are no longer harvested . . . . Flour has replaced Indian millet and other wild seeds; canned spinach has replaced the Rocky Mountain bee weed, . . . *Amaranthus*, and other native greens; and many other plants, too numerous to mention, have been replaced by other white man's products. (Elmore 1943:9)

Flora Bailey (1940) reported a similar situation. Young women knew significantly less about wild plants than their older kinswomen. She also noted that certain food plants were getting harder to find. The use of wild plant foods declined significantly after the turn of the century, if not earlier—a change particularly pronounced where Bailey and Elmore worked, in areas of strong Anglo-American influence. Some minor use of these foods continued in the eastern region (Bailey field notes), and significant use persisted in the west. As late as 1910, western Navajos were "still entirely dependent on gardens and wild plants for vegetables and flour" (Luomala 1938:51–52).[16]

Piñon nuts represented an important exception to the general decline in gathering.[17] Piñon trees produce nuts in an uneven seven-year cycle: two excellent years, two fair years, and three years with no crop (Hegemann 1963:323). In productive years, Navajos earned relatively high incomes from gathering and selling the nuts. In the early 1920s, traders were paying between 10¢ and 20¢ per pound for them (RCIA 1922:5), and between 12¢ and 35¢ per pound in the early 1930s (Hegemann 1963:323). To take advantage of these prices, Navajos collected piñons more for their commercial value than for home consumption. In 1922 Navajos from Eastern earned an estimated $150,000 from piñon sales (PB SR 1922:26), and families from Southern sold $116,400 worth (N SR 1922:34). The best year for piñons was probably 1926, when Navajos from Southern sold 2,800,000 pounds for an estimated $420,000 (N NR 1926:14).

Trade

The intertribal trade network declined to relative insignificance during the early twentieth century, largely because trading posts expanded their operations and took over most of the business. In the past, intertribal trade had depended on blankets and livestock, but in the 1890s, Navajos began to prefer machine-woven Pendleton blankets to those they made themselves (McNitt 1962:222; Kluckhohn and Leighton 1960:87). We suspect that a similar change took place among other tribes, undermining the trade in Navajo blankets. Traders contributed to the decline of intertribal trade by encouraging rug weaving and buying up the entire output of weavers. About the turn of the century, they also began to purchase livestock regularly, removing the other vital prop of intertribal trade. Knowing that Navajos could obtain some essential trade items only from surrounding tribes, traders began to stock baskets, buckskins, and other Indian products, eliminating the need for direct exchange between the Navajos and their Indian neighbors.

Though greatly diminished in economic importance, some aspects of intertribal trade survived the competition. When the demand for wearing blankets fell off, some Navajos continued to trade saddle blankets directly to members of other tribes. Eastern Navajos traded saddle blankets for turquoise at Jemez Pueblo.[18] In the north, Navajos still traded directly with Utes and Paiutes for baskets, buckskins, and beadwork, although many of these items were available at local trading posts. Navajos traded for salt from the sacred lake south of Zuni because it satisfied the requirements of certain religious ceremonies and was thought to possess curative qualities (W. Hill 1940c:8). Even in the 1920s, Zunis traded salt to Navajos in farming areas of the Chuska Valley, usually in exchange for silver jewelry (Bailey field notes). In the western area, Navajos continued to trade livestock for Hopi farm produce (WN NR 1918:24).

In 1891 there were only seven licensed trading posts on the reservation (Jenkins to Sec. of Int., Feb. 11, 1891, RBIA LR GR), but as economic conditions improved after 1900, both the number of posts and the volume of trade they handled increased rapidly. Volume equaled between $150,000 and $200,000 in 1899 (RCIA 1899:157), $500,000 in 1903 (RCIA 1903:126), $1,000,000 in 1906 (RCIA 1906:182), and approximately $2,415,000 in 1911

(Lake Mohonk Conference 1913:68). Increases in wool prices and wool production, the introduction of new trade items, and high demand for Navajo rugs were responsible for this rapid and far-reaching change.

By 1910, thirty-nine licensed trading posts were doing business in the various Navajo jurisdictions, in addition to several on the Hopi reservation and numerous unlicensed, off-reservation posts. Complete data on the volume of Navajo trade do not exist for the period after 1911, but narrative statements indicate that the growth trend continued into World War I. Fragmentary data show that the number of licensed trading posts doubled between 1910 and 1918, also corroborating this trend (fig. 13).

By the late teens and early 1920s, the trading post had become an established economic and social institution on the reservation. Few families, if any, lived more than a half day's travel from one. After the war, the number of posts declined slightly. Older traders often said that some trading posts went bankrupt because of the postwar drop in wool prices (Bailey field notes).[19] As economic conditions improved in the middle and late 1920s, the number of posts increased slightly (fig. 13).

As the volume of trade and the number of posts expanded, trading practices began to change. At the turn of the century, purchases could be made by an exchange of goods or by pawning valuables—usually jewelry (Bailey field notes). The superintendent of Northern Navajo described the pawn system in 1922:

> In the spring when he sells his wool he usually pays his trader for his winter bill of goods—that is, he takes out his pawns. Then he immediately goes to pawning again and runs in debt until he sells his lambs in the fall. Some hides and pelts are disposed of during the year. But what money an Indian gets between the spring wool season and the fall stock selling he gets by hauling freight, working for wages away from the reservation, gathering pinon nuts, and from the sale of blankets. (SJ NR 1922:38)

Neither this account nor an economic survey of Northern made in 1924 mentioned unsecured credit, although the survey revealed that traders were holding $36,078.30 in pawn (SJ NR 1924:50a). However, in 1929 a committee from San Juan County, New Mexico, conducted an independent investigation of Northern Navajo and found that regional trading posts had open credit accounts for "dependable" customers, but that they required pawn from others: "silverware," jewelry, turquoise, guns, blankets, buckskins. The amount of credit extended by these posts almost equaled the total value of their goods in stock (*Farmington Times Hustler*, May 3, 1929).

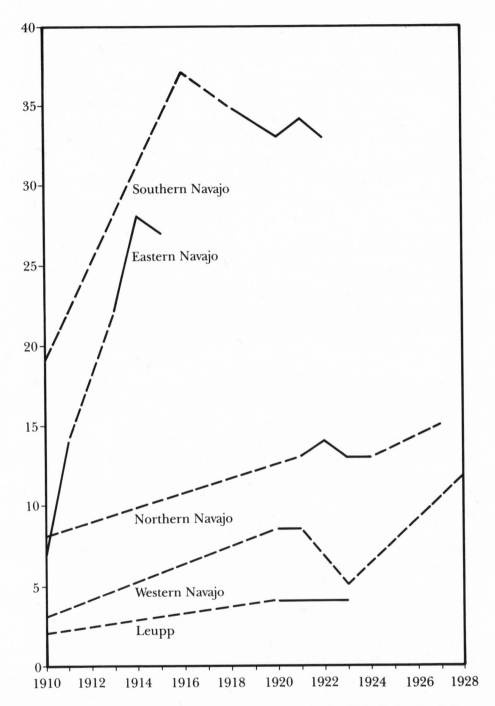

Figure 13. Number of trading posts by agency, 1910–1928. Broken line indicates missing data.

As a way of doing business, credit may have emerged during World War I when wool prices were extremely high and competition between traders exceptionally keen.[20] Because most traders ran small, undercapitalized operations, they took considerable economic risk in extending unsecured credit. If they could do so at all, they depended on customers to clear their debts with some regularity. Consequently, the practice of extending credit probably developed along with the marketing of lambs, which enabled sheepmen to settle their accounts twice a year: wool in the spring and lambs in the fall. In Eastern, Northern, and probably Southern, traders were extending limited credit to the most reliable and affluent families by the mid-1920s, but the practice did not become common in the west until the 1930s (Bailey field notes). The slight decline in trading posts in the early 1920s may be attributed at least in part to the inability of undercapitalized posts to extend credit, thereby losing their better customers to posts that could.

Unsecured trading post credit became an economic necessity for many Navajos, as well as a status symbol. The commercially oriented herding economy was vulnerable to seasonal and long-term market fluctuations.[21] Income from these sources was unreliable, and credit sometimes protected sheepmen from the vagaries of the market.

The Commercialization of Crafts

Although the Navajos had traded blankets and silver jewelry to other tribes as well as to whites before 1892, true commercialization of crafts did not appear until the late 1890s. From that time on, they began to produce items which in both form and function had no counterpart in Navajo material culture, and which were produced solely for the Anglo-American market.

As late as 1887, it was estimated that Navajos produced only 2,700 blankets per year, or about one for every two adult Navajo women. Of these, approximately two-thirds were coarsely woven textiles which were traded to the Apaches, Utes, and other tribes (RCIA 1887:172). Tourists and soldiers occasionally bought pieces, but no significant Anglo-American market existed. In order to develop this market, Navajo weavers would have to produce an item both useful and aesthetically appealing to Anglo-Americans. Blankets failed on both counts.

The economic collapse of the 1890s made Navajo weavers open to suggestions, and traders guided them into the production of marketable items. About the turn of the century, interior decorating underwent one of its periodic Indian "crazes." In response to this demand, Navajo weavers began to shift from blankets to rugs:

> No one person was responsible for the partial transition of the
> Navajo blanket from blanket to rug; efforts of many traders who
> sought a commercial outlet were combined in this, and the
> Navahos' own increasing preference for machine-manufactured
> trade blankets, notably from the Pendleton mills, was a strong fac-
> tor. (McNitt 1962:211)

It is impossible to state with any certainty when Navajos wove their first
"rugs."[22] Navajo wearing blankets typically measured 4 feet by 6 feet, and
the first "rugs" were nothing more than blankets advertised and sold as
rugs by traders. In 1894 an Indian Service employee purchased a Germantown "blanket" measuring 5.9 feet by 16 feet (*Farmington Daily Times*, Oct.
4, 1955). Germantown yarn is a little fine for rugs, and this piece may have
been woven as a portiere (doorway hanging) or couch cover. Regardless of
its intended use, the size of the piece alone indicates that it was woven for
trade instead of use as a wearing blanket, and that by 1894 at least some
Navajo weavers were producing "new" items for the Anglo-American
market.

Another example of weaving geared to Anglo-American customers
occurred during the Spanish-American War. Weavers started making
American flag blankets to capitalize on the current patriotic fever (*San Juan
Times*, Aug. 26, 1898). It is not known who originated the idea, weavers or
traders.

In spite of attempts to commercialize Navajo weaving, the market grew
slowly during the 1890s. In 1890 Navajos traded only about $24,000 worth
of blankets (RCIA 1890:162), and as late as 1899, income from weaving
amounted to only $50,000 (RCIA 1899:157). A significant market had yet
to be found.

In 1899 and 1900, new marketing outlets revolutionized Navajo weaving.
In the spring of 1899, Richard Wetherill announced that he would buy all
the blankets Navajo weavers could produce. In the fall the Hyde Exploring
Expedition, with which he was associated, opened a store in New York City
to sell Indian goods (McNitt 1966:181, 183). The following year, Fred Harvey and the Santa Fe Railroad jointly inaugurated the "Indian Building"
in Albuquerque and began promoting Indian crafts (Amsden 1975:190).
These two companies, which did much of their trade in Navajo textiles,
may have created the "Indian craze," or may only have been responding
to it. In 1900 the *Santa Fe New Mexican* commented on the fashion:

> Local curio dealers report that there is an unusual demand for
> Navajo blankets and the various weapons and implements used by the

Indians of New Mexico for the decoration of what are called "Indian dens" in New York. (quoted in the *San Juan Times*, Mar. 23, 1900)

The expanding national market for Indian crafts had a tremendous impact on the Navajo economy in general. In particular, the rug trade flourished. In 1903 the governor of New Mexico reported that the Navajos were marketing between 40,000 and 50,000 "blankets" a year, receiving about $1.00 per pound for rugs that averaged seven pounds (RGNM in RDI 1903:173). Thus, between 1899 and 1903 the annual rug trade had grown from $50,000 to somewhere between $280,000 and $350,000.

The volume of goods sold and the prices paid for them continued to increase. By 1907 Navajo weavers were getting between 75¢ and $3.50 per pound for their rugs, and even $5.00 per pound was not an exceptional price (*Farmington Enterprise*, Nov. 15, 1907). Although textiles had always been important to the Navajos as a trade item, now their economic importance increased dramatically. By 1908 rugs were described as the main source of income for the Navajos in the San Juan area (*Farmington Times Hustler*, Nov. 27, 1908). Income from the rug trade continued to climb until the outbreak of World War I (fig. 14).[23] Rug sales brought $675,000 in 1911 (Lake Mohonk Conference 1913:68), between $600,000 and $700,000 in 1913 (RCIA 1913:38), and approximately $700,000 in 1914 (RCIA 1914:34).

It is important to note that the rug and wool trades were intricately related, and in this sense, rug weaving developed as an alternative means of marketing wool. A Navajo family could weave all or part of their wool into rugs, which brought a higher price per pound than raw wool. Thus, rug production increased when wool prices were relatively low, and decreased when wool prices were high (PB NR 1920:8; EN NR 1928; N NR 1916:15; L NR 1927). This option gave the Navajos some control over their yearly income—an important advantage, given the fluctuations in the wool market (appendix B).

Considering this relationship, it is not surprising that when wool prices rose at the outbreak of World War I, the production of rugs declined. In 1918 the Navajos marketed only $316,643 in rugs (RCIA 1918:134, 136). After the war the price of wool fell to an average of 17.3¢ per pound, slightly more than its prewar value (appendix B); and rug production increased rapidly, peaking at about $700,000 in 1920 (RCIA 1920:113, 115), approximately its prewar level. The market value of wool recovered somewhat by 1923, but while remaining relatively high through the late 1920s, never approached wartime levels (appendix B). Rug production declined gradually during the mid and late 1920s, and before the depression Navajos were marketing about $400,000 in rugs each year (fig. 14).

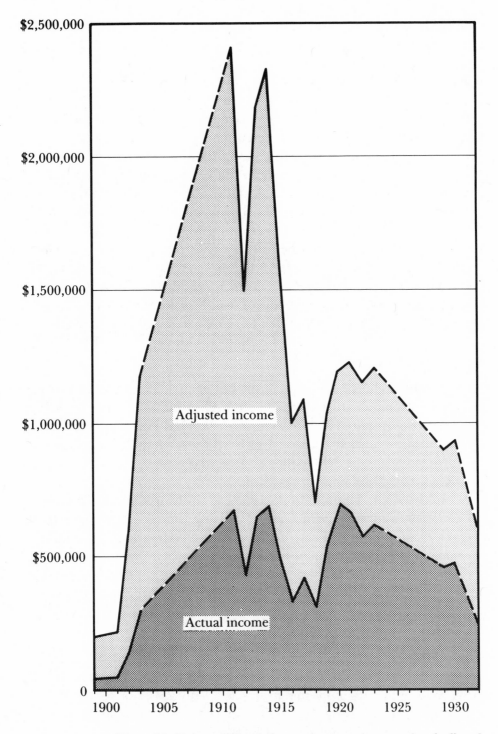

Figure 14. Estimated Navajo income from weaving, actual and adjusted (1967=100), 1899–1932. Broken line indicates missing data.

When comparing prewar and postwar income from rug weaving, it is critical to note the high rate of inflation during World War I and the years immediately following. Although rug income recovered its prewar level in dollar figures, the money would buy only about half as much (fig. 14).

Although silverwork followed a course similar to weaving, it did not achieve the same degree of commercialization.[24] After the turn of the century, silversmiths produced two different lines of goods: for Navajos, heavy silver and turquoise bracelets, rings, ketohs (bow guards), concha belts, and necklaces; and for the Anglo-American market, lightweight silver rings and bracelets as well as new items such as eardrops, belt buckles, tie clasps, and watchbands, meat forks, gravy ladles, spoons, sugar shells, and paper knives (Morris 1938:29; PB NR 1910:2; SJ NR 1921:38; Dolfin 1921:57). However, more silverwork was made for the Navajo market than for the Anglo market.

Some of the people responsible for the commercialization of weaving also had a hand in the partial commercialization of silversmithing. C. N. Cotton, a Ganado trader who had encouraged Navajo weavers to make rugs about 1890, was also one of the first to recognize the commercial potential of Navajo silverwork (McNitt 1962:210–11). However, according to John Adair (1944:25),

> the commercialization of the craft began in 1899 when the Fred Harvey Company first started to order silver made up expressly for white consumption. Before that time, the Fred Harvey Company had bought pawned Navajo silver from the traders. It had proved to be too heavy for sale to the tourists, who wanted lighter jewelry which they could wear in the East.
>
> In 1899 Mr. Herman Schweizer, . . . in charge of the Harvey Company's curio department, . . . took . . . stones and some silver to a trading post at Thoreau, New Mexico. He asked the trader there to have Navajo smiths make jewelry lighter in weight than that which they made for their own use.

The Harvey Company soon made similar agreements with traders at Sheep Springs, Smith Lake, and Mariano Lake, and the commercial Navajo jewelry industry was born (Adair 1944:25–26).

In contrast to weaving, income from silversmithing stayed extremely low in the early years of the twentieth century. As a result, superintendents rarely made estimates of income from sales of silverwork or commented on it in their reports. Commercial silversmithing was concentrated in the southern portions of Southern and Eastern Navajo.

Limited data indicate that income from sales of silver jewelry increased late in the period, when weaving income declined. Navajos in Southern Navajo sold approximately $25,000 worth of jewelry in 1926 (N NR 1926:14), $65,000 in 1929 (SN SR 1930:24), and $80,400 in 1930 (SN SR NM 1931:5; SN SR AZ 1931:5). In Northern Navajo, the market improved in spite of the depression. Traders in this jurisdiction encouraged Navajos to produce more silver jewelry (NN NR 1932:9), and income jumped from an estimated $12,875 in 1931 (NN SR AZ 1932:7; NN SR NM 1932:7; NN SR UT 1932:7) to $28,080 the following year (NN SR AZ 1933:7; NN SR NM 1933:7; NN SR UT 1933:8). In spite of the strong growth of silversmithing at the very end of this period, it remained a minor source of income for Navajos.

Wage Labor

To a limited degree, Navajos began working for wages almost as soon as they returned from Bosque Redondo. The U.S. Army employed a few scouts, particularly during the campaigns against the Apaches. From time to time the Fort Defiance Agency hired Navajos as laborers or interpreters, and larger numbers as reservation police. However, the government never employed many Navajos during this period, and the economic impact of wage labor was minimal.[25]

During the 1880s, Navajos had little reason to seek wage labor. The herds were large, and people prospered. When the herds declined in the 1890s, the entire Southwest was suffering from the same economic reversal that affected the Navajos. Wage labor could not be found. Only when economic conditions began to improve in the late 1890s did some jobs became available.

Starting in the mid-1890s, Navajos became increasingly interested in wage labor, both on and off the reservation. More than 300 applied for work on the construction of the Tsa-a lee irrigation ditch, north of Fort Defiance, in August of 1894 (*San Juan Times*, Aug. 31, 1894). In his 1900 report, Agent Hayzlett wrote, "They are beginning to realize that they must work [at wage labor] in order to live" (RCIA 1900:191). The following year, he added, "They are each year more anxious to procure work" (RCIA 1901:180). In 1904 William Shelton, the superintendent of Northern, commented, "The Navaho are a hard-working industrious people and never lose an opportunity to secure work. At different times, when I have sent out for 10 to 15 men to cut wood or work on the roads, from 50 to 100 would apply for employment" (RGNM in RDI 1904:280).

While Navajos had a strong desire to find paying work, the government offered only a small number of permanent jobs at the agencies or on temporary construction projects. Likewise, the trading posts hired a relatively small number of Navajos, and most had to look for work off the reservation. Since few Navajos spoke English or had marketable skills, it was difficult for them to find jobs away from home, as well.

The Santa Fe Railroad was the most important single private employer of Navajos. During the winter of 1898–99, the Santa Fe employed 302 Navajos for a total of about $20,000 in wages; the following spring and summer, 320 Navajos earned a total of about $7,000 per month (RCIA 1899:157). Although railroad officials complained that many Navajos quit "work just as the company had them taught to understand how the work should be done" (RCIA 1899:157), the experiment was generally considered a success (San Juan Times, June 23, 1899). The railroad employed about 400 Navajo workers in 1900 (RCIA in RSI 1900:191); nearly 300 in 1901 (RCIA 1901:180); and while no estimate was made of the numbers hired in 1902, Navajos earned a total of $70,135 for the year (RCIA 1902:156). Railroad officials quickly came to prefer Navajo workers to Spanish-Americans and other Indians, and paid them $1.10 per day— 10¢ more than other laborers (RGNM in RDI 1904, 2:275–76; RCIA in RSI 1904:141).

The sugar beet farms of eastern Colorado, western Kansas, and northeastern New Mexico also emerged as a major source of employment for unskilled Navajo workers. In 1900 about 200 Navajos worked on American Beet Sugar Company farms in eastern Colorado. In the spring of 1901, the company hired 20 Navajos and asked agency officials, traders, and missionaries to help them find others. Promising to provide rail transportation from Gallup to Rocky Ford, Colorado, if the workers assembled at Fort Defiance, the company also offered to withhold half their wages to make sure they would have some money when they returned (Chase to Hitchcock, Apr. 19, 1901, RBIA LR GR). American Beet Sugar managed to recruit only 42 Navajos at $1.00 per day (RCIA 1901:180), but because there was only enough field work to keep them employed half time, they returned with very little money. In 1902, 169 Navajos went to the Colorado beet fields, but found only about sixty days of work (RCIA 1902:156).

Although the pay was often poor, Navajos continued to work in the beet fields. The schools initiated a program of summer "outings" to generate income and provide students with an educational experience. In 1910 between 400 and 500 teenage Navajo boys spent their summer working in the Colorado beet fields for 15¢ per hour (Lake Mohonk Conference 1910:43), and in 1913 Navajo students worked in the beet fields of western

Kansas and northeastern New Mexico (L NR 1913:7). The schools continued to send students to the beet fields at least as late as 1926 (PB NR 1926:7).

Navajos worked at a variety of other jobs around the turn of the century.
Some found seasonal employment on Anglo-American farms and orchards
in the San Juan Valley (Lake Mohonk Conference 1896:32; BINM
1908:39). Others worked as herders and seasonally as shearers for white
ranchers in areas adjoining the reservation (RDC 1900, San Juan County,
Sch. 1, Pop.; *Farmington Enterprise*, Mar. 13, 1908; *Farmington Times Hustler*,
Apr. 14, 1904; Bailey field notes). When Anglo-Americans went on strike
at the Durango smelter in 1903, 25 Navajos were hired to work there (*Farmington Times Hustler*, Sept. 3, 1903, Sept. 10, 1903, Nov. 5, 1903). In 1905
the Denver and Rio Grande Railroad hired Navajo laborers to complete the
roadbed and do section work, maintaining the track on the Durango to Farmington spur (*Farmington Enterprise*, Oct. 13, 1905). In 1906 about 200
Navajos were reported to be harvesting "rubber weeds" (a source of rubber gum) near Durango (*Farmington Times Hustler*, May 24, 1906). Others
worked in the mines, presumably in Colorado (RCIA in RSI 1904:141;
RCIA 1905:167), and on government projects on the Zuni reservation
(RCIA in RSI 1904:141).

In 1904 Reuben Perry, superintendent of Southern Navajo, wrote of the
willingness of Navajos to look for wage work:

> Wherever labor is wanted the Navaho is employed. They secure
> employment in the beet fields, at various mines, and on the rail-
> roads, and generally are given preference over other Indians and
> Mexicans. . . . I have encouraged the Indians to leave the reserva-
> tion to find employment, and they are willing to go almost any
> place to secure work. (RCIA in RSI 1904:141)

Navajos living off the reservation or near its boundaries had a better
chance of finding work than those living in isolated areas. In 1910 the
superintendent of Western Navajo, the area of the reservation that had the
least contact with major Anglo settlements, wrote that none of the people
in his jurisdiction had "ever worked any place off the reservation" (WN NR
1910:8). Five years later, however, the Tuba City School organized its first
"outings," sending the boys to the beet fields in Colorado and placing the
girls as maids and housekeepers in Flagstaff (WN NR 1915:23).

Prior to World War I, Navajos resorted to wage labor to satisfy immediate and temporary needs, rather than as a permanent livelihood. Income
from wage labor often went into rebuilding depleted herds. For example,

Old Man Pete and his son worked at the Durango smelter and on the railroad in 1903, then quit their jobs and used their savings to buy a small herd of sheep at Zuni Pueblo (*Farmington Times Hustler*, Nov. 5, 1903). Other Navajos also bought sheep with their earnings (N NR 1914:20; Johnson and Hoffman 1978:26; NMSRCA McNitt Collection, S. Akeah to Frank McNitt, Jan. 4, 1958; Bailey field notes). Not an end in itself, wage labor enabled Navajos to buy livestock, rebuild their herds, and carry on their former means of livelihood. As the herds recovered, income from wage labor leveled off, and interest in wage labor began to wane (compare figs. 6 and 15).

Severe postwar economic problems quickly brought the Navajos back into the wage labor market. They left the reservation in unprecedented numbers to look for seasonal jobs throughout the Southwest. The Santa Fe Railroad remained the major employer, and in 1927 the superintendent of Southern Navajo estimated that the company had paid Navajo workers about $190,000 that year (SN SR 1927:16a). Starting about 1928, the railroad began to replace Navajos with illegal Mexican aliens. Indian Service officials and local traders attributed the shift to the Navajos' unwillingness to buy provisions from the Holmes Supply Company, a firm they alleged was set up by Santa Fe officials and their wives to furnish labor and operate the commissaries. The implication was that workers would be kept in servitude through indebtedness to Holmes. Santa Fe officials denied the accusation, explaining that "when directed by the medicine men . . . they cease their labors and go . . . to participate in their rituals, leaving their work unfinished and . . . our property . . . unprotected" (U.S. Congress 1932, 18:9607–12). For whatever reason, the Santa Fe hired fewer Navajos from then on, and in 1928 the railroad paid them only $80,000 in wages (SN SR 1928:15a).

Navajos managed to find work with a variety of other employers, including the Denver and Rio Grande Western Railroad (NN NR 1927:23) and the Zuni Mountain Railway (PB NR 1919:6). They continued to work in the beet fields of Colorado, Kansas, and New Mexico (PB NR 1926:7; N NR 1918:13; WN NR 1925:8). After the war they began picking cotton in the Salt River Valley of southern Arizona (WN NR 1919:16; WN NR 1922:30; RBIC 1923:41); working in the potato fields near Flagstaff, Arizona, and Monte Vista, Colorado (WN NR 1919:16; WN NR 1922:19–20; *Farmington Times Hustler*, Sept. 21, 1923); and harvesting in southern California (WN NR 1919:16). Navajo pick and shovel crews helped build the Durango-Silverton highway in Colorado (SJ NR 1920:29; *Farmington Times Hustler*, July 18, 1918), the Gallup-Shiprock-Farmington highway, and other roads in New Mexico (NN NR 1927:22; PB NR 1924:23). Navajo miners

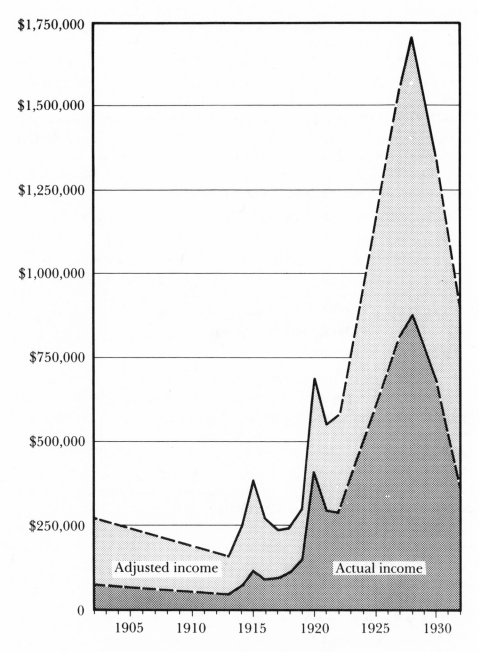

Figure 15. Estimated Navajo income from wage labor, actual and adjusted (1967 =100), 1902–1932. Broken line indicates missing data.

worked the hard rock mines at Rico and Telluride, Colorado, and at Jerome, Arizona (NN NR 1929:12); and the coal mines near Gallup (N NR 1919:13; N NR 1922:11). Others found jobs at the sawmills and the lumber camps of McGaffey, New Mexico (PB NR 1919:6); at McNary and Williams, both in Arizona (NN NR 1929:12; N NR 1922:11); and in Colorado (NN NR 1927:22). After the discovery of oil on the reservation in 1922, Navajos worked in the San Juan Basin oil fields (NN NR 1927:22). Still others worked on farms and ranches adjacent to the reservation (SJ NR 1920:29).

In 1924 the superintendent of Northern Navajo praised the industry, endurance, and thrift of Navajo workers:

> No task is so dirty, no task is so hard, no conditions so unpleasant as to cause them to refuse. . . . It is true that they are timid about accepting work that requires them to migrate to distant places. I have seen them working for themselves, performing, with worn out tools, tasks that seem impossible. They cut their hay with a scythe, or lacking that, with a sickle or lacking a sickle with a knife. . . . The ability, combined with a great desire, to labor is one of the outstanding characteristics of the Navajo. From their earliest infancy they are taught to labor and to save. (SJ NR 1924:13)

Because of their reputation as hard workers, Navajos did not have much trouble finding work. In 1920 offers from prospective employers surpassed the number of Navajos seeking work in Northern Navajo (SJ NR 1920:29), and other superintendents reported similar experiences (PB NR 1926:8; WN NR 1929, 4:8). The agencies offered programs to help Navajos find jobs, but with such a high demand for their services, they were "not seriously in need of assistance" (NN NR 1927:23).

After the war, Navajo income from wage labor increased rapidly from an estimated $110,000 in 1918 to almost $411,000 in 1920. The figure dropped slightly in 1921 and 1922, began to rise again in the mid-1920s, and reached almost $875,000. Income declined in 1929, and as the depression took hold, continued its downward trend. In 1932, Navajos earned only $370,000 from this source (fig. 15).

The nature of wage labor changed significantly during the 1920s. Although many workers continued to spend their savings to rebuild or establish herds,[26] wage work became more than just a response to immediate and temporary economic need. As the men in many families began to accept off-reservation seasonal employment every year, income from wage labor became an integral part of the economy.

Entrepreneurs

Although limited in numbers and economic importance, the Navajo entrepreneurs of the late nineteenth and early twentieth centuries demonstrated the adaptive abilities of the Navajos more dramatically than any other group. Entrepreneurs developed in three major areas: coal mining, freighting, and trading.

The development of Navajo-owned coal mines is rather obscure. Traditionally, Navajos believed coal to be the property of Haashch'ééshzhinî, the Black Yei (a supernatural being), and considered its use both dangerous and sacrilegious. They refused to use it for fuel or even to eat food prepared on a coal-burning fire (Bailey field notes). As late as 1910, probably referring to people living in the immediate vicinity of Fort Defiance, the Franciscan Fathers (1968:66) stated, "Coal is not mined [by the Navajos] as it is not in demand for domestic purposes." In other areas, the situation was already changing. Navajos may have mined coal in the Table Mesa area south of Shiprock in the 1890s (*Indians at Work* 1937:34), but the first reliable evidence dates from 1905. In that year, the superintendent of Southern Navajo paid $2,547.16 to Navajos for coal and wood (RCIA 1905:167), presumably delivered to the agency and schools. Mining first developed on a significant scale in Northern Navajo. In 1906 a coal mine was opened near the Hogback to supply fuel for the San Juan Indian Training School and agency in Shiprock (RCIA 1906:280; *Farmington Times Hustler*, June 28, 1906). Navajos mined the coal, and children at the school ate food cooked over a coal fire.

Navajos soon realized the commercial potential of coal, which in some areas was readily available. Possibly as early as 1913, they opened a small number of their own mines and started to sell coal to local trading posts and white settlers in the San Juan Valley (Bailey field notes). In 1923 it was estimated that twenty Navajos in the Northern agency received $10,000 from coal sales to private parties, trading posts, and oil companies (SJ SR 1923:58). The following year, Navajo miners sold $11,800 worth of coal to traders, slightly more than $7,800 worth to the agency, and an unspecified figure to oil companies (SJ NR 1924:50a). Most Navajo miners worked part time, selling coal to supplement income from livestock, farms, and other sources (Bailey field notes).

In the 1880s, the agency began hiring Navajos to freight goods from the railroad at Manuelito to Fort Defiance. Throughout the late nineteenth century, Navajo freighters handled a relatively small volume of goods, mainly in the southern portion of the reservation. For example, as late as

1898 they transported only 582,000 pounds of goods for a total income of $1,421 (RCIA in RSI 1898:617).

Freighting evolved into an important source of income only after the turn of the century, when the volume of trade expanded rapidly. Navajos quickly took over the local business, and in 1916 handled more than 90 percent of the freight (*Farmington Times Hustler*, May 18, 1916). Navajos controlled freighting in every jurisdiction but Western, where Hopis from Moencopie did most of the hauling (WN NR 1913).

In the early years, any Navajo with a wagon and team could hire out as a freighter. Freighting as a specialized occupation did not develop until the early 1920s, when local men began to haul oil field equipment in Northern Navajo. In 1926 the superintendent wrote,

> They are slow to take up a new line of work, but once having acquired the nack [sic] they are excellent at almost any task. A few years ago there was not a freighter among them that could be classed as "fair", to-day they swarm to Farmington and unload 150,000 pounds of four inch iron pipe and have it all on their wagons and headed for the oil fields in four hours time. They will handle boilers weighing from 10,000 to 14,000 pounds and deliver them at the oil fields. In fact they do not stop at any piece of freight large or small and the more there is of it the better they like it. . . .
> They have become expert in this work. (SJ NR 1926:38–39)

The weights of these loads indicate that Navajo freighters had advanced well beyond the use of light farm wagons and teams of "Indian ponies." By 1927 some were using teams of "American" horses to haul wagons (NN NR 1927:19), and in 1926 one bought a commercial Ford truck (*Farmington Times Hustler*, May 14, 1926).

Some people became involved in trading, long an integral part of Navajo economic life. The earliest known Navajo trader, Chee Dodge, went into partnership with Stephen H. Aldrich, an Anglo-American, at Round Rock Trading Post in the Chinle Valley in 1890 (Hoffman 1974:192; McNitt 1962:279). The growth in trading after 1900 encouraged other Navajos to go into business. Of the nineteen traders in Southern Navajo in 1910, five were full-blood Indians, and one was of mixed blood (N NR 1910). A trader of mixed blood operated one of the two trading posts at Leupp in 1910 (L NR 1910:4), and Navajo owners were said to be operating two posts on Northern Navajo in 1919 (SJ NR 1919:7). Because Navajos ran small businesses and did not have to apply for trading licenses, these estimates are probably low. Some traded goods out of their homes; others set up tents in the farming districts. Mostly independent businessmen dealing in a limited range of goods, Navajo traders sometimes formed partnerships with Anglo-Americans (Bailey field notes; Bailey and Bailey 1982:305).

The activities of Navajo traders reached their height during the teens, and by the early 1920s, most of the small posts had closed. It is not entirely clear why Navajo trading posts declined at that time. For one thing, competition had gotten keener. With limited capital, Navajo businessmen had to join general merchandise wholesalers in order to survive. Wholesalers sold goods on credit to the owners of trading posts, or took wool or rugs in payment (Bailey field notes; Adams 1963:168). In turn, owners sold on credit to their customers. Although we cannot say for certain, it was probably the inability of native Navajo traders to secure credit from the large wholesale houses that led to the decline in the number of these posts.[27]

Economic Recovery and Change

At the turn of the century, the Navajos were still suffering from the economic collapse of the 1890s. Although their herds had recovered somewhat from the mid-1890s low, livestock could not even support the expanding Navajo population at subsistence level: in 1900 the ratio of Navajos to sheep and goats was 1:19. To make matters worse, wool, the major trade commodity, was bringing only 13.7¢ per pound—better than the 1895–96 price of 10.3¢, but below the 16.3¢ of 1892 (appendix B). Depleted herds and low wool prices forced Navajos to seek other forms of income. Wage labor and weaving became the primary instruments of economic recovery, and surplus income generated by these activities was used to purchase sheep, accelerating the rebuilding of their herds.

After 1900 the Navajo economy took a new lease on life. In 1903 the herds increased by at least 30 percent (RCIA in RSI 1903, 1:126). Range conditions improved. In 1906 the governor of New Mexico wrote, "For the past two years the sheep business [in New Mexico] has probably been the most valuable of any in the West. . . . Abundant moisture . . . has produced an excellent stand of grama grass" (RGNM in RDI 1906:76). As the herds expanded, Navajo weavers produced more rugs to meet the increasing demand. The economy got another boost when the price of wool jumped to 23.1¢ per pound in 1906, its highest level since 1880 (appendix B). The economy continued to grow. In 1914 income from rug weaving reached an estimated $700,000, and in 1915 the sheep and goat herds peaked at slightly more than 1,800,000.

On the eve of World War I, the Navajo economy differed from that of the pre-1892 period in several respects. While herding remained primarily subsistence oriented in 1914, some livestock was being marketed. Navajos produced wool and rugs for market, and the commercialization of crafts, particularly the shift from blankets to rugs, generated most of the economic growth. Important in the late 1890s, wage labor declined between 1900 and 1914 as the herds recovered, and as income from rugs increased.

During World War I, the prices of wool and livestock reached their highest levels in memory, a circumstance at least partly responsible for the decline in rug weaving and wage labor. In 1916 an official remarked, "Never before in the history of this reservation has there been such a prosperous year in the livestock industry" (N NR 1916:13). Income from the sale of wool and livestock remained high through 1918 (WN NR 1918:25). However, most of this income was generated by the sale of productive stock. By the end of the war, livestock sales had reduced the number of sheep and goats to 956,012 in 1919, or slightly more than half of the prewar level.

Wartime inflation drove up all commodity prices, wool and livestock included. When the war ended, however, wool and livestock dropped sharply, while the prices of most other goods continued to rise. The Navajos found themselves in an economic squeeze. Necessary items often cost more or not much less than they had during the war years, and with the herds drastically diminished, Navajos did not have much to sell.

The tribe reoriented its economy during the early 1920s, reacting to changing economic conditions. Rug production increased rapidly, although in terms of purchasing power, it recovered only about half of its prewar level. The major changes took place in the herding economy and wage labor. Taking regional variation into consideration, the Navajos generally shifted from subsistence-oriented herding to commercial herding, emphasizing the production of wool and feeder lambs. Income from wage labor, which was becoming a regular, seasonal activity, made the greatest proportional increases.

The reoriented Navajo economy was a success. In 1926 Samuel Stacher, the superintendent of Eastern Navajo, wrote, "I doubt very much if there has ever been as much prosperity among the Indians of this jurisdiction than the year just closing" (PB NR 1926:8). Stacher was in a good position to make such an assessment. Serving at Eastern since 1909, he had witnessed both the prewar and wartime economic booms. Economic conditions continued to improve, and in 1928 Superintendent A. H. Kneale stated that the Navajos had "multiplied their annual income by two or two and a quarter in the past five years" (NN NR 1928:10).

THE EROSION OF CULTURAL ISOLATION

Prior to 1900, few Navajos came into regular contact with whites. Even in the 1890s, their exposure to Anglo-American culture and material goods was extremely limited. The situation changed rapidly after 1900, as the creation of the six agencies brought Navajos into more frequent contact with government officials. An expanding road system connecting the major administrative centers with each other and with Anglo-American communities also contributed to the erosion of isolation. Many families acquired wagons, and in the mid-1920s some wealthy Navajos bought automobiles and trucks. Trading posts proliferated, and by the teens all but the most isolated Navajo families traded there regularly. The number of schools increased both on and off the reservation, and by the end of this period, almost half of Navajo children were attending school. Missions and missionaries spread throughout the region. A substantial number of Navajos worked off the reservation and came into daily contact with Anglo-Americans, producing major changes in Navajo material culture. By the early 1930s, most material items used by the Navajos were either wholly or partially of Anglo-American manufacture, as Navajos increasingly came to accept the technology of their Anglo-American neighbors.

Roads and Transportation

In the late nineteenth century, the washes, canyons, mesas, and mountain ranges typical of Navajo country made travel difficult at best. The San Juan and Colorado Rivers on the north and the Little Colorado to the southwest were frequently difficult to cross, if not impassable. Bridges were nonexistent. Most wagon roads were confined to the San José and Little Colorado valleys in the south, connecting Fort Defiance with the military post at Fort Wingate, and with the settlements at Gallup, Holbrook, Joseph City, and Winslow. In the mid-1870s, Mormons built the "Mormon Wagon Road" through western Navajo country from the Little Colorado Valley to Lee's Ferry. Built in the mid-1880s, the "Togay Trail" ran north from Fort Wingate to Fort Lewis on the San Juan (MacDonald and Arrington 1970:17, 113–14, 116). However, the vast interior of Navajo country remained accessible only on horseback. Living in such rough country, Navajos showed little interest in acquiring wagons until roads and bridges were built in the early decades of this century.

The San Juan River constituted one of the major barriers to contact between Navajos and whites. For the most part, Anglo-Americans lived on the north side of the river, Navajos on the south. In the early years of white settlement, crossings were made by ferry, and Navajos could trade at Anglo-American stores. However, at certain times of the year the San Juan ran swiftly, and ferry crossings could be difficult and dangerous (U.S. Congress 1912:2, 6). In 1904 a footbridge was completed across the San Juan at Farmington (*Farmington Times Hustler*, Mar. 3, 1904), and in 1910 the first wagon bridge opened at Shiprock (U.S. Congress 1912:2).[28] After a flood destroyed both of them in October 1911 (Bailey field notes; U.S. Congress 1912:4), the Shiprock bridge was soon replaced; but a new wagon bridge did not span the river at Farmington until 1919 (*Farmington Times Hustler*, May 8, 1919; U.S. Congress 1932, 18:9748).

A program of road development started in the late 1890s. In 1897 the government repaired 200 miles of roads on the reservation and built another 25 miles of new road (RCIA in RSI 1897:499). In 1898 the government built another 50 miles of new road (RCIA in RSI 1898:617). While repairs and new construction affected only a small part of the reservation, they confirmed the government's commitment to road development.

Eventually, each jurisdiction supervised its own road building program. Navajos did most of the work, taking wagons, plows, and tools in payment from the agency. However, some agencies organized mandatory work projects. As early as 1914, the business council in Southern required Navajos to work on the roads every year (N NR 1914:13). From 1926 to 1930, Navajos living in Western had to do two days of road work per year without pay (WN NR 1928, 4:3; WN NR 1930, 4:5), and a similar situation existed at Leupp (L NR 1930, 4:2).

Most of the effort went into building local roads, but a few major highways were also constructed. In 1915 the highway from Shiprock to Gallup (*Farmington Times Hustler*, Apr. 15, 1915) joined the Shiprock-Hogback road, which had been finished in 1911 (*Farmington Enterprise*, Feb. 3, 1911). While classified as "improved," the Shiprock-Gallup highway was not paved until 1927,[29] when it was dubbed "the million dollar highway of Navajo land" (*Farmington Times Hustler*, Jan. 6, 1928). With partial funding from the Indian Service, in 1929 the state of Arizona completed a highway from Flagstaff north to the Utah border, passing through the western portion of the reservation and crossing the Colorado at Lee's Ferry (Measeles 1981:61).

The construction of bridges and roads increased the demand for wagons. Although some Navajos bought wagons from traders, the government was the major supplier in the early years of this century, giving them in payment for labor (WN NR 1910:11; PB NR 1913:6; L NR 1911:14). When the agencies introduced the reimbursable plan, Navajos could buy wagons on credit at the wholesale price. In 1926 Southern Navajo was selling wagons for $145.61; a local trader was charging $184.00 for the same model. Under this plan, a customer could pay the agency $50 down, and pay off the balance later (RCIA 1926:23).

In 1900 very few Navajo families owned wagons, and most of those who did probably lived in the vicinity of Fort Defiance (Frisbie and McAllester 1978:30). By 1907 the number of wagons on the reservation was increasing (*Farmington Enterprise*, Nov. 15, 1907). Navajos prospered from the sale of wool and rugs, and wagons were one of the most desirable consumer items of the day. The *Farmington Enterprise* (June 14, 1907) reported that the demand for wagons and buggies was so high that one trader had purchased an entire boxcar load of them.

Wagons were acquired by steadily increasing numbers of Navajos during this period, but with significant regional differences. As in other aspects of Navajo culture change, Western was the slowest to change. In 1913 the "average" resident of the region had "very little use for roads as he rides a horse and uses the trails" (WN NR 1913, 4:5). As late as 1917, wagons and buggies were just starting to come into common use (WN NR 1918:4), and horses were still the principal means of travel (WN NR 1917:24).

Even before wagons came into universal use, some well-to-do Navajos bought motor vehicles. The date of the first such purchase is not known. Superintendent Kneale (1950:368) stated that in 1923, no Navajo in the Northern region owned an automobile. Harvey Meyer, the superintendent of Western Navajo, reported that ten trucks and automobiles belonged to Indians in his jurisdiction in 1924 (WN SR 1924:4), but most or all of them probably belonged to Hopis who lived in Moencopie. By 1925, however, some Navajos in Northern had purchased motor vehicles. Deshna Cheschillege, tribal chairman from 1928 to 1932 (Young 1955:204), and Nalget Yazzie from Shiprock were driving new Fords in the summer of 1925 (*Farmington Times Hustler*, July 3, 1925). J. C. Morgan, chairman from 1938 to 1942, had a new sport model Dodge (*Farmington Times Hustler*, July 17, 1925).[30]

Automobiles and trucks quickly became popular with the more prosperous Navajo families. In 1926 the superintendent of Eastern Navajo reported that "some" Navajos in his jurisdiction owned automobiles (PB NR 1926:6), and in the same year Navajos in Western were "rapidly getting away from the use of teams and wagons and taking up auto trucks instead" (WN NR 1926, 4:1). In 1926 the superintendent of Leupp expressed concern that "the lure of the automobile is threatening the existence of some of the herds": in order to purchase cars, families were selling their livestock to off-reservation traders to circumvent agency restrictions on the sale of breeding stock (L NR 1926, 4:2). Automobiles had become "quite an obsession among these Indians," wrote the superintendent, who had counted fifty Navajo-owned automobiles at closing exercises on the last day of school (L NR 1927:6). In spite of the sudden popularity of motor vehicles, many Navajo families did not even own a wagon in the early 1930s, and continued to travel by horseback.

Education

In 1890 only 89 Navajos out of a school-age population of 6,090 were enrolled in school. Johnston (1966a:362, 367) estimated that in that year, only 2.35 percent of Navajos twenty years of age or older had ever attended school, and few of those had stayed long enough to learn English.

The government started to support education for American Indians in the late 1880s by establishing a network of large government-operated boarding schools. The first such school was established at Grand Junction, Colorado, in 1886, followed in 1891 by schools in Phoenix, Arizona, and Santa Fe, New Mexico. Fort Lewis Indian School was established in southwestern Colorado in 1892; Theodore Roosevelt School in Fort Apache, Arizona, in 1893; and Sherman Institute in Riverside, California, in 1902 (Young 1954:103; Underhill 1956:223). Eventually, Navajo students enrolled in all of these schools. Because of its emphasis on the construction of boarding schools, the government established only one school on the reservation during the 1890s—Blue Canyon Day School (WN NR 1915:2).

The government had originally contracted Indian schools on the reservation to missionary societies and churches. Reaching a high in 1893, "contract" schools declined in number during the mid and late 1890s, and the government dropped the system in 1901 (Warner 1970:217).

Financed by various churches, mission schools were established on the reservation. The earliest mission school was established in Jewett, New Mexico, in 1896 and eventually became Navajo Methodist Mission School (Malehorn 1948:14–15; Lake Mohonk Conference 1897:63; MacDonald and Arrington 1970:91). The Franciscans dedicated St. Michaels Mission in 1898, but the school was not opened until December 3, 1902 (*Padres' Trail*, Oct. 1953). In 1897 a nondenominational mission was established at Tolchaco, Arizona (L NR 1931:1–2), which included a school later on (L NR 1912, 1:1–2).

A number of new mission schools were founded after the turn of the century. The Christian Reformed Church opened Rehoboth in 1901 (Young

1954:103; Underhill 1953:227). The Presbyterian Church moved its Jewett school to Ganado in 1912 (Malehorn 1948:17–22; Warner 1970:214). In 1904 a nondenominational mission school was holding classes in Aneth, Utah (RGNM in RDI 1904:279). The Presbyterians had a school near Leupp in 1920 (L SR 1920:9), and the Catholics were operating a day school at Lukachukai in 1930 (SN NR 1931:6).

Commissioner of Indian Affairs Francis Leupp focused on education as a means of acculturation and assimilation. Considering it more advantageous to "carry civilization to the Indian" than to "carry the Indian to civilization" (Leupp 1910:135), he opposed off-reservation government boarding schools. During the administration of Leupp and his immediate successors, the number of reservation boarding and day schools increased rapidly. Boarding schools opened in Tohatchi in 1900, Tuba City in 1901, Shiprock in 1907, Leupp in 1909, Chinle in 1910, Crownpoint in 1912, Toadlena in 1913, Marsh Pass in 1914, and Fort Wingate in 1925 (Underhill 1956:223; Young 1954:103; WN NR 1914). In addition, day schools were built at Cornfields, Lukachukai, and Pinedale (N NR 1910; N SR 1920:10; PB NR 1917:1).[31]

As the number of schools increased, so did enrollment. In 1898, 185 Navajos were attending school (about 3 percent of the school-age population), 770 in 1908, and 1,881 in 1918. Rapid increases in attendance took place during the 1920s, until by 1932, enrollment had climbed to 5,719 students, or approximately 4 percent of the school-age population (Young 1954:104; fig. 16). In 1900 only an estimated 3.7 percent of adult Navajos had any education, but by 1930 the figure had grown to 32.2 percent, or almost one-third of the adult population (Johnston 1966a:367).

Because Navajo parents resisted sending their children to off-reservation boarding schools (N NR 1912), few attended during the early years of the twentieth century. Education at home was a different matter. In Southern Navajo, voluntary applications for enrollment exceeded the number of available places in 1915 (N NR 1915:12). By the early 1920s, reservation schools were filled to capacity, and the number of children attending off-reservation schools rose sharply (Bailey and Bailey 1982:fig. 28). This change in attitude towards off-reservation schooling may have resulted from a growing conviction on the part of many Navajos that education in general, and English language skills in particular, would give their children an economic advantage. During the early 1920s, only older students attended off-reservation schools such as Phoenix, Albuquerque, Santa Fe, Sherman Institute, and Haskell in Kansas. Other Navajos attended reservation

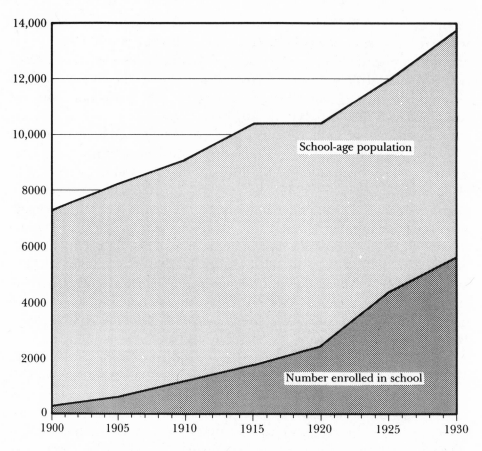

Figure 16. Navajo school-age (6-18) population and number enrolled in school, 1900-1930. Adapted from Johnston (1966b:362).

schools in Fort Apache, Truxton Canyon, and Fort Mohave (all in Arizona), and Ignacio, Colorado (L SR 1920, 4:9; L SR 1921, 4; SJ SR 1920, 3:15; SJ SR 1924, 3:2; L SR 1928, 2:2).

Educators often found themselves at odds with traditional Navajo culture. For example, in 1916 the new superintendent of Western reported, "Up to last year the vicious custom [of previous school administrators] of permitting Indian parents to exchange a smaller child in the family for an older child who had attended school from two to four years was very much in vogue" (WN NR 1916:11). Parents needed their children at home to help with herding and other chores. The superintendent put a stop to this practice. Returning from off-reservation schools, students often found it difficult to capitalize on their newly acquired skills, and faced economic hardship: "Because of their long absence from the reservation they lose their recognized birth right to sheep, cattle, and grazing grounds on the reservation and, returning without assets, they are not in a position to establish themselves again" (WN NR 1926, 3:3). Indeed, some educators did not want students to resume their traditional way of life. The prevailing attitude was that Indian culture inhibited the assimilation of the Indians into the larger national community, and that since Indian culture was going to die out anyway, the sooner it was eliminated, the better.

Missionary Activity

Missionary activity among the Navajos remained sporadic and ineffectual until the 1890s, when a wide variety of denominations established missions on or adjacent to the reservation. Missions were founded by the Women's National Indian Association, an interdenominational group, near Two Gray Hills in 1890; the Ladies Home Missionary Society of New York in the San Juan Valley in 1891 (Malehorn 1948:3–5; Warner 1970:215); the Gospel Union Mission in Tuba City in 1894; the Christian Reformed Church at Fort Defiance in 1896, with an outstation at Tohatchi in 1899–1900; the Episcopalians at Ft. Defiance in 1897 (Dolaghan and Scates 1978:30–31, 35; Warner 1970:216); a nondenominational group at Tolchaco in the Little Colorado Valley, also in 1897 (L NR 1931:1–2); and the Catholics south of Ft. Defiance in 1898 (*Padres' Trail*, Oct. 1953). Nevertheless, historian Michael Warner (1970:217) described the missionary work of the 1890s as "far from extensive and pervasive."

The level of missionary activity increased considerably after the turn of the century. The Presbyterians opened a mission at Ganado, and the Gospel Missionary Union of Kansas City started one at Tuba City. Baptist missionaries took over the work in the Two Gray Hills area from 1901 until 1906, when the mission was transferred to the Christian Reformed Church.

The government continued to make land grants for missionary activity, as it had in 1890 to the Women's National Indian Association (Warner 1970:216–17, 219). Between 1903 and 1912, the Catholics received 160 acres in the Chinle Valley, the Presbyterians 80 acres in Ganado, the Baptists 40 acres in Eastern, the Mennonites half an acre in the west, and the Tolchaco mission 45 acres. By 1914 a total of forty-eight missionaries were actively at work among the Navajos (RCIA 1914:90).

Whether they were run by the government or a church, schools served as the centers of Christian missionary activity. Missionaries actively proselytized students at mission schools such as Rehoboth (Christian Reformed), St. Michaels (Catholic), Ganado (Presbyterian), and Navajo Methodist

Mission. At the encouragement of officials, they also worked at government schools and often held religious services there (L NR 1910:21; L NR 1911:1; PB NR 1920:2-3).

Several missionary groups worked through medical missions or hospitals. The Episcopalian Church established the first such mission to the Navajos, which grew into Good Shepherd Hospital at Ft. Defiance in 1897 (Dolaghan and Scates 1978:30); and San Juan Mission near Farmington in 1917 (Bailey and Bailey 1982:472; Warner 1970:221). The Presbyterians opened a hospital at Ganado in 1904 (Underhill 1953:229). About 1911 a small medical mission under the sponsorship of the Massachusetts Indian Rights Association was treating Navajos in Blanco Canyon, New Mexico (PB NR 1911), and the Presbyterians were operating a medical mission at Indian Wells in Leupp Agency in 1916 (L NR 1916:2).

Some missionaries claimed large numbers of converts, but Indian Service officials and even some churchmen believed that missionary work had a negligible effect on Navajo religious beliefs. In 1912 the superintendent of Western noted, "In spite of the work of the three missionary organizations on the [Western] reservation, hardly any apparent progress has been made in Christianizing them." Though the Hopis at Moencopie seemed somewhat more disposed to accept Christianity, not even the missionaries claimed any Navajo converts (WN NR 1912, 1:13). In 1926 the superintendent of Western said the reservation was "infested with Missionaries," but he could vouch for no more than twenty-five Christians, either Navajo or Hopi (WN NR 1926:3). Leupp agency likewise reported very few converts, and what few there were reverted to traditional practices whenever they were ill and in need of a sing (L NR 1927; L NR 1931, 1:4). The strongest condemnation of missionary work came from a missionary, James D. Verplanck, who had worked with the Navajos for years. In 1934 he wrote, "The Navajos and Hopis as tribes are no more Christian than the Hottentots in Africa. There are a few following for the 'loaves and fishes' " (Verplanck 1934:51).

Some Navajos experienced genuine conversion, however, to the extent of becoming missionaries themselves. A Navajo missionary was working at Cedar Springs in Leupp Agency in 1930 (L NR 1930:2), and J. C. Morgan, a Christian Reformed convert, established a church in Farmington, New Mexico, during the 1920s (Bailey and Bailey 1982:472). Previously mentioned as the owner of one of the first automobiles on the reservation, Morgan was also a political activist, and served as tribal chairman from 1938 to 1942 (Young 1961:603).

Changes in Material Culture

As early as the 1890s, what had been a very mobile population began to settle into more permanent camps—a change that was to affect the kind of structures Navajos lived in (C. Mindeleff 1898:482). This process accelerated during the early twentieth century, when the acquisition of wagons allowed families to haul stone and logs, and occupy areas where such building materials were not available (Bailey field notes). Settlement patterns also changed: people no longer occupied areas that were inaccessible to wagons, such as mesa tops. Also, the availability of water and firewood became less important criteria for choosing the location of a camp, because now they could be hauled in by wagon (Downs 1964:84–85).

Navajos built and lived in some houses (as opposed to hogans) during the nineteenth century, but a major increase in house construction did not take place until the twentieth century (Ostermann 1917:26). A minority of Navajos actually owned houses, though the percentage varied from agency to agency. As part of the 1916 census, the superintendent of Southern Navajo reported 2,075 hogans and 766 houses in his jurisdiction (N NR 1916:4)—about 25 percent houses. Estimates from the other agencies appear to be little more than informed guesses. In Northern Navajo, houses comprised approximately 14 percent of the dwellings in the early 1920s (SJ SR 1920:4; SJ SR 1921:4); in Leupp, less than 10 percent (L SR 1920:4; L SR 1921:4); and in Eastern, 17 percent (PB SR 1921:4). By 1925 houses made up 33.3 percent of the dwellings in Eastern Navajo (PB SR 1925:4). Western Navajo appears to have lagged behind the other agencies in house building: in 1928 it was reported that people who had previously lived only in hogans were building new homes (WN NR 1928, 3:5).

Houses built by the Navajos during this period varied considerably in materials, size, and construction technique. Some were made of stone, others of adobe or logs. Log structures took the form of Anglo-American log cabins or Spanish-American jacals. Some houses had gabled roofs, while others had flat, dirt-covered roofs. Owners probably built most of the houses, although some were built by hired Navajo workmen who had studied carpentry and masonry at one of the Indian schools (Bailey and Bailey 1982:330). As the superintendent of Southern wrote in 1916, "The houses run . . . all the way from costing $5,000 and up to date to a one room affair without either floor or windows" (N NR 1916:4).

Important changes also took place in the design and construction of hogans, although white observers took little note of them. Even in the early twentieth century, Navajos continued to prefer the old conical forked-stick and corbeled-log hogans, which were covered with dirt (Bailey field notes), to stone, palisaded-log, and cribbed-log hogans, which had started to appear in the late nineteenth century and which were built with increasing frequency in the twentieth. The origin of hogan types is obscure. Stone hogans date back to at least the eighteenth century. Although most scholars agree that palisaded-log and cribbed-log hogans date from the late nineteenth century and owe their form to Anglo-American contact, there is some evidence of an earlier origin (Jett and Spencer 1981:67, 77–78, 99–101). Most researchers attribute the increasing popularity of cribbed-log hogans to stylistic changes, but the change correlates more plausibly to the availability of steel axes (Jett and Spencer 1981:78).

Stone, palisaded-log, and cribbed-log hogans had vertical walls, in contrast to the inward slanting walls of the conical forked-pole and corbeled-log hogans.[32] Vertical walls produced a more spacious structure, better suited to Anglo-American furnishings, and the adoption of the new hogan forms can be viewed as a compromise between the old forms and Anglo-American houses. The one-room Navajo houses of this period differ from the vertical-walled hogans mainly in shape: the houses were square, the hogans round.

Anglo-American tents began to transform even temporary summer camps, where in the past, temporary dwellings usually consisted of little more than brush shades (conical forked-pole shades, palisaded shades, lean-to shades, ramadas, and windbreaks) (C. Mindeleff 1898:494–96; Jett and Spencer 1981:34–41, 18, 22). In the nineteenth century and even in the early twentieth century, some Navajos used a crude form of tipi—little more than a conical pile of poles loosely wrapped in canvas (Robert Roessel 1980:190; Newcomb 1966:39 facing page). Their use was limited to very few areas, notably Aneth, Utah (Jett and Spencer 1981:46), and the Newcomb-Burnham area of New Mexico. Although some Navajos lived in tents during their confinement at Bosque Redondo (Underhill 1956:128), the agency did not list them as annuity goods after they returned, and apparently they dropped out of use until the end of the nineteenth century.[33] Cosmos Mindeleff (1898) did not mention tents of any kind, but in 1890 Walter Marmon noted that some of the wealthier Navajo families had wall tents or officer tents (U.S. Bureau of the Census 1894:147). A decade later, U. S. Hollister (1972:72) reported, "In recent years the common Sibley tent has been used in summer to some extent."[34] After 1900 Navajos began to use tents more extensively during the summer (L NR 1916:5; Dolfin 1921:143–44). By the late teens, they were buying commercial canvas tents from trading posts, and poorer families made their own by sewing flour sacks together (Dolfin 1921:144; Bailey field notes). The high price of tents kept them from coming into universal use, however, and many families continued to use brush shades in their summer camps (Reichard 1969:7).[35]

Changes also took place in the furnishings of Navajo dwellings. Although people living near the agency and railroad may have acquired stoves before 1900, most Navajos had only a simple, open fireplace in the center of the hogan for cooking and heating. Navajos acquired two kinds of commercially produced stoves between 1900 and the early 1930s: the common cast-iron, potbelly stove; and a small, portable box stove made out of sheet metal, known as a shepherd's stove. In addition, Navajos frequently made their own stoves out of fifty-gallon steel oil drums.

Officials referred to the use of stoves only at Northern, Eastern, and Leupp. As early as 1910, Northern reported that "a considerable number of the Indians have cook stoves" (SJ NR 1910:13)—perhaps something of an exaggeration. Fifteen years later, some of the families near Toadlena wanted stoves for their houses (SJ NR 1925:14), and in 1928 the number of cook stoves had "greatly increased" (NN NR 1928:10), indicating that many families in Northern Navajo still lacked stoves in the late 1920s. In Eastern, people acquired stoves even more slowly (PB NR 1911:5; EN NR 1931, e:1), and the superintendent of Leupp did not mention them until the late 1920s (L NR 1927:6).

In the 1920s Navajos began using the smoke hood, a homemade device that funneled smoke out of the hogan.[36] In 1926 the superintendent of Eastern wrote, "Many Indians now use powder cans, gasoline cans or other constructed pipe over the fire and projects [sic] above the top of hogan creating a better draft and eliminating the smoke nuisance to a great extent" (PB NR 1926:3). The hoods spread rapidly among the Navajos, and in 1927 the superintendent of Northern gave a detailed description of those used in his agency:

> In the best of hogans, the owners have constructed a smoke conveyor usually consisting of an old wash tub with a hole in the bottom, suspended over the central fire and connected with this tub are several old bottomless buckets, telescoped, and extending from the tub through the central hole in the roof. (NN NR 1927:5)

The superintendent was so taken with the idea that he placed an order at a local tin shop for some hoods made from galvanized iron (NN NR 1927:5–6). Although the use of smoke hoods spread rapidly during the 1920s, stoves and smoke hoods were described as "unusual" in the northwestern part of the reservation as late as 1925 (Verplanck 1934:22), and one trader reported that people in the Oljeto area did not have them when he arrived in 1939 (Bailey field notes).

Traditionally, the hogan was devoid of furniture: Navajos slept on piles of sheep pelts at night, or sat on them during the day. Extra clothing, utensils, food, tools, and miscellaneous items were hung from the walls or stored on the floor around the walls of the hogan. As late as the turn of the century, only the wealthiest and most progressive Navajos owned much in the way of Anglo-American furniture. While Earle Forrest (1970:106) was visiting the northern portion of the reservation in 1902, he commented that outside of trading posts, a Navajo named Sandoval owned the only chair he had seen on the reservation. In 1910 the Franciscan Fathers (1968:327–28) wrote, "While these [houses] are furnished with chairs, tables, and other modern furniture, the Navaho hogan dispenses with these luxuries." A few years later, Father Ostermann (1917:27) noted that Navajo houses were "furnished with stoves, tables, chairs and bedsteads, with mattresses, and other consequences of civilization."

These statements suggest that early in the twentieth century, the acquisition of Anglo-American style furniture accompanied the occupation of houses, and that the furnishings of hogans remained unchanged. "Their chief furniture are sheep and goat skins," it was said of the Northern Navajos in 1910. "From time to time pieces of rude furniture are added, which have been made from boxes and other like material" (SJ NR 1910:13). Slowly, furniture found its way into hogans, possibly as a result of changes in their design. A substantial increase in the use of furniture took place during the 1920s, when the superintendent of Eastern Navajo reported "more cupboards" being used to store food (EN NR 1927:3). A few years later, he reported, "Many of the houses and hogans are furnished with tables, chairs, bedsteads, stoves, and cupboards" (EN NR 1931, 3:9). In the west, Navajos acquired Anglo-American furnishings at a much slower rate. Most families in Leupp continued to sleep on sheep pelts, and "very few" had beds, chairs, or tables (L NR 1927:6).[37]

Even before stoves and other furnishings appeared in sizable quantities, the production of pots and baskets experienced a significant decline. Forrest (1970:108, 136) wrote that Navajos rarely made pottery in the northern part of the reservation, mentioning that he had been served with a tin plate and cup in 1902. In 1910 the Franciscan Fathers (1968:219, 287–89) also observed that Navajos were making very little pottery. Except for clay cooking pots, which continued to be made for domestic use in limited numbers, china, tin, brass, and enamelware had almost completely replaced pots by that time.[38] Similarly, Navajos no longer made baskets for utilitarian purposes by 1910, except for pitched-basket water bottles and in a few instances, wicker carrying baskets (Forrest 1970:125–26; Franciscan Fathers 1968:291–99). Not many years passed before canteens and wooden kegs replaced these water bottles as well in most areas (Bailey field notes; Hegemann 1963:272).[39] Generally, Navajos continued to make baskets and pots during this period for religious rather than domestic purposes.

Navajo clothing styles underwent drastic changes. During the 1890s, Pendleton blankets and shawls replaced native Navajo blankets, and calico blouses and skirts replaced traditional woolen dresses as articles of everyday dress (Kluckhohn and Leighton 1960:29; Amsden 1975:97, 103). By the 1920s, if not earlier, velveteen blouses and satin skirts had become popular (Bailey field notes; Carson Trading Post Ledger 1929–1930; Hegemann 1963:272). Women continued to buy fabric from the posts and make their own clothing, but sewing methods learned in school by Navajo girls began to produce subtle changes in styles of dress. Though still uncommon, sewing machines were coming into wider use towards the end of the period. In the early 1920s, Eastern issued fifteen sewing machines (PB SR 1920:37; PB SR 1921:37; PB SR 1922:37), and Navajos in Northern Navajo agency sought them eagerly in the mid-1920s (SJ NR 1925:14).

Men's clothing underwent even greater changes. More and more Navajos bought manufactured "western" style clothing from the trading posts, and as early as the turn of the century, the new styles had nearly replaced calico clothing in the San Juan region (Forrest 1970:126–29). Usually, only the older and more traditional men continued to wear calico shirts and pants. In 1906 Superintendent Shelton of Northern Navajo wrote,

> Practically all of the Indians dress partly in civilized garb, the men wearing the cheaper grades of clothing. . . . Blankets are used in winter in preference to overcoats, better suiting the convenience of the wearer inasmuch as the Navaho finds it necessary to carry his bed with him. (RCIA in RSI 1906:280)

To meet the new demand, most of the posts carried a large stock of men's clothing. In 1929 Carson Trading Post in Eastern Navajo carried overalls, pants, shirts, belts, Mexican weskits (a sort of waistcoat), lumber jackets, gloves, hats, caps, coats, sweaters, and mufflers (Carson Trading Post Ledger 1929–1930). As isolated as it was, even Shonto stocked men's cotton workshirts, workshoes, Levi pants, and Stetson and Mallory hats in 1930 (Hegemann 1963:272).

Navajos did not adopt Anglo-American footwear quite so readily. Photographs taken in the San Juan Valley between 1897 and 1902 failed to show a single Navajo wearing either shoes or boots (Bailey and Bailey 1982:293). Although an official reported that Navajos were wearing shoes in Northern in 1906 (RCIA 1906:280), photographs taken in Northern and Eastern in the late 1920s and early 1930s show some Navajos were still wearing moccasins for everyday use. As late as 1927, the superintendent of Leupp claimed that half of the Navajos in his jurisdiction still wore moccasins (L NR 1927:7).

Highly localized changes in Navajo material culture were also taking place during this period, and no two trading posts stocked exactly the same goods. About 1914 or 1915, Mrs. Franc Newcomb of Newcomb Trading Post visited Red Rock Trading Post and found that it emphasized "clothing for men, while our grocery department was larger and carried a greater variety of canned goods, fruit, and smoked meat" (Newcomb 1966:91). When Joseph Schmedding purchased Keams Canyon Trading Post from Lorenzo Hubbell, Jr., in 1916, he discovered a large inventory of baby bottles and nipples, which he had never seen in a trading post before. Hubbell explained that Navajos in that area used baby bottles to feed orphan lambs and that he had done a brisk business in them (Schmedding 1974:319). Thus during the first three decades of the twentieth century, Navajos were introduced to an endless array of Anglo-American material goods, some of which were only adopted locally.

As Navajos became increasingly familiar with Anglo-Americans and their culture during this period, attitudes towards the use of Anglo-American material goods began to change. Navajos not only wanted to own the products of the foreign culture—they came to depend on them. By later standards, exposure to Anglo-American culture reached only minimal proportions, but it far surpassed that of the late nineteenth century. As Frank Mitchell (Frisbie and McAllester 1978:35–36) noted, in the late nineteenth century Navajos rejected some elements of Anglo-American culture—clothing, for example—as "alien." By the 1920s this attitude was certainly losing ground, if it had not disappeared altogether in many areas. As attitudes changed, so did buying habits, and increasing numbers of Navajos, especially students returning from school, emulated the lifestyle of their Anglo-American neighbors. However, these changes were far from universal. Navajos living in isolated areas of the reservation took longer to accept and acquire goods than those who had regular dealings with Anglo-Americans. Even in regions exposed to Anglo-American influence, differences of attitude and economic means significantly affected the speed with which such items were adopted.

THE NAVAJOS DURING THE EARLY TWENTIETH CENTURY

The Navajo culture that started to emerge during the first decade of the twentieth century and which coalesced during the 1920s was quantitatively and qualitatively different from that of the late nineteenth century. Economic necessity led to a great dependence on and integration with the broader national economy. At the same time, increased exposure to Anglo-American culture resulted in a greater acceptance of material goods such as wagons, cars, and clothes, compounding the need for integration.

The Navajo economy of this period did not merely resurrect that which had collapsed in the 1890s. Given the rapidly growing population and a limited land base for grazing livestock, the reestablishment of the older, intensified herding economy was impossible. In order to succeed, the new economy had to be capable of generating increased productivity, not just to meet the basic subsistence and material needs of the expanding population, but also to generate income to purchase the ever-expanding range of Anglo-American material goods that Navajos were coming to need, or at least, to want.

To meet these demands, the Navajos diversified into commercial stock raising and wage labor. Even though limited rangeland prevented Navajo herds from expanding indefinitely and thereby meeting the needs of a growing population, the productivity of the herds could still be increased. It is important to note that market and subsistence value of livestock are not synonymous. An animal may have a higher market value than another, while having equal or lower subsistence value. During the early twentieth century, the Navajos began qualitatively changing their herds, substituting animals of higher market value for animals of high subsistence value. Many non-Navajos had accused the Navajos of being unable to distinguish between quality and quantity, arguing that the Navajos were interested only in the quantity of animals produced. Few accusations could be more ethnocentric, or for that matter, further from the truth. The Navajos did make qualitative judgements about the various breeds of livestock, but unlike Anglo-American ranchers, who based their decisions solely on market value, based their judgments on both market and subsistence value.

Instead of totally commercializing their herds, the Navajos successfully maintained high subsistence value while raising the market value of their livestock. By crossing native animals with different breeds and changing their herding patterns, they increased both the value and quantity of goods for market with minimal sacrifice of subsistence value. In large part, rug weaving enabled them to achieve this balance. In addition to the major livestock products marketed by the Navajos—wool and feeder lambs—rug weaving gave a dimension to their herding economy that Anglo-American and Spanish-American ranchers lacked. By marketing wool as rugs, Navajos greatly enhanced its value. While the human population of the tribe continued to increase, its economy expanded by means of modifications in stock raising patterns.

Even with a modified herding economy, Navajos were not able to totally meet the growing economic needs of their population. As a result, a pattern of regularized seasonal wage labor emerged in the 1920s, generally limited to poorer families. Seasonal wage labor was integrated with their herding economy in such a way that additional income could be generated without the disruption of herding activities.

The 1920s witnessed a coalescence of this new economic system of partially commercialized herding and wage labor, bringing a decade of relative prosperity. Wider exposure and lessening resistance to Anglo-American culture resulted in the adoption of a broad range of Anglo-American ideas and material goods. Major regional differences characterized these changes, and Navajos living in regions that were more exposed to Anglo-American influences changed to the greatest extent. Thus, during the decade of the 1920s the Navajos became an increasingly culturally heterogeneous population.

CHAPTER FOUR

The End of Independence: 1930–1949

Well into the twentieth century, economic self-sufficiency and isolation from Anglo-American society sharply distinguished the Navajos from other North American tribes. Because the government gave the prosperous Navajos little direct support, it lacked the economic leverage to enforce its programs. Consequently, Navajos experienced little of the heavy-handed paternalism that most other tribes endured. Contact with Anglo-Americans increased significantly during the early 1900s, but remained minimal compared to that of other tribes. At least within the confines of the reservation, federal officials were usually content to leave the Navajos alone.

As late as the 1920s, most Navajos still had little experience of the world outside their own culture. Although Anglo-Americans were becoming a major annoyance, they did not yet threaten Navajo cultural integrity or sociopolitical identity. At most, only a few educated Navajos viewed themselves as members of a subordinate, dependent, relatively powerless minority in what had become an Anglo-American dominated world—a view that was to gain increasing acceptance in the years ahead.

During the relatively prosperous 1920s, it is doubtful that any Navajos realized the magnitude of the changes which were going to transpire in the coming quarter century. They were facing three major problems. First, the economic self-sufficiency of the 1920s differed markedly from that of the late nineteenth century. In the 1920s, their prosperity resulted from partially integrating their economy into the national economy and depended in large part on market prices paid for wool, lambs, mohair, and livestock, as well as the demand for rugs and the local availability of wage labor. Regional and national economic trends could now affect them directly. Second, their economy was still based on herds of sheep, goats, and cattle. While the size of Navajo herds appears to have stabilized during the 1920s as a result of increased commercialization, their numbers still far exceeded the carrying capacity of the range. The Navajos were living in a counterfeit paradise. Even though the range could accomodate the herds for a while, it was only a matter of time before overgrazing led to disaster. Third, the Navajo population continued to expand rapidly, exerting a steady pressure on the economy to keep pace.

A combination of factors precipitated the climax. The Great Depression severely damaged Navajo economic self-sufficiency. Under the leadership of Commissioner of Indian Affairs John Collier, the Indian Service seized the opportunity of the depression and the resulting economic dependence of the Navajos to reshape their economy and assert the dominance of the service in Navajo affairs. One of the critical elements of Collier's policy was livestock reduction. The size of the herds was drastically and forcibly reduced. Regulations were developed and implemented that limited the economic importance of herding and forced an ever increasing number of Navajos into the labor market. World War II permanently changed the Navajos' view of themselves and their relation to the white world. Within less than a generation, the Navajos saw their relative prosperity, economic self-sufficiency, and autonomy vanish, to be replaced by poverty, economic dependence, and bureaucratic domination.

THE DEPRESSION

Navajos felt the first effects of the depression in the spring of 1930, when stockmen found that their wool brought a substantially lower price than it had in previous years. The price of wool dropped from 30.2¢ per pound to 19.5¢ on the national market, the lowest price since the disastrous spring of 1921 (appendix B). On the reservation, wool fell from 25¢ to 17¢ per pound. In the fall of 1930, Navajo lambs were bringing only 4¢ to 5¢ per pound, half of the 1929 price (NN NR 1930:18).

On the national level, wool and lamb prices continued to decline, and by 1931 had fallen to their lowest level since early in the century. At the same time, Navajos were spending only slightly less for goods than they had before the crash (appendix B). That fall traders were paying only $1.75 to $2.00 per head for lambs, and before they could resell them, the bottom dropped out of the lamb market. One trader reported selling his lambs for a mere $3.00 per dozen (*Farmington Times Hustler*, Feb. 5, 1932, Feb. 10, 1932). By 1931 the price of Navajo rugs had fallen to half of what it had been two or three years earlier (NN NR 1931:4). Traders extended credit "to the fullest" during the fall and early winter of 1931 (*Farmington Times Hustler*, Dec. 11, 1931), but in early February, they were forced to stop (*Farmington Times Hustler*, Feb. 5, 1932).

Conditions went from bad to worse in the winter of 1931–32. Snow came early and so deep that sheep could not find forage (*Farmington Times Hustler*, Dec. 11, 1931). The agencies distributed hay and oil cakes (feed made of cottonseed and soybean meal) to some families, but deep snow kept wagons and trucks from reaching all of the herds (*Farmington Times Hustler*, Dec. 25, 1931, Jan. 22, 1932). The editor of the *Farmington Times Hustler* wrote,

> Both the Navajo and white stock men seem to have the cards stacked against them this year. With the lowest market prices in years for livestock much of the stock shipped out barely brot [sic] in enough to pay the freight bill. Then unusually early and heavy snows made extra feeding necessary for the stock that was not shipped out, and many head of cattle and sheep have perished in the snow. (Jan. 8, 1932)

While the winter exacted a heavy toll on Anglo herds, its effect on Navajo stockmen was even more disastrous. The following summer, sheep dip counts revealed that the herds had declined by 13 percent during the winter (*Farmington Times Hustler*, Oct. 7, 1932).

In the spring of 1932, wool prices dropped to 8.6¢ per pound, their lowest level since at least 1869 (appendix B). Anticipating that economic conditions would not improve in the near future, Superintendent Stacher of Eastern urged Navajos to "raise everything you can, and put away as much as you can for your own winter use; especially corn" (*Farmington Times Hustler*, Mar. 25, 1932). The Navajos took his advice to heart, and in the spring of 1932, they planted approximately 2,000 additional acres along the San Juan, along with a "considerable area of dry farms" (NN NR 1932:4).

With the depression in full swing, opportunities for off-reservation wage labor declined (NN NR 1932:5). Competition between Navajos and whites for the few available jobs in communities adjacent to the reservation became intense. In Farmington, a contractor hired a crew of Navajos on a gas pipeline, only to be confronted by an enraged group of unemployed Anglo-Americans who surrounded his car, demanding that he fire the Navajos and hire them. The contractor refused, and eventually the mob dispersed (*Farmington Times Hustler*, Sept. 16, 1932). To alleviate the unemployment problem, the Indian Service began hiring fewer full-time and more part-time employees, stretching available funds so that more Navajos could have jobs (*Farmington Times Hustler*, Mar. 18, 1932).

While its economic effects were not as disastrous for the Navajos as those of the 1890s collapse, the Great Depression brought an end to the era of self-sufficiency and presented Indian Service officials with the opportunity to effectively control the tribe. From this time on, the Navajos would in large part be economically dependent on the largess of the United States Congress and the federal bureaucracy.

THE NAVAJOS AND THE NEW DEAL

The election of Franklin Delano Roosevelt in 1932 and his appointment of John Collier as commissioner of Indian affairs in 1933 marked the beginning of a new era in Indian policy.[1] Under Collier's administration, the Indian Service took control of reservation resources for the first time, and in spite of opposition from Navajos, forced obedience to policies created by Anglo-American officials. The Collier era saw a drastic change in the power relationship between the Navajos and the federal government: for the first time since 1868, Navajos were made to feel that they were indeed dependent and powerless.

The depression, which had increased their economic dependence on the government, made the Navajos particularly vulnerable to such a loss of power at this time. They were put at a further disadvantage because agency officials finally had the personnel, funding, and political backing to openly and successfully challenge Navajo autonomy. Because Commissioner Collier was personally involved in formulating and implementing programs on the Navajo reservation, he could put the full weight of his office behind them.

With a population of more than 42,000, the Navajos were the largest tribe under Collier's jurisdiction, and presented what he considered by far his most difficult and pressing problems. The depression had drastically lowered livestock, wool, and crafts prices. Wage labor was becoming increasingly difficult to find. Erosion was destroying large areas of range-land, already overstocked and overgrazed, and no relief was in sight. Because livestock constituted the major source of income, further range deterioration and continuing population growth seemed likely to result in an economic collapse of unprecedented proportions. The situation was hardly better off the reservation. Approximately one-fifth of the Navajos were living on public lands, where they competed directly with white ranchers. The division of Navajo administration into six decentralized agencies compounded Collier's worries. According to Ruth Underhill (1956:234–35),

> he had no way of knowing that President Roosevelt, who had appointed him, would be in office for almost four terms and that he could therefore make a twelve-year approach to the Navajo problem. He felt sure only that, for one presidential term, he had money and backing. And he believed that any plans he had for the Navajos must be pushed through before, perhaps, some reactionary was put in his place.

The new administration had hardly been installed before work began on the Navajo "problem." Four basic objectives were defined: the reduction of livestock on the reservation and a program of erosion control; public works programs designed to minimize the economic impact of stock reduction, and in the long run, to permanently reduce dependence on livestock; congressional legislation to expand reservation boundaries and consolidate off-reservation landholdings; and consolidation of Navajo administration into a single agency, along with a restructuring of tribal government. Collier and his staff tried to implement all of these changes simultaneously.

Livestock Reduction

Certainly in the minds of the Navajos, the livestock reduction program was by far the most controversial component of Collier's programs.[2] Indian Service officials saw the problem as overgrazing, resulting in erosion and permanent deterioration of the range, and stock reduction as the only solution. In contrast,

> The Navajos did not associate too many sheep with erosion and the consequent need to reduce livestock to save the range. Rather, they perceived a different set of factors which produced the erosion — namely, the reduction of stock "caused the rain clouds to diminish,"

which kept the grass from growing, and this in turn resulted in the erosion. The vast majority of the Navajos never accepted or understood the need for livestock reduction. (Roessel and Johnson 1974:x).

Given their different cultural perceptions of the problem, Navajo resistance to stock reduction is not surprising. To them, stock reduction was not only irrational, it was detrimental (Roessel and Johnson 1974). Although the need for such a drastic measure had been noted for several years, previous administrations had chosen to ignore the problem. Thus, it fell to John Collier to take action and bear the accompanying blame.[3]

Although Navajo herds remained well below their prewar levels in the late 1920s, they considerably surpassed the carrying capacity of the range. In 1928 a survey of range conditions on the reservation revealed that Navajos owned 1,300,000 sheep units in sheep, goats, cattle, and horses, and that livestock ownership was not equally distributed (Muck 1948:1, 7). The survey included no estimate of range capacity, nor of the degree of overgrazing at that time. The Tribal Council and the Indian Service held their first joint discussion of overgrazing late in 1928, after the survey was completed. As a result of this meeting, the council adopted a resolution requiring any family with more than 1,000 sheep and goats to pay 15¢ per head per year as a grazing fee or to decrease the size of its herd. However, the regulation was never enforced (Aberle 1966:53).

In 1929 and 1930, a more intensive study of overgrazing led to the conclusion that the number of sheep units on the reservation would have to be reduced from 1,300,000 to 400,000. Congressional hearings in 1931 also called for reduction of Navajo livestock (Aberle 1966:53–54; U.S. Congress 1932, 18:9121–32, 9268–93). Although the problem had been defined, neither the Indian Service nor Congress took any action, and John Collier inherited the problem. According to Aberle (1966:52), Collier's approach to livestock reduction during the 1930s can be divided into two phases: "voluntary" reduction from 1933 to 1936; and "systematic" reduction, involving a permanent regulatory program, from 1937 to 1941.

In October 1933, Collier met with the Navajo Tribal Council, telling it that Navajo herds had to be reduced and an erosion control program developed. He suggested eliminating 200,000 sheep and 200,000 goats, informing the council that while he had the authority to impose restrictions on herd size unilaterally, he wanted their approval. As an inducement, he offered more reservation land, day schools, irrigation projects, and other programs that would employ large numbers of Navajo workers. Participation in the stock reduction program would be voluntary, and the animals would be purchased by the Indian Service. Whether out of fear, hope of economic gain, or a combination of factors, the council adopted the program.[4] At the time, Navajo leaders such as Chee Dodge predicted that a voluntary program was doomed to failure because livestock owners would be willing to sell only their culls (U.S. Congress 1937, 34:17986–7; Aberle 1966:55–56).

Using Federal Emergency Relief Administration (FERA) funds, officials sought to quickly implement the program. The first reduction called for the purchase of 100,000 sheep, and in the fall of 1933, the government assigned each agency a quota of sheep to be purchased. Leupp was responsible for 8,000, Hopi for 10,000, Eastern and Western for 15,000 each, Northern for 20,000, and Southern for 32,000. Agency officials soon realized that few Navajos would willingly sell their stock, and that a truly voluntary program was unworkable. As a result, the government imposed a general 10 percent reduction on every stockowner regardless of herd size, with the further requirement that ewes make up 75 percent of the animals sold. There was considerable opposition to the program, and only 86,000 sheep were purchased (Aberle 1966:56).

The initial reduction, far from solving the problem, did little more than arouse the suspicion of Navajos. Having introduced legislation in Congress to extend the boundaries of the reservation, in March 1934 Collier informed the Tribal Council that passage of the measure depended on further stock reduction. Responding to his pressure, the council agreed to a reduction of 150,000 goats, with the understanding that only large stockowners would have to comply, and that families with less than 100 animals would not be affected. Uneasy over the turn of events, the council did not agree on a plan for implementing goat reduction until July, and at the same time, approved the optional sale of 50,000 sheep (Aberle 1966:57).

Poor management on the part of the government and growing resistance from Navajos hindered the 1934 reduction, and considerable pressure from tribal police had to be applied on stockowners to "voluntarily" sell portions of their herds. East of the reservation, the Indian Service sent Navajo police to the dipping vats, where they forced each owner to sell half his or her herd of goats for $1 per head (Counselor and Counselor 1954:367–68). Similar tactics were employed in other areas (Bailey field notes). The disposal of goats proved a major problem, and created lasting bitterness. Some animals were herded to railheads and shipped, but the market was so limited that most of them had to be disposed of on the reservation. In some areas, the animals were butchered, and the meat given to their owners. In other instances, the animals were shot, piled up, drenched with gasoline, and burned (Aberle 1966:57). Thousands of others were allowed to starve to death in holding pens (Downs 1964:92–93). By these methods, enforcement officials removed approximately 148,000 goats and 50,000 sheep from the range in 1934 (Aberle 1966:57).

The following year, $250,000 in FERA funds made it possible for the program to continue, but by that time Navajo opposition had become so intense that the council refused to approve any such continuation. Only about 16,000 sheep and 15,000 goats were purchased in the fall of 1935 (Aberle 1966:59), and the so-called voluntary phase ended with these purchases.

Aberle (1966:59–60) found that the initial phase of stock reduction had not proven very effective. Between the fall of 1933 and the fall of 1935, the Indian Service purchased a total of 152,742 sheep and 163,060 goats from the Navajos. In the summer of 1933, just before the first purchase, dip records listed 544,726 mature sheep and 164,999 mature goats belonging to Navajos and Hopis on the reservation. In the summer of 1936, following the 1935 reduction, the dip records showed 459,285 mature sheep and 73,600 mature goats (Aberle 1966:70). Although more than 150,000 sheep had been purchased, the total number of mature sheep on the reservation had declined by only about 85,000, and the number of mature goats by about 90,000. Thus, the government had purchased almost 316,000 sheep and goats during this phase of the program, but the number of mature animals on the reservation had actually fallen by only about 175,000 (Aberle 1966:70). Usually, families sold only culls and saved their most productive stock in an attempt to rebuild their herds as quickly as possible.

An emergency measure designed to reduce livestock levels as quickly as possible, the "voluntary" phase was never conceived as a final solution to the problem of overgrazing. Officials anticipated that the herds would soon regain their pre-reduction levels if not controlled, and recommended a program that would further reduce herd size and stabilize Navajo livestock holdings at or below the grazing capacity of the range. Planning for the second phase began before the first phase ended. The Soil Conservation Service was created by Congress in 1935, and as one of its first projects, undertook a comprehensive survey of the Navajo reservation in terms of population distribution, soils, vegetation, water resources, and livestock holdings (Spicer and Collier 1965:187). To facilitate economic planning and livestock control, the service divided the reservation and adjacent off-reservation areas into eighteen[5] geographical and administrative units called land management units or districts (map 6). Vegetation studies were made of each district, allowing the carrying capacity of the range to be determined on a district-by-district basis.

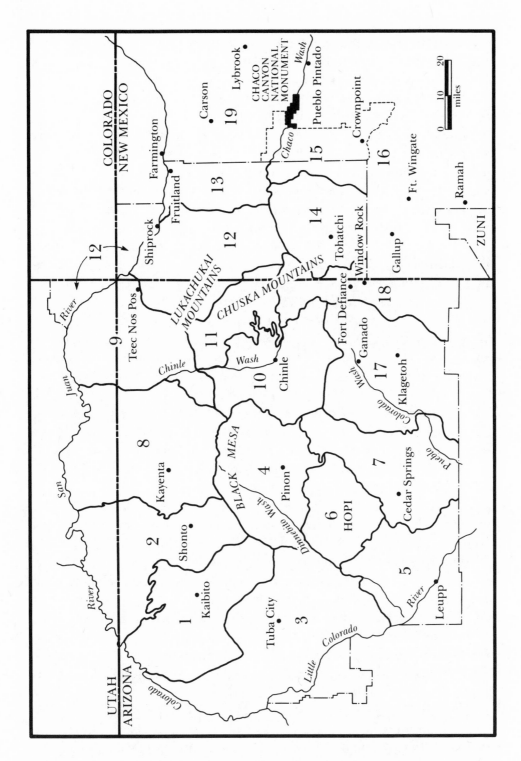

Map 6. Land management districts. Adapted from U.S. Indian Service (1941).

During the second phase of reduction, the government did not trust routine enforcement of livestock regulations to the Navajo police, and in the spring of 1937, a new type of agency official appeared: the range rider. Mostly Anglo-American cowboys, about thirty riders patrolled the reservation (Ward 1951:30; Parman 1976:114). In 1937 the Indian Service employed both range riders and tribal police to conduct the first and only comprehensive Navajo livestock census. Census takers counted sheep and goats during dipping, and rounded up all the cattle and horses on the reservation. They were counted and held until their owners came for them. Although the census tried to establish the number and ownership of animals in each district (Aberle 1966:66), the count was not completely accurate. Some families hid their sheep and goats, refusing to have them dipped. In one incident, tribal police beat three Navajos for failure to comply (*Farmington Times Hustler*, Aug. 20, 1937).

The census listed a total of 379,078 sheep, 57,679 goats, 17,380 cattle, and 38,159 horses. Only mature animals were counted. The figures were converted to sheep units on the following basis: a goat was considered to consume as much forage as a sheep, a cow four times as much, and a horse five times as much. Thus, in 1937 Navajos living on the reservation owned the equivalent of 702,072 sheep. The Soil Conservation survey and stock census revealed that the reservation was overstocked by about 190,000 sheep units. While the problem was common to all districts, it was far more severe in some than in others. With an estimated carrying capacity of 23,372 sheep units and a livestock count of 51,259 sheep units, District 4 was the most seriously overgrazed region. In contrast, District 17 had a carrying capacity of 74,895 sheep units and a livestock count of 77,327 sheep units. The other districts fell somewhere between these two extremes (U.S. Soil Conservation Service 1938:table XIV; Young 1961:168).

From these data a systematic program was developed to reduce Navajo herds and control livestock on the reservation in the future. The program was based on two principles: first, livestock was to be managed at the district level, and Navajos in districts with serious overgrazing would be required to reduce their herds more than those in districts where the problem was less pronounced; second, because grazing resources were limited, and all Navajos had an equal right to use them, the program was to be as "equitable" as possible.

The animals of each stock owner within a land management unit were counted and converted to sheep units, and owners ranked according to the number of sheep units they owned. The total number of sheep units estimated as the carrying capacity was subtracted from the total livestock count

TABLE 6. *Maximum Permit Size by District:*

District	Maximum Permit	District	Maximum Permit
1	225	10	153
2	161	11	105
3	280	12	104
4	72	13	200
5	280	14	61
6 (Hopi)	n.a.	15	88 (on-reservation)
7	237	16	off-reservation
8	154	17	275
9	83	18	238

Source: Aberle 1966:67, table 3.

for a particular land management unit, and the difference cut from the herds of the wealthiest owners. In this manner, officials determined maximum herd size in terms of sheep units. If every large owner in the district reduced the size of their herds to this maximum, then the number of livestock in the district would match its carrying capacity. Those who conceived of the plan thought that only the wealthy families would be affected, since small herds would fall under the maximum.

Since maximum herd size was determined separately for each district as a function of range conditions and carrying capacity, there was significant variation. Stockowners in District 14 were allowed no more than 61 units, the lowest maximum; but in districts 3 and 5, they were allowed 280 units (table 6). Once these calculations were made, each owner received a "sheep" permit, which entitled them to graze a specific number of units within the district (Aberle 1966:66–67, table 3). Permittees could decide for themselves how to allocate their units. For example, a stockowner who had a permit for 200 sheep units could keep 200 sheep, or 200 goats, or 50 cows, or any combination of these categories, as long as the number of mature animals did not exceed the specified forage intensity of 200 sheep units. However, regardless of the size of their allowance, no owner could keep more than two horses on a permit (Aberle 1966:67). The permit system only applied to reservation lands. Navajo families living off the reservation on allotments and using public domain lands came under the Taylor Grazing Act, which we will discuss later in this chapter.

Between 1937 and 1940, the total number of sheep units on the reservation dropped by about 100,000 (Aberle 1966:68, 70). However, the history of livestock reduction in the late 1930s is not well known. Aberle (1966:68) wrote, "Exactly what the Government did during these years is by no means clear," and we have been unable to clarify it.

The permit system was worked out on paper soon after the livestock census of 1937, but for some reason, the government delayed formal issue of the permits until 1940. The system proved far from flawless. Owners who had hidden their herds in 1937 found themselves without permits. Others discovered that their stock had been counted with a relative's, and that only the relative was going to receive a permit. If the oversight or mistake were pointed out, officials would make corrections (Aberle 1966:68; Bailey field notes).

Forced stock reduction under the permit system lasted little more than a year. When the United States entered World War II, most of the range riders were discharged (Parman 1976:286), and the attention of officials shifted to other, more pressing problems.

Commissioner Collier realized that stock reduction would have severe economic repercussions, and to cushion the impact, both temporary and permanent sources of income would have to be found or created. In the 1930s, the federal government sponsored a host of national public work projects to alleviate unemployment caused by the depression, and a wide range of these programs—mainly construction projects—were put into effect on the reservation. The Soil Conservation Service, the Civilian Conservation Corps (CCC), and the Indian Service employed Navajos to build and upgrade roads, drill more than 300 water wells, install windmills, and construct almost 2,000 water reservoirs (Ricketts and McPhee 1941:13). Some 25 CCC camps were opened on the reservation in 1933, and Navajos rushed to enroll. At Southern, a quota of 1,200 workers was almost reached in four days. Navajo CCC workers made truck trails for logging and fire access, put out poisoned grain to kill prairie dogs, and built storage tanks and dams. They were paid $30 a month and received literacy and job training, and a balanced diet. To prevent further erosion, the Soil Erosion Service, which became the Soil Conservation Service, employed 705 Navajos to build dams and terraces, reseed grass, and plant trees. The service established 13 demonstration stations on the reservation, restoring the depleted range by letting it lie fallow, fencing, better animal husbandry methods, and the exclusion or limitation of goats and horses. A large hospital, which opened in 1938, was built with Works Progress Administration money at

Fort Defiance, and in 1934 and 1935, 43 day schools were built on the reservation. Other Navajos worked on the construction of the tribal headquarters at Window Rock, and in 1940, the tribal sawmill was dedicated, employing about 100 Navajos (Parman 1976:34–35, 81–89, 96, 98, 186, 195, 225, 264; U.S. Bureau of Indian Affairs 1949:9–10).

Income from reservation wage labor jumped from about $200,000 in 1932 (Young 1961:212) to more than $1,500,000 in 1936 (U.S. Soil Conservation Service 1938:table IV; see table 9), indicating that work programs had substantial short-term economic benefit. However, the Indian Service "had hoped that the Indians would save their earnings and sell off marketable livestock through the trading posts to pay for living expenses as they had in the past. Instead, the security-minded tribesmen had kept their animals and used their wages to buy goods at the trading posts" (Parman 1976:97–98). During the late 1930s, the number of projects and income from wage labor declined rapidly. Superintendent E. R. Fryer laid off one-half of the CCC workers in 1938, and the program was discontinued after Pearl Harbor (Parman 1976:270–71).

The Land Question

The land question still had not been resolved when John Collier took office.[6] Large numbers of Navajo families continued to occupy portions of the public domain (mainly in New Mexico, but also in Arizona) both with and without legal allotments. Early in 1932, H. J. Hagerman[7] submitted a report recommending the addition of approximately three million acres to the reservation by purchase, exchange, and consolidation. The report also recommended the immediate discontinuation of individual allotments (Kelly 1968:128; Mosk 1944:47; Parman 1976:132).

Based on these recommendations, bills were introduced in Congress in 1932 and 1933 to enlarge the reservation in Arizona and New Mexico. While the Arizona congressional delegation was agreeable, the New Mexico delegation vigorously opposed these extensions, and both bills were defeated. In order to gain at least some ground, in 1934 Collier had the legislation divided into two separate bills: one for Arizona, and one for New Mexico. Congress quickly passed the bill extending the reservation in Arizona (U.S. *Statutes at Large* 48, 1:960), but the bill for the extension in New Mexico died in the House (Mosk 1944:48; Kelly:1968:128–29; Parman 1976:133).

Sanford Mosk (1944:52–53) believed that the 1934 enactment of the Taylor Grazing Act, intended to provide for the management of public domain lands and protect them from overgrazing and soil deterioration, also hindered passage of the New Mexico bill. The act provided for the division of public domain land into grazing districts to be administered in part by locally elected grazing committees. Since many Navajos were illiterate, they would not have been eligible to vote or hold positions on these committees. In addition, use allocations of public domain lands were to be based on improvements—mainly those providing water for livestock—owned by individual ranchers. Few Navajos owned such improvements. In January 1935, the Grazing Service was created as a division of the Department of the Interior to carry out the provisions of the Taylor Grazing Act; specifically, to manage federal lands, organize grazing districts, and begin systematic planning for their use. The Taylor Grazing Act had a major impact on off-reservation Navajos in New Mexico because it authorized the Grazing Service to take control of federal lands adjacent to their allotments (Mosk 1944:54–55).

Perhaps sensing a loss of congressional support, Collier pushed to secure passage of the bill. In 1936 a subcommittee of the Senate Committee on Indian Affairs held hearings in New Mexico to discuss a new extension bill. Local Navajos were as concerned about Collier's stock reduction program as they were about the land extension bill, however, and much of their testimony consisted of diatribes against him and his appointed officials (U.S. Congress 1937, Pt. 34). Members of the Twin Lake Chapter wrote the subcommittee, "We hope the President of the United States, Mr. Roosevelt, will appoint another man which will be kind and build up the tribe, instead of pushing them back with threats and fear as the man now in office is doing" (U.S. Congress 1937, Pt. 34:17972). Because of this confusion of issues, the Indian Service and the Navajos failed to present a united front.

Local white ranchers, who had exercised virtually no control over the use of public domain lands before passage of the Taylor Grazing Act, were revising their position on the extension issue.[8] Only a portion of these ranchers had opposed extension of the reservation during the early 1930s. The "checkerboard" of lands owned by Indians, whites, the railroad, and federal and state governments had proven disadvantageous to all parties, and many white ranchers believed it was only a matter of time before the reservation was extended. As late as March 1, 1935, the *Farmington Times Hustler* reported that San Juan Basin stockmen supported the Indian Service plan to consolidate Indian landholdings and extend the boundary of the reservation. Local non-Navajo support for consolidation and extension quickly disappeared the following year, probably for a variety of reasons. Certainly, statements by Collier, Secretary of the Interior Harold Ickes, and

Superintendent E. R. Fryer about white stockmen did not create harmonious relations. Before the arrival of the Senate subcommittee, Ickes and Collier stated that if the Navajos "are not given more grazing land there will be bloodshed following disputes with white stockmen." Fryer accused white ranchers of cheating the Indians, and said that Navajos were "in desperate condition. Their lands are being grazed out by white sheep men, some of whom drive sheep from Colorado for the winter" (*Farmington Times Hustler*, June 5, 1936).

The passage of the Taylor Grazing Act also affected public opinion. According to Mosk (1944:54), many white ranchers who had been willing to exchange their land for land outside the extended boundaries of the reservation came to oppose expansion, perhaps because by 1936 it had become clear that the act would benefit them more than it would benefit Navajo allottees. In his testimony before the Senate subcommittee in 1936, Hugh Calkins, regional director of the Soil Conservation Service, stated:

> The act and the Secretary's regulations pursuant thereto contain certain provisions that would appear to have a somewhat adverse effect upon the welfare of Indian livestock owners. . . . Indians in the eastern Navajo country would in many cases . . . be under a disadvantage in attempting to secure [grazing] permits. . . . Frequently it might be found that property qualification was inadequate. This is particularly true because stock water, often stipulated as a necessary qualification, has in the majority of cases been developed by the Government and is, therefore, not the property of the individual range users. . . . A further disadvantage is that the Navajos would have difficulty in securing adequate representation on the [local district] advisory board, which is largely responsible for administration of grazing under the regulations of the Secretary. . . . Many Navajos are unable to write and would, therefore, be ineligible to vote. (U.S. Congress 1937, 34:17619–20, quoted in Mosk 1944:54–55)

Navajos also realized the inequalities of the Taylor Grazing Act. Robert Tso, a Navajo from the Cuba area, contended, "Stockmen favor putting the Navajo Indians under the Taylor Grazing Act, [because] young Indians owning no allotments would have no right to a grazing permit within the Taylor Grazing District" (*Farmington Times Hustler*, Mar. 25, 1938).

In the face of growing local opposition, Collier failed to have the Navajo reservation extended in New Mexico, and off-reservation families came under the supervision of the Grazing Service. In 1939, however, designation of the area occupied by off-reservation Navajos as a "special grazing district"—that is, one not exclusively reserved for commercial ranchers (Mosk 1944:55–56)—partially alleviated the disadvantages pinpointed by Calkins in 1936. Each grazing district had one advisory board dominated by local ranchers, but in addition, the special grazing district had a second advisory board composed of representatives of locally active government agencies such as the Indian Office, the Soil Conservation Service, and the Forest Service.

The Restructuring of Navajo Administration

By 1933 the government recognized the need for a centralized administration to develop and implement programs for the Navajos, as well as the need for a more effective tribal governing body. The discovery of oil in the San Juan jurisdiction in 1922 first demonstrated the need for reform. Acting on the premise that the San Juan mineral resources belonged to all Navajos and not just those within the jurisdiction, in 1923 the government created an elected Navajo Tribal Council and the position of commissioner to the Navajos (Kelly 1968:49, 62–64). This position was created primarily to manage tribal resources such as oil and timber, but also for general supervision of the six agencies (Williams 1970:22). However, the position did not produce any integration of programs among the agencies.

John Collier believed that Navajo economic development depended on a single, well-coordinated administrative program. In 1935 the six agencies were consolidated into a single Navajo Agency with its administrative offices at Window Rock (Young 1961:598–601).[9] Collier also advocated tribal self-government, and to this end, in 1934 he secured passage of the Indian Reorganization Act, also known as the Wheeler-Howard Act. Under the terms of this act, any tribe could organize a constitutional government if it chose to do so. Under pressure from Indian Service officials, most tribes quickly agreed to reorganize, but more from opposition to Collier's administration than from dissatisfaction with the terms of the act, the Navajos rejected the idea (Williams 1970:23).

However, the tribe could not resist governmental pressure for very long (Williams 1970:23).[10] In 1934 the Tribal Council increased its membership from twelve to twenty-four (Young 1961:377), and in 1936 it appointed a committee to draft a tribal constitution (Williams 1970:23). Secretary of the Interior Ickes rejected the proposed constitution in 1937 (Young 1961:380–81), and in July 1938, at Collier's request and without Navajo consent, he issued a set of bylaws creating a new Tribal Council. The positions of chairman, vice chairman, and seventy-four delegates were to be filled by popular election. Since the bylaws did not define any limits to the authority of either the council or its officers, the new tribal government possessed much broader powers than the 1923 council (Williams 1970:23–24).

While strengthening the Tribal Council, the Collier administration withdrew its support from the "chapter" system. According to Solon Kimball and John Provinse (1942:24),

> When the Chapters became centers of gossip and agitation they were quickly disowned [by the government]. . . . An artificial system like the chapters had vitality only so long as it was subsidized by the government. When that subsidy was withdrawn, they collapsed. The reason for the collapse can be attributed to the fact that Navajos with power and prestige took little active part and the chapters were foreign to Navajo thinking and experience.

Evidently, the government withdrew its support from the chapters because these "centers of gossip and agitation" resisted official policy. Even though the number of active chapters declined from eighty to forty between 1937 and 1943, the survival of those forty in the face of government opposition indicates that in spite of their artificial nature, they satisfied an important need (Williams 1970:38, 40).[11]

By the late 1930s, Collier had been successful in implementing most of his policies. Besides administrative centralization and reform of tribal government, he witnessed changes in the relationship between officials and the tribe. The superintendent now had to deal only with the Tribal Council, whose membership and powers had been expanded, and the resources at his disposal for supervising and policing the reservation had increased dramatically. At the same time, the economic relationship between the Navajos and the federal government had shifted radically in the direction of increased dependence. Along with the inability of Navajos to secure off-reservation employment, livestock reduction had considerably undermined Navajo economic self-sufficiency. Under these conditions, the need for temporary government jobs handed officials the economic leverage they had previously lacked.

WORLD WAR II

Beginning in 1938, federal programs on the Navajo reservation started to wind down. It had become obvious that the problems in Europe would eventually involve the United States, and domestic spending declined as the country began to increase its level of military preparedness (Parman 1976:281).

Navajos took an active part in World War II.[12] The Citizenship Act of 1924 had made them legal citizens of the United States (Strickland 1982:143) and subject to the draft. Registration centers were set up at 125 points on the reservation (Parman 1976:281). In January 1941, nine Navajos from San Juan County, New Mexico, were drafted—the first taken from that part of the reservation, although Navajos from other areas may have been drafted slightly earlier (*Farmington Times Hustler,* Jan. 17, 1941). By December 1941, approximately 5,000 Navajos had registered, of whom 200 had been drafted, and 150 enlisted (*Indians at Work* 1941b, 9:4, 18). Some Navajos joined the New Mexico National Guard and were in the Philippines in December 1941 when the Japanese attacked. Navajo national guardsmen fought the Japanese from December 8, 1941, to April 8, 1942, until the American surrender on Bataan. There were 21 Navajos among the 6,700 Americans taken prisoner. Ten Navajos, including the son of Tribal Chairman J. C. Morgan, did not survive the captivity (Johnson 1977:20–21, 27; LaRouche 1943:17).

At first, Navajos expressed some of the same attitudes towards this war as they had towards the last. Largely out of a deep-seated suspicion of the government, many young Navajos failed to register for the draft when registration began in October 1940. Some thought that draft registration was somehow related to livestock reduction. At least one Navajo leader argued that Navajos should not become involved unless the Germans actually invaded the United States (Parman 1976:281–82). However, after the Japanese attack on Pearl Harbor, Navajo attitudes toward the war started to change, and the majority of Navajos came to look upon the war as "their war." Tribal Chairman J. C. Morgan and the Tribal Council supported the war effort from the outset (Parman 1976:282–83). A Navajo marine said his "main reason for going to war was to protect my land . . . I wanted to live on the earth in the future" (Johnson 1977:61).

Even after Pearl Harbor, some Navajos were reluctant to go to war. In the Fruitland area, local Navajos organized a mounted patrol to help register eligible males who had avoided registering for the draft (*Farmington Times Hustler,* Jan. 30, 1942). By December 1942, approximately 1,400 Navajos were serving in the army, marines, or navy, but of this number, only about 350 had volunteered (LaRouche 1943:17). Many spoke little or no English, presenting the military with communication problems. Of those who were called for the draft, 88 percent were found to be illiterate (Sanchez 1948:25). At Wingate Indian Service Vocational School, the army set up a special "Preinduction School" to prepare Navajos over eighteen for military service, teaching "military English" and basic military skills (LaRouche 1943:17).

Not long after the United States entered the war, a Marine Corps officer named Philip Johnston, who had spent his childhood among the Navajos, came up with the idea of transmitting battlefield messages in the Navajo language so the enemy could not understand them (Parman 1976:287). Several Indian languages had been used during World War I for battlefield communications, but the complexity of the Navajo language and the large pool of native speakers made it especially suitable. In May 1942 the first platoon of Navajo "code talkers" completed training, and proved so successful that other units were soon formed (Paul 1973; Underhill 1956:242–43).

Besides serving in the armed forces, Navajos worked at a variety of war-related occupations. In the summer of 1941, the army started to convert Fort Wingate into an ordnance depot and hired about 800 Navajos to work on its construction (*Indians at Work* 1941a:12, 25). About 1,500 Navajos had worked on the project by its completion, many of whom continued to work there. Local army engineers were so impressed with the work of Navajo construction workers on the Fort Wingate project that another 1,500 were hired to work on the Bellemont depot, near Flagstaff, Arizona. The Bellemont post commander thought that besides being unquestionably loyal to their country, Navajos were the best workers available, and the army even allowed them and their families to live in tents and hogans within the depot enclosure (LaRouche 1943:18–19). After construction was completed, about 500 Navajos were kept on, including a woman who policed the main entrance at night (Johnson 1977:48–49). In 1943 more than 100 Navajos worked as carpenters, plumbers, and laborers on the construction of a helium plant near Shiprock, and management wanted to retain Navajos as regular employees after the plant was completed in 1944 (*Farmington Times Hustler*, Dec. 10, 1943).

As the war progressed and labor shortages became more acute, labor recruiters for ordnance depots, railroads, and farms scoured the reservation in search of Navajos who were willing to work:

> Big stake body trucks stopped at remote trading posts all over the reservation. Drivers offered the few English speaking Navajos a dollar a head or two dollars a head, or whatever dollars it took to gather up a truckload of workers. . . . Navajo men . . . were packed in trucks to standing room only. (Boyce 1974:130)

Recruiters searched even the most isolated areas of the reservation, such as Shonto:

> The war brought labor recruiters into every part of the Navaho country for the first time. Prior to 1940, Navahos had been regarded as a significant labor force only in localized agricultural areas; the great majority of Shonto men had never held a paying job, except perhaps for a few days or weeks on a local construction project. . . . By 1943 recruiters were in every part of the reservation, assisted by traders, and any able-bodied Navaho, regardless of education, could have his pick of steady, well-paid jobs, with housing and free transportation thrown in. . . . Before World War II not more than six men in the community had ever earned wages except on temporary Government projects, and none had served in the armed forces. At the end of the war only two men had been in the army, but at least 50 out of a total labor force of around 70 had been employed either in the Navajo Ordnance Depot near Flagstaff or on the Santa Fe Railroad. Many also engaged in seasonal agricultural work in Utah and Idaho. (Adams 1963:50)

Most Navajos preferred jobs close to home, but a sizable number migrated to the west coast for jobs in aviation plants, shipyards, and naval installations (LaRouche 1943:18).

By the end of the war, some 3,600 Navajos had served in the military throughout the world (Underhill 1956:242), and approximately 15,000 others had worked in various war-related industries on and off the reservation (*Farmington Times Hustler*, May 23, 1947)—significant statistics, considering that the Navajo population in 1945 was estimated at 59,009, of whom only 24,784 were over nineteen years of age (Johnston 1966a:367). In one way or another, whether by military service, employment in war industries, or participation in scrap metal drives (LaRouche 1943:19), the war effort involved the vast majority of adult Navajos.

While the war was being fought, many of the more controversial government programs were scaled down. Lack of funds and personnel resulted in the closing of five hospitals and eighteen day schools. From a Navajo perspective, the most significant change occurred in the enforcement of stock reduction regulations. Most Navajos probably had no way of knowing that the change reflected reductions in spending and manpower shortages, rather than a revision of government policy. Superintendent Fryer, who had become the personification of stock reduction, left the reservation to take charge of the relocation of west coast Japanese. His replacement, James

Stewart, reportedly "lacked Fryer's forcefulness and devotion to the livestock program." Stewart used a low-key approach based on persuading the Navajos to adhere to the stock reduction program. Even if he had wanted to force reduction, reduced funding and the layoff of many range riders would have made it extremely difficult (Parman 1976:285–86).

CHANGES IN THE NAVAJO ECONOMY
AND THE POSTWAR COLLAPSE

The Collier administration's program of stock reduction succeeded in that the number of animals on the reservation eventually fell below the estimated carrying capacity of the range. In 1933, the year that stock reduction began, the Navajos and Hopis were grazing 999,725 sheep units on the reservation, including 544,726 sheep, 164,999 goats, 20,000 cattle, and 42,000 horses. The stock reduction program caused a steady decline in these figures during the 1930s and early 1940s, and even though the program was neglected during the war, livestock numbers continued to fall.[13] By 1944 the reservation was supporting only 548,000 sheep units, approximately 35,000 above carrying capacity (Aberle 1966:70; Young 1961:168). Although numbers of livestock declined in all categories, the relative composition of the herds in terms of sheep units changed significantly (appendix A). Goats underwent the sharpest decline, making up 16.5 percent of the herds in 1933 and only 7.6 percent in 1944. In the same time, cattle decreased from 8 percent to 5.8 percent, sheep increased from 54.5 percent to 62.8 percent, and in spite of official attempts to rid the range of "useless" horses, horses increased from 21 percent to 23.7 percent.

In order to compensate Navajos for income lost through the forced reduction of herds, the government developed programs to increase the commercial value of the remaining stock. Research conducted at the Southwestern Range and Sheep Breeding Laboratory, established at Fort Wingate in 1935 as a cooperative program of the Department of the Interior and the Department of Agriculture (Blunn 1940:99; Parman 1976:127–30), helped improve the weight and quality of Navajo fleeces as well as the weight and market value of lambs. The laboratory was trying to develop a sheep that was well suited to the environmental and climatic conditions of Navajo country, and at the same time, one that would serve the economic needs of the people. Hoping for an animal with heavier fleece, wool that was suitable for weaving, and heavier lambs, they produced a hybrid cross: one-quarter Romney, one-quarter Corriedale, and one-half native sheep.

Because the wool of the hybrid was too fine for weaving and the weight increases were not as large as anticipated, the laboratory experimented with other crosses after 1942, striving for the "perfect" hybrid.

In response to more immediate needs, the Navajo Service (Department of the Interior) initiated a massive stock improvement program with Rambouillet rams in the late 1930s (Parman 1976:128–30). By the late 1940s, the Navajo herds were primarily Rambouillet; the wool they produced was less than ideal for weaving:

> The Rambouillet wool is kinky and heavy in grease. This makes it almost impossible to hand card, and requires that it be scoured before carding, which was not necessary with the old Navajo straight and almost greaseless wool. . . . [The new wool] . . . will naturally reduce the number of rugs produced. . . . Rugs woven of hand-carded Rambouillet wool are not of as good quality as those made of the straight wool. (U.S. Bureau of Indian Affairs 1949:26)

Nevertheless, the Navajo livestock industry made general gains in all areas. Between 1933 and 1935, the weight of a Navajo fleece averaged only 4.1 pounds, but rose to 6.5 pounds by 1945–1947 (U.S. Bureau of Indian Affairs 1949:21). This increase kept wool production relatively stable in spite of reduced numbers of animals (table 7). The production of marketable lambs made similar progress. Despite reduced numbers of mature sheep on the reservation, the number of marketable lambs produced each year increased from 273,168 in 1933–35 to 314,324 in 1942–44, but fell back to 253,239 in 1945–47, probably because of increased domestic consumption after the war (table 7). From 1933 to 1947, the average weight per lamb jumped from 54.5 pounds to 64.5 pounds, the result of hybridization (U.S. Bureau of Indian Affairs 1949:22). Cash income from sales of livestock increased steadily (table 7). Adjusting for inflation in terms of 1935 dollars, the average annual income from livestock in 1945–47 still represented about a 60 percent increase over the 1933–35 figure (U.S. Bureau of Indian Affairs 1949:20–21). The market value of wool and lambs increased far more rapidly than the rate of inflation during this period. Wool climbed from 20.6¢ per pound in 1933 to 42¢ per pound in 1947, and during the same period the price of lambs per hundredweight went from $5.04 to $20.50 (appendix B). Thus, the increase in cash income from livestock resulted more from market conditions than from the effects of Indian Service programs.

Increased income from livestock, resulting in part from the commercialization of Navajo herds, was achieved at the expense of the Navajo rug

TABLE 7. Wool and Lamb Production, and Annual Cash Income from Livestock:
1933–1947

Period	Wool per Year (pounds)	Lambs per Year	Annual Cash Income
1933–35	2,089,121	273,168	$ 953,619
1936–38	2,316,403	288,572	1,006,950
1939–41	2,425,976	317,220	1,757,053
1942–44	2,189,681	314,324	1,874,004
1945–47	2,046,597	253,239	2,429,149

Source: U.S. Bureau of Indian Affairs 1949:20–21.

industry—not a trivial sacrifice. In 1924 rugs accounted for an estimated 22.2 percent of the income in Northern Navajo, but in 1936, with high income from wage labor and low demand for rugs, they accounted for only 6 percent of the tribe's income as a whole (U.S. Soil Conservation Service 1938:table III). In 1940, when income from wage labor had fallen off considerably, weaving accounted for 9 percent of the total Navajo income (U.S. Bureau of Indian Affairs 1941:table III).[14]

Although government policies focused on raising the commercial value of livestock and livestock products, officials tried to break up the large herds and more "equitably" distribute sheep permits as part of the reduction program: two essentially contradictory approaches. In defense of the second, officials stated:

> It is obvious that there is no room for the commercial Navajo livestock operator on the reservation and the efforts of the government are now being directed toward the elimination of the "big fellow" to give breathing space for the horde of subsistence and below-subsistence operators. (Ricketts and McPhee 1941:6–7)

Navajos claimed that a herd of between 400 and 500 sheep and goats could support a family at subsistence level (Farmington Times Hustler, Feb. 28, 1941; Minutes of Navajo Tribal Council, June 1940:128). The Indian Service put the figure at 250 mature sheep (Krug 1948:29). Presuming the Navajos were including mature and immature animals in their figure, the difference in the two estimates would not be significant. Not a single family on the reservation received a sheep permit in the 400 to 500 range, and less than 200 families received permits in excess of 250 sheep units (Krug 1948:30). Thus, even according to the government's assessment of subsistence levels, Navajos were not allowed to own enough livestock to succeed at commercial ranching.

Given such small livestock permits, subsistence herding represented the most effective economic use of livestock, but by concentrating on commercial value, officials actually lowered the subsistence value of the herds.[15] For example, milk goats had a far greater subsistence value than sheep, but because of their low commercial value suffered the sharpest decline of all categories of livestock during stock reduction. The resulting drop in the subsistence value of the herds caused Navajos to become more dependent on trade and the cash economy.

The Collier administration turned to farming as a possible alternative to herding, favoring the development of irrigation projects to increase farm production. In early addresses to the Navajo Tribal Council, John Collier suggested developing 25,000 acres of additional farmland, but did not specify where or when the land was to be developed (Parman 1976:117 n.). Orval Ricketts and John McPhee (1941:13) stated that eight new irrigation projects were completed on the reservation between 1933 and 1941, and seventeen older projects either expanded or improved. Randolph Downes and Elizabeth Clark (1946:36) noted that the number of acres under ditch increased from 11,169 in 1933 to 23,400 in 1945.

Construction of the Fruitland ditch, the largest and most important irrigation project, began in the fall of 1933 (*Farmington Times Hustler*, Nov. 10, 1933). Collier secured substantial funding through the newly created Works Progress Administration, and work accelerated. If things went according to plan, the ditch would encompass 5,100 acres along the San Juan, including farmland under three earlier ditches, and 255 families would settle on 20-acre farms along its length (*Farmington Times Hustler*, July 20, 1934; Parman 1976:117). The first section of the project was finished in 1935. Farm assignments were made to 51 Navajos, but Superintendent Fryer refused to approve the assignments because of the limited farming resources of the reservation, the wealth in livestock of some of the recipients, and their failure to agree to livestock reductions. Fryer believed that subsistence farming, not commercial farming, should be the goal at Fruitland. A new plan reduced the farms to 10 acres and limited assignments to Navajos who owned no livestock or who agreed to dispose of what livestock they had (U.S. Congress 1937, 34:17848; Parman 1976:117–19).

Chaos resulted. Families who farmed land under the old ditches were allowed to proceed with their planting, but others refused to accept farms

Two Navajo girls, c. 1864-68. The dark woolen dresses were typical for women during most of this period. Photographer unknown, courtesy Museum of New Mexico #38208.

Agent Arny and Navajos, perhaps a party of the Navajo police, at Fort Defiance, c. 1874-75. The man in the middle with a dark shirt and hat is Manuelito. The white cotton shirts and pants were typical attire for Navajo men during this period. Photographer unknown, courtesy Smithsonian Institution.

Navajo man at a summer camp, c. 1890. Photographer Ben Wittick, courtesy School of American Research Collections in the Museum of New Mexico #16017.

A temporary Navajo sheep camp consisting of a brush windbreak in a small stand of junipers, c. 1890. The woman on the right appears to be wearing a striped Navajo blanket, while the woman holding a baby to the left is wearing a Pendleton. Photographer Ben Wittick, courtesy School of American Research Collections in the Museum of New Mexico #15926.

Pesh-laki-ilhini (on the left), a silversmith, winter 1892-93. Forked-stick hogans such as this one were the kind of dwelling most frequently constructed during this period. Silversmithing tools included a bow drill operated by the man at the right and a bellows next to the boy. Photographer James Mooney, courtesy Smithsonian Institution.

A temporary Navajo camp, c. 1890. All three women are wearing machine-manufactured blankets and calico blouses and skirts. The man is wearing Anglo-American clothing, including the hat and either boots or shoes. In the foreground are two tin coffee pots, commercial ceramic bowls, other metal utensils, and a wooden water keg. Photographer Ben Wittick, courtesy School of American Research Collections in the Museum of New Mexico #15930.

By the early decades of the twentieth century, trading posts had become a focal point of economic and social life. This group at Carson's reflects this increasing importance. The men are dressed in shirts, pants, hats, and boots purchased at the post, while the women wear machine-made Pendleton blankets and dresses made of purchased cloth. Photographer unknown, courtesy Sam Drolet.

Starting in 1928, the chapters became the center of community political activity. This photograph was taken at the dedication of the Huerfano chapter house in 1931. Photographer unknown, courtesy Sam Drolet.

The annual community dipping of sheep for scabies had become part of Navajo life. The sheep were driven from the corral in back into the solution-filled trough. Photographer unknown, courtesy Sam Drolet.

Although wagons had become common by the late 1920s, and some wealthy families even owned automobiles, most Navajos still traveled on horseback. Photographer unknown, courtesy Sam Drolet.

Weaving remained a critical source of income. Rugs had replaced blankets, however, with design elements frequently created and standardized by traders instead of weavers. The design of this Crystal-style rug appeared in the J. B. Moore 1911 mail-order catalog. Photographer Frasher.

Larger vertical- and horizontal-log hogans were becoming the style. A chimney protrudes from the smokehole at the top of the roof. The women are wearing high button shoes. Photographer Mullarky.

After the war, government officials recognized the pressing need for better education for the Navajos. Here, youngsters learn the language of sheep husbandry at Hunter's Point School, c. 1950. Photographer unknown, courtesy Navajo Tribal Museum.

212

Traditional ways of life and technological innovation meet on the reservation, c. 1950. A Navajo family traveling by horse and wagon pause for a chat. In the background, a work crew erects a power line. Photographer unknown, courtesy Navajo Tribal Museum.

A horse-drawn wagon and its descendants—pickups, c. 1950. Old and new construction methods are represented by the log structure and the framed, pitched-roof buildings. Photographer unknown, courtesy Navajo Tribal Museum.

Navajos became increasingly dependent on wage labor after 1950. The excavation crew for the Lupton Highway Project poses in front of Indian Trails Trading Post, June 9, 1959. Photographer W. W. Wasley, courtesy Arizona State Museum.

Increasingly, Navajo preachers took over the job of spreading the gospel on the reservation. The sign announces the Rudy Yazzie revival, Upper Fruitland, October 1985. Photographer Scott Sandlin, courtesy Scott Sandlin.

Government-built housing, Window Rock, Arizona, 1981. Photographer unknown, courtesy Navajo Tribal Museum.

under the new conditions. When attempts to relocate families from outside the region failed, the new farmland was left unplanted. The final assignments were not made until the late 1940s, nine years after the project was completed (Bailey and Bailey 1982:396–400; *Farmington Times Hustler*, Aug. 11, 1939; Sasaki 1960:44).

The Navajos felt they had been betrayed at Fruitland, and a legacy of distrust followed the government to other areas. Concerning the last-minute change in allotted farm acreage, Maria Chabot (c. 1941:35) wrote,

> The Government's vacillation and failure to keep its promises to the Navajos in regard to this project, even if justified on the grounds of greater good to a greater number of people, is the source of much of the bitterness and distrust surrounding irrigation projects in other parts of the reservation, today.[16]

Some families resisted government irrigation projects elsewhere on the reservation because they were afraid that they would lose their old farms; others, because they thought the government would take their surplus crops. In 1945 Navajos were actually farming only 16,590 acres (Downes and Clark 1946:36).

As a result of stock reduction, a damaged subsistence base, and the failure of farm development projects that might have compensated at least in part for other losses, Navajos became increasingly dependent upon trading posts for food. In about 1940, the trader at Outlaw Post noted that "80 percent more meat [had] sold in the last two years," and the trader at Mexican Water estimated a "20 percent increase in the Navajo's cost of living. Goat reduction didn't hurt money income," he explained, "but hurt them at home because they had to replace with stuff bought at store" (Chabot c. 1941:19). Government surveys confirmed this trend. A 1936 study estimated that in dollar value, Navajos produced 53 percent of the food they ate (U.S. Soil Conservation Service 1938:table XXIV), but by 1940, a similar survey put the figure at only 35 percent. Thus, by 1940 Navajos were obtaining almost two-thirds of their food by trade, and in some districts, well over 70 percent (U.S. Bureau of Indian Affairs 1941:table XXXI).

This change had important economic consequences for the Navajos. With the herds reduced, not just the poor, but virtually every family had to find wage work to meet basic needs. Federal work programs provided numerous opportunities for wage work in the mid-1930s, and Navajo income from on-reservation wage labor increased from $200,000 in 1932 to $800,000 the following year (Young 1961:212). Youngblood (1935:24) found that "during the latter half of 1933, the trading posts enjoyed

TABLE 8.   *Average Gross Sales of Trading Posts: 1929–1933*

Year	Number of Trading Posts	Average Sales	Percentage of 1929
1929	20	$60,380.39	100.0
1930	26	41,267.72	68.4
1931	26	35,525.41	58.8
1932	29	26,163.57	43.3
1933	32	34,852.50	57.7

Source: Youngblood 1935:24.

increased business resulting from Public Works payrolls." The average gross sales of posts increased by approximately 33 percent between 1932 and 1933 (table 8), and the *Farmington Times Hustler* (Dec. 15, 1933) described the Navajos as "lousy with money."

In spite of stock reduction and the depression, the mid-1930s were relatively prosperous years for the Navajos. Both the number of government projects on the reservation and the number of Navajos they employed continued to increase, until in 1936 Navajo income from on-reservation wage labor totaled $1,546,590, and per capita income from all sources came to $141.71 (tables 9, 10). This was a relatively high level of income for Navajos during this period.

These prosperous times did not last long. In the late 1930s, the government reduced the herds still further and began phasing out public works programs, which had cushioned Navajos against earlier reductions. By 1940 Navajo income from on-reservation wage labor had fallen to only $892,350, and per capita income to $78.81 (tables 9, 10). As economic conditions deteriorated, trading posts, which had become the principal source of food for the Navajos, were forced to cut back on credit to their poorer customers. Food shortages were reported, and malnutrition increased (Chabot c. 1941:19, 27–29). Financed with federal funds, the Navajo Service had begun reservation-wide distribution of commodities as early as the winter of 1936–37 to combat malnutrition. By 1937 about 5 percent of Navajos were on relief (Parman 1976:125–27). In 1941 the relief program distributed only $36,685 worth of commodities (Young 1961:296), or less than $1 per person.

Prosperity returned to the reservation during World War II because of income from military service and war-related industries. Per capita income increased to $199.60 by 1944, surpassing the prosperous mid-1930s, even

TABLE 9. *Individual Income by Source: 1936, 1940, and 1944*

Source	1936 Amount	1936 Percentage	1940 Amount	1940 Percentage	1944 Amount	1944 Percentage
Wages	$1,546,590	34.0	$ 892,350	28.3	$ 5,168,790	45.8
Livestock	1,389,870	30.6	1,400,630	44.4	2,676,198	23.7
Agriculture	1,023,970	22.5	521,800	16.6	437,680	3.9
Rugs	288,840	6.3	283,480	9.0	180,000	1.6
Miscellaneous	299,410	6.6	54,070	1.7	191,620[b]	1.7
Unearned	0	0.0	0	0.0	2,629,674[c]	23.3
Totals	$4,548,680[a]	100.0	$3,152,330[a]	100.0	$11,283,962[d]	100.0

Sources: 1936, U.S. Soil Conservation Service 1938:table III.
        1940, U.S. Bureau of Indian Affairs 1941:table III.
        1944, E. Clark 1946:table 5.
[a]These totals are just for on-reservation Navajos, and exclude District 6, which was Hopi.
[b]Included in this figure are private business ($24,000); native products, such as piñons, furs, and skins ($28,870); silverwork ($106,800); leather and beadwork ($10,000); "other" ($5,480); and "miscellaneous" ($16,500).
[c]Included in this figure are servicemen's allotments ($2,160,000); AAA benefits ($144,084); relief ($42,250); social security assistance ($1,500); timber sales ($40); leases, permits, and royalties ($100); and "other" ($281,700).
[d]These totals are for both on- and off-reservation Navajos.

TABLE 10. *Adjusted Individual Navajo Annual Per Capita Income: 1936–1946*

Year	Per Capita	Consumer Price Index[e]	Adjusted Per Capita	Percentage of 1936 Income
1936[a]	$141.71	41.5	$341.45	100.00
1940[b]	78.81	42.0	187.64	54.95
1944[c]	199.60	52.7	378.75	110.92
1946[d]	80.00	58.5	136.75	40.05

[a]U.S. Soil Conservation Service 1938:table III.   [d]*Farmington Times Hustler,* July 5, 1946.
[b]U.S. Bureau of Indian Affairs 1941:table III.   [e]Appendix B.
[c]Clark 1946:16.

taking wartime inflation into account (table 10). In 1944 allotments to the families of servicemen amounted to $2,160,000, and Navajo military personnel and war plant workers earned approximately $4,000,000. Thus, about $6,000,000, or almost 60 percent of Navajo income from all sources in 1944, was directly related to the war (E. Clark 1946:table 5).

When the war ended, Navajos were laid off at the war plants, Navajo servicemen were discharged, and allotment benefits to Navajo dependents ended. The tribe did not experience the full impact of stock reduction until workers and veterans returned from various parts of the country and the world. In 1932, the year before the program began, the Navajos owned eighteen sheep and goats per capita; ten in 1941, at the start of the war; and eight when the war ended, as a result of slightly reduced livestock numbers and a continuously increasing population (Aberle 1966:71). Returning Navajos discovered that their herds and farms could not support their families even at bare subsistence, and that opportunities for wage labor were minimal. To make matters worse, approximately 88 percent of Navajo men between the ages of eighteen and thirty-eight were illiterate (Sanchez 1948:25). Many had been able to find employment during the war only because of extreme labor shortages.

These conditions led to the collapse of the Navajo economy in 1945. Between 1944 and 1946 the annual per capita income fell from $199.60 to $80 (table 10), about the same as the 1940 figure. Between 1940 and 1946, however, inflation severely cut into the buying power of those dollars. By converting the Navajo income estimates for these years into 1967 dollars, we can see that the adjusted per capita income of Navajos in 1946 was 40 percent of what it had been in 1936, 73 percent of the 1940 figure (a poor year), and only 36 percent of the 1944 figure (table 10). Thus, between 1944 and 1946 the buying power of Navajos dropped by almost two-thirds: an economic collapse of devastating proportions.

Lacking any other means of support, many families were forced to butcher productive animals in order to survive, further depleting herds of sheep and goats. Between 1944 and 1947, the number of sheep on the reservation dropped from 344,000 to 245,000, and the number of goats from 42,000 to 29,000 (appendix A). In three years, sheep and goat herds had declined by almost 30 percent.

By the fall of 1947, deteriorating economic conditions on the reservation were beginning to attract national attention. On November 3, 1947, *Time* magazine reported,

> [The Navajos] are among the most destitute and underprivileged of U.S. minorities. But last week these deprivations seemed like minor matters. Great numbers of the Navajos are facing starvation . . . from 25,000 to 30,000 Navajos are lingering in the state between malnutrition and starvation. The whole tribe's diet averaged only 1,200 calories [per person] and many have nothing to eat but bread

and coffee. . . . By January, if the winter is hard, there would be snowdrifts on the reservation and many of the children and old men will be dead. (quoted in Boyce 1974:221)

Local Indian Service officials tried to head off disaster as these conditions developed, but relief funds averaged only $5.00 per person per month (*Farmington Times Hustler*, May 23, 1947). The *Time* article brought donations from private charities, which moved far more quickly than the federal government. On November 21, 1947, the *Farmington Times Hustler* reported that the Denver relief committee had sent a large shipment of food and clothing to the Navajos, and in early December, the Mormon Church sent two truckloads of food and clothing to Navajos living in northern New Mexico, Arizona, and Utah (*Farmington Times Hustler*, Dec. 5, 1947).

On December 2, 1947, after the problem had become a national issue, President Truman called on Congress for emergency aid, and a week later, the National Congress of American Indians sought both emergency and permanent relief from Congress (Boyce 1974:221). A special session of Congress appropriated $500,000 in January 1948 to help Navajos and Hopis through the winter (*Farmington Times Hustler*, Jan. 21, 1948). The program, which went into effect on February 1, 1948, and which was supposed to render further private contributions unnecessary (*Farmington Times Hustler*, Jan. 30, 1948), increased the amount of relief payments and the number of recipients. Reportedly, five times as many Navajo families were on relief in 1949 as had been in 1947, with the average family receiving $38.72 per month in cash (*Farmington Times Hustler*, Dec. 5, 1949). However, Indian Service officials knew that larger relief payments did not represent a permanent solution to the economic problems of the Navajos, and that action would have to be taken to place them on a stronger economic footing.

NAVAJO ATTITUDES TOWARDS ANGLO-AMERICANS

During the 1930s and 1940s, the way Navajos saw themselves and their relation to Anglo-American society underwent important changes. Researchers have analyzed changes in Navajo attitudes as a result of livestock reduction (Aberle 1966) and World War II (Adair 1947; Vogt 1949; Adair and Vogt 1949), but there has been no attempt to gauge the cumulative outcome of two events that took place in such rapid succession, yet produced such different effects.

During the late nineteenth century, Navajos continued to look upon Anglo-Americans as the "enemy," and showed overt hostility to aspects of their culture such as clothing and houses. Neither the government nor civilians seriously challenged the tribe's cultural autonomy, but without military power, Navajos had to tolerate the Anglo-American presence. As officials, traders, and missionaries came to the reservation, and increasing numbers of Navajos enrolled in government schools and found jobs away from the reservation, the social and economic isolation of the tribe began to erode. Navajos, particularly men, began to adopt Anglo-American clothing, and if only as status symbols, the more affluent families built houses. Nevertheless, these signs of acculturation did not indicate any significant degree of assimilation. The perception of Anglo-Americans as "enemies" may have lost ground, but Navajos continued to view themselves as a people different and apart from Anglo-American society.

As Navajos became ostensibly receptive to Anglo-American material goods, underlying feelings of hostility towards Anglo-Americans persisted. Before stock reduction, several incidents which in themselves had little significance illustrate this submerged hostility when considered together. First, during World War I, rumors that Navajos would be drafted caused some traders to move their wives and children off the reservation, fearing armed resistance on the part of the Navajos (Faunce 1981:289–95). Second, and the most overt expression of Navajo antagonism, in July 1920 Navajo medicine men prophesied that the world was about to be flooded, and that the Anglo-Americans would drown. "When the flood was over," wrote the superintendent of Northern Navajo, "if there were any white people left the Navajos could kill them easily and thus be rid of the white man and his ways forever" (SJ NR 1920:4). Third, in 1932 an Anglo-American truck driver fatally injured a Navajo in Shiprock, and a mob of enraged Navajos, including a tribal policeman, surrounded the driver and threatened to lynch him (*Farmington Times Hustler*, Aug. 12, 1932). Finally, in the summer of 1933, government officials tried to recruit 600 Navajos from Northern to work on reforestation projects. Even though wage work was in short supply, and in spite of assurances from officials to the contrary, some Navajos refused because they considered the required physical examinations tantamount to military enlistment (*Farmington Times Hustler*, June 9, 1933, June 23, 1933). In view of the usual willingness of Navajos to accept this kind of work, their reluctance indicated deep distrust of government officials and hostility toward military service.

Bernard Barber (1941:667) thought that anti-white sentiment emerged in the 1930s in response to livestock reduction, but based on these incidents, we believe that Navajo suspicion of and antagonism towards Anglo-Americans were already present. Still a tribal people, the Navajos had not even reconciled themselves to the presence of Anglo-Americans, let alone accepted foreign domination. Rather than being the cause of anti-white sentiment, livestock reduction revealed and intensified feelings that already existed.

Certainly, stock reduction was one of the most psychologically traumatic events in Navajo history. Not since Bosque Redondo had the government attempted to exercise such total control. Tribal police, range riders, and other Indian Service personnel dictated how many animals would have to be sold and the price they would sell for, meeting resistance with threats of physical force or force itself. Stockowners had no choice but to acquiesce to the demands placed on them. As one older Navajo said, "They were afraid" (Bailey field notes). The manner in which the government disposed of the purchased animals disturbed the Navajos as much as forced sales. Destruction of livestock by shooting and starvation were "perfectly understandable in white economic terms," but "viewed as utter barbarism by the Navajo" (Downs 1964:93), to whom the waste of so many animals was incomprehensible (Bailey field notes).

Many Navajos suspected the government of trying to destroy them. In 1936, Robert Martin, an educated Navajo businessman from Fruitland, complained to Senator Elmer Thomas of the Senate Committee on Indian Affairs, "Under the present reservation administration attempts are being made to drive our people as though they are slaves." Mrs. Y. N. Yazzie of Toadlena wrote the committee, "We don't want no more reduction of our sheep, because it is our everlasting money. . . . Why should the Government rob us out of our sheep, it is our money" (U.S. Congress 1937, 34:18016–17). An Anglo-American supervisor for Emergency Conservation Work Act (Civilian Conservation Corps) projects on the reservation noted uncharacteristic inefficiency on the part of Navajo road and dam workers. Navajo laborers were known for diligence and efficiency, but this work was costing more and going more slowly than similar projects in other parts of the United States. The supervisor eventually learned that his workers distrusted the government's objectives, and had to convince them they were working for the good of the tribe before the pace accelerated (Bailey field notes).

The response to a 1938 epidemic of typhoid on the reservation best illustrates the Navajos' extreme suspicion of the government. When the epidemic broke out, health officers promptly launched a massive vaccination campaign to keep it from spreading, but a rumor started to circulate among Navajos that the anti-typhoid vaccine was intended to sterilize Navajo children and would cause their deaths within three years. To overcome their distrust, J. C. Morgan set an example by having himself publicly vaccinated (*Farmington Times Hustler*, Feb. 11, 1938). Beyond losing faith, it appears that by 1938 many Navajos actually believed the government was trying to murder them.

Major political and religious movements began to evolve on the reservation in the 1930s. One of the original representatives from Northern Navajo on the 1923 Navajo Tribal Council (Kelly 1968:69–70), J. C. Morgan vigorously fought government policy on a number of issues in the late 1920s. His opposition became so vehement that in 1927 Superintendent Kneale of Northern Navajo wrote to Commissioner Hagerman,

> [Morgan] is a bigot, unreasonable, unreliable, and an ever present and apparently ever growing menace. . . . Worse than all he is an admirer of John Collier and Representative [James] Frear and eagerly devours every word that these gentlemen write, . . . the veracity of which he places on a par with Holy Writ. (quoted in Kelly 1968:120)[17]

In January 1932 a group of about 600 Navajos met in Farmington to express their opposition to Indian Service policies (*Farmington Times Hustler*, Jan. 7, 1932). That summer, returned students from every part of the reservation organized the Returned Students' Association (*Farmington Times Hustler*, Aug. 26, 1932) to influence the tribe's future economic development. Organized by Morgan, the association found its greatest support among Navajos living in the Northern jurisdiction, where many Navajos were dissatisfied with the government's handling of oil lease royalties. According to the *Farmington Times Hustler* (July 17, 1932), Morgan and another Northern Navajo, Dashne Clah Cheschillege, were "developing as real leaders" in the early 1930s.

J. C. Morgan had admired John Collier in the 1920s, but by the early 1930s, Morgan had emerged as the leader of educated Navajos and opposed the pro-traditionalist Collier. Neither he nor the Returned Students' Association supported Collier's nomination for Commissioner of Indian Affairs (*Gallup Independent*, Feb. 4, 1933; Parman 1976:27–28, 39)—a refusal that marked the beginning of the political break between the two men.[18] In 1935 their struggle focused on the implementation of the Indian Reorganization Act (Wheeler-Howard Act), one of Collier's key projects. Morgan opposed reorganization, and later, Collier indirectly accused him of telling the Navajos that a vote for the Indian Reorganization Act was a vote for stock reduction (Collier Biweekly Report 6, June 6, 1935, JCP).[19] As a tribe, the

TABLE 11.   *Vote on Navajo Reorganization*

Jurisdiction	For	Against
Keams Canyon (Hopi)	1,322	63
Eastern Navajo	1,131	1,917
Southern Navajo	3,272	2,921
Northern Navajo	536	2,771
Leupp	700	74
Western Navajo	834	468
Totals	7,795	8,214

Source: Kelly 1968:169.
Note: Parman (1976:76) and Iverson (1981:34) show slightly different totals, listing 7,679 for and 8,197 against. Williams (1970:23) has still a third count of 7,608 for and 7,992 against. Kelly's final totals are from the *Albuquerque Journal*, Williams's counts are "official" tabulations, while Parman and Iverson's totals are from the Santa Fe *New Mexican*. We have no explanation for the discrepancies.

Navajos rejected the act by a vote of 8,214 to 7,795. Four of the six jurisdictions actually voted in favor of the measure, but voters in the Northern and Eastern jurisdictions, where Morgan's influence was strongest, rejected it soundly (table 11).

In a letter to Collier analyzing the defeat of the Indian Reorganization Act, Roman Hubbell, the trader at Ganado, noted that opposition had been the strongest where missionaries and Indian Service personnel had been the most active (Hubbell to Collier, June 16, 1935, JCP)—in other words, in regions that had experienced the most intensive contact with Anglo-Americans. Hubbell's statement indicates that Morgan's charisma and the loyalty of his followers were not solely responsible for the bill's rejection.

In July 1937, 600 Navajos formed the Navajo Progressive League and called for the dismissal of Commissioner Collier, the election of a new Tribal Council, a congressional investigation of the misrule of the Indian Service, and issued a denunciation of livestock reduction (*Farmington Times Hustler,* July 30, 1937). Although Morgan instigated the league's organization, he attempted to stay in the background and held no official position in it (Parman 1976:177–78).

The Navajos elected Morgan tribal chairman in 1938. In the past, he had benefited politically from his opposition to stock reduction and other government programs. As chairman, however, he had gained power and wanted to keep it, even if it meant supporting government grazing policy. In a change of attitude that was probably politically motivated, he came out in favor of selling surplus horses and branding other horses, an act with serious political repercussions. Many of his supporters abandoned him. Dashne Clah Cheschillege, previously Morgan's colleague and ally, established the rival Navajo Rights Association in October 1940 to oppose stock reduction. Starting in the Shiprock area, Cheschillege and his followers tried to expand the association, recruiting new members and financing the work by charging $1 per person in membership fees. By the following spring, membership had increased to between 5,000 and 6,000 Navajos from all parts of the reservation, and at the outbreak of World War II, the Navajo Rights Association was the center of anti-government activities on the reservation (Parman 1976:240–63, 272–73; Philp 1977:193).

Changes in Navajo religious beliefs coincided with increased political activity. In the mid-1930s, Navajos began to join the Native American Church as a result of contact with Ute peyotists living on the Ute Mountain reservation. Aberle (1966) was not able to determine precisely when the first Navajos became involved with the Native American Church, but as early as 1935, several Navajo road men (peyote ceremonial leaders) were conducting meetings in the northern portion of the reservation. Two centers of peyotism developed during the late 1930s: the first in the north, including the Shiprock, Aneth, Mancos Creek, Teec Nos Pos, and Beclabito areas; the second in the south, including the Crystal, Tohatchi, Sawmill, Fort Defiance, and Window Rock areas. The church probably became active in the south by 1938, and was definitely in existence by 1940 (Aberle 1966:109).

Traditionalists and Christian Navajos alike reacted against the spread of the peyote religion on the reservation. According to the Law and Order files of the agency, in January 1938 two peyote church leaders were arrested for "possessing dope (peyote)," apparently an isolated incident (Aberle 1966:110). By 1940 the presence of peyotists had become widespread enough to generate opposition from Navajo traditionalists as well as Christian missionaries. Navajo opponents of the Native American Church seized upon the same arguments that had been used in Oklahoma: peyote was said to arouse people sexually, and peyote meetings were characterized as little more than sexual orgies in which incest was practiced (Bailey field notes; Parman 1976:258). In these early years, J. C. Morgan, a Christian missionary as well as tribal chairman, led the opposition to the church. With his encouragement, the Tribal Council adopted an anti-peyote resolution in the summer of 1940, making its sale, use, or possession punishable by imprisonment for a maximum of nine months, a $100 fine, or both.

Although Commissioner Collier did not personally oppose the use of peyote, he supported the resolution on the principle of tribal self-government. However, he ultimately undermined the law by preventing Navajo tribal police, who were paid with federal funds, from enforcing it (Aberle 1966:110–14). Throughout the 1940s, the law was only weakly enforced.

Concurrent with the early growth of the Native American Church, but not directly related to it, "visionary stirrings" were reported in the northern and eastern areas of the reservation.[20] In 1936 White Shell Woman, a Navajo holy figure, reportedly visited a woman from the Huerfano area; and in 1936 or 1937, Band Rock Boy, another such figure, visited a woman living near Farmington. During the late 1930s, a Shiprock woman reportedly saw the child Jesus, who told her, "I will lead you out of these terrible troubles that the whites are making for you." In 1941, a woman from either the Largo or Blanco Canyon area had a vision of a field of white men's skulls; she claimed that the Japanese were the Navajo mythological heroes Born of Water and Monster Slayer, who had come back to rid them of the white man (Aberle 1966:73–74).

The policies of the Collier administration served as a catalyst, causing the growing dissatisfaction of Navajos to crystallize into the religious and political movements of the 1930s and early 1940s. Stock reduction stirred up distrust of the government and hostility towards whites in general, but it did not create these feelings, which had existed long before the Collier era. Navajos in all areas experienced intensified anti-white sentiments and suspicion of the government at this time, but especially in the north and east. The major incidents of anti-white behavior, anti-government political movements, the early activities of the Native American Church, and the rash of visionary prophecies all centered in these two areas, which had experienced the greatest degree of change.

In the early twentieth century, changes in Navajo society accompanied economic changes, and people began to revise their perception of themselves in relation to Anglo-American society. School teachers, missionaries, government officials, and to a lesser extent traders caused Navajos to begin questioning traditional values and behavior, resulting in erosion of Navajo culture and a weakening of traditional mechanisms for social control. As contact with Anglo-Americans increased, Navajos became aware that many local whites considered them their cultural and social inferiors, causing inevitable damage to their sense of worth. Together with the economic problems caused by the depression, these factors contributed to the cultural conflicts that emerged in the years immediately preceding stock reduction.

What followed demonstrated to the Navajos that they were a dependent, dominated people, powerless against the federal government, and controlled by people whose actions at times seemed irrational and unpredictable to them. Under these conditions, it is not surprising that they distrusted the government, its programs, and its personnel, even to the extent of believing that it was deliberately trying to destroy them. The most "progressive" Navajos—those who had been educated or become Christians—turned to political organization to fight government programs; while conservative, less educated Navajos turned to religious movements in an attempt to restore some order to their disintegrating world.

World War II, which began before the tribe could adjust to the changes brought about by the Collier administration, also produced far-reaching effects on Navajo culture. In one way or another, the war directly influenced the lives of virtually all young Navajo adults, and almost one-third of the total Navajo population—especially those who did military service. Except for the "code talkers," the 3,600 Navajos who served in the armed forces were usually assigned to non-Indian units where they had little contact with other Navajos, or for that matter, Indians from any tribe. Isolated and immersed in non-Navajo society, they soon became integrated into it, and their wartime experiences had a lasting effect on their attitudes and cultural orientation.

John Adair (1947:6) wrote, "This second World War has exerted a great impact on the cultures of these [Navajo and Pueblo] peoples, perhaps the greatist [sic] since the arrival of the Spaniards." The war had a particularly pronounced effect on the attitudes of Navajo servicemen towards whites:

> At home . . . the Navajo from the back regions of the reservation behaved in certain ways towards Whites because pressure was brought to bear by his elders. In the Service much of this reserved as well as resentful attitude towards Whites was modified by necessity. As a result some of the psychological barriers which had always been present in relations between the Indian and the White were torn down. (Adair 1947:7–8)

Besides tearing down social and psychological barriers, World War II had a profound effect on the basic cultural orientation of many Navajos. Indian schools had frequently given students a "veneer" of Anglo-American culture, but the military carried the process of acculturation much further. In the case of John Nez, a returning Navajo veteran, Evon Vogt (1949:17–18) noted,

The total effect of his service experience was positive. When John reached home after his discharge, white ways were more than a "veneer." They were internalized as integral parts of his motivational system. His attitudes have changed in almost every phase of culture. In material culture, he favors a change from the Navajo hogan to the white-style cabin. One of the first things he did was to buy a bed, and he has not slept on a sheepskin since his return home. He owns and wears white-style clothing more like "city" clothing than that worn by local rural whites. He misses white food and has tried making biscuits and pies at home. He is also a vigorous promoter of schooling and teaching white ways to *all* Navajo children. John now expresses strong doubts about Navajo ceremonials . . . . He questions the existence of Navajo ghosts and witches . . . . With his strong aspirations to follow the "white way" and his loss of belief in the "Navajo way," John Nez has found himself in a hopeless situation between two worlds.

While Vogt stated that John Nez could not be considered typical, his reaction to the war was similar to that of hundreds of Navajo veterans. It is likely that Navajo war plant workers, particularly those who migrated to the west coast, also experienced pervasive changes in cultural orientation.

Aberle (1966) contends that the spread of the Native American Church is best understood as a response to livestock reduction. Adair (1947) and Vogt (1949) emphasize the effects of World War II on Navajo cultural values. We prefer to examine the cumulative effects of livestock reduction and World War II, and to interpret them as a single, protracted historical event. There is no doubt that in 1945, the "typical" Navajo had a far different view of himself, his culture, and Anglo-Americans than his counterpart in 1933. During those twelve years, the Navajos watched their world getting turned upside down, and were subjected to repeated psychological upheavals. Their own cultural values, their idea of Anglo-American culture, and their relationship with the dominant society had been shattered. Together, stock reduction and World War II forced Navajos to redefine their relationship with Anglo-American society, resulting in a cultural reorientation of even greater magnitude than had occurred early in the century.

Covering a period of less than fifteen years, the Collier era did not culminate in any new coalescence or restructuring of Navajo culture, but it was a time of rapid change, dramatic economic fluctuations, and vastly increased exposure to Anglo-American society. Although stock reduction and World War II did not in themselves initiate changes, they set the stage for the far-reaching changes that were to follow. Herding could no longer form the basis of Navajo economy. The Navajos would have to become dependent on wage labor, and as a result, more fully integrated into and dependent upon regional and national economies. The psychological and social barriers which had kept Anglo-American culture and society at a distance were breached. In terms of long-term cultural effects, stock reduction and World War II had an even greater impact on the Navajos than their experience at Bosque Redondo, and prepared the way in the late 1940s for what Ruth Underhill called "a new beginning."

CHAPTER FIVE

The Modern Navajos: 1950–1975

Indian Service officials recognized the Navajo "problem" before it received national attention and initiated a series of studies to gain a better perspective on the situation. Dr. George Sanchez's study (1948) of Navajo education, Lee Muck's survey of reservation range resources and the state of the Navajo livestock economy, and A. L. Wathen's report on the general economic conditions on the reservation (Young 1968:71–72) pinpointed the major areas of concern. These reports, as well as studies of welfare and living conditions on the reservation by Downes and Clark (1946) and the Navajo Agency (Young 1968:71), emphasized that social and economic conditions on the reservation were rapidly deteriorating.

By the late 1940s, the Navajo population had reached about 65,000 (Johnston 1966b:151). It was estimated that a Navajo family would have to earn an annual income of $1,200 to support itself at what officials considered a minimal subsistence level, but average annual family income stood at less than $400. Economic surveys also indicated a bleak situation. If all the known economic resources on the reservation were developed to the maximum level, the reservation would be capable of supporting only 6,950 families with annual incomes of $1,200, or about 35,000 people (Krug 1948:8, 38, 49). The population of the tribe was growing at an annual rate of 2.5 percent, compounding the problem (Johnston 1966b:153).[1]

Some families were able to survive only by consuming their productive stock, and as a result, Navajo herds declined (appendix A). Malnutrition was described as "widespread" (Krug 1948:8), and some Navajos were on the verge of starvation. This immediate and critical problem was not going to solve itself. Even if reservation resources were developed to the fullest, large numbers of Navajos would have to be relocated. Livestock could no longer provide a major source of income. Although it was imperative that the Navajos find employment as wage laborers, such a dramatic shift was not going to be easily accomplished. Few Navajos had marketable skills. Over 80 percent of the Navajos called for the draft during the war were illiterate (Sanchez 1948:25), and only a minority of school-age children were attending school. Only prompt action by the federal government could avert disaster.

In 1948 Secretary of the Interior Julius Krug presented the so-called "Krug Report" to Congress. This report summarized the social, economic, and health conditions of the reservation and made a series of recommendations for the "rehabilitation" of the Navajos. The objectives of the proposed program were to "(1) enable the Navajo people to attain economic self-sufficiency through their own efforts; (2) assist them in becoming healthy, enlightened citizens, capable of enjoying the full benefits of our democracy; and (3) carry out the legal and moral obligations of the Federal government to the Navajo Tribe" (Krug 1948:24).

The Krug Report formed the basis of the Navajo-Hopi Long Range Rehabilitation Act, passed by Congress in 1950. This act in itself would have produced far-ranging effects on the Navajos. However, Secretary Krug and officials of the Bureau of Indian Affairs (BIA)[2] did not anticipate that regional development of mineral resources both on and off the reservation during the 1950s would transform Navajo culture more than any act of Congress. Starting in 1950 with the passage of the Rehabilitation Act and the almost simultaneous exploration and development of mineral resources in the region, the Navajo economy began to expand and change rapidly. Wage labor and welfare became the major sources of income, and herding, farming, and weaving declined to the point of little overall significance. As income from wage labor and welfare increased, real income (adjusted for inflation) increased by a factor of five between the late 1940s and mid-1970s (see table 21; U.S. Commission on Civil Rights 1975b:20). Concurrently, education became virtually universal for the first time, missionaries flooded the reservation, the road system was expanded, and the large-scale acquisition of motor vehicles quickly eroded geographical isolation. In the wake of these changes, Navajos adopted Anglo-American material culture to such an extent that by the mid-1970s they continued to use few items of native manufacture. As we will see, although it was a time of rapid and steady economic expansion, adoption of Anglo-American material culture and life-style, and acceptance of Anglo-American beliefs, Navajo social identity remained intact.

THE NAVAJO-HOPI LONG RANGE REHABILITATION ACT

A ten-year project designed to alleviate rather than cure some of the tribe's social and economic ills, the Navajo-Hopi Long Range Rehabilitation Act originally authorized the expenditure of $88,570,000, and a 1958 amendment authorized an additional $20,000,000 (table 12). Of these funds, approximately $74,000,000 was earmarked for the construction and improvement of facilities on the reservation: schools, hospitals, roads, water systems, communication networks, and housing. Significantly less went to economic development programs (the acquisition of trading posts, the establishment of tribal enterprises to produce cement, clay, and wood products, and the attraction of large industries to the reservation) than to the construction of service facilities (Harper 1953:29). Although the construction projects employed Navajos, the act went far beyond public works legislation designed to create temporary jobs. As facilities were developed, Congress had to increase the annual appropriation for the operation of the Navajo Agency to staff and maintain them. Slightly more than $20,000,000 was authorized for development of irrigation projects, soil conservation, range improvement, studies of timber and mineral resources, and the development of industries and business on the reservation (table 12).

The Rehabilitation Act also called for the resettlement of Navajo families as a means of alleviating overpopulation on the reservation. In 1945 the Mohaves and Chemehuevis had reached an agreement with the Indian Service allowing members of other tribes to relocate on part of the Colorado River Indian reservation in western Arizona and making about 75,000 irrigable acres available to them (Young 1961:201). The first Navajo family moved there that summer, and 23 additional families were voluntarily relocated in the late 1940s. Secretary Krug proposed resettling 1,000 Navajo families on the Colorado River reservation in 1948 (Krug 1948:49), and the passage of the Rehabilitation Act accelerated the program. Ninety-two Navajo families settled there in 1950 and 1951, bringing the number of resident Navajo families to 108. The sudden influx of Navajos caused the Colorado River Tribal Council to rescind its agreement, however, putting

TABLE 12. *The Navajo-Hopi Long Range Rehabilitation Act, Funds Authorized and Allocated: 1951–1962*

Purpose	Authorized	Allocated
School construction	$ 25,000,000	$24,997,295
Hospital and health facilities	4,750,000	4,750,000
Agency, institutional, and domestic water	2,500,000	1,356,670
Irrigation projects	9,000,000	6,616,775
Roads and trails	40,000,000	38,237,680
Soil and moisture conservation, range improvement	10,000,000	7,097,175
Development of industrial and business enterprises	1,000,000	238,000
Resettlement on Colorado River irrigation project	5,750,000	3,449,750
Surveys and studies of timber, coal, and minerals	500,000	436,895
Off-reservation placement and relocation	3,500,000	194,600
Telephone and radio communications systems	250,000	250,000
Revolving loan fund	5,000,000	1,800,000
Housing and necessary facilities and equipment	820,000	26,300
Common service facilities	500,000	495,100
Totals	$108,570,000[a]	$89,946,240

Source: Young 1961:5.

[a]The Navajo-Hopi Long Range Rehabilitation Act originally authorized only $20,000,000 for the construction of roads and trails out of a total authorization of $88,570,000. In 1958 the act was amended by adding an additional $20,000,000 to roads and trails for the completion of routes 1 and 3.

an end to resettlement. Most of the resettled Navajos apparently found the area unsuitable, and by 1960, 72 families had left (Young 1961:203–6).

The Rehabilitation Act authorized $3,500,000 for the relocation of Navajos in other areas, but only $194,600 was ever appropriated for this purpose, probably because the BIA established a national relocation and employment assistance program in 1952 (Hodge 1969:8; Young 1961:5). The national program eliminated the need for a separate Navajo-Hopi program, and named the cities of Los Angeles, San Francisco, Oakland, San Jose, Denver, Chicago, Dallas, and Cleveland as relocation sites. The BIA paid the moving expenses of Indian families who wanted to relocate, helped them find work, and provided some money until they did. Between 1952 and 1960, 3,273 Navajos were resettled under this program (Young 1961:234–36).

Thus, the Navajo-Hopi Long Range Rehabilitation Act took a multifaceted approach to the Navajo problem. Congress eventually funded most of the projects, although some were either dropped or scaled down, and by 1961, $89,946,240 of the $108,570,000 authorized had been appropriated (table 12).[3]

DEVELOPMENT OF MINERAL RESOURCES AND TRIBAL REVENUE

The potential mineral wealth of the Navajo reservation had been recognized long before the 1950s.[4] Even before the turn of the century, potentially valuable coal deposits had been noted by geologists in the eastern and northern portions of the reservation. In the 1920s, oil was discovered in the northeast, and developers opened a few oil fields. These resources were left underdeveloped for the most part, primarily because of their distance from major markets and the region's poorly developed transportation system.

The situation changed abruptly after the war, when a nationwide economic boom greatly increased the consumption of fuels, especially natural gas. Between 1945 and 1950, the use of natural gas in the United States increased 50 percent, and over 300 percent between 1945 and 1960 (U.S. Bureau of the Census 1975:587–88). During the same period, the population of the United States was moving westward. Between 1940 and 1960, the population of New Mexico increased from 532,000 to 951,000, and that of Arizona, from 499,000 to 1,302,000. As a result, the potential regional market for Navajo resources more than doubled during this twenty-year period. The population of the west coast was increasing even more rapidly. Between 1940 and 1960, the population of California went from 6,907,000 to 15,717,000 (U.S. Bureau of the Census 1975:24–25, 32). This growth and the associated industrial expansion in the postwar years resulted in energy demands that far exceeded locally available resources on the west coast. The large-scale development of Navajo mineral resources came primarily as a response to this expanding market.

In the summer of 1950, El Paso Natural Gas Company was granted a right-of-way by the Navajo tribe across the reservation (*Farmington Daily Times*, July 31, 1950), and by August construction was underway on a pipeline to connect the gas fields of the San Juan Basin with the expanding markets in Arizona and southern California (*Farmington Daily Times*, Aug. 4, 1950). With the completion of this pipeline in 1951, the pace of gas-well drilling in the basin quickened. In 1950, 112 gas wells were drilled; in 1953, 676; and in 1956, 750 (*Farmington Daily Times*, Oct. 16, 1957). Because most natural gas deposits occurred in the eastern portion of the basin, off the reservation, their development had only local effects on the Navajos. Some off-reservation families in this region benefited from lease bonuses and royalties because their allotments were in the gas fields.

In the early 1950s, oil companies began looking again to the reservation proper. Only one producing well was actually drilled between 1950 and 1954 (Young 1958:397), and the output of all reservation wells was only about 142,000 barrels of oil in 1950 and 174,000 barrels as late as 1955 (Young 1961:267). However, oil companies planning future exploration on the reservation paid the tribe over $11,000,000 in lease bonuses between 1951 and 1954 (Young 1961:269). In 1957 and 1958, several oil companies began intensive exploration of the reservation, paying the tribe almost $60,000,000 in lease bonuses (Young 1961:269), and the number of productive oil wells on the reservation climbed from 127 to 238 (Young 1958:397). To transport the anticipated increases in production, two new pipelines were completed by 1958, and in 1960, 860 reservation wells yielded 34,272,928 barrels of oil (Young 1961:265–66).

Oil and gas development generated three different kinds of revenue for the tribe: lease bonuses, royalties, and rentals. On behalf of the tribe, the BIA auctioned leases for oil and gas exploration on specified tracts of land, and the successful bidder paid lease bonuses immediately. In addition, if oil or gas were discovered, the oil company would be required to pay royalties ranging from 12.5 percent to 16.6 percent of gross production. Finally, companies had to pay annual rentals of $1.25 per acre for the duration of the lease (Young 1961:265).

In the late 1940s, uranium and vanadium were discovered on the reservation. In terms of tribal revenue, the most important uranium discoveries were made on the east side of the Chuska Mountains and near Cameron and Kayenta. A number of mines opened in these regions in the late 1940s and early 1950s, with production increasing steadily between 1950 and 1954 and remaining relatively stable through the 1950s (Young 1961:268). These mines produced enough uranium that Kerr-McGee Corporation established an ore processing plant at Shiprock in 1954 (*Farmington Daily Times*, July 12, 1954, Nov. 1, 1954, June 19, 1955). At about the same time, mills were also established at Tuba City and Mexican Hat (Reno 1981:134).

In the 1950s, technological advances made it possible for coal-fired generating stations to produce electricity inexpensively. In 1957 Utah Mining and Construction (later Utah International Incorporated) and the tribe negotiated a contract allowing the company to strip-mine coal from an area just south of the San Juan River. Arizona Public Service Company agreed to build a coal-fired electric generating station (later named the Four Corners Power Plant) next to the mine. The plant and mine began operations in 1962 (Reno 1981:107). In 1966 Peabody Coal Company secured a mining lease on portions of Black Mesa, and in 1968 the tribe approved the construction of a second on-reservation electrical generating station at Page, Arizona. Coal for the Page station was delivered by conveyor belt and railroad (Reno 1981:108).[5] Also, a slurry pipeline for the shipment of coal was laid between the Black Mesa mine and a generating station at Bullhead City, Nevada.

The 1950s marked tremendous growth in the development of oil, gas, uranium, and vanadium resources on the reservation. Large-scale coal mining operations started in the early 1960s, and mineral revenue increased rapidly. The tribe received $445,000 in 1950; $1,398,657 in 1951; and a windfall, primarily in lease bonuses, in 1957 and 1958—over $65,000,000. As the fields were developed, income dropped, although it remained substantial. During the 1960s, the tribe averaged about $14,250,000 a year from oil, gas, and coal leases, bonuses, and royalties. By the first half of the 1970s, income from this source had declined to about $11,200,000 a year (table 13). In the 1950s, well over 80 percent of tribal income was generated by mineral resources, two-thirds during the 1960s (although there were yearly fluctuations), and only about half by the early 1970s. The decrease resulted from increases in income from other sources, as well as from a decline in mineral income. The tribe invested much of its mineral revenue, and in 1975 interest income amounted to $4,223,697, or approximately 15 percent of the total tribal income of $27,549,392 for that year (Benson 1976:4). Whether from leases, rentals, royalties, or interest from capital investments, tribal income played a crucial role in reshaping the relationship between the Navajo tribe and the federal government.

NAVAJO POLITICAL GROWTH

The Tribal Council and chapter governments created in the 1920s were designed to help the Indian Service manage tribal affairs rather than to serve the Navajos, to whom these institutions had little political legitimacy. Subsequently, the Collier era marked the lowest point in Navajo political autonomy since Bosque Redondo. Although resistance to Collier's policies on the part of Navajo leaders proved futile, these men led the opposition to government policy, and the council and chapters became the major forums

TABLE 13. *Navajo Tribal Income by Source: 1950–1975*

Year	Oil and Gas[a]	Coal[b]	Total Income Minerals[c]	Percentage[d]	Total Income[d]
1950	$ 378,931	$?	$ 445,015	?	?
1951	1,245,278	403	1,398,657	?	?
1952	1,428,546	3,073	1,732,590	?	?
1953	5,161,912	3,450	5,637,072	?	?
1954	5,310,201	3,423	5,973,640	?	?
1955	1,544,061	1,409	2,110,117	?	?
1956	1,479,697	1,983	2,045,311	?	?
1957	34,807,982	1,478	35,504,883	?	?
1958	29,194,756	2,539	29,606,866	93	$30,629,792
1959	15,323,947	12,453	16,025,725	85	19,540,713
1960	11,688,646	13,210	12,383,331	79	18,536,890
1961	15,139,135	?	?	82	20,058,220
1962	13,068,219	?	?	77	16,942,904
1963	14,172,456	?	?	76	18,036,182
1964	30,880,185	?	?	88	34,030,227
1965	18,212,468	?	?	77	17,960,805
1966	13,679,026	?	?	65	12,841,958
1967	7,178,195	?	?	62	13,253,804
1968	8,740,513	?	?	69	16,333,341
1969	10,090,779	?	?	62	16,526,743
1970	6,254,341	?	?	42	19,043,792
1971	n.a.	?	?	51	26,448,508
1972	11,001,123	?	?	41	19,561,915
1973	6,853,270	?	?	28	26,316,176
1974	13,977,646	?	?	49	20,583,984
1975	12,858,797	?	?	70	27,549,392

[a]Oil and gas income figures for 1950 through 1960 are from Young 1961:269; data for 1961 through 1975 are from Reno 1981:125.
[b]Young 1961:268.
[c]Adapted from Young 1961:268–69.
[d]Reno 1981:131.
Note: There are discrepancies between sources and within this table. Reno (1981:125, 131) presents slightly different revenue figures for oil, gas, and coal prior to 1961. For 1965 and 1966, the income figures given by Reno (1981) for oil, gas, and coal exceed the total tribal income figures given for those years. Reno's (1981) percentage of tribal income derived from mineral resources for the years 1958, 1959, and 1960 do not precisely match Young's (1961) report for these years nor his figures for total tribal income.

for such opposition. Unintentionally, Collier's policies helped transform the Tribal Council and chapter system. About 40 percent of the chapters continued to operate after Indian Service support had been withdrawn, demonstrating that while most Navajos may not have accepted these institutions as legitimate, they had come to realize their necessity in dealing with the federal government.

The significance of this change did not become fully apparent until the late 1940s. In 1945 Collier was forced out as commissioner of Indian affairs (Parman 1976:289), and with his departure the government's philosophy changed radically. Many politicians felt that the time had come to get out of the "Indian business," as some called it; that is, to end government control and supervision of Indian tribes and their properties (Taylor 1972:48–60). In August 1953, this philosophy culminated in the passage of House Concurrent Resolution 108, the so-called Indian Termination Act (Strickland 1982:170–72), which was meant to end federal management of tribes. On a tribe-by-tribe basis, the act called for agencies to be closed and tribal property either divided among tribal members or turned over to tribal corporations. With termination, all government responsibilities towards Indians as tribal members would cease.[6]

The relationship between the Navajo people and the federal government changed significantly after 1950.[7] Because officials considered them neither economically nor socially ready, they were never considered for termination, but classified as a Group 3 tribe—one that would continue under government supervision for an "indefinite time" (Taylor 1972:188). However, the general policy of reducing government involvement in Indian matters allowed an invigorated and aggressive Navajo tribal government to assume some control over its own affairs. Greatly facilitated by tribal income from the development of mineral resources, which gave them the opportunity to develop programs independent of federal funding, Navajo leaders were able to expand and strengthen this control during the 1950s and 1960s.

Some scholars have traced this change back to 1947, when Norman Littell, an Anglo-American, was employed as the first Navajo tribal attorney (Shepardson 1963:85; Iverson 1981:52–53). Unquestionably a competent attorney and political advisor, Littell facilitated the growing Navajo "nationalism," but he did not invent it. Collier's policies, particularly stock reduction, had inspired a "nationalistic" feeling with little precedent in Navajo history; but before such a movement could surface, Navajo leaders needed an opportunity to assert themselves.

The year 1950 proved to be a watershed in Navajo relations with the federal government in that the Rehabilitation Act allowed the Navajo Tribal Council to allocate its own tribal revenues (Iverson 1981:55; Young 1961:3). At the time, since tribal income was extremely limited, the decision seemed insignificant. Little did officials suspect that during the next quarter century tribal income would rise as rapidly as it did, giving the Tribal Council allocation powers over revenues well in excess of 400 million dollars.

As the Navajo Tribal Council began to take greater control of tribal affairs, the BIA weakened. In 1954 Congress enacted legislation (Public Law 568) transferring Indian health care from the BIA to the Public Health Service. Effective on July 1, 1955, this action divided responsibility for the Navajos between two federal agencies (Young 1961:69). Within the year, the BIA reorganized Navajo administration. The reservation and off-reservation areas were divided into five subagencies: Tuba City, Shiprock, Crownpoint, Chinle, and Fort Defiance. The main offices of the Navajo Agency remained at Window Rock (Young 1961:602; map 7).

Also in 1955, the Navajo Tribal Council strengthened its position with the tribe and indirectly with the federal government by formally recognizing and incorporating the chapter system into tribal government. Although many chapters disintegrated after the Collier administration withdrew its financial support and recognition of the chapter system (Kimball and Provinse 1942:24), others continued to function, and in the early 1950s, approximately 40 of the original 100 chapters still existed (Williams 1970:40). A two-level political system had evolved: the Tribal Council at the tribal level; and although not officially recognized by the council, chapter governments at the community level. No formal, structural relationship existed between the two political systems until June 1955, when the council recognized the chapters as local governing bodies under its authority. The council resolved that chapters would be organized where the system had never been instituted and reorganized where it had disappeared (Williams 1970:40–41). This fusion of tribal and local political systems strengthened the Tribal Council by bringing the chapters under its control, and the chapters by extending financial support to them.

At the request of the Tribal Council, the secretary of the interior established a tribal grazing committee in each land management district in October 1952 and approved the grazing regulations drafted jointly by the grazing committee chairmen and an advisory committee in April 1956. Practically, the new regulations transferred enforcement responsibility to the tribe; technically, the ultimate authority remained with the secretary of the interior (Young 1961:157–59).

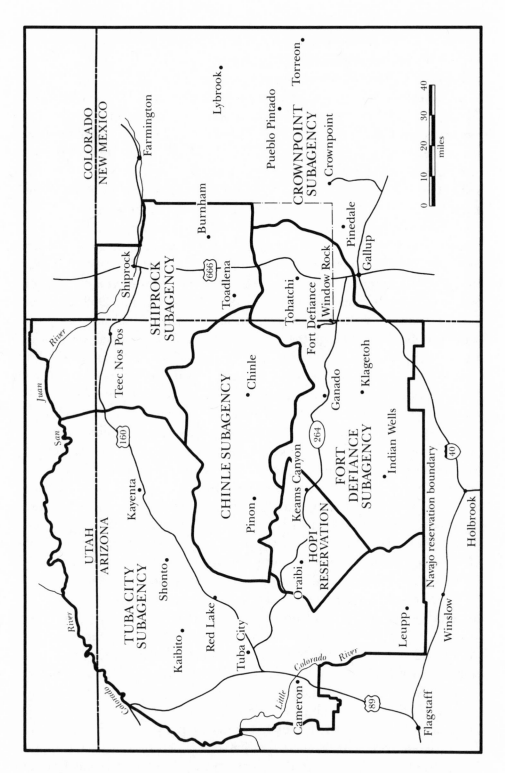

Map 7. Navajo subagencies later elevated to agencies. Adapted from Young (1961:x).

The reservation court and law enforcement systems also experienced important changes during the 1950s. In 1951 the BIA decided that instead of being appointed by the commissioner of Indian affairs, court judges would be elected by popular vote during regularly scheduled tribal elections (Young 1961:284–85; Iverson 1981:68). In 1953 the Tribal Council agreed to hire six additional Navajo police officers with tribal funds to patrol the eastern off-reservation area (Young 1958:140–41). Nevertheless, the courts and police remained under the direct control of the BIA until 1959, when the Tribal Council assumed control. With the approval of the secretary of the interior, the Tribal Council created a judicial branch composed of judges appointed by the chairman and approved by the council. The judicial branch consisted of a trial court with seven judges and an appeals court with three judges; its jurisdiction was limited to civil and domestic problems, and offenses committed by Indians on the reservation in violation of the Navajo Law and Order Code (Iverson 1981:74–76). Also in 1959, the tribe took over control of the Navajo police from the BIA. Tribal support of the police had increased through the 1950s, until by 1959 the council was providing over 93 percent of the cost of maintaining the force (Iverson 1981:76).

At first, there was considerable confusion over the jurisdiction of the new Navajo courts and police. In accordance with the general philosophy favoring the termination of federal involvement in Indian affairs, in 1953 Congress passed Public Law 280, transferring jurisdiction of criminal and civil cases arising on Indian lands from federal and tribal courts to state courts. Although the law transferred jurisdiction in only five states (California, Oregon, Nebraska, Minnesota, and Wisconsin), it allowed for other state courts to eventually assume jurisdiction over reservations in their states (Strickland 1982:175–77). The law created ambiguities concerning the jurisdiction of the new Navajo court system, as well as that of the Arizona, New Mexico, and Utah state courts on the Navajo reservation. These ambiguities were clarified within the year by two landmark decisions handed down in federal court. First, in 1958 a reservation trader went to state court in Arizona and secured an attachment for indebtedness on the property of a reservation Navajo. *Williams v. Lee* was appealed in 1959 to the Supreme Court, which held that the Navajo tribal courts, not the state court, had exclusive jurisdiction in the matter (Strickland 1982:237, 359). Second, in 1959 the Native American Church brought suit against the Navajo Tribal Council on the grounds that the tribal law prohibiting the use, sale, or transport of peyote violated their freedom of religion. The Tenth Federal Circuit Court ruled in favor of the Tribal Council on the grounds that although tribes are "states" in the generic sense, they "are not states of the union within the meaning of the Constitution, and the constitutional limitations on states do not apply to tribes" (Strickland 1982:664–65). Thus, in the same year that the tribal government assumed control of courts and police, federal courts recognized that the Navajo Tribal Council had at least limited sovereignty, and that the Navajo tribal courts were not subordinate to the state courts.

In his political history of the Navajos, Peter Iverson (1981:82) wrote, "The 1950s had . . . witnessed the birth of the Navajo Nation. The 1960s would reveal its gradual maturation." During the 1960s, the Tribal Council created a host of new tribal agencies to fill voids in existing federal services, using tribal revenues and funding from a variety of federal programs. In 1959 the Navajo Tribal Utility Authority was created to supply electric power to the growing community of Shiprock. This agency later managed the development of electric, natural gas, water, and sewer utilities for the whole reservation (Iverson 1981:166). In 1960 a tribal corporation, Navajo Forest Products Industries, took over management of the timber industry on the reservation (Young 1961:185). In the same year, the council established a tribal newspaper, the *Navajo Times*, published semimonthly until it became a weekly in 1961 (Grove, Barnett, and Hanson 1975:291). In 1953 the council set up a small scholarship fund for higher education, and in 1958 and 1959 used mineral revenues to establish a $10,000,000 trust fund supporting this program (Robert Roessel 1979:39). Initially, the council and the BIA administered the scholarship program jointly, but the tribe assumed sole responsibility in 1961. In 1964 the newly created Navajo Housing Authority, funded through the Department of Housing and Urban Development, began its first low-rent housing project (Smith 1966:58, 59). The Navajo Division of Education was created in 1971 to assure "the preservation of the Navajo cultural heritage" (quoted in Iverson 1981:151), and in 1972 the Navajo Health Authority was established (Iverson 1981:158).

The Office of Navajo Economic Opportunity (ONEO) proved the most influential, effective, and controversial tribal office created during this period. When the federal government authorized the Office of Economic Opportunity (OEO), BIA officials tried to administer OEO project funding on the reservation. The Tribal Council protested this control in 1964, organizing local Navajo groups to submit requests for funding directly to OEO, and in the spring of 1965 the Office of Navajo Economic Opportunity was established to manage the $920,000 worth of programs that had been funded for the Navajos. By that fall, ONEO had created preschool programs, a Neighborhood Youth Corps, and a center for the development of small businesses. In 1966 and 1967, ONEO expanded its programs to encompass legal aid, alcoholism, community development, home improvement training, off-reservation labor placement, and Head Start. In one way or another, these extensive and varied programs influenced the lives of most Navajos. Between 1965 and 1968, ONEO received over $20,000,000 in federal grants (Iverson 1981:89–91).

From 1950 to 1975, the influence of the BIA over Navajo affairs declined steadily, balanced by a steady growth in the power of Navajo tribal government. By 1975 the Navajos had succeeded in reclaiming much of their political autonomy, at least in regard to the daily management of internal Navajo affairs and programs.

THE CHANGING ECONOMY OF THE NAVAJOS

In spite of a rapidly growing population, the Navajo economy expanded so quickly during the quarter century after 1950 that per capita income increased dramatically. As the economy expanded, the relative importance of herding, farming, crafts, wage labor, and welfare shifted. Navajo economic growth during this period resulted mainly from increased income from wage labor and welfare. Herding, the most important component of the economy since the 1870s, had fallen to a position of only minor importance by the mid-1970s. As significant as these shifts in the relative importance of income sources were, in many cases the components themselves underwent profound qualitative changes. For example, during the early 1950s most Navajo wage-labor income came from seasonal, off-reservation employment. In contrast, during the early 1970s, permanent, on-reservation jobs generated most of that income. Thus, it is necessary to discuss the changes that occurred in the various economic components independently, then to discuss the overall growth in income and general patterns of change.

Livestock

In the late 1940s, because most permittees owned far fewer animals than their permits allowed, Navajo herds stood well below the grazing capacity of the range. The overall size of the herds began to increase in the early 1950s, and by the mid-1950s had about reached the estimated maximum carrying capacity of the range—512,922 sheep units (appendix A). After the regulation of grazing was transferred from the BIA to the tribe in 1956, Navajo herds began to exceed permitted levels (Young 1961:159–62). By

1960 reservation herds had increased to 556,095 sheep units, and by 1974, to 870,433 (appendix A).

In absolute numbers, the Navajos owned more sheep, goats, cattle, and horses in 1975 than they had owned in 1936 (fig. 17, appendix A). However, because the Navajo population had grown rapidly during this period, relative numbers of livestock had declined. Between 1941 and 1951, the ratio of sheep and goats to Navajos had fallen from about 10:1 to 4:1 (Aberle 1966:71), and remained more or less steady for the following quarter century.

The distribution of livestock ownership, on the other hand, showed some change between 1950 and 1975. After the original issue of permits, younger couples could only acquire stock permits through inheritance or purchase, and a family could only increase the size of its allowance by buying permits from others (Bailey field notes). In 1946–1947 there were about 7,500 sheep permits (Muck 1948:12) distributed among approximately 12,000 families (Krug 1948:1), meaning that about 62.5 percent of the families had permits. In 1975, 11,001 sheep permits were in effect on the reservation (U.S. Bureau of Indian Affairs, OLO, Range Unit Records, Window Rock), a number equal to only about 44 percent of the total number of families on the reservation. It is difficult to make a correlation between the number of permits and number of families raising stock. Some families had permits but no livestock, while others kept stock illegally. Younger couples frequently ran stock on their parents' permits. Many older Navajos "gave" their permit to their children, enabling them to keep their stock on the permit and still meet welfare qualifications (Bailey field notes). Nevertheless, the decline in the number of stock permits relative to the number of families seemed to indicate a general decline in the number of families raising stock.

When a permittee died, the permit would be divided among the surviving children. Fragmentation of permits through inheritance increased the number of permits and reduced the size of the average permit, as shown by data from the 1940s and 1950s. In 1946, 73 percent of all stock permits allowed between 1 and 100 sheep units (Muck 1948:exhibit C), a figure that rose to 80 percent in 1957 (Young 1958:391). The number of permits in excess of 100 sheep units declined both in percentage of total permits and in absolute numbers.

As many permits were being fragmented through inheritance, a few wealthy Navajos were in the process of buying them up (table 14). In 1948 Lee Muck (1948:25, 32) suggested that the buying and selling of stock permits be prohibited, and in response, the secretary of the interior ended their

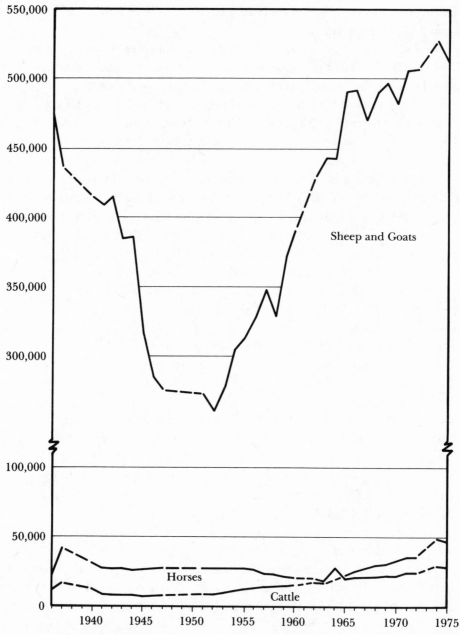

Figure 17. Livestock numbers, 1936–1975. Broken line indicates missing data.

negotiability in June 1948. However, the regulation was reversed in October 1952 (Young 1961:157–58). During the 1960s and early 1970s, a small number of wealthy stockmen expanded their holdings and consolidated permits, although overall growth in the total number of permits indicated continued fragmentation (Bailey and Bailey 1982:513–16).[8]

TABLE 14. Distribution of Stock Permits by Size: 1946 and 1957

| Size | 1946[a] | | 1957[b] | | |
	Number	Percentage	Number	Percentage	Change
1–50	3,386	45.0	4,094	51.0	+6.0%
51–100	2,071	28.0	2,356	29.0	+1.0
101–150	966	13.0	858	11.0	−2.0
151–200	576	8.0	429	5.0	−3.0
201–300	422	6.0	292	4.0	−2.0
301 +	32	0.4	48	0.6	+0.2
Totals	7,453	100.4	8,077	100.6	

[a]Adapted from Muck 1948:exhibit C.
[b]Adapted from Young 1958:391.

The size and relative composition of the herds underwent significant changes between 1951 and 1975.[9] Numbers of sheep and goats increased rapidly from 1951 to 1965 and fluctuated slightly from 1966 to 1975. Horses declined steadily from 1951 to 1963, when Navajos were changing from wagons to cars and trucks, but began to increase again in the mid-1960s. By 1974 and 1975, there were more horses on the reservation than at any time since 1940. We have no explanation for this reversal. Cattle increased moderately from the 1950s until the mid-1960s, when their numbers rose sharply—an event that appears to correspond with the leveling off in the growth of the sheep and goat herds (fig. 17).

The composition of Navajo herds changed considerably between the early 1950s and the early 1970s, as shown by relative herd composition. While horses declined from 30 percent to 16.4 percent during this period, and sheep and goats remained relatively constant, cattle climbed from 8.6 percent to 20.7 percent (table 15). By the mid-1960s, the Navajos owned more cattle than horses for the first time (fig. 17).

TABLE 15. Composition of Herds

	1951–54	1971–75
Sheep and Goats	61.4%	62.9%
Cattle	8.6	20.7
Horses	30.0	16.4

Source: Adapted from appendix A.

These increases in the absolute and relative numbers of cattle reflect important changes in the role of herding in Navajo life. Cattle, unlike sheep and goats, do not require continuous care, and are left to graze on their own for much of the year (Downs 1972:65–68). If, as many Navajos contend, sheep are more profitable than cattle (Bailey field notes),[10] stockowners may have been sacrificing part of their herding income for less labor-intensive herding practices. As wage labor became increasingly vital to the Navajo economy, people with permanent, full-time jobs no longer had time to tend sheep and goat herds, and began to favor cattle. Thus, the growth in cattle numbers indicated the increasingly subordinate role that stock raising in general played to wage labor in the Navajo economy. In earlier periods, Navajos had to accommodate seasonal wage labor to the needs of the herd; now, the demands of wage labor took precedence.

Farming

The Krug Report of 1948 listed 78 existing irrigation projects on the reservation, incorporating about 23,000 acres of irrigated farmland. Within the project areas, 2,468 families owned farms that averaged 9 acres: far too small to support a family or succeed as commercial enterprises. If the farms were enlarged to 40 to 60 acres, the estimated minimum size for subsistence support, only about 400 families could have been accommodated on the existing irrigated acreage (Young 1961:123, 126).

Although the Navajo-Hopi Long Range Rehabilitation Act of 1950 authorized $9,000,000 for the development of irrigation projects on the reservation, as late as 1962, only $6,616,775 had been appropriated for the work (table 12). In the 1950s, irrigation projects were concentrated along the San Juan River and had only minor economic benefit. Of the 5,134 acres brought under irrigation between 1951 and 1960, almost 3,400 were developed as part of the Fruitland and Hogback projects. Farms in the newly developed areas included 20 to 30 acres, still too small to support a family even at subsistence level. However, irrigation developments had slight economic impact on the Navajos during the 1950s, and by 1960 only 124 families (620 people) had benefited from the projects (table 16), less than 1 percent of the Navajo population.

Increases in irrigated acreage had no appreciable effect on the intensity of Navajo farming, at least not on the number of acres farmed. Navajo farmers continued to plant only a small portion of the available acreage. In 1951, when project construction began, the Navajos planted only 10,008 acres out of approximately 23,000 under ditch. In 1959, after several

TABLE 16. *Irrigated Farm Acreage Developed: 1951–1960*

Project	Acreage	New Farms	Number of People Benefited
Fruitland	400	20	100
Hogback	2,975	44[a]	220
Many Farms	274	13	65
Ganado	485	16	80
Red Lake	1,000	31	155
Totals	5,134	124	620

Source: Young 1961:125.

[a]Young provides no figures for the number of new farms and people benefited for one tract of 1,200 acres that was developed in the Hogback project. We assume that farms had not yet been assigned on the tract.

projects had been completed and several thousand new acres developed, they planted only 10,213 acres. In the intervening years, irrigated acreage planted fluctuated from a high of 17,816 in 1952 to a low of 9,696 in 1956 (Young 1961:125). Between 1965 and 1975, the major San Juan projects showed no noticeable trend towards increased utilization of farmland, in spite of population pressure (Bailey and Bailey 1982:521). Evidently, the growth of Navajo farming between 1950 and 1975 was inconsequential, if in fact it took place at all.

In the 1950s, the government and the tribe shifted their attention from the construction of small irrigation projects to a single, massive plan: the Navajo Indian Irrigation Project (NIIP). Since the turn of the century, several people had suggested using water from the San Juan to irrigate large areas of the northern Chaco Plateau, just south of the river (Reno 1981:66). In 1956 Congress passed Public Law 485, providing for Navajo Dam and Reservoir, which would supply water for the project; and in 1961 authorized the project itself, with the goal of developing 110,630 acres of irrigated land for the Navajos (Young 1961:129–31). Construction started in 1964, and although completion was originally set for 1970, water did not actually reach the first 10,000-acre tract until 1976 (Reno 1981:67). Although initial plans called for division into individual family farms, by the time water was brought to the first irrigation tract, it had been decided that individual family farm assignment was not economically feasible. Instead, Navajo Agricultural Products Industries, a tribal corporation, was created to farm the NIIP.

Unfortunately, separate estimates for income from farming and livestock are not available for this period, and we have to examine them as a unit. These two sources provided an estimated 58.5 percent of all Navajo income as late as 1940, but fell to 22.7 percent by 1952, 9.1 percent by 1960, 2 percent by 1974, and 1.6 percent by 1978. Farming and livestock earned $4,719,124 for Navajos in 1952, or adjusting for inflation, $5,936,000 (1967 =100); $3,950,000 in 1960, adjusted to $4,453,213; and $6,747,000 in 1978, or the equivalent of only $3,452,917 (tables 17, 18). Thus, we see a steady but gradual decline in the absolute value of farming and stock raising, corresponding to a sharp decline in the economic importance of farming and stock raising relative to other sources of income after 1950. Wage labor and welfare displaced both farming and herding as sources of income, which even combined, had little overall importance in the Navajo economy by the mid-1970s.

Craft Income

The craft industries experienced major fluctuations in economic importance during this period. In 1940 individual income from arts and crafts (primarily rugs) came to $441,700, or approximately 11 percent of the Navajos' total individual income (U.S. Bureau of Indian Affairs 1941:tables III, XIV). After 1940, crafts underwent a rapid decline in economic importance. In his discussion of the Navajo trade in the early 1930s, Youngblood (1935:9) noted, "The rug income is of greater economic significance to the Navajos than the values involved would indicate. It is practically the only income they can normally depend upon between wool and lamb marketing seasons." While rug weaving once filled these seasonal gaps, after 1950 they were filled by sources of income such as wage labor and welfare, ending the compelling economic urgency to weave that had characterized earlier periods.

In addition, depressed rug prices during the 1940s and 1950s gave the average weaver little in return for her labor. As late as 1959, it was estimated that most weavers earned only about 6¢ an hour (*Farmington Daily Times*, Jan. 18, 1959).[11] As a result, young women in particular lost interest in the craft (*Farmington Daily Times*, Jan. 18, 1959), and weaving suffered a serious decline. In 1950, Gilbert Maxwell, a trader at Farmington, New Mexico, purchased 3,402 rugs; ten years later he was able to purchase only 1,364 (Maxwell 1963:61). According to Luther Manning, another trader, Bruce Bernard's Trading Post in Shiprock handled an average of 400 to 500 rugs a year from the 1920s until World War II, but in 1958, the store bought only 225 (interview with Luther Manning, Aug. 14, 1958, McNitt Collection, NMSRCA). In 1958 the total Navajo income from craft sales was estimated at $450,000, or only about 1 percent of their total income (Young 1958:105).

TABLE 17. Individual Income by Source: 1952

Wage Labor[a]		
Railroads and seasonal farm work		
Railroads	$ 5,180,000	24.9%
Railroad compensation	1,450,000	7.0
Seasonal farm labor	3,025,000	14.6
	$ 9,655,000	46.5%
On-reservation government employment		
Bureau of Indian Affairs payroll	1,750,000	8.4
Navajo tribal payroll	825,885	4.0
	$ 2,575,885	12.4%
Other employment		
Public utility service occupations	122,000	
Mining	240,000	
Forestry	280,000	
Construction	275,000	
Manufacturing	70,000	
Government defense projects	600,000	
"Self-placed" (estimated)	250,000	
Sub-total	$ 1,837,000	8.9
Total for wage labor	$14,067,885	67.8%
Livestock and Farming (sold and consumed)[b]		
Livestock	3,541,748	17.1
Farming	1,177,396	5.6
	$ 4,719,124	22.7%
Unearned Cash Income[c]	1,750,794	8.4
Arts and Crafts	?	?
Mineral Leases (individual allotments)[d]	218,958	1.1
Total Individual Income	$20,756,781	100.0%

[a]Young 1954:124.
[b]Young 1954:115.
[c]Young 1961:301.
[d]Young 1961:268, 270.

Starting in the late 1960s, the United States experienced another of its periodic "Indian crazes." Indian rugs, pottery, and basketry again became popular decorator items, and Indian-style jewelry, particularly silver and turquoise, became fashionable. The market for both old and new craft items expanded quickly, and prices rose rapidly.

The number of active weavers and rug production increased with the demand. A survey conducted by Navajo Community College reported that weaving income reached $2,799,232 in 1972, and a survey made in 1973 estimated that 28,000 Navajo women knew how to weave. Even though rugs were bringing higher prices, weaving remained a low-paid occupation. In 1973 it was estimated that Navajos earned only about 30¢ an hour from their weaving (Ruth Roessel 1983:595–96). Silversmithing made even more impressive gains. As the demand for silver jewelry increased, the price of silver bullion went up. Interest was so widespread that even major department stores across the United States were handling Indian jewelry (Kluckhohn and Leighton 1974:4–5). As prices increased, so did the number of Navajo silversmiths and their output (King 1976:12–16; Bedinger 1973:199–200). John Adair (1944:202) estimated that in 1940, there were about 600 Navajo silver workers; the 1973 Navajo Community College survey estimated that there were about 1,300. In 1972 Navajo silversmiths earned an estimated $2,719,724 from their work. In contrast to weaving, silversmithing provided a comfortable income, and some of the best silversmiths were making more than $15,000 a year (Ruth Roessel 1983:599, 601).

The market for Indian craft items stimulated the revival of pottery and basketry, crafts that had been on the verge of extinction. A survey of Chinle subagency in the mid-1950s located only two Navajo potters in that jurisdiction, and by the mid-1960s, probably fewer than a dozen Navajo basketweavers were working in all jurisdictions. In 1966 Rough Rock Demonstration School began teaching pottery and basketry, and later on, Navajo Community College instituted crafts programs. Educational opportunities and the demand for Indian goods quickly revived these crafts. By 1973 there were over 100 basket weavers on and off the reservation, and 125 potters in Chinle Agency alone (Ruth Roessel 1983:602–3). At least in part, commercialization stimulated the revival of these crafts. In the western portion of the reservation, some Navajo potters started making new and exotic forms of pottery intended solely for the non-Indian market.[12] In the Oljeto area, basketweavers began producing baskets with *yei* figures woven into their designs. While such baskets could not be used in religious ceremonies, they found a ready market with non-Indians (Bailey field notes; Ruth Roessel 1983:600, fig. 8). The Indian fad even stimulated the development of a new craft. In the Sheep Springs area, artists started gluing sand paintings (dry paintings) to particle board so they could be hung vertically. The paintings found a ready market with tourists, and the craft spread quickly to other areas of the reservation (Parezo 1982:81–82).

Both production and income from crafts increased rapidly in the late 1960s and early 1970s. Between 1958 and 1974, income from crafts jumped from 1 percent to about 6 percent of the Navajos' total individual income (Kelley 1977:182). Although significantly higher than it had been in the early 1950s, the percentage of income from arts and crafts sales did not regain its pre-World War II level.

Wage Labor

Navajos became increasingly dependent on seasonal and permanent wage labor after 1950, a far-reaching change, and one primarily responsible for the surge in per capita income. In the late 1940s, fewer than 1,000 Navajos out of a population of more than 25,000 aged twenty or older had permanent, year-round jobs (Iverson 1981:56; Johnston 1966a:367). Still primarily agricultural, the reservation and adjacent areas offered little full-time work. Because most adult Navajos could not speak English, and even fewer had marketable job skills, their opportunities were limited to railroad work and seasonal agricultural work.

World War II created major labor shortages for the railroads, and as early as 1942 they were again actively recruiting Navajos to work on section crews and as members of extra gangs (Young 1961:224). By the mid-1940s, it was estimated that the railroads employed about 5,000 Navajos per year (*Farmington Times Hustler*, Oct. 4, 1946). To supply the railroads with such large numbers of workmen, an efficient recruiting system evolved on the reservation, with traders serving as recruiting agents. In a survey of trading posts conducted in 1948 and 1949, Moris S. Burge (1949:table 4) found that 92 percent of the trading posts in his sample recruited labor for the railroads. At first, only the Santa Fe Railroad sought Navajo employees, but later, the Union Pacific and the Denver and Rio Grande also began recruiting on the reservation. In 1949 it was estimated that railroads employed about 7,000 Navajos, over half of the number working off-reservation (U.S. Bureau of Indian Affairs 1949:14). The number of placements in railroad jobs fluctuated during the early 1950s.[13] In a nine-month period during 1951, the railroads hired 11,468 Navajos, but in 1954, only 4,514 placements were made. By the mid-1950s, skilled Navajos were working as metal workers, car inspectors, diesel mechanics, pipefitters, and machinists (Young 1955:63; Harper 1952:33).

Navajo income from railroad work increased sharply between 1945 and 1955. In the mid-1940s, Navajos were earning a total of about $1,000,000 per year from this source (*Farmington Times Hustler*, Oct. 4, 1946), including wages and retirement—a figure that rose to an estimated $6,750,000 in 1950 (Young 1954:123) and $10,673,756 in 1955 (Young 1955:63). By then, railroad work had become the single most important source of income for Navajos, accounting for almost one-third of their total income (Young 1955:65).

Part of the rapid increase in income from railroad work can be explained by wage raises. In 1945 the Union Pacific paid Navajo laborers 97¢ per hour (*Farmington Times Hustler*, Nov. 21, 1947), but by 1959, railroad employees were earning an average of $2.06 per hour (Young 1961:225).[14] Wage raises proved a mixed blessing, soon forcing the railroads to mechanize their maintenance operations to reduce labor costs. Increased mechanization started to displace Navajo workers as early as 1957, and in 1958, the number of placements dropped to 1,543 (Young 1961:224–25).

By the late 1950s, the railroads were also trying to trim expenses by increasing the number of full-time employees and reducing the number of seasonal workers. In the spring of 1959, the *Farmington Daily Times* (Apr. 6, 1959) reported,

> The railroads are trying to cut costs. They want to do away with free transportation. Also, they want Navajos to leave the reservation permanently and work the year-round on section crews, so that the expense of unemployment compensation can be trimmed. Some Navajos have left the reservation for such full time jobs, but others, for good reasons, are reluctant to do this.

The railroads convinced many Navajo workers to accept full-time employment, as indicated by the declining number of claimants for railroad unemployment compensation. Navajos made 2,800 such claims in January 1958, 675 in January 1959, and 564 in January 1960. In 1960 the railroads paid $1,971,200 in wages to 1,400 Navajos, and $1,255,800 in unemployment benefits (Young 1961:225). Thus, within five years the number of Navajos working for the railroads had declined by almost 80 percent, and railroad income by about 70 percent (tables 17, 18).

Railroad employment reached its height of economic importance during the mid-1950s. Although some Navajos were still working as permanent and seasonal laborers in the mid-1970s, the work no longer constituted an important source of income for the Navajos as a whole.

Navajo involvement in off-reservation agricultural work dated from around the turn of the century. However, beginning in the late 1940s and early 1950s, Navajos began to seek farm work in much greater numbers.[15] Before 1950, farmers in Colorado, Utah, Arizona, and New Mexico had obtained Navajo workers directly through the trading posts, but in that year, the New Mexico and Arizona state employment services began recruiting labor for farmers in their respective states and for other states (Uchendu 1966:153). In 1952 the New Mexico State Employment Service set up offices in Shiprock, Huerfano, Farmington, and Gallup to recruit Navajo farm laborers (*Farmington Daily Times*, Feb. 18, 1952). That fall the service sent a sound truck around to the various trading posts to broadcast in Navajo and English a call for workers to harvest potatoes in the San Luis Valley of Colorado (*Farmington Daily Times*, Sept. 24, 1952). Although the state employment services eventually became the major agents for Navajo agricultural workers, some traders continued to act in this capacity, and some Navajos found jobs on their own. Victor Uchendu (1966:172) estimated that the state employment services placed about 75 percent of the workers in 1965; representatives of employers, working through traders, placed 10 to 15 percent; traders placed 5 percent; and between 5 and 10 percent of the employees found jobs on their own.

In the late 1940s, it was estimated that approximately 4,000 Navajos a year were employed as seasonal farm workers (U.S. Bureau of Indian Affairs 1949:14). For 1950–51, the BIA reported 6,655 placements (Young 1954:123), but many people had multiple placements, and the statistics did not include those who found jobs on their own or who were recruited by traders. We can only surmise that during the early 1950s, well over 6,000 Navajos engaged in farm work each year. Navajos worked mainly in five Rocky Mountain states. According to a 1951 report by the Arizona State Employment Service, 2,300 Navajos worked in Arizona that year, 2,500 in New Mexico, 1,000 in Colorado, 1,800 in Utah, and 1,450 in Idaho (Young 1954:124). During the late 1950s and early 1960s, about 6,000 Navajos worked each year harvesting pinto beans, sugar beets, potatoes, broom corn, and vegetables in Utah, Colorado, and Idaho, and smaller numbers in New Mexico and Arizona (Uchendu 1966:141–42, 145, 147, 154, 164).

During the early and mid-1950s, as many Navajos worked on farms as for the railroads, and maybe more. However, farm labor paid less, did not last as long, and did not qualify workers for unemployment compensation, and as a result, brought in significantly less income. In 1950–51, it was estimated that Navajo farm workers received a total income of $2,500,000, about one-third the amount received from railroad work (Young 1954:123); and in 1955, $2,000,000, or less than one-fifth of railroad income (Young 1955:65).

By 1960 income from seasonal farm labor had fallen to $1,368,000 (Young 1961:228–29). As on-reservation employment opportunities increased, farm work ceased to be an important source of income during the late 1950s and early 1960s, although some Navajos continued to work as seasonal agricultural laborers in the 1970s.

On-Reservation Wage Work

Largely because of the Navajo-Hopi Long Range Rehabilitation Act, which created temporary jobs in construction and laid the way for the major expansion of government services and associated full-time government jobs, on-reservation employment became increasingly available during the 1950s. In addition, tribal revenues from mineral resources created permanent jobs in the tribal bureaucracy and funded temporary construction jobs.

In 1952 Navajo income from federal employment amounted to $1,750,000 (table 17). By 1960 the federal government (BIA and Indian Health Service) had become the largest employer of Navajo workers in terms of both numbers of employees and income generated (Young 1961:228–31). In that year, the government paid Navajo workers $9,197,842 in wages and salaries (table 18).

Similar growth took place in tribal employment. In 1952, income from tribal employment equaled $825,885 (table 17), but rose to $3,707,500 in 1960. The tribe also had its own public works program, which paid Navajo workers an additional $4,000,000 in wages in 1960 (table 18).

The tribe sought to develop its own industries and attract private industry to the reservation to improve job opportunities. Tribal and federal funds created eighteen tribally owned businesses between 1951 and 1954, including three trading posts, two motels, a coal mine, a low-cost housing project, a clay products factory, a leather products industry, and a wool textiles industry (Young 1961:190). Even though nearly $900,000 in federal funds and $40,000 in tribal funds went into starting these industries, most of them failed quickly, and only seven of these businesses were still operating in 1955 (Gilbreath 1973:37–38).

Despite the high rate of failure, the tribe continued to establish new industries. Since the late nineteenth century, the BIA had operated lumber mills on the reservation to supply local needs. A study of reservation timber resources led the Tribal Council to appropriate $7,500,000 in 1958 for the establishment of Navajo Forest Products Industries (NFPI), and in 1960

TABLE 18. *Individual Income by Source: 1960*

Wage Labor		
Railroads and seasonal farm work		
Railroad work	$ 1,971,200	4.8%
Railroad compensation	1,255,800	3.0
Farm labor	1,368,000	3.3
	$ 4,595,000	11.1%
On-reservation government employment		
Bureau of Indian Affairs payroll	7,590,000	18.3
Public Health Service	1,607,842	3.9
Navajo tribal payroll	3,707,500	9.0
Navajo Public Works	4,000,000	9.7
Well and spring development	786,000	1.9
	$17,691,342	42.7%
Other employment		
Forest Products Industries	666,581	
Glen Canyon Dam	260,000	
Ordnance depots	1,110,000	
Uranium mills	1,049,854	
Reservation mining	1,000,000	
Natural gas companies	700,000	
Public schools	389,270	
Off-reservation employment	1,323,000	
Sub-total	$ 6,498,705	15.7
Total Wage Labor Income	$28,785,047	69.5%
Livestock and Farming	3,950,000	9.5
Arts and Crafts	500,000	1.2
Mineral Leases (allotments)	803,178	1.9
Miscellaneous	1,500,000	3.6
Unearned Cash Income (welfare)	5,863,552	14.2
Total	$41,401,777	99.9%

Source: Young 1961:228–29.

the BIA relinquished control of the tribal sawmill to the fledgling enterprise (Young 1961:182–83, 185). By far the largest of the tribal enterprises, NFPI also proved to be the only unqualified success. In 1959 the tribal sawmill employed 166 Navajos and paid them $487,530 in wages; by 1975, NFPI employed 564 Navajos and paid them $3,048,742 (Reno 1981:92).

After the failure of most of the tribal enterprises in the mid-1950s, tribal leaders turned their attention to private industry (Gilbreath 1973:38). A number of privately owned uranium mines were operating on the reservation in the late 1940s and early 1950s, and several mills were established to process the ore in the mid-1950s, but otherwise, private employment on the reservation was extremely limited. To attract private industry, in 1956 the Tribal Council appropriated $300,000 to subsidize companies willing to locate there (Young 1961:192, 225). Of the first four companies attracted by payroll subsidies and other inducements, three closed their facilities as soon as they had exhausted their subsidies (Gilbreath 1973:38). By 1961 only the Babyline Furniture Company, with nineteen Navajo employees, remained in operation (Young 1961:192).

These failures did not permanently discourage tribal leaders from trying to attract private industry. In March 1964, the Tribal Council announced that it "invites and encourages investment by private capital to develop the extensive natural and human resources of the Navajo Reservation" (quoted in Iverson 1981:100), and by late 1966 the council had earmarked $1,000,000 for the development of industries on the reservation (Iverson 1981:100).

Subsidized by the tribe, Fairchild Semi-Conductor, a division of Fairchild Camera that manufactured electronic components, opened a large plant just south of Shiprock in 1965. Fifty Navajos worked at the plant when it opened in 1965 (*Farmington Daily Times*, Aug. 26, 1969), but the number increased to 922 by 1974 (Navajo Tribe 1974:24). In 1975 members of the American Indian Movement occupied the building (*Farmington Daily Times*, Feb. 24, 1975, Mar. 4, 1975). The occupation followed a 20 percent layoff, attributed by the company to a sluggish economy adversely affecting the electronics industry. Grievances listed on petitions included adverse working conditions and the inadequacies of the Public Health Hospital in Shiprock. Following the occupation, which lasted for eight days and resulted in damage to office facilities, Fairchild permanently closed the plant (Bailey field notes). Tribal subsidies and cheap labor also appealed to General Dynamics Corporation, which established a small plant at Fort Defiance (Iverson 1981:101) and was employing 75 Navajos in 1974 (Navajo Tribe 1974:24).

Some of the industries that came to the reservation under the new program may have been more interested in tribal subsidies than in developing successful businesses. In 1970 Armex Corporation of New Jersey established a plant at Mexican Springs to manufacture tennis shoes, and Westward Coach opened a plant at Mexican Hat to build trailers and campers. Both operations went under quickly, and "all too soon . . . it would become evident that the tribe had been swindled by both corporations" (Iverson 1981:101).

Other industries hoped to utilize Navajo energy resources, and in so doing, improved employment opportunities on the reservation. In 1962 Arizona Public Service opened the Four Corners Power Plant, and Utah International began operating the associated Navajo Mine near Nenahnezad (Reno 1981:107). By 1974 Arizona Public Service employed 113 Navajos at its plant, and 303 Navajos were working for Utah International (Navajo Tribe 1974:24–25). By the early 1970s, the Page Power Plant and the associated Black Mesa Mine were in operation (Reno 1981:108), and employed 85 and 180 Navajos by 1974, respectively (Navajo Tribe 1974:24–25).

During the 1960s and early 1970s, Navajo wage labor shifted from seasonal, off-reservation work towards a greater dependence on permanent, full-time work on the reservation. The number of full-time, on-reservation jobs went from about 1,000 in the late 1940s to at least 4,000 in 1960 (the data for this year are incomplete) and 14,280 in 1974 (table 19). In addition, many Navajos found permanent employment in nearby non-Indian

TABLE 19.   On-Reservation, Full-Time Employment: 1960 and 1974

Industry	1960	1974[c]
Mining	297[a]	518
Agriculture and forestry	177[b]	840
Tourism	?	217
Manufacturing and processing	205[b]	1,281
Commercial trades and services	?	892
Transportation, communications, and utilities	135[b]	333
Construction	70[b]	741
Public services	3,155[b]	9,458
Totals	4,039	14,280

[a]Young 1958:105.
[b]Young 1961:230–31.
[c]Navajo Tribe 1974:23.

communities, some of which were experiencing rapid economic growth, while continuing to live at home on the reservation or in off-reservation Navajo communities. Many families moved to towns where they could find work and still be close to home (Kelley 1977:198).

Welfare Programs

Congress passed the Social Security Act in 1935, and in 1936 New Mexico and Arizona established state welfare agencies to manage categorical aid: old age assistance, aid to dependent children, and aid to the blind. However, because the states considered Navajos the sole responsibility of the federal government, they did not qualify for benefits (Young 1968:70).

As economic conditions on the reservation deteriorated in the late 1930s, the federal government began to establish relief programs. Starting in 1941, a very limited program distributed $36,685 worth of commodities to needy families, but with 1,244 families (5,558 people) on relief, this assistance amounted to only $4.73 per household per month. The distribution of commodities continued throughout the war years, but economic conditions had improved by 1944, and only 121 families received assistance that year (Young 1961:296).

No preparations had been made for the collapse of the Navajo economy after World War II, and help came slowly. As late as 1947, only $50,000 in federal funds were available, woefully inadequate to meet the need. In 1948, after President Truman's appeal for emergency relief funds, assistance rose to $611,662: $510,075 from the federal government, $73,341 from the Red Cross, and $28,246 from the Tribal Council, increasing the number of families that could receive relief and allowing higher payments. The following year, the federal government and the Red Cross increased their spending to a total of $961,826, and in 1950 the federal government assumed the whole financial burden of the relief program (Young 1961:296).

The Navajo-Hopi Long Range Rehabilitation Act recognized the need for a well-organized welfare program. With federal subsidies, the states of New Mexico, Arizona, and Utah agreed to accept Navajos in their welfare programs, making payments to dependent children, as well as to aged, blind, and disabled recipients on the reservation. In addition, the federal government continued to provide some programs of its own, and the Navajo tribe used mineral revenues to develop special assistance programs (Young 1961:296–98).

After the establishment of these programs in the early 1950s, welfare benefits paid to the Navajos increased rapidly. From a total of $50,000 in

1947, welfare benefits rose to $1,173,000 in 1950 (Young 1961:296) and $5,863,552 in 1960 (table 18). By 1966 an estimated 10 percent of the Navajo families in New Mexico depended entirely or in part on welfare payments (Smith 1966:56). Although data are not available, we suspect that a similar situation existed in Arizona by the mid-1960s.

In the late 1960s and early 1970s, the number of Navajo families receiving welfare continued to increase rapidly. A 1974 survey found that about 37 percent of the Navajo families in the sample received welfare payments, and of these, about 22 percent obtained over 90 percent of their total income from welfare (Wistisen, Parsons, and Larson 1975:223). By the mid-1970s, income from various forms of welfare provided about 24 percent of Navajo income, exceeded only by wage labor (Kelley 1977:182).

Individual Income from Mineral Rights

The Navajos who received allotments on the public domain during the early decades of the twentieth century acquired mineral rights as well as surface rights. During the 1950s, oil, natural gas, and uranium were discovered on many of the allotments just east of the reservation line in New Mexico. In addition, oil was discovered in the vicinity of Aneth, Utah. In such cases, developers paid lease bonuses, royalties, and rentals to the allottees or their heirs instead of the tribe, and between 1950 and 1960, allottees received almost $8,500,000 (table 20).

Many of the original allottees in the off-reservation area had died by the mid-1950s, and the income had to be divided among their heirs—on the average, five heirs per allotment. Navajos often owned portions of several allotments. In 1958 developers leased the mineral rights to approximately 1,200 allotments for anywhere from $200 to $36,000, and approximately 3,600 Navajos received from $40 to several thousand dollars (Young 1958:109). Mary Charley, whose allotment was located in the Gallegos Canyon area of New Mexico, received a record payment of $116,310.40 from the 1955 lease sale (Navajo Indian Agency 1955a, 1955b). The largest profits went to off-reservation Navajo families, but in some cases, heirs of allottees had married into families on the reservation who also benefited from these payments. Income from rental payments and royalties continued to be paid to these allottees or their heirs throughout the 1960s and early 1970s, but in most cases the size of the payments declined significantly by the mid-1970s (Bailey field notes).

TABLE 20. *Individual Income from Oil, Gas, Uranium, Vanadium, and Sand and
Gravel on Allotted Lands: 1950–1960*

Year	Uranium and Vanadium	Sand and Gravel	Oil and Gas	Totals
1950	—	—	$ 101,107	$ 101,107
1951	—	$ 975	68,040	69,015
1952	$ 2,692	—	216,266	218,958
1953	28,911	25	130,705	159,641
1954	45,345	1,126	278,572	325,043
1955	21,294	1,411	98,628	121,333
1956	27,352	806	1,111,675	1,139,833
1957	19,151	3,218	1,982,003	2,004,372
1958	595,560	6,450	1,643,443	2,245,453
1959	119,975	5,556	1,182,744	1,308,275
1960	212,504	396	590,278	803,178
Totals	$1,072,784	$19,963	$7,403,461	$8,496,204

Source: Adapted from Young 1961:268, 270.

Changes in the Relative Importance of Income Sources

Largely as a result of wage labor and welfare, the individual income of
Navajos increased more than five times over between 1946 and 1970.
Annual per capita income was calculated at $80 in 1946, $290 in 1952, $521
in 1960, and $776 in 1970 (table 21)—somewhat deceptive figures, since the
dollar lost almost half of its purchasing power during that twenty-five year
period. Even so, adjusting for inflation (1967 =100), per capita income rose
from the equivalent of $136.75 in 1946 to $667.24 in 1970.[16]

Meanwhile, sources of income were shifting—sometimes abruptly—in
relative economic importance. Stock raising and farming, the primary components of the economy for almost two hundred years, declined rapidly during this period. As late as 1940, it was estimated that 61 percent of Navajo
income was derived from livestock and farming (table 9), but only 22.7 percent in 1952, 9.5 percent in 1960 (tables 17, 18), and 2 percent in 1974 (Kelley 1977:182). Although the 1940 estimate included the value of livestock
and farm produce consumed by the Navajos, unlike the 1952, 1960, and
1974 estimates, the decline was substantial.

TABLE 21. *Individual Annual Per Capita Income: 1946–1970*

Year	Income	Adjusted Income (1967 =100)
1946	$ 80.00[a]	$136.75
1952	290.00[b]	364.78
1960	521.00[c]	587.37
1970	776.00[d]	667.24

[a]*Farmington Times Hustler*, July 5, 1946.
[b]See table 17.
[c]Adapted from Young 1961:228; see table 18.
[d]U.S. Commission on Civil Rights 1973:A-59, for on-reservation Navajos. Gilbreath 1973:4 gives the figure of $831.00.

Income from crafts production followed a slightly different course. Weaving and silversmithing income fell from approximately 11 percent of Navajo income in 1940 to slightly more than 1 percent in 1960 (table 18), but rose sharply in the late 1960s and early 1970s. In 1974 it was estimated that about 6 percent of their income was derived from this source (Kelley 1977:108). For most Navajos, craft income, like that from livestock and farming, had been reduced to a role of supplementing income from wage labor and welfare, the primary sources.

Wage labor had been the largest single source of income for Navajos during the mid-1930s and World War II, but these were only temporary phenomena, and wage labor did not take a permanent place as the most important source of income until the late 1940s and early 1950s. In 1940 wage labor constituted only 28.3 percent of the total Navajo income (table 9), but by the early 1950s, it accounted for approximately two-thirds, and continued to do so through the mid-1970s. The growth of income from wage labor never really stopped. In absolute terms, it increased dramatically, reflecting economic growth on the reservation; but in relative terms, it was offset by welfare income, which jumped from 8.4 percent in 1952 (table 17) to about 24 percent in 1974 (Kelley 1977:182).

THE END OF ISOLATION

Navajos remained culturally isolated in spite of increased exposure to Anglo-Americans during World War II. For many, the war had been like a tour of some exotic foreign country, in which the tourists see the natives and their way of life, but have little if any meaningful contact with them. Although psychological barriers began to erode, and Anglo-American culture did not seem quite as foreign as it had, servicemen and war plant workers again found themselves isolated after they returned to the reservation. Even among war plant workers, only a minority of adult Navajos could speak fluent English. Once again, they were isolated from Anglo-American society in general, and contact was limited to government employees, traders, and missionaries. Nevertheless, the war had made many Navajos conscious of their isolation and had given them some idea of what they were isolated from. Some, perhaps the majority, were relieved to be home, back with the familiar. Others had only whetted their appetites for Anglo-American culture.

After 1950 the geographical and cultural isolation that had severely limited exposure to and acceptance of Anglo-American culture began to break down rapidly. The construction of roads and the shift from wagons to motor vehicles put an end to the geographical isolation of the reservation. Wage work, a surge in school attendance, and increasingly frequent shopping trips to nearby off-reservation white communities raised the level of contact with Anglo-Americans and their culture. Crash programs in education and the establishment of "universal" education for Navajo children gave young people a broader acquaintance with Anglo-American culture and greatly increased the number of English-speaking Navajos. Missionaries descended upon the reservation in unprecedented numbers, bringing with them a variety of religious beliefs and cultural practices. Finally, changes in settlement patterns and the gravitation of Navajos to urban centers made the goods and services of Anglo-American culture increasingly available.

Roads and Motor Vehicles

Before 1950 only four paved highways served the Navajos: New Mexico State Highway 44 cut across a portion of the eastern off-reservation area and connected Cuba and Bloomfield; U.S. 66, later Interstate 40, skirted the south; in the west, U.S. 89 crossed a section of the reservation between Flagstaff, Arizona, and the Colorado River; and U.S. 666, between Gallup, New Mexico, and Cortez, Colorado, cut through the eastern part of the reservation (map 8). These highways had been built to meet the needs of Anglo-American communities, and except for U.S. 666, were peripheral to the vast internal expanse of the reservation, accessible only by dirt roads that were really little more than primitive wagon trails.

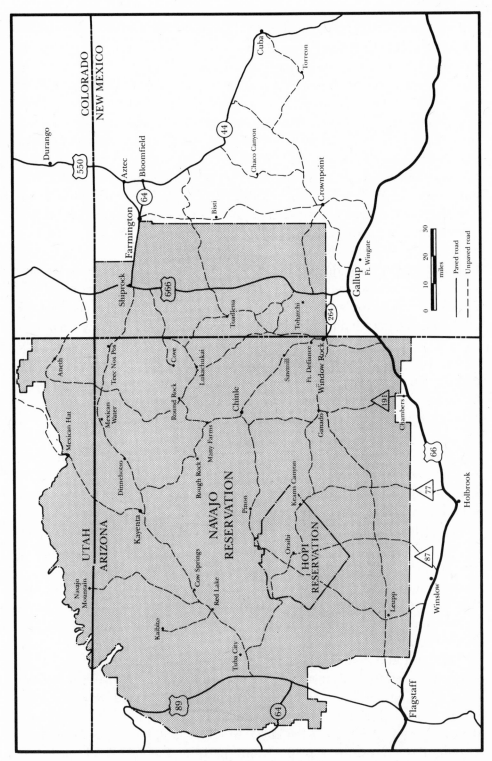

Map 8. Roads, 1950. Adapted from Young (1961:140).

In his investigation of education on the reservation in 1947, George San-chez (1948:62–66) learned that many schools lacked coal for the winter because after heavy rains or snow, many roads were impassable. Even in good weather, coal trucks could not always get in. In 1948 the Krug Report declared that the rehabilitation of the Navajo reservation depended on a road construction program, recommending the construction of 636 miles of primary (all-weather, but not necessarily paved) roads and 633 miles of secondary roads. To begin, the Navajo-Hopi Rehabilitation Act authorized $20,000,000 for road construction, and an additional $20,000,000 was authorized in 1957. By June 30, 1961, 291 miles of paved and 360 miles of gravel roads had been constructed on the reservation, and two new bridges had been built across the San Juan: one at Farmington, New Mexico, and another near Montezuma Creek, Utah (Young 1961:134–43).

Road construction during the 1950s and early 1960s increased paved mileage on the reservation from about 205 miles to 517 miles, mostly to meet reservation needs (Young 1961:143). During the 1960s and early 1970s, additional federal funding brought the network of paved highways to a total of 1,370 miles in 1972. Even though the Navajo reservation averaged only 60 miles of paved road per 1,000 square miles in 1973, compared to 154 miles of paved roads per 1,000 square miles in the southwestern states (U.S. Commission on Civil Rights 1975b:21, 41), the road system on the reser-vation had undergone vast improvement since 1950. Paved roads penetrated almost every region, greatly facilitating Navajo travel (map 9).

Relatively rare on the reservation in the late 1940s, motor vehicles may actually have been more common among the Navajos in the 1930s (Bailey field notes).[17] During the war years, motor vehicles were difficult to obtain, and immediately after the war, Navajos as a group were far too impoverished to purchase them. In the mid-1940s an estimated one fam-ily in fifty owned an automobile or truck (Kluckhohn and Leighton 1974:71), but as economic conditions improved after 1950, Navajos pur-chased them eagerly. Between 1950 and 1975, cars and trucks replaced wagons as the standard mode of transportation, and by the end of this period wagons had virtually disappeared from even the remotest parts of Navajo country.

The Fruitland area (District 13), in the northeasternmost corner of the reservation, led the shift from wagons to motor vehicles. A 1949 survey rev-ealed that families living along the Fruitland ditch owned only 10 motor vehicles, a number that increased to 50 in 1951, and to more than 150 by the summer of 1952 (Sasaki 1960:102). In about 1951, when Hatch Brothers Trading Post (across the San Juan from the Fruitland farms) sold their last

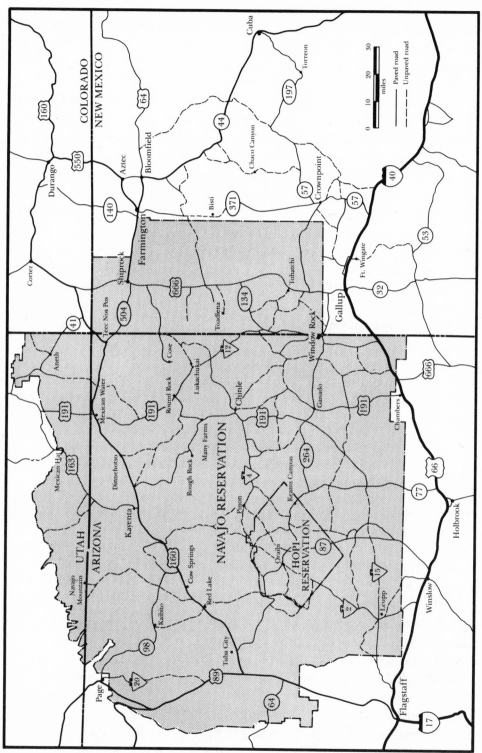

Map 9. Roads, 1975. Adapted from Young (1961:140) and Arizona and New Mexico state highway maps.

wagons in stock, demand was so low that they decided not to order any more. By the mid-1960s, virtually every Navajo camp in this area had at least one car or truck, although limited use of wagons continued until about 1970.[18]

According to James Downs (1964:23–24), the number of motor vehicles owned by families in the Pinon or Black Mesa area of Arizona almost doubled in 1960 and 1961, but only about one-third to one-half of the families had access to either a car or a truck. While the sales of wagons had decreased, horses and wagons remained the primary mode of travel, and every camp had at least one horse. Similarly, about the time Downs was in Pinon, Mary Shepardson and Blodwen Hammond (1970:12) noted that the acquisition of pickup trucks was breaking the isolation of Navajo Mountain residents, although here too, horses and wagons remained the primary means of transportation.

The work of Downs, Shepardson, and Hammond shows that wagons and teams were disappearing from even the isolated parts of the reservation. In 1972 Martin Topper reported from the Tuba City area, "It is a rare sight to see even a very traditional Navajo family driving around in a wagon. Most of them now have pick-up trucks" (Topper 1972:76). A 1974 survey found that approximately 62 percent of all Navajo households owned either a car or pickup (Wistisen, Parsons, and Larson 1975:140). Given that most families lived in multihousehold camps, the vast majority must have had at least limited access to a motor vehicle by the mid-1970s.

The Decline of Trading Posts

Road construction and the acquisition of cars and trucks greatly increased Navajo mobility. Trips that had taken several days by wagon took only hours by car, a circumstance that along with increased income from wage labor rapidly weakened the economic hold of trading posts on the reservation.

As the Navajo economy expanded in the 1950s, trading posts flourished, and the number of posts on the reservation increased 34 percent. Although the economy continued to grow during the 1960s, the number of trading posts began, paradoxically, to decline. By 1970 the count had fallen almost to its 1949 level (table 22), and the decline continued into the early 1970s (Bailey field notes).

In order to understand the rise and decline of trading posts, it is necessary to examine their role in Navajo life. William Y. Adams (1963:154) wrote that by the end of World War I, "the trading post had become, as it

TABLE 22.   Licensed Trading Posts

Year	Number	Percentage Change
1939[a]	93	—
1949[b]	102	+ 9.6
1960[c]	137	+ 34.3
1970[d]	100	– 27.0

[a]Van Valkenburgh n.d.
[b]Burge 1949:5.
[c]Iverson 1981:169.
[d]Gilbreath 1973:11–12.

largely remains, a late version of the old general store which was the cornerstone of the American rural economy throughout the 19th century." This analogy is too simplistic: the trading post served far more complex economic and cultural functions than the general store. One has only to examine Adams's (1963) own study of Shonto and earlier studies by Burge (1949) and Youngblood (1935) to note significant differences. Certainly a general store in that it provided groceries, dry goods, hardware, and other necessary items, the trading post also purchased virtually any items that its customers had to sell (wool, livestock, hides, rugs, piñon nuts, farm produce); served as a bank, making loans in the form of credit or cash for pawn; and incorporated the functions of an employment office, post office, and welfare office. In addition, prior to the 1930s, the trading post linked the local Navajo economy to the national economy, to say nothing of Anglo-American society in general.

Initially designed to meet the specialized needs of isolated, small-scale sheep raisers, the trading post evolved with the wool and lamb trade into the unique, multifaceted institution just described. Production of wool and lambs varied annually, as did prices. Because Navajos marketed wool in the spring and lambs in the fall, they had significant income only twice a year, and this income varied greatly from season to season and from year to year. To compensate for these fluctuations, trading posts extended unsecured credit and accepted pawn. In theory, debtors were expected to clear their bills and redeem pawn after the next wool or lamb sale; in practice, low prices or low production frequently forced them to carry over their debts to another season.

Stock reduction dealt an economic blow to the trading posts. As the herds declined in size, traders had to cut back on credit to most of their customers—an estimated one-third reduction by about 1940. In the 1930s, most posts did not extend credit to workers on temporary government projects because the jobs were too short-lived and income from them too unpredictable and sporadic, further weakening the economic relationship between the traders and the Navajos (Chabot c. 1941:18–20).

In the late 1940s and the 1950s, however, the availability of seasonal, off-reservation wage labor led to an increase in the number of posts. Trading posts became recruiting centers for the railroads, the major employers of Navajos. In 1949, 23 of the 25 posts surveyed recruited workers for the railroads, and 15 of them recruited labor for other employers (Burge 1949:table 4). Like stock raising, income from off-reservation employment was seasonal, and fluctuating income made credit a necessity for the families of off-reservation laborers. The 1949 survey also noted that informally or officially, 24 of the 25 posts handled mail for their customers (Burge 1949:table 4), which meant that traders handled income checks sent home by workers. Some Navajos complained that traders opened the checks, had the recipients endorse them, and gave them the cash that was left after their bills were paid (Bailey field notes).

The judicious use of credit by many traders minimized the amount of cash that was available to the Navajos, maximized the income of the posts, and gave traders tremendous economic control over their customers. As labor recruiters, they knew who was working and how much they made, and could raise credit allowances to a calculated limit. By encouraging families to use the maximum amount of credit, some traders were able to ensure that much of the income generated by off-reservation wage labor would be spent at their posts.[19] As a result, when income from off-reservation wage labor increased during the late 1940s and early 1950s, the trading posts profited and increased in number (Bailey field notes).

Without these advantages, high prices and limited stock would have made it difficult for traders to compete with off-reservation stores. Although some people had shopped in nearby off-reservation communities since the nineteenth century, a relatively small percentage of Navajo income flowed directly into the towns. During the early years, geographic isolation made regular shopping in town impractical, and lack of cash made it impossible. As roads and motor vehicles eliminated that isolation during the 1950s, however, only lack of money discouraged Navajos from off-reservation shopping.

In the early 1950s, merchants in nearby off-reservation communities became aware of the economic potential of the Navajo trade, and radio stations in Gallup and Flagstaff started broadcasting advertisements in Navajo (Bailey field notes; Johnson and Hoffman 1978:124). As radios became more common on the reservation, the number of stations with Navajo programming also increased, and by the early 1960s, a number of stations in off-reservation communities offered such broadcasts (Shepardson and Hammond 1970:12; Vogt 1961:322).[20]

In the middle and late 1950s, the relationship between traders and customers began to change. Railroad employment declined. In New Mexico and Arizona, state employment offices opened facilities on the reservation and began to supplant the trading posts as the major clearinghouse for jobs. Seasonal, off-reservation employment started to decrease, and permanent, on-reservation employment emerged as the major source of wage labor income. As income from permanent employment increased and Navajos had a steadier flow of cash, credit became less important, and trading posts began to lose their economic leverage.

During the 1960s, the tendency of ever increasing numbers of Navajos to spend their income in off-reservation communities further undermined the trading posts' control of Navajo trade.[21] A 1974 survey found that over 43 percent of the respondents left the reservation at least once a week, primarily to shop in nearby towns (Wistisen, Parsons, and Larson 1975:158, 161). A 1974 study of food stamp redemption disclosed that over 70 percent of the food stamps issued to reservation families in New Mexico were redeemed by off-reservation stores (Navajo Tribe 1974:36), indicating that by that time, most posts had become little more than local convenience stores, selling groceries and gasoline. Almost invariably, Navajos bought clothing, hardware, furniture, trucks, cars, and other expensive items off the reservation. By 1973 an estimated 83.75 percent of expended Navajo income was spent in off-reservation stores (adapted from U.S. Commission on Civil Rights 1975b:26).[22] Even on the reservation, trading posts faced competition: new supermarkets offered greater variety as well as lower prices. In 1968 Fed Mart opened a large store at Window Rock (Aberle 1969:247; Kluckhohn and Leighton 1974:6), and within a few years, Imperial Mart opened in Chinle (Navajo Tribe 1974:31).

Thus, as the primary source of Navajo individual income shifted toward permanent, on-reservation employment during the 1960s, the economic importance of the trading posts began to decline rapidly. In increasing numbers, Navajos turned to off-reservation stores or supermarkets on the reservation. As competition from off-reservation stores increased, some trading posts survived by changing their methods of operation, catering to a limited segment of Navajo trade. Some survived as convenience stores for younger Navajos, some stocked a limited range of goods for their older and less affluent customers, some became primarily arts and crafts stores, and some off-reservation posts became pawn shops.[23]

Growth in Education

While the Collier administration supported Indian education, it vehemently opposed off-reservation boarding schools. Navajo education languished as the government attempted to shift to community day schools. Limited resources kept the number of new on-reservation schools built during this period to 50 (U.S. Bureau of Indian Affairs 1949:9–10)—woefully inadequate to meet the educational needs of the Navajos. In the initial stages of this program, Navajo enrollments declined in absolute numbers as well as percentage of school-age children attending school: from 5,555 students in 1930, or 40.5 percent of the school-age children, to 5,159 in 1935, or 32.7 percent. The establishment of other day schools in the late 1930s increased enrollments to 5,962 in 1940 and 6,869 in 1945. However, the Navajo population was growing so rapidly during these years that the percentage of children enrolled remained relatively constant—32.8 and 32.9 percent in 1940 and 1945, respectively (Johnston 1966a:362).

While the percentage of Navajo children attending school remained relatively constant between 1935 and 1945, the percentage of Navajos over twenty years of age with some formal education rose from an estimated 32.17 percent in 1930 to 49.64 percent in 1945 (Johnston 1966a:367). The significance of this increase should not be overestimated: in 1945, adult Navajos had attended school for a median figure of 0.9 years (Downes and Clark 1946:88), and the vast majority had not stayed long enough to acquire basic English language skills.

Following the war, government officials recognized the pressing need for better education for the Navajos and the inadequacy of existing facilities.[24] It was obvious that future economic growth would depend on wage labor, but the overwhelming majority of Navajos lacked the basic language and labor skills necessary to obtain such employment. When the government hired Dr. George Sanchez to study problems in Navajo education, he found the system deficient in almost every respect. In particular, he found the day school approach inappropriate to the Navajos' dispersed settlement pattern. Furthermore, overcrowded facilities on the reservation could not meet the needs of even the relatively small percentage of Navajo students enrolled (Sanchez 1948:25–42).

For the first time, government officials conceived of bringing universal education to the Navajos. As they saw it, this called for providing facilities for younger children as well as for solving the more urgent problem of educating teenage Navajos who had never been to school. In 1946 the Special Navajo Education Program, developed for students between the ages of twelve and eighteen who had never attended school or who had attended rarely, introduced a special five-year curriculum to teach basic English and job skills (Robert Roessel 1979:18; Bailey field notes). With no suitable facilities on the reservation and no funding for the construction of new schools, officials decided to use older, off-reservation boarding schools, many of which were on the verge of being closed (Robert Roessel 1979:18–19). In the fall of 1946, the first group of 290 students arrived at Sherman Institute in Riverside, California (Young 1968:80), and by 1949 approximately 2,000 older Navajo students were enrolled in nine boarding schools in California, Oregon, Arizona, New Mexico, Nevada, and Oklahoma (U.S. Bureau of Indian Affairs 1949:10–11; Young 1968:80). To accommodate the growing number of Navajo students in the program, a vacant army hospital at Brigham City, Utah, was converted into Intermountain Indian School, a facility which would be exclusively devoted to the instruction of older Navajo students. Intermountain opened in 1950, with housing and classrooms for over 2,000 students (Young 1968:80).

By using off-reservation boarding schools and existing on-reservation schools, BIA officials increased Navajo enrollment from 6,869 in 1945 to 11,202 in 1950. Even so, only 46.6 percent of Navajo school-age children were attending school by that time (Johnston 1966a:362). Officials were faced not only with a chronic lack of facilities, but also a shortage of funding to create them.

The Navajo-Hopi Long Range Rehabilitation Act went a long way towards providing needed funding. The act authorized $25,000,000 over ten years for renovating existing schools and building new ones, but the construction took time, and enrollment increased only slightly in the early 1950s. Concerned with the slow rate of growth, in March 1954 the Tribal Council empowered the commissioner of Indian affairs to take whatever action he deemed necessary to bring about universal education. This resolution soon resulted in the Navajo Emergency Education Program, which set as its goal the creation of an additional 7,946 classroom seats for Navajo students by September 1954. Over $4,500,000 was used for construction of new facilities and for redesigning facilities so that more students could be housed and taught. The BIA brought trailers to the Reservation as temporary school buildings and set up 37 "trailer schools" in various parts of the reservation by 1954–1955 (Young 1961:18, 33; Young 1954:4). The program established temporary dormitories in towns, and agreements were reached with eight nearby off-reservation school districts to allow additional Navajos to attend public school in their communities (Young 1961:33, 39–42).

The program surpassed its goal (Young 1961:17–18), and in 1955, 23,679 Navajo students were enrolled in school, or 85.3 percent of the school-age population (Johnston 1966a:362). Enrollment exceeded 30,000 by 1960 (Young 1961:65) and 50,000 during the 1970s (Robert Roessel 1979:96). Although enrollment percentages fluctuated somewhat from year to year, almost 90 percent of the school-age population was enrolled each year during the 1960s and 1970s (Robert Roessel 1979:96–97). For the first time, virtually every Navajo child was receiving some formal education, and by 1972 median educational achievement had risen to five years. Only a high dropout rate among junior high and high school students kept the annual enrollment percentage from going higher (U.S. Commission on Civil Rights 1975b:58–59).

Gains in Navajo education during the 1950s resulted in large part from improvisation and use of existing facilities. The system was a patchwork of government boarding and day schools, public schools, and mission schools. At first, government schools enrolled the greatest number of students: 77 percent during the 1951–52 school year, compared to 14 percent for public schools and 9 percent for mission schools and others (Young 1961:65). The Navajo-Hopi Long Range Rehabilitation Act provided for the eventual transfer of responsibility for Navajo education from the federal government to local public school systems (Young 1961:16). Meanwhile, the problem was one of meeting immediate educational needs by whatever means available.

Public school systems existed both on and off the reservation, an increasingly significant distinction towards the end of this period. In the early decades of the twentieth century, several small public schools had been established on the reservation for children of non-Indian government employees unable to attend local Indian schools, as well as a few Navajo students (Robert Roessel 1979:152). In addition, a small number of Navajo students had gone to public schools in nearby off-reservation, non-Indian communities as early as the 1920s. However, the off-reservation schools had never encouraged Navajo enrollment, and in 1939 only 98 Navajos—less than 2 percent of Navajo students—were attending public schools either on or off the reservation. Although public school attendance had increased to 1,837 by the 1951–52 school year, this number represented no more than 14 percent of total Navajo school enrollment (Robert Roessel 1979:96–97; Young 1961:65).

In the 1950s, the government encouraged on-reservation and off-reservation public schools to enroll Navajos by offering various kinds of subsidies. Under the authority of the Johnson-O'Malley Act of 1934, the Department of the Interior contracted with off-reservation public school systems to provide education for reservation Indians. At first, off-reservation communities showed little interest in such funding. In 1950 Congress passed Public Law 874, primarily intended to compensate local school districts for educating the children of military personnel, but which also applied to reservation Indians; and Public Law 815, which earmarked money to build schools in these districts (Robert Roessel 1979:152–54). By the early 1950s, off-reservation school districts began to see the economic advantage of enrolling Navajo students. In addition to public laws 815 and 874, the Navajo Emergency Education Program supplied a one-time payment of $1,000 per student to districts that agreed to enroll a specified number of Navajo students for a period of twenty years. With such incentive, eight off-reservation school districts, mostly in communities adjacent to the reservation, quickly contracted with the BIA to accept a total of 2,235 Navajo students (Young 1961:39–40).

Public schools on the reservation were initially denied funding under public laws 815 and 874, but after these laws were amended in the mid-1950s, the schools grew rapidly. Of 11 school districts on the reservation in 1976–77, incorporating 37 schools, some fell entirely within the reservation and served Navajo students almost exclusively; while others extended into off-reservation areas, and had both Navajo and non-Navajo students (Robert Roessel 1979:154, 91).

The expansion of public schools diminished the role of the BIA in Navajo education. Although the enrollment of Navajo students in BIA schools more than doubled between 1951–52 and 1969–70, the percentage of total Navajo enrollment in these schools fell from 77 percent to 48 percent. During the same period, Navajo enrollment in public schools jumped from 1,837 to 21,703, and the percentage of Navajo students attending increased from 14 percent to 46 percent. In the early 1970s, the absolute number of Navajos enrolled in government schools began to decline for the first time, and public schools took the lead in Navajo education. By 1975–76 only 33 percent of Navajo students were in government schools, while 59 percent were enrolled in public schools (table 23).

After 1950 the role of mission schools in Navajo education became less significant. In the 1960s and early 1970s, they suffered a general decline in enrollment. As private, religious institutions, they did not qualify for funding under Public Law 815 or Public Law 874, but depended entirely on private donations and tuition. When missionary activity intensified during the 1950s, some existing schools expanded and several new schools were established, none of which challenged the old mission schools in terms of enrollment or influence. In 1960 mission schools on and off the reservation enrolled about 1,300 Navajos (Young 1961:49–51). In the 1960s and early

TABLE 23. *Navajo Student Enrollments by School System*

Year	Bureau of Indian Affairs	Public School	Mission and Other	Total
1951–52[a]	10,123 (77%)	1,837 (14%)	1,175 (9%)	13,135
1960–61[a]	16,881 (59%)	10,564 (37%)	1,379 (5%)	28,824
1969–70[b]	22,971 (48%)	21,703 (46%)	2,816 (6%)	47,490
1975–76[c]	18,057 (33%)	32,369 (59%)	4,673 (8%)	55,099

[a]Young 1961:65.
[b]U.S. Bureau of Indian Affairs 1969:9.
[c]Robert Roessel 1979:96. These figures are not entirely comparable to the figures for other years. Roessel's statistics are for all Navajo students regardless of age, while the other statistics are only for Navajo students between the ages of six and eighteen.

1970s, however, many of the smaller mission schools closed, and as a group, mission schools ceased to be a necessary component of Navajo education.

Contract schools—unlike public schools, completely controlled by local Navajos—emerged during the 1960s. The first such institution, Lukachukai Demonstration School, was established in 1965 with funding from the Office of Economic Opportunity, and by the late 1970s, nine contract schools had a total of 1,280 students. Through a creative curriculum and textbook development geared to Navajo cultural experiences, contract schools have had a much greater influence on Navajo education than their numbers indicate. In the opinion of some educators, BIA opposition has limited the growth of these schools (Robert Roessel 1979:47–48, 93–94).

Since 1950, higher education of Navajos has experienced a high rate of growth. The first Navajo received a college degree in the 1920s, but prior to 1950, very few Navajos had even graduated from high school. During the late 1930s, an average of 10 Navajos attended college each year, and by the late 1940s, the number had increased to only 35. The Tribal Council provided a major boost to higher education by establishing a scholarship program for Navajo students enrolled in colleges and universities. The Navajo scholarship office, which also received funding from the BIA, made 35 grants in 1953–54, the first year of its existence. The number increased to 316 by 1960–61. Between 1953–54 and 1960–61, the total number of Navajo college students rose from 84 to 401, and by the early 1970s, almost 2,000 grants were being awarded annually (Young 1961:63; Robert Roessel 1979:39). Estimates of the total number of Navajo students enrolled in college during the early 1970s have not been obtained, but the number of applicants for scholarships exceeded the number of awards. At least some

Navajos were attending college on the G.I. Bill, or paying for it with their own money (Bailey field notes).

Increased Navajo enrollment in institutions of higher learning can be attributed at least in part to improved accessibility. Navajo Community College was established at Tsaile in 1968, and two years later, the Presbyterian Church established the College of Ganado, a two-year community college (Robert Roessel 1979:82). State institutions also became more readily accessible. In the 1970s, Northern Arizona University at Flagstaff started to offer extension courses on and near the reservation, and several two-year campuses were already in existence in communities adjacent to the reservation in northwestern New Mexico. New Mexico State University established a branch campus at Farmington in 1956 and one at Grants in 1968, and the University of New Mexico opened a Gallup campus in 1968 (Williams and McAllister 1981:94).

The universal education of children had a much more profound influence on Navajo life and attitudes than economic change. This was particularly true during the 1950s and even into the early 1960s. Indian schools trained students in skills they needed to survive in the Anglo-American world, but also indoctrinated them with Anglo-American cultural values. One of the mission schools during this period had a large sign near its gate that read, "Tradition is the Enemy of Progress" (McCombe, Vogt, and Kluckhohn 1951:82). This attitude prevailed in most Indian schools well into the 1960s. Besides being taught to read and write English, students were exposed to Anglo-American ideas, values, and material goods in the classrooms and dormitories of boarding schools. While not necessarily alienating them from Navajo culture, education exposed them to cultural alternatives that their parents were not aware of.

Religious Practices

Although missionaries had been active in limited numbers among the Navajos since their return from Bosque Redondo, as a group the Navajos remained relatively immune to their influences until the 1950s. At that time, Navajos began to accept non-Navajo religious beliefs and practices in increasing numbers. This acceptance was not limited to Anglo-American Christian religions—Catholic, Protestant, and Mormon—but included the Native American Church, which used peyote in its ritual.

Because of the rapid growth of the Protestant denominations during this period, Dolaghan and Scates (1978:41) called 1950 to 1977 "The 27 Unbelievable Years," a title that could also be applied to the other religious groups. These years witnessed rapid growth in Navajo membership in the Protestant, Mormon, and Native American churches. Precisely what effect this change has had on traditional Navajo religion is subject to question.

It is important to note that the Native American Church, though Indian in origin, was and still is considered by many traditional Navajos to be a "foreign" religion, and therefore associated with Catholicism, Protestantism, and Mormonism. During the late nineteenth and early twentieth centuries, the peyote religion spread rapidly among the plains, prairie, and some southwestern tribes (La Barre 1969:109–23). During this early period, the Navajos remained aloof from its influence, and it was not until the 1930s that some of them became adherents. By 1951 Navajo peyotists numbered somewhere between 8,400 and 9,800, or between 12 and 14 percent of the tribe. By 1960 an estimated 30,000 Navajos, or about one-third of the population, belonged to the church. This growth took place in spite of increasing opposition from tribal officials and stricter enforcement of the anti-peyote ordinance (Aberle 1966:110; Dustin 1960:16). Persecution of peyotists became an issue in the tribal election of 1963. By pledging to end the harassment of church members, Raymond Nakai gained their support, helping him defeat the incumbent chairman, Paul Jones (Iverson 1981:84). In 1967 the Navajo Tribal Council repealed the anti-peyote law (Aberle 1983:567). The church continued to grow, and Dolaghan and Scates (1978:23) estimated that 40 percent of the Navajos participated by the 1970s. Although the Native American Church "represented the largest new religious movement in the Navajo country" (Aberle 1982a:222), strong opposition to the peyote church from some older Navajo traditionalists and Navajo Christians remained (Bailey field notes).

The Mormon Church suspended official missionary work among the Navajos in the late nineteenth century, and did not resume until the 1940s (Flake 1965:84; Blanchard 1977:113). The church conducted an aggressive missionary program on the reservation in the 1950s, and by the late 1970s, claimed 47 Navajo congregations with a membership of about 20,000 Navajos, of whom about half were said to be active members (*Navajo Times*, July 27, 1978).

According to Dolaghan and Scates (1978:41), "In the 1950's there was no great increase in number of Christians or organized churches, but there was a great influx of [Protestant] missions and missionaries due in part to national awareness of the Navajo." This influx set the stage for a rapid increase in the number of Navajo Christians in the 1960s and early 1970s.

A critical aspect of this change was the evolution of a Navajo clergy. Before 1950, Anglo-American missionaries often had to rely on Navajo interpreters to get their message across, and Navajo Christians did not have the education required for ordination. By denying Navajos leadership roles in missionary work, however, the various churches only limited their own effectiveness. The situation changed radically during the 1950s, when fundamentalist sects such as the Assembly of God, the Pentecostals, and the Baptists, with few formal requirements for clergy, quickly absorbed Navajos into leadership roles. From 1950 to 1977, Navajo congregations were served by 203 Navajo pastors. Most of the 73 Navajos who were Indigenous Pentecostal pastors had served as apprentices to experienced pastors in lieu of any "formal college or seminary training," and only a few had gone to a bible training school (Dolaghan and Scates 1978:41, 43). While Protestantism as a whole increased among the Navajos during this period, only the sects that readily accepted Navajo ministers can be said to have flourished. Between 1950 and 1977, the number of Baptist congregations grew from 1 to 62, and the Assembly of God Church and the Pentecostal Holiness Church increased from no congregations to 32 and 24, respectively. In contrast, older established churches such as the Presbyterian and Episcopal declined in number of congregations, and the Methodists experienced only slight growth (Dolaghan and Scates 1978:41–42).

Of the major religious groups proselytizing among the Navajos during this period, the Catholics appear to have been the least effective. Catholic missionary work made rapid progress among the Navajos between 1898 and 1939, but after 1950, it failed to keep pace with the other Christian denominations. By the 1970s, the main strength of the church resided in the south-central portion of the reservation (Trockur 1973; Aberle 1982a:224).

The religious movements in the quarter century after 1950 had little effect on traditional Navajo religious beliefs. Until the 1960s, some people predicted that the peyote religion would cause a decline in traditional Navajo ritual practices, but instead, most Navajos came to look on the church as another ritual (Wyman 1983:536). Leland Wyman (1983:536) argues that Navajos have incorporated the peyote ritual into the traditional Navajo ceremonial system, so that to many Navajos it is just another "sing" or ceremony. Nor did Navajo adherents of the peyote religion believe that membership in the Native American Church required them to reject traditional Navajo religious beliefs or rituals. The attitude also characterized Navajo converts to Christianity. Mormon church leaders complained,

> Some Navajo members . . . won't replace authority of the medicine man with that of church leaders. . . . LDS [Latter Day Saints, or Mormon] church leaders on the reservation have problems with

Navajo members who see no reason why they can't belong to the Mormon faith as well as the Native American Church at the same time. (*Navajo Times*, July 27, 1978)

Kendall Blanchard (1977:225) found that even Navajo converts who openly rejected traditional Navajo religious practices did not experience fundamental change:

> In the process of religious change, traditional ideological value systems of the Rimrock Navajos are not being replaced nor even dramatically altered by Christian theological tenets. Rather, the converts are synthesizing elements of their customary thought patterns and implicit philosophical premises with selected elements of the new doctrines. This accommodation legitimates certain new behaviors without, in most cases, seriously modifying traditional belief systems. Therefore, the event of a Navajo's rejecting traditional religious activities and joining a Christian congregation is actually not as "radical" or "surprising" as some anthropologists have previously suggested.

In times of illness, Navajo Christians frequently turned to traditional healing rituals or sings. According to some older Navajos, even J. C. Morgan, the most famous Navajo missionary, secretly had a sing performed to cure him of an illness toward the end of his life. As one traditional leader remarked, regardless of church membership, "they're still Navajos" (Bailey field notes).

In a recent study of religious affiliations of Navajos living in a portion of the western Navajo reservation, John Wood (1982:177) found that only a minority of household heads listed a single religious affiliation: 53 percent gave two or more, while slightly over 14 percent listed three. Many Navajos see no contradiction in being a traditionalist and a peyotist and a Protestant at the same time, or for that matter, a traditionalist and a Protestant and a Catholic.

In some respects, Dolaghan and Scates (1978:41) were correct in their assertion that traditional Navajo religion was declining. Both in absolute numbers and in proportion to the population, the number of traditional singers was decreasing, as well as the number of major ceremonies that singers knew how to perform (Henderson 1982). At the same time, it can be argued that new religious rituals and practices are being integrated into Navajo ritual practices, and that since the 1950s, the Navajo ritual inventory has actually expanded, rather than diminished.

Changes in Material Culture and Life-Style

The breakdown of isolation exposed the Navajos to a wide range of cultural alternatives—particularly in terms of material goods—that they had never before experienced. Trading posts had offered an extremely limited range of Anglo-American products. The old BIA off-reservation boarding schools tended to isolate Navajo students, giving them only what officials considered acceptable cultural alternatives. Similarly, Navajo railroad and agricultural laborers usually worked in all-Navajo work parties, preventing them from learning English, and perpetuating their isolation from non-Navajos.

During the 1950s in particular, these barriers began to break down, and for the first time, Navajos came into contact with the complete range of goods produced by the Anglo-American world. At the same time, larger incomes allowed them to acquire these products on a massive scale. Before 1950, some Navajos owned beds, tables, chairs, couches, chests of drawers, radios, sewing machines, lamps, clocks, and other Anglo-American household goods and furnishings, but by 1975 such items had become almost universal. A 1974 survey found that 88 percent of the households had "furniture," 60 percent had stoves, 42 percent had sewing machines, and 54 percent had radios (Wistisen, Parsons, and Larson 1975:350). Before 1950, only a few Navajos living in the reservation's major administrative centers had indoor plumbing or electricity. By the mid-1970s, although sewage lines and electricity had been installed in a limited number of areas, 27.6 percent of the households had indoor plumbing, and 47.4 percent had electricity. With electricity came electric lighting and many appliances that had not been available on the reservation before 1950. By the mid-1970s, 38 percent of the households had television sets, 36 percent had refrigerators, 21 percent had stereos, 17 percent had washing machines, 14 percent had vacuum cleaners, and 5 percent had dryers (Wistisen, Parsons, and Larson 1975:350).

Clothing styles also changed. While "cowboy" clothing remained the norm for Navajo males, an increasing number of men wore suits or Anglo-American work clothes. Velveteen blouses were rapidly becoming obsolete as women (especially young women) purchased their clothing in off-reservation department stores (Bailey field notes). Young women also began to wear levis and slacks, although as late as 1958, conservative Navajos considered such attire inappropriate at best, or at the worst, scandalous (Kluckhohn and Leighton 1974:7). While some Navajos continued to wear moccasins, for the most part commercially manufactured Kaibab moccasins replaced the homemade product (Bailey field notes). In short, Navajos made few items of their material culture by the end of this period, adopting Anglo-American goods as far as income and living conditions would allow.

Changes in Settlement Patterns

Wage labor, motor vehicles, universal education for children, an increasing desire on the part of young Navajos to emulate Anglo-American life-styles, and a number of government programs led to a rapid shift in Navajo settlement patterns during this period. Rural camps became more permanent and began taking on the general characteristics of small Anglo-American ranches, while at the same time, small urban centers began to appear on the reservation.

By the early 1950s, the very nature of Navajo camp life was changing.[25] The family camps experienced acute labor shortages. Before then, children had played the key role in herding sheep, but universal education and boarding schools kept them away from home most of the year. Also, the need for income from wage labor resulted in the seasonal absence of the majority of able-bodied men during the 1950s. In the 1960s and 1970s, these changes were accentuated by a shift toward greater dependence on full-time reservation wage work and the enrollment of children in reservation day schools. The accessibility of the camps to jobs and school became a major concern. In addition, the desire of many Navajos to live in areas with electricity, sewers, and telephones resulted in the movement of camps to locations that were more convenient to roads and utilities.

Changes in the factors determining camp location coincided with an attempt by the federal government to redefine land use on the reservation. In order to delineate "Traditional Use Areas," the BIA and local grazing committees instituted a program to map and define areas that were used and could be used by owners of sheep permits. Up until this time, a sheep permit allowed its owner to graze a specified number of animals within a grazing district. After the definition of use areas, a sheep permit was directly linked to the use of a particular tract of rangeland. At about the same time, a program was initiated to fence use-area boundaries. Fencing progressed slowly because of the expense and a requirement that permittees on both sides of the boundary line agree to the project. Such mutual approval was often slow in coming, if indeed it came at all (Bailey field notes).

The division of reservation rangeland into traditional use areas and the fencing of use-area boundaries restricted the movement of livestock and reduced the need for seasonal camps. Along with the shortage of available labor and the increasing influence of roads and utilities, these changes caused many families to stop maintaining seasonal camps. In most cases, the winter camp evolved into a permanent year-round residence.[26] Families with small herds could find year-round forage and water within easy grazing distance of a single camp, and larger herds could be tended with the use of motor vehicles. Families with large herds often built corrals in different parts of their use area so that livestock could be moved seasonally. From the permanent camp, a herder could drive out to tend the animals every day (Bailey field notes).

As the camps developed into more permanent residences, different kinds of structures, usually adapted from Anglo-American models, began to appear: storage sheds, coal sheds, outhouses, chicken houses, dog houses, fenced yards, and even an occasional barn or garage. In some areas, Navajo camps began taking on the appearance of Anglo-American rural homesteads (Bailey field notes).

Camp dwellings became more substantial as it became practical for families to take on the additional expense and effort of building a house (Tremblay, Collier, and Sasaki 1954:218). Although Vogt (1961:322) noted "a strong trend toward White-style cabins or frame or rock houses," by the end of the 1950s, hogans remained the most common kind of dwelling. A survey of seven Navajo communities in 1958–59 found tremendous variation in the use of houses and hogans. In Fort Defiance and Shiprock, houses had replaced hogans almost entirely, but in most of the other communities surveyed, hogans continued to predominate. In Tuba City, Dinnebito, and Klagetoh, the percentage of hogans ranged from 58.5 percent to 87.8 percent, and in Tonalea, all permanent dwellings surveyed were hogans (Young 1961:308).

During the 1960s, houses gained increasing acceptance. In the Black Mesa area, Downs (1972:129) noted,

> In five years permanently located rectangular houses, which were constructed with pitched roofs and made of logs or cement blocks, had replaced perhaps a quarter of the hogans that had existed in 1960. In addition, a new-style log hogan, nearly twice as large as the traditional-style one, had appeared; the larger size, which requires roofing of rafters and composition paper, . . . [was] a response to the increased use of beds rather than sheepskins and blankets.

With funds provided by the Department of Housing and Urban Development, in 1964 the Navajo Housing Authority started work on its first 40-unit housing project in Shiprock (Smith 1966:58) and by 1976 had built more than 1,000 Anglo-American style homes (Jett and Spencer 1981:224). In 1955 William Adams and Lorraine Ruffing (1977:61–62) found only one Navajo house in Shonto, but by 1972 "nearly every" camp had at least one house, and it was said that a new hogan had not been built in the community for the previous eight years.

Starting in 1970, Stephen Jett and other researchers did an extensive survey of Navajo dwelling types and their distribution. Of the 5,222 dwellings recorded in the survey, 31 percent were hogans, and 69 percent were houses. However, the percentage of hogans varied greatly from one area to another, ranging from a high of 73 percent to a low of 7 percent (Jett and Spencer 1981:234–37). A 1974 study found that only 16 percent of the Navajos were living in hogans. On a district-by-district basis, the percentage of hogans ranged from 36 percent to 4 percent (Wistisen, Parsons, and Larson 1975:86, 91). The differences between the two surveys probably reflected sampling bias as well as the rapid replacement of hogans by houses in the early 1970s.

As the number and percentage of houses increased, larger houses were being built, tending to be more closely modeled after Anglo-American structures than were earlier dwellings. Before 1950, people were building mostly small, single-room structures with flat roofs (Young 1961:308), but during the 1950s and particularly the 1960s, they favored multiroom structures with gabled roofs (Downs 1972:129; Adams and Ruffing 1977:61–62; Bailey and Bailey 1982:540). In the mid-1970s, a survey reported that approximately 76 percent of Navajo dwellings had two or more rooms (Wistisen, Parsons, and Larson 1975:92).

The change from hogans to houses had far more profound significance for Navajo culture than a change in the predominant kind of dwelling. The only appropriate place to conduct certain ceremonies (Frisbie 1980:165; Tremblay, Collier, and Sasaki 1954:216–17), hogans have a strong religious significance to Navajos (Kluckhohn and Leighton 1974:88–89).[27] Earlier in the twentieth century, a Navajo family might build a house as a status symbol, using it for storage and living in a nearby hogan (Jones et al. 1939:82; Lockett 1952:137; Haile 1954:11). Navajo opposition to the occupation of houses had apparently lost ground by mid-century, for as Marc-Adelard Tremblay, John Collier, Jr., and Tom Sasaki (1954:217) noted, "In the Fruitland community, negative sanctions no longer exist against those who wish to build a modern type house." Precisely what kinds of sanctions existed or why there was such pronounced opposition to houses is difficult to say.

Believing that ghosts frequented a dwelling where someone had died, Navajos abandoned or destroyed such buildings—a practice that made them reluctant to invest very much time or money in an Anglo-style house. As hospital facilities were expanded during the 1950s, seriously ill Navajos were taken to hospitals more frequently, and by the 1960s, the majority of Navajos died in hospitals (Lamphere 1977:162), a change that helped eliminate this reluctance.

Thus, changes that took place in Navajo dwellings during the 1950s and 1960s indicated other and more profound changes in Navajo beliefs and life-style. However, even in areas strongly oriented towards houses, hogans continued to be required for ceremonial purposes, and for this reason, most camps maintained at least one (Bailey field notes; Kluckhohn and Leighton 1974:88).

For reasons discussed, the old Navajo settlement pattern of dispersed family camps began to break down during this period (McIntire 1967:94). By the 1960s, attracted by employment opportunities, public schools, housing, and public utilities, many Navajo families began to move into urban centers such as Shiprock, Window Rock, Fort Defiance, Navajo, Kayenta, Tuba City, Crownpoint, Chinle, and Ganado (Bailey field notes; Kluckhohn and Leighton 1974:3).[28]

During the 1960s, the availability of jobs on the reservation and in adjacent, off-reservation communities showed a dramatic increase. A survey conducted in the early 1970s found that of 17,228 full-time and part-time jobs on the reservation, 82 percent were concentrated in just eight communities: Chinle (2,284), Crownpoint (1,149), Fort Defiance (1,925), Kayenta (571), Navajo (697), Shiprock (3,616), Tuba City (1,762), and Window Rock (2,100) (Navajo Tribe 1974:26). Other employment opportunities were found in the off-reservation communities of Farmington, Gallup, Winslow, Flagstaff, and Holbrook. Because jobs were highly concentrated in a few areas, Navajo workers had to travel long distances to their jobs each day. Round trips of 50 to 100 miles were not unusual (Bailey field notes), and many Navajos found it desirable to move closer to their place of employment.

As we have seen, during this period an ever increasing percentage of Navajo school children went to public day schools on or off the reservation. In some areas, school bus routes developed, but elsewhere, parents had to drive children to school. To avoid the long, tiring drive, parents of school-age children often tried to move closer to schools or bus routes (Bailey field notes).

Families also moved into urban areas to take advantage of public utilities (Bailey field notes). Because Navajos lived over such a large, thinly populated area, it was impossible to bring public utilities and services to every camp. Few rural camps had electricity, running water, natural gas, sewers, or telephones; and therefore, no electric or gas ranges, refrigerators, electric lights (unless they used gas generators), indoor plumbing, television sets, or telephones.

Young Navajo couples in particular wanted the conveniences that urban life afforded. Many who wanted to leave the isolated family camps and relocate near schools and jobs were assisted by the Navajo Housing Authority and the Navajo Tribal Utilities Authority, which sponsored housing projects in these areas. Other families moved to off-reservation communities. Between 1940 and 1970, the Indian populations of Farmington, Flagstaff, Gallup, Winslow, and Holbrook increased from 376 to 6,560 (Kelley 1977:198). Although not all of the newcomers were Navajos, certainly the vast majority were.

As a result of this shift in Navajo population, Navajos were becoming more tightly clustered in a few areas of the reservation, leaving more remote areas to older and less educated members of the family. This pattern did not necessarily result in an economic or social break between young people and their families. In many cases, a strong economic tie continued to exist, as many couples kept livestock in the family herd, and a constant coming and going of family members between the various residences maintained economic and social ties (Bailey and Bailey 1982:573–78). However, it did weaken family ties.

PATTERNS OF CHANGE IN NAVAJO CULTURE

Navajo culture underwent far-reaching changes in the quarter century following 1950, and in the mid-1970s, the changes did not give any sign of ending or slackening. In fact, the rate at which Navajo culture was changing accelerated throughout this period and continued to accelerate up to the present day—the mid-1980s. This chapter ends with the mid-1970s solely because of the lack of available data. Within the first decade of this period, most of the remaining cultural, geographical, and economic barriers that for the preceding century had isolated the Navajos from the onslaught of Anglo-American culture were swept away. An expanding population and rapidly changing economic conditions and needs forced the Navajos into the Anglo world, bringing widespread acceptance and adoption of Anglo-American ideas, values, and material items. As a result, virtually every aspect of Navajo culture underwent major changes: political organization, religion, material culture, settlement patterns, land use, and family structure. Only the relatively low income of Navajos inhibited their acceptance of Anglo-American culture during this period. If employment opportunities and income had been greater, the changes in Navajo life-style would have been even more dramatic.

Neither Navajo culture nor social cohesiveness disintegrated under this onslaught. Socially, the Navajos remained as they had always been—a population separated from the rest of American society by a strong sense of tribal identity. Navajo culture proved to be extraordinarily flexible and adaptive as it absorbed a major infusion of new cultural items, incorporating ideas, beliefs, and technology while limiting cultural loss through displacement or replacement to minor items of material culture. As a result, far from destroying Navajo culture, these changes expanded the cultural inventory.

The effects of culture change during this period varied geographically and from generation to generation. Economic developments, as well as contact with merchants, missionaries, and other non-Navajos, accentuated regional differences that had already existed.[29] For the first time, major generational differences started to appear, overriding regional variations in Navajo culture.[30] By the late 1960s, for example, most younger Navajos had gone to school and spoke English, while most of their parents and grandparents had attended school briefly or not at all, and did not speak English.

To some degree, differences in economic status had always existed in Navajo society, but during this period, they began to assume new forms and meaning. In the past, resources that in theory had been equally available to everyone allowed great economic mobility: a bright, ambitious young couple could build up a herd and become prosperous. Livestock controls and the sheep permit system virtually closed this traditional avenue of economic advancement. Most young couples could secure a sheep permit only through inheritance, and even then, regulations limited the ultimate size of their herd. Ambitious Navajos turned to wage labor, in which educational background and job skills determined income and advancement opportunities. The lack of such training severely limited earning potential. For the first time, varying accessibility of resources (livestock, farms, or wage labor) resulted in major discrepancies of income level and income source from family to family. In earlier periods, the wealth of a family had been measured solely by the quantity of goods it owned—horses, sheep, jewelry. Once the Navajo people found themselves totally caught up in a cash economy, however, dependent on Anglo-American industry for virtually all of their material goods, differences of wealth came to be expressed in qualitative terms. Navajos chose houses over hogans, motor vehicles over travel by horse or on foot, butane stoves over wood stoves, television sets over radios. As life-styles became differentiated through this process, Navajo culture became increasingly heterogeneous.

Late-nineteenth-century acculturationists had advocated the "individualization" of the Indian. "American Indians" were to become "Indian Americans." While regional cultural differences have existed among the Navajos since before Bosque Redondo, significant differences began to appear at the family level only after 1950. Income level, income sources, religious practices, educational backgrounds, and material culture became increasingly heterogeneous as the period progressed. Even within an extended family residence unit, pronounced differences existed between households, between generations, and between siblings. Although the post-1950 period witnessed the "individualization" of the Navajos, this process has yet to erode their cultural cohesiveness and social solidarity.

Conclusion: Why the Navajos are Different

The Navajo people seldom feel any threat to their social identity as Navajos. Their sociological and ideological institutions have proved resilient enough to adapt to changes in the more material aspects of Navajo culture and to absorb what the people wanted of Anglo-American culture. Navajo identity is not endangered to the point where overt markers of "Indianness" are necessary; a Navajo is free to wear tennis shoes while performing a religious ceremony or to eat doughnuts and sno-cones instead of "Indian food" at "Indian events."

Few North American Indian tribes have maintained such cultural continuity during the past century. The core institutions of most tribes have disintegrated, and their members have been at least partially assimilated into surrounding populations. Some tribes exist only in the legal fiction of the federal bureaucracy and the courts. Unlike many other North American Indians, the Navajos were never completely dominated for a long period of time by other societies, and so their cultural autonomy has never been seriously challenged (Spicer 1954:675; Vogt 1961:329; Downs 1964:96–97).

Why have the Navajos survived and flourished alongside of the dominant Anglo-American society, while other tribes were assimilated or struggled to maintain their sociocultural identity? The histories of tribes living east of the Rocky Mountains and south of the Great Lakes in North America have much in common with one another. Collectively, these tribes experienced European contact much differently from the way the Navajos did.

Disease and warfare—the direct or indirect results of European settlement and trade—destroyed some eastern tribes and severely weakened others that had never even seen a European (Dobyns 1976, 1983). Even before Europeans actually settled in some areas, their diseases preceded them, decimating many native populations. As the colonists moved westward, the disruption of Indian communities worsened, reaching well in advance of the actual line of settlements and even beyond the limits of European trade networks.

For some surviving tribes, not all the initial effects of European contact were disastrous. The introduction of horses and metal tools allowed some groups to flourish with their core institutions intact, adapting and integrating alien traits into their cultures. However, this renaissance did not last. As Euro-American expansion continued, so did warfare, epidemics, and population loss. Tribes were displaced farther westward into areas sometimes quite different ecologically from their homelands. The steady destruction of wildlife ruined or at least weakened the economic stability of all the tribes.

At one time or another in its history, each tribe faced some catastrophic event. For the Natchez, it was war with the French (Swanton 1911); for the Mandan, it was a series of epidemics which killed most of their population (Bruner 1961). Southeastern tribes were forced to move to new reservations west of the Mississippi (Eggan 1966:15–44), and the Plains tribes finally fell victim to the destruction of the bison herds.

Nothing in their past experiences prepared the tribes for disasters of such magnitude, and no modifications of their traditional social institutions could have saved them from the effects of these episodes. Some institutions vanished overnight. Sociopolitical structures, religious beliefs and rituals that had held the tribal communities together, and even languages began to disappear. Smaller tribes were absorbed by larger ones: the Natchez by the Cherokee, the Mandan by the Hidatsa (Bruner 1961). Other tribes fragmented. Individually and in families, the Munsee and "New York" Indians of Kansas scattered and were assimilated into other tribes and even into non-Indian communities.

If governmental pressures for assimilation had been greater during the eighteenth and nineteenth centuries, most of the Indian tribes of the eastern United States would have been absorbed into the Euro-American and

Afro-American populations. As it was, the fear and hostility that most Anglo-American settlers felt for Indians convinced the government to isolate Indian communities and so reduce the chances of conflict, a policy that continued until the late 1800s. For the most part, reservations were created in regions well removed from areas of Euro-American settlement, and as the frontier moved westward, tribes were often moved to reservations in even more remote territory.

Geographical isolation allowed new institutions to evolve among the eastern tribes and fill the voids left when the old ones disappeared. Some of the new institutions were tribal and some pan-tribal, but most were religious movements: the Long House religion of the Iroquois (Wallace 1972), the Big House religion of the Delawares (Prewitt 1981), the Cherokees' Night Hawk society (R. Thomas 1961), and the In-lon-schka society of the Ponca, Kaw, and Osage (G. Bailey 1973). The peyote religion, later named the Native American Church, was the latest and most important religious movement because it was pan-tribal. Most of these religious movements combined Indian and Euro-American cultural traits. As they developed within the tribes, these movements often became new core institutions into which the vestiges of the fragmented tribal cultures were integrated. It is difficult to know whether any of these movements had any real potential for revitalizing tribal cultures; in most cases, they never had the opportunity.

In the late nineteenth and early twentieth centuries, the federal government began a policy of assimilating the Indians into the non-Indian community through a process of "individualization." Tribal landholdings were broken up and allotted with titles in fee simple to individual Indians, and surplus lands were then opened to white settlers. Some Indians sold their landholdings to non-Indians. Eventually most Indian groups became minorities within the boundaries of their former reservations. Indian children were forcibly enrolled in schools to learn English and be indoctrinated into Anglo-American culture, and "objectionable" religious activities such as the sun dance and the peyote religion were often banned. When reservation and tribal governments were dissolved, Indians had to deal as individuals with local non-Indian governmental offices. Without the protection or intervention of the tribe, they had to compete on their own for survival in a non-Indian world. These changes, along with frequent intermarriage with non-Indians, eroded the social boundaries and cultural differences that separated tribal populations from the larger non-Indian society.

After allotment, the pressures for assimilation increased, and cultural traits became either "Indian" or "non-Indian." "Indian" cultural traits, increasingly peripheral to the daily lives of tribal members, served primarily to maintain a group's tribal identity and distinct ethnic status. "Indianness" came to be identified with the past, and surviving Indian cultural institutions became static, frozen in time. Fearing that Indian ways would be lost forever if they were changed, Indians resisted any kind of change at all. The only permissible way to expand a tribe's cultural inventory was to reach back in time and attempt to revive a defunct tribal institution. The Kiowa-Apaches did this with the Blackfoot society (Bittle 1971:32), the Kiowas with the gourd dance (Howard 1976). In the 1940s, the Crows revived the sun dance, which they had not performed since 1875 (Voget 1984).

Meanwhile, a pan-Indian social identity was evolving that also threatened the survival of separate tribal communities. Intertribal marriages and the increasing tendency of tribal members to leave home in search of work weakened cultural identities and community cohesiveness. More and more, urban Indians and people of tribally mixed ancestry began to identify themselves as Indians rather than as members of a tribe.

While tribal culture tends to be exclusive, pan-Indian culture has the ability to include any trait generally identified as Indian. The institutional core of pan-Indian culture became the powwow, a secular, nontribal social event (Howard 1955). The Native American Church also emerged as a pan-Indian institution, and in recent years, the Kiowa gourd dance (Howard 1976). For small, disintegrating tribal communities, pan-Indianism offered the last opportunity for survival of an Indian identity.

While the encroachment of Europeans had disastrous results for the eastern tribes, the Navajos managed to maintain both livelihood and cultural integrity. What were the particular qualities of Navajo society that enabled it to endure? The answer lies not only in historical differences but also in differences between the traditional cultural institutions of the Navajos and the eastern tribes in general.

Most of the eastern tribes had tightly integrated, well-defined political, social, and religious units. Political leadership was invested in certain offices, often hereditary within a family or clan. A rigidly structured social organization usually revolved around clans that had clearly defined social, political, and religious functions within the tribe. Highly trained religious leaders bore responsibility for performing ceremonies required by a religious calendar. Seasonal economic pursuits were often organized at the community level. In short, these tribes had many culturally defined requirements for the maintenance of their institutions—requirements that made it all the more difficult for such maintenance in periods of dramatic change.

A catastrophic event was one that made it impossible for a society to maintain one or more of its major institutions, resulting in deculturation. The Natchez Indians' war with the French almost completely destroyed their political and religious leadership. Although hundreds of Natchez survived and established a village among the Cherokees, it was virtually impossible for them to reconstitute their political and religious institutions without trained leaders. The Natchez people survived only as a "Cherokee" community (Swanton 1911). The Osages consisted of twenty-four patrilineal clans, and every Osage religious ceremony had twenty-four parts, one for each clan. The *Non-hon-zhin-ga*, religious leaders, were trained in their clan's ritual duties. Warfare, disease, and starvation reduced the Osage population until eventually several of the smaller clans became biologically extinct. Without them, tribal ceremonies could no longer be performed, and the religious structure collapsed (G. Bailey 1973).

Navajo institutions, in contrast, were unstructured and informal; communities were fluid in membership and loosely defined. The true core institution in Navajo culture was the resident extended family, a self-contained, self-sufficient, multigenerational unit that transmitted culture from the oldest and most conservative members to the children. Communal economic activities were rare. Navajo political leadership was at best only slightly formalized, and there were no hereditary positions. Religious leaders, though highly trained, were concerned mainly with curing; there was no ritual calendar and no required tribal ceremonies. If a particular ceremony became extinct, it endangered neither the tribe nor the continuation of other religious ceremonies. The Navajos were divided into matrilineal clans, but these had few functions other than the regulation of marriage. With little formal, institutionalized superstructure, Navajo society was less complex and thus more adaptive than that of most eastern tribes. This is not to say that the Navajos were immune to catastrophic events— only that they were less vulnerable to them.

The eastern tribes subsisted on various combinations of hunting, fishing, and farming. After the Europeans arrived, most tribes developed a vigorous trade in furs, robes, or hides, but geographical displacement and the destruction of game animals eventually eliminated these activities. During the nineteenth century, most eastern tribes found it impossible to support themselves by traditional means, and they had lost any economic base that might have allowed them to gradually integrate into the national economy. As a result, at one time or another the majority of these tribes were dependent upon government rations or other types of assistance for their support.

Like many of the eastern tribes, the Navajos relied on hunting and gathering during the early historic period. In the early to mid-1700s, however, they were able to integrate the herding of sheep, goats, and cattle into their economy—a development that later proved crucial in Navajo economic adaptation. Though their herding remained on a subsistence level at first, during the early twentieth century they made the shift to commercial herding and thus managed to integrate their economy into the national system.

Events that had devastating effects on other Indian populations were short-lived in Navajo history, or didn't happen at all. For example, most eastern tribes were confined on small reservations where government officials could scrutinize their behavior and persist in attempts to change their culture. Because they depended on the government agency for food and clothing during the late nineteenth and early twentieth centuries, tribal members were unable to oppose these violations of their cultural autonomy.

Except during their relatively brief imprisonment at Bosque Redondo and during the Collier administration, the Navajos' reservation experience did not follow this pattern of dependence and cultural manipulation by government officials. When the Navajos reestablished their herds and their economic independence in the late 1800s, they denied the few government employees at Fort Defiance much control over their scattered and inaccessible population. It was not until the 1930s and the economic devastation of the Great Depression that government officials were able to regain effective control over the Navajos. Then in the 1950s, the Navajo tribal government began using the clout of its new energy-development wealth to reassert itself. Politically and culturally, the Navajos have maintained greater autonomy than most other native American tribes throughout their reservation experience.

The Navajos also escaped damage from the assimilationist policy that evolved in the late nineteenth century. Although some Anglo-Americans in New Mexico pressed for allotment of the reservation and the opening of "surplus" lands to white homesteaders, the federal government never gave the idea serious thought. On the contrary, Indian Service officials worked diligently throughout the late nineteenth and early twentieth centuries to expand the reservation. They realized that the Navajo population was still growing and would require more land, and that only a few Euro-American ranchers were interested in the rangeland that made up most of the reservation. Besides, the Navajos were economically self-sufficient, and it was in the best interests of both the tribe and the government to keep them that way. Thus, the Navajos were never reduced to a minority on the reservation, and the geographical boundaries separating them from the surrounding non-Indian population remained relatively well defined.

Continuity in Navajo culture is, then, a product of historical accident as well as the intrinsic nature of Navajo cultural institutions. If the Navajo reservation had been allotted; if the imprisonment at Bosque Redondo had been permanent; if the tribe had been moved to Oklahoma in 1868 as some officials recommended; if the Navajos' economy had been based primarily on hunting and farming instead of farming and herding; if their political, social, and religious organization had been more highly structured — then the history of the Navajo tribe might have been quite different.

Yet none of these ifs happened. The Navajos' reservation was established in their old homeland, geographically isolated from the main thrusts of Euro-American expansion and settlement. The basic social institution — the resident extended family — survived. Along with geographical isolation, economic self-sufficiency insulated the Navajos from political control by the government. The Navajos' economy, successfully integrated into the national economy, underwent a transition from subsistence herding and farming to wage labor. Indeed, the Navajos' economic history since 1868 hinges on the rise and fall of two main economic strategies — the intensified herding strategy and the commercialized herding strategy — and the beginnings of a new one, the wage labor strategy.

Shortly after their return from Bosque Redondo, the Navajos began to intensify the herding aspect of their economy by expanding their flocks to levels well beyond subsistence needs. The surpluses could then be traded to compensate for the shortages created by cutting back other aspects of their economy: farming, hunting, crafts, and so forth. The success of this strategy depended upon the availability of enough land to support more animals than the Navajos needed for daily consumption. Its success also varied regionally across Navajo territory, depending on the location and quality of water and forage. The intensified herding strategy required peace in the region and relative security for the herds, conditions that had not been met earlier. It also demanded trade institutions capable of exchanging surplus animal products for other needed goods. Because the earlier intertribal trade network was inadequate, the development of trading posts was crucial.

This adaptive strategy came into practice between about 1880 and 1892. In the 1890s, it collapsed. The immediate cause was drought; the underlying cause, population pressure. Both the Navajo people and their herds were growing in numbers, but by the 1880s, continued expansion of their landholdings was blocked by Anglo-American and Spanish-American settlers who occupied the range up to the borders of Navajo country.

Recovery from the collapse of the 1890s required a new economic strategy—commercialized herding. In the first decade of the twentieth century, with their herds depleted, the Navajos had to maximize the trade value of livestock and livestock products. Sheep began to be raised as a money crop, sacrificing the subsistence value of the herds and necessitating even more trade to compensate for the loss. Crossbreeding raised both the quantity of wool produced (yield per fleece) and the quality (price per pound). The Navajos changed their herding practices to produce items specifically for the Anglo-American market: lambs, cattle, mohair, wool, and rugs.

The success of the commercialized herding strategy depended upon the simultaneous development of what we call the "classic" trading post, an institution capable of managing a great quantity and complexity of trade. Again, the strategy was more or less effective in different parts of the reservation, depending on population densities and the amount of contact with non-Navajos, primarily Anglo-Americans. In some northwestern portions of the reservation, population density was so low that the older intensified herding strategy persisted with only slight modification. In parts of the central reservation, rug weaving was a sufficient economic supplement to meet the needs of a larger population. The most commercialized areas were those east of the Chuska Mountains and in the southern part of the reservation adjacent to the railroad.

Commercialized herding in turn collapsed with the Great Depression and stock reduction. At the same time, the Navajo population had grown so large that herding and farming resources on the reservation could no longer supply even basic subsistence needs. Wage labor was the only available alternative. Before the Navajos could become successful wage laborers, however, they had to acquire Anglo-American cultural skills that few of them possessed in the 1930s. For this reason, the evolution of the wage labor strategy has taken longer than the earlier transitions in herding. Even after forty years, this strategy has not fully taken hold, nor will it until the number of jobs open to the Navajos on or adjacent to the reservation meets their need for employment.

Since about 1940 Navajo culture has been changing at an accelerating rate, and regional differences within the reservation have become even more pronounced. Distinct cultural pockets have evolved where jobs are available and where the Navajo Housing Authority has established housing. With increased levels of education and dependence on wage labor, "individualization" is gaining ground.

What do these changes hold in store for the Navajos? The basic social unit, the resident extended family, has been primarily responsible for continuity in Navajo culture. By its very nature, this multigenerational, economically interdependent grouping of nuclear families forces conformity on its members. Those who are most likely to be affected by Anglo-American ways, the young people, are held in check by their elders. Changes in Navajo culture occur at the level of the extended family rather than the level of the individual. This will continue to be the case if wage labor remains sporadic and families within the resident extended group remain economically dependent on one another. But as permanent, reliable wage labor becomes more readily available, and nuclear families become economically independent, the cohesiveness and moderating influence of the extended family will be threatened. We are beginning to witness just such a change. If the extended family vanishes as an institution, continuity in Navajo culture change will vanish with it.

Appendix A

TABLES 24 - 28

Livestock Estimates: 1868-1975

TABLE 24.   Estimated Number of Livestock by Category: 1868-1935

Year	Sheep	Goats	Total	Cattle	Horses[a]	Sources
1868	1,025	940	1,965	—	1,570	RCIA 1868:165
	—	—	4,190[b]	—	—	Affidavit of C. Whiting, Dec. 29, 1870, RBIA LR NMS
1869	—	—	—	—	—	
1870	15,000	2,300	17,300	—	8,000	Arny for Indian and Census Service in N.M., 1870, RBIA LR NMS
1871	—	—	30,000	—[c]	8,000	RCIA 1871:378, 795
	—	—	40,000	—	—	Pope to Parker, July 6, 1871, RBIA LR NMS
1872	—	—	100,000[b]	6	10,000	RCIA 1872:53, 409, 793
	—	—	125,000	—	—	RCIA 1872:688
	—	—	130,000	—	—	RCIA 1872:378
1873	—	—	175,000	—[d]	10,000+	RCIA 1873:272, 643, 266
	—	—	250,000[b]	—	—	RCIA 1873:266
1874	—	—	125,000	1 cow	10,080	RCIA 1874:307, 437
	—	—	130,000	—	—	RCIA 1874:62
1875	—	—	—	6,000	11,100	RCIA 1875:130, 632
1876	—	—	400,000[b]	1,000	15,200	RCIA 1876:513, 634
1877	—	—	—	1,500	20,225	RCIA 1877:709
1878	—	—	500,000[b]	1,500	20,225	RCIA 1878:802-3; Sherman to McCrary, Sept. 9, 1878, RBIA LR NMS
1879	—	—	700,000[b]	1,600	23,000	RCIA 1879:115
	—	—	500,000[b]	—	—	Sherman to Lincoln, Oct. 7, 1881, RBIA LR NMS
1880	—	—	700,000[b]	500	41,500	RCIA 1880:131-32
1881	800,000	200,000	1,000,000	800	40,500	RCIA 1881:361
1882	—	—	1,100,000	800	40,500	RCIA 1882:419

TABLE 24. *(continued)*

Year	Sheep	Goats	Total	Cattle	Horses[a]	Sources
1883	—	—	1,000,000[b]	200	40,050	RCIA 1883:297
	1,000,000+	200,000	1,200,000+	300	35–40,000	Gardner to Sec. of Int., Oct. 15, 1883, RBIA LR GR
1884	—	—	1,000,000[b]	300	35,075	RCIA 1884:357
1885	—	—	1,500,000[b]	—	76,000	RCIA 1885:388-89
1886	800,000	300,000	1,100,000	1,050	253,500	RCIA 1886:203
1887	750,000	300,000	1,050,000	2,000	245,800	RCIA 1887:171
1888	800,000	300,000	1,100,000	3,500	245,800	RCIA 1888:189-90
1889	700,000	200,000	900,000	5,000	251,500	RCIA 1889:255
1890	700,000	200,000	900,000	6,000	251,600	RCIA 1890:162, 473
	—	—	800,000[b]	—	—	Morgan to Belt, Nov. 17, 1890, RBIA LR GR
1891	—	—	1,583,754[b]	9,000	118,798	RCIA 1891:309
1892	—	—	1,715,984[b]	9,876	125,529	RCIA 1892:802-3
1893	—	—	1,250,000	1,000	100,600	RCIA 1893:711
1894	1,000,000	250,000	1,250,000	1,200	100,500	RCIA 1894:586-87, 589
1895	all livestock estimates taken from 1894 report					RCIA 1895:582-83
1896	all livestock estimates taken from 1895 report					RCIA 1896:539
1897	all livestock estimates taken from 1896 report					RCIA 1897:499
1898	all livestock estimates taken from 1897 report					RCIA 1898:616-17
1899	all livestock estimates taken from 1898 report					RCIA 1899:582-83
1900	—	—	401,882	6,858	38,260	RCIA 1900:659
1901	380,000	67,000	447,000	6,000	38,260	RCIA 1901:709
1902	380,000	67,000	447,000	8,000	47,260	RCIA 1902:651
1903	400,000	60,000	460,000	8,000	52,000	RCIA 1903:529
1904	646,000	108,000	754,500	12,100	65,626	RCIA 1904:617, 623, 627
1912	—	—	1,461,776	30,290	330,000	Gregory 1916:77
1913[e]	1,182,821	255,455	1,424,776	30,470	324,931	See tables A-3, A-4, and A-5
1914[e]	—	—	1,687,726[f]	37,180	176,141[f]	See tables A-3, A-4, and A-5
1915[e]	—	—	1,819,000	29,310	184,244[g]	See tables A-3, A-4, and A-5
1916[e]	—	—	1,209,300	29,618	76,675[g]	See tables A-3, A-4, and A-5
1917[e]	—	—	1,162,300	29,018	71,475[g]	See tables A-3, A-4, and A-5
1918[e]	—	—	1,197,000	30,256	68,570[g]	See tables A-3, A-4, and A-5
1919[e]	—	—	956,012	28,810	60,860[g]	See tables A-3, A-4, and A-5

TABLE 24. *(continued)*

Year	Sheep	Goats	Total	Cattle	Horses[a]	Sources
1920[e]	—	—	1,090,254	36,222	58,288[g]	See tables A-3, A-4, and A-5
	—	—	1,064,093	36,422	62,588	See tables A-3, A-4, and A-5
1921[e]	—	—	951,191	35,280	61,391	See tables A-3, A-4, and A-5
1922[e]	—	—	966,350	36,780	66,190	See tables A-3, A-4, and A-5
1923[e]	—	—	1,319,398	34,445	56,068	See tables A-3, A-4, and A-5
1924	—	—	942,000	36,000	—	Hagerman 1924
1925[e]	—	—	—	31,454	60,750	See tables A-3, A-4, and A-5
1926[e]	—	—	—	—	—	
1927[e]	—	—	—	—	—	
1928[e]	—	—	1,151,500	63,100	43,610	See tables A-3, A-4, and A-5
1929[e]	—	—	1,208,300	28,775	38,310	See tables A-3, A-4, and A-5
1930[e]	—	—	1,303,951	25,575	32,026	See tables A-3, A-4, and A-5
1931	—	393,885	1,370,554	—	—	*Farmington Times Hustler*, Oct. 13, 1932
1932	—	347,169	1,180,230	—	—	*Farmington Times Hustler*, Oct. 13, 1932
1933	—	329,994	1,152,492	—	—	U.S. Congress 1937:17979
1934	—	294,851	1,086,648	—	—	
1935	—	145,823	944,910	—	—	

[a]We have included estimates for burros, mules, asses, jacks, etc. with those for horses.
[b]Although the accounts give these estimates for "sheep," we have assumed here that they meant both sheep and goats.
[c]The report of the commissioner of Indian affairs for 1871 stated that they had "a few" cattle.
[d]The report of the commissioner of Indian affairs for 1873 stated that they had "a large number" of cattle.
[e]These estimates are for the five strictly Navajo reservations; figures from Hopi are not included.
[f]In 1914 burro figures were grouped with the estimates of sheep and goats.
[g]From 1915 to 1920, estimates of burros were grouped with swine and poultry.

TABLE 25. Estimates of Mature Livestock by Category: 1936–1975
(On-reservation, Hopi excluded)

Year	Sheep	Goats	Total	Cattle	Horses	Total Sheep Units
1936[a]	408,500	66,000	474,500	12,000	23,500	639,000
1937[a]	380,000	55,000	435,000	17,000	41,000	708,000
1938	—	—	—	—	—	—
1939	—	—	—	—	—	—
1940[a]	357,000	57,000	414,000	13,000	31,000	621,500
1941[a]	357,000	52,000	409,000	9,000	27,500	585,000
1942[a]	362,000	52,000	414,000	8,000	27,000	583,500
1943[a]	338,000	47,000	385,000	8,000	27,000	552,000
1944[a]	344,000	42,000	386,000	8,000	26,000	548,000
1945[a]	284,000	32,500	316,000	7,000	26,000	477,000
1946[a]	257,000	29,000	286,000	7,500	26,500	449,000
1947[a]	245,000	29,000	274,000	8,000	27,000	440,000
1948	—	—	—	—	—	—
1949	—	—	—	—	—	—
1950	—	—	—	—	—	—
1951[b]	234,619	39,014	273,633	9,205	27,439	449,808
1952[b]	220,476	41,997	262,473	8,847	27,802	436,871
1953[b]	233,109	45,196	278,305	9,997	27,309	454,838
1954[b]	252,261	52,678	304,939	11,149	26,972	484,395
1955[b]	257,042	55,945	312,987	12,583	26,890	497,769
1956[b]	266,185	62,509	328,694	13,678	25,783	515,965
1957[b]	275,515	71,130	346,645	14,594	23,920	524,621
1958[b]	287,785	62,509	328,694	14,590	23,051	538,400
1959[b]	291,804	80,557	372,361	14,897	22,067	539,323
1960[c]	—	—	390,767	15,482	20,680	556,095
1961	—	—	—	—	—	—
1962[c]	—	—	429,141	17,948	20,071	601,288
1963[c]	—	—	442,936	17,731	18,438	606,050
1964[c]	—	—	441,302	—	27,314	—
1965[c]	—	—	490,979	22,801	20,355	683,958
1966[c]	—	—	491,741	26,655	21,426	705,491
1967[c]	—	—	470,756	28,459	21,687	693,012
1968[c]	—	—	489,213	30,016	21,030	714,427
1969[c]	—	—	496,860	31,009	22,069	731,241
1970[c]	—	—	482,146	34,025	21,525	725,871
1971[c]	—	—	506,027	35,836	24,167	782,202
1972[c]	—	—	506,027[d]	35,836[d]	24,167[d]	782,202[d]
1973	—	—	—	—	—	—
1974[c]	—	—	526,864	49,201	29,353	870,433
1975[c]	—	—	510,301	47,524	28,949	845,142

[a]Aberle 1966:70.   [c]Window Rock Agency, Office of Land Operations, Range Unit Records.
[b]Young 1961:167.   [d]Apparently repeated 1971 count.

TABLE 26. *Estimated Number of Sheep and Goats by Agency: 1913–1930*

Year	Leupp	Southern (Navajo)	Western	Eastern (Pueblo Bonito)	Northern (San Juan)	Total	Source
1913	25,000	700,000	118,500	146,776	448,000	1,424,776	RCIA 1913:221, 223
1914[a]	150,150	800,000	151,800	147,076	439,000	1,687,726	RCIA 1914:175, 177
1915	160,000	920,000	150,000	149,000	440,000	1,819,000	RCIA 1915:189, 191
1916	155,000	420,000	150,000	146,000	238,300	1,209,300	RCIA 1916:178, 181
1917	153,000	520,000	150,000	146,000	193,300	1,162,300	RCIA 1917:184, 187
1918	155,000	520,000	200,000	137,000	185,000	1,197,000	RCIA 1918:203, 205
1919	156,012	250,000	240,000	115,000	95,000	956,012	RCIA 1919:195, 196
1920	135,524	375,000	235,000	160,000	185,000	1,090,524	RCIA 1920:180, 183
	124,093	375,000	235,000	160,000	170,000	1,064,093	See SR 1920 for all agencies
1921	124,191	300,000	235,000	122,000	170,000	951,191	See SR 1921 for all agencies
1922	124,850	350,000	235,000	102,000	154,500	966,350	See SR 1922 for all agencies
1923	67,900	723,998	275,000	98,000	154,500	1,319,398	See SR 1923 for all agencies
1924	—	—	—	—	—	—	
1925	67,900	350,000	—	122,000	174,000	—	See SR 1925 for all agencies
1926	—	—	—	—	—	—	See SR 1926 for all agencies
1927	41,000	—	—	—	—	—	See SR 1927 for Leupp
1928	88,000	401,000	340,000	160,000	162,500	1,151,500	See SR 1928 for all agencies
1929	48,000	485,300	330,000	170,000	175,000	1,208,300	See SR 1929 for all agencies
1930	48,000	498,951	337,000	180,000	240,000	1,303,951	See SR 1930 for all agencies

[a]In 1914 burros were grouped with sheep and goats.

TABLE 27. *Estimated Number of Cattle by Agency: 1913–1930*

Year	Leupp	Southern (Navajo)	Western	Eastern (Pueblo Bonito)	Northern (San Juan)	Total	Source
1913	1,340	10,000	2,680	10,550	5,900	30,470	RCIA 1913:221, 223
1914	2,630	15,600	2,600	10,550	5,800	37,180	RCIA 1914:175, 177
1915	2,835	15,625	2,600	2,550	5,700	29,310	RCIA 1915:189, 191
1916	2,785	14,431	2,600	2,750	7,052	29,618	RCIA 1916:178, 181
1917	2,735	14,431	2,600	2,200	7,052	29,018	RCIA 1917:184, 187
1918	2,235	14,431	4,110	2,400	7,080	30,256	RCIA 1918:203, 205
1919	2,635	15,000	4,125	1,775	5,275	28,810	RCIA 1919:195, 196
1920	3,112	20,000	4,330	3,580	5,200	36,222	RCIA 1920:180, 183
	3,112	20,000	4,530	3,580	5,200	36,422	See SR 1920 for all agencies
1921	3,000	20,000	4,530	2,550	5,200	35,280	See SR 1921 for all agencies
1922	3,000	20,000	4,530	4,050	6,200	36,780	See SR 1922 for all agencies
1923	2,000	20,000	4,195	2,050	6,200	34,445	See SR 1923 for all agencies
1924	—	—	—	—	—	—	
1925	2,000	20,000	1,954	2,300	5,200	31,454	See SR 1925 for all agencies
1926	—	—	—	—	—	—	
1927	1,800	—	—	—	—	—	See SR 1927 for Leupp
1928	1,450	47,300	7,200	2,050	5,100	63,100	See SR 1928 for all agencies
1929	1,350	12,000	7,950	2,075	5,400	28,775	See SR 1929 for all agencies
1930	1,000	8,000	7,950	2,075	6,650	25,675	See SR 1930 for all agencies

TABLE 28. *Estimated Number of Horses by Agency: 1913–1930*

Year	Leupp	Southern (Navajo)	Western	Eastern (Pueblo Bonito)	Northern (San Juan)	Total	Source
1913	1,150	162,000	12,200	10,651	138,931	324,931	RCIA 1913:221, 223
1914	6,250	22,000	12,200	10,351	127,040	176,141[a]	RCIA 1914:175, 177
1915	6,100	28,080	10,700	10,505	128,859	184,244[a]	RCIA 1915:189, 191
1916	6,400	25,570	10,700	10,505	21,500	76,675[a]	RCIA 1916:178, 181
1917	5,400	27,570	10,700	6,305	21,500	71,475[a]	RCIA 1917:184, 187
1918	4,350	27,570	12,800	6,300	17,500	68,570[a]	RCIA 1918:203, 205
1919	4,350	24,650	12,850	5,260	14,250	60,860[a]	RCIA 1919:195, 196
1920	7,983	24,430	12,800	6,225	6,850	58,288[a]	RCIA 1920:180, 183
	8,883	24,430	14,200	7,725	7,350	62,588	See SR 1920 for all agencies
1921	8,111	24,430	13,800	7,700	7,350	61,391	See SR 1921 for all agencies
1922	8,250	24,430	13,800	10,200	9,510	66,190	See SR 1922 for all agencies
1923	7,060	24,430	13,260	1,808	9,510	56,068	See SR 1923 for all agencies
1924	—	—	—	—	—	—	
1925	7,060	24,430	10,100	9,650	9,510	60,750	See SR 1925 for all agencies
1926	—	—	—	—	—	—	
1927	—	—	—	—	—	—	
1928	3,700	10,500	9,010	5,900	14,500	43,610	See SR 1928 for all agencies
1929	1,425	9,500	8,460	6,400	12,525	38,310	See SR 1929 for all agencies
1930	1,300	10,354	8,460	6,402	5,510	32,026	See SR 1930 for all agencies

[a]In 1914 burros were grouped with sheep and goats, while from 1915 to 1920 they were grouped with swine and poultry.

Appendix B

TABLE 29

Market Values of Wool, Stock Sheep, Sheep, and Lambs;

and Consumer Price Index: 1869-1970

TABLE 29.   Market Values of Wool, Stock Sheep, Sheep, and Lambs;
and Consumer Price Index: 1869-1970

Year	Wool Price[a] Per Pound	Stock Sheep[b] Value Per Head	Sheep[c] Value Per Cwt.	Lamb[d] Value Per Cwt.	Consumer Price Index[e] All Items (1967 =100)
1970	35.4¢	$24.70	$7.64	$26.40	116.3
1969	41.9	22.00	8.24	27.20	109.8
1968	40.5	19.20	6.55	24.40	104.2
1967	39.8	19.70	6.35	22.10	100.0
1966	52.1	19.70	6.84	23.40	97.2
1965	47.1	15.80	6.34	22.80	94.5
1964	53.2	14.00	6.00	19.90	92.9
1963	48.4	14.40	5.76	18.10	91.7
1962	47.7	12.90	5.63	17.85	90.6
1961	42.9	14.60	5.20	15.80	89.6
1960	42.0	16.50	5.60	17.90	88.7
1959	43.2	20.30	6.00	18.70	87.3
1958	36.4	19.40	7.20	21.00	86.6
1957	53.4	14.90	6.05	19.90	84.3
1956	44.3	14.30	5.60	18.50	81.4
1955	42.7	14.90	5.78	18.40	80.2
1954	53.2	13.80	6.14	19.10	80.5
1953	54.9	15.70	6.67	19.30	80.1
1952	54.1	28.00	10.00	24.30	79.5
1951	97.1	26.50	16.00	31.00	77.8
1950	62.1	17.80	11.60	25.10	72.1
1949	49.4	17.00	9.27	22.40	71.4
1948	49.2	15.00	9.69	22.80	72.1
1947	42.0	12.20	8.39	20.50	66.9
1946	42.3	9.57	7.48	15.60	58.5
1945	41.9	8.45	6.38	13.10	53.9
1944	42.3	8.68	6.01	12.50	52.7
1943	41.6	9.68	6.57	13.00	51.8
1942	40.1	8.66	5.80	11.70	48.8

TABLE 29. *(Continued)*

Year	Wool Price[a] Per Pound	Stock Sheep[b] Value Per Head	Sheep[c] Value Per Cwt.	Lamb[d] Value Per Cwt.	Consumer Price Index[e] All Items (1967 =100)
1941	35.5	6.77	5.06	9.58	44.1
1940	28.4	6.35	3.95	8.10	42.0
1939	22.3	5.74	3.90	7.78	41.6
1938	19.1	6.13	3.58	7.05	42.2
1937	32.0	6.02	4.52	8.88	43.0
1936	26.9	6.35	3.77	8.05	41.5
1935	19.3	4.33	3.75	7.28	41.1
1934	21.9	3.77	2.85	5.90	40.1
1933	20.6	2.91	2.38	5.04	38.8
1932	8.6	3.44	2.24	4.47	40.9
1931	13.6	5.40	3.11	5.64	45.6
1930	19.5	9.00	4.74	7.76	50.0
1929	30.2	10.71	7.19	11.90	51.3
1928	36.2	10.36	7.65	12.20	51.3
1927	30.3	9.79	7.01	11.50	52.0
1926	34.0	10.53	7.20	11.70	53.0
1925	39.5	9.63	7.56	12.40	52.5
1924	36.6	7.94	6.57	10.80	51.2
1923	39.4	7.50	6.55	10.52	51.1
1922	27.1	4.79	5.96	9.90	50.2
1921	17.3	6.34	4.55	7.13	53.6
1920	45.5	10.59	8.17	11.64	60.0
1919	49.5	11.49	9.26	12.83	51.8
1918	57.7	11.76	10.75	13.96	45.1
1917	41.6	7.06	9.58	12.71	38.4
1916	26.1	5.10	6.28	8.34	32.7
1915	22.1	4.39	5.30	6.98	30.4
1914	16.6	3.91	4.83	6.36	30.1
1913	16.7	3.87	4.52	5.99	29.7
1912	17.3	3.42	4.25	5.62	29
1911	15.8	3.83	4.01	5.17	28
1910	21.7	4.06	4.99	6.16	28
1909	22.2	3.42			27
1908	16.3	3.87			27
1907	20.5	3.81			28
1906	23.1	3.51			27
1905	22.2	2.77			27
1904	16.3	2.55			27

TABLE 29. (Continued)

Year	Wool Price[a] Per Pound	Stock Sheep[b] Value Per Head	Sheep[c] Value Per Cwt.	Lamb[d] Value Per Cwt.	Consumer Price Index[e] All Items (1967 =100)
1903	15.4	2.62			27
1902	13.7	2.62			26
1901	13.7	2.96			25
1900	13.7	2.97			25
1899	14.5	2.80			25
1898	13.7	2.51			25
1897	11.1	1.84			25
1896	10.3	1.71			25
1895	10.3	1.57			25
1894	11.1	1.97			26
1893	14.5	2.64			27
1892	16.3	2.60			27
1891	16.3	2.51			27
1890	17.1	2.29			27
1889	18.0	2.14			27
1888	17.1	2.06			27
1887	18.0	2.05			27
1886	16.3	1.95			27
1885	14.5	2.19			27
1884	14.5	2.40			27
1883	17.1	2.53			28
1882	20.5	2.35			29
1881	22.2	2.35			29
1880	23.1	2.18			29
1879	18.0	2.01			28
1878	18.8	2.12			29
1877	21.4	2.03			32
1876	19.7	2.20			32
1875	25.7	2.39			33
1874	25.7	2.33			34
1873	26.5	2.60			36
1872	31.7	2.51			36
1871	27.4	2.10			36
1870	22.2	1.87			38
1869	22.2	1.65			40

[a]U.S. Bureau of the Census 1975:517–18.
[b]U.S. Bureau of the Census 1975:519–20.
[c]U.S. Bureau of the Census 1975:519–20.
[d]U.S. Bureau of the Census 1975:519–20.
[e]U.S. Bureau of the Census 1975:210–11.

Notes

CHAPTER 1

1. The actual number of Navajos killed by troops during the campaign is unknown. Richard White (1983:214) states that Carson's troops killed less than fifty.

2. Frank Mitchell (Frisbie and McAllester 1978:15) recalled that his family killed and ate its dog. Navajos considered dogs unclean because they were camp scavengers, and unlike some other tribes—particularly those on the Great Plains—did not normally eat them (Bailey field notes).

3. For detailed studies of the Navajo war, see Kelly (1970), Lynn R. Bailey (1964), and Trafzer (1982).

4. Although the first large parties of Navajo prisoners were not taken to Bosque Redondo until the spring of 1864, several small groups were sent in the late summer and fall of 1863. The first party of fifty-one Navajos began its trek on August 27, 1863 (Correll 1979, 4:85).

5. Lynn R. Bailey (1970) and Gerald Thompson (1976) wrote accounts of the Navajo imprisonment at Bosque Redondo. See Thompson (1976:161–65) for a discussion of its effects on Navajo culture.

6. For archaeological findings and interpretations of Navajo and Southern Athabaskan prehistory, see Wilcox (1981), Gregory (1981), Brugge and Schaafsma (1981), and Brugge (1983).

7. Downs (1964:43 n.) believed the Navajos learned herding techniques from escaped Navajo slaves whom the Spaniards had used as herders. This may have been the case, but it is more likely that they learned from Pueblo refugees.

8. Klara B. Kelley (1980:320–21) arrived at an estimate of 240 sheep per household for the 1850s, or a ratio of about 1:50. We do not know how she arrived at this figure.

9. The number of sheep and goats required for subsistence-level support is a critical question concerning the Navajo economy during the nineteenth and twentieth centuries. What few estimates have been made are frequently ambiguous. In 1941 the Navajo Rights Association claimed that a "larger Navajo family" needed from 400 to 500 sheep (*Farmington Times Hustler*, Feb. 28, 1941). The Krug Report (1948:14) estimated that no less than 250 "sheep units" would support a family. George Sanchez (1948:14) wrote that a family needed 500 sheep "to make a modest living." Frank Bradley, a tribal council-man, made the most precise estimate in 1940: "My personal opinion as to the amount of sheep needed for the support of a family runs between 400 to 500. I am just referring to where a person absolutely depends on livestock alone . . . for the support of a family of six to ten children" (Minutes of Navajo Tribal Council, June 1940:128).

10. Only indirect references have been made to the relative economic importance of hunting during the mid-nineteenth century. During the 1840s Navajos were still trading buckskins (Bieber 1936:198–99), indicating a surplus. By the 1870s and 1880s, the Navajos suffered from a shortage of leather and had to trade for it, from which it can be inferred that available game had declined.

CHAPTER 2

1. There were two Fort Wingates. The first, established in 1862 in the San José Valley near present day Grants, New Mexico, was later abandoned. When the Navajos returned from Bosque Redondo in 1868, the army established a new Fort Wingate at Ojo del Oso, about forty miles further west, and closer to the Navajo reservation (Williams and McAllister 1981:39; McNitt 1972:117).

2. Little is known of Navajo political organization before 1863. Richard Van Valkenburgh (1936:17) wrote:

> Aged informants state that there were twelve chiefs: six War Chiefs and six Peace Chiefs . . . a Navajo leader's rank being determined by his ability. A prevailing tone of democracy ran through the entire organization. Choice of leaders was by popular selection from the rank and file based upon an individual's particular abilities. . . . Supreme power was exercised individually as vested in them by the tribe, and their authority was never impaired in their districts. Their sub-chiefs or representatives enforced the injunctions at the meetings of the tribe or council.

Tribal assemblies with ceremonial connections, *Nah-sit*, met at two-year and four-year intervals (Van Valkenburgh 1936:18). W. W. Hill (1940b) also considered war chief and peace chief to be formal leadership positions. Together, Hill and Van Valkenburgh represent one extreme in anthropological thought concerning early Navajo political structure. Using ethnographic data and secondary historical summaries, Aubrey Williams (1970:4–7) presented a more modified view. He accepts a dual war chief and peace chief structure at the band level and formal accession to office, but questions a more centralized structure and the degree of authority exercised by these chiefs over their followers.

3. Describing the political and administrative structure of the reservation during this period, Van Valkenburgh (1945:71–72) stated,

The "Head Chief" was appointed by the Agent with the approval of the Secretary of the Interior. The regional *naat'aánih* were issued cards in place of canes and medals. There were some 30 recognized *naat'aánih* in 1900. Should some untoward event take place in a certain region, the Agent would contact the "Head Chief" who would send a messenger to the *naat'aániah* of that region, with orders to report to Fort Defiance in so many days.

When the *naat'aánih* arrived, the problem of his region would be discussed with the "Head Chief" and any leaders who might be involved. Since the Agent was supported by the military at Fort Wingate, there was very little dickering or disobedience. The *naat'aánih* was directly responsible to the "Head Chief" who was responsible to the Agent.

Few councils of the whole tribe were held. About once a year all *naat'aánih* were "called in," and then only problems of tribal importance were discussed. . . . This system was of course synthetic, a continuance of the old military system at Fort Sumner in 1865.

Shepardson (1963:78) apparently accepted Van Valkenburgh's model, but Aberle (1966:33–34) wrote, "Van Valkenburgh describes a system far more structured than could be imagined from reading agents' reports—so much so that I am inclined to think that he has overformalized it." We agree with Aberle. Primary sources give no evidence of such a highly structured system, and abundant data to the contrary.

4. Major Price reported dissatisfaction with Arny, who on several occasions went to Washington instead of settling two local murder cases. Arny's son, W. E. Arny, was accused of using almost 1,000 yards of manta to sack wool that he purchased from the Navajos and returning only a few bolts of "inferior" material. The Navajos thought Arny had "been stealing from them" (Price to Mahnken, Oct. 9, 1875, RBIA LR NMS). Arny attributed many of his difficulties to "squaw men" (Anglos who lived with Navajo women) and the "whiskey sellers" who turned the Navajos against him when he tried to halt their activities (Arny to Smith, Sept. 14, 1875, RBIA LR NMS; Affidavit of W. F. M. Arny, RBIA LR NMS).

5. In 1883 a courier sent by Agent Riordan secured the release of two medicine men and one medicine man's wife accused of practicing witchcraft southwest of Fort Defiance (Riordan to Price, Mar. 15, 1883, RBIA GR).

6. The chiefs' fear of witchcraft is interesting in light of an interview conducted by Williams (1970:16), whose questions are in brackets:

A *natani* in the days before the council was always seen on the same horse, and he talked to the people from horseback. [Why did he ride the same horse all the time?] A *natani* always rode the same horse to show the people that he was not afraid of witchcraft, and he let the horse go (defecate) just any place and would let it just lie there and never bother to scoop it up. [How does horse manure relate to his position of leadership?] It has everything to do with it. A leader was showing his disregard for witchcraft, and anyone who wanted to try and harm him was free to try by using the horse manure, but the fact that the leader always rode the same horse showed that he was capable of warding-off any witchcraft practiced against him, and in this way he indicated he was a strong healthy leader.

In 1878, with the exception of Ganado Mucho, *naat'anii* obviously did not feel so confident.

7. Witchcraft may even have been practiced against officials. Joseph Thacker, a trader, reported that in the early summer of 1880 some Navajos held a dance near his post:

> They drew figures of the Sun, Moon, and certain persons and enacted peculiar ceremonies around them, a buffalo hide being also used; that a representation of Captain Frank T. Bennett . . . in effigy was made; that one of the Indians . . . was given some mixture to cause sickness and at the proper time to vomit over the said effigy. (Affidavit of Joseph Thacker, June 6, 1880, RBIA LR NMS)

This description bears a marked resemblance to Kluckhohn's description (1962:27) of a "bad sing."

8. Frank Mitchell (Frisbie and McAllester 1978:129) reported in his autobiography, "While I was working away from home . . . the Shirley family offered Chee Dodge's old mother-in-law to me. I refused her because that group wanted to use me like a servant to take care of their property. I told them I already had a woman. And when they asked how well off she was I said, 'Her people have some cattle.' "

9. See Bailey and Bailey (1982:73–75).

10. In the summer of 1872, Navajos took 35 horses from the Abiquiu area that belonged to either the Utes or the Jicarillas (Keam to Pope, June 26, 1872, RBIA LR NMS). Later that summer, 10 "animals" were taken near Tierra Amarilla (Keam to Pope, July 4, 1872, RBIA LR NMS). These may have belonged to the Jicarillas. Two days later the chiefs turned over 46 stolen horses and mules, and Acting Agent Keam sent some of the animals back to the Jicarilla Agency (Keam to Pope, July 6, 1872, RBIA LR NMS).

11. In August 1872, a group of Navajos stole Mescalero horses from a pasture near Fort Stanton (Pope to Walker, Aug. 27, 1872, RBIA LR NMS).

12. In October 1869, Navajos attacked a Zuni, killed him, and took a burro and other property (Cooper to Clinton, Nov. 8, 1869, RBIA RNMS). Ten cows and four horses were taken from Acoma in late January 1870 (Evans to Cooper, Feb. 10, 1870, RBIA RNMS).

13. Spanish-American herds were the prime target of Navajo raiders. The largest numbers of animals reported stolen were 3,000 sheep taken from the Rio Puerco area in June 1869 (Chavey to Clinton, Aug. 4, 1869, RBIA RNMS); 46 sheep, 1 horse, and 2 burros taken near Las Lunas on Aug. 7, 1870 (Price to Bennett, Aug. 26, 1870, RBIA LR NMS); 200 sheep taken on March 21, 1871 from the San Pallo area (Watts to Parker, May 19, 1871, RBIA LR NMS); 226 sheep and 2 burros taken on Feb. 10, 1871 from the Piedra Luna region (Watts to Parker, received Apr. 29, 1871, RBIA LR NMS); and approximately 500 sheep taken in early April 1872 from along the Rio Puerco (Miller to Pope, Apr. 16, 1872, RBIA LR NMS).

14. Few Anglo-Americans lived in the region at this time, and most of those who lost horses and mules were either travelers or ranchers (Claim of Balthazar Marfin, 1870, RBIA LR NMS; Watts to CIA, Apr. 5, 1872, RBIA LR NMS; Armstrong to Dudley, Feb. 23, 1873, RBIA LR NMS; Hardison to Smith, June 21, 1875, RBIA LR NMS; McCarty to Parker, Aug. 10, 1870, RBIA LR NMS).

15. "Larago" led Navajo raiders against Mormon settlements in Kane, Washington, and Iron counties (Utah) in November 1869. During December 1869 and January 1870, a group of about 100 Navajo raiders led by "Barawezeta" struck Beaner and Iron counties and drove off a large number of horses and mules, as well as some cattle (Testimony of John Francisco . . . Feb. 22, 1870, RBIA LR NMS; Fenton to Parker, Nov. 25, 1869, RBIA LR NMS).

16. See Bailey and Bailey (1982:73–77).

17. Late in 1870, an Acoma stole two horses from Barboncito (Bennett to Pope, Jan. 1, 1871, RBIA LR NMS).

18. During the winter of 1873–74, a party of Mormons attacked a Navajo trading party in southern Utah, killing three Navajos, wounding another, and taking their horses (Arny to Dudley, Feb. 16, 1874, RBIA LR NMS).

19. We have no explanation for the sharp drop in the number of horses in 1891, except to suggest a revision of the estimates. Also, economic conditions were deteriorating in the early 1890s, and Navajos were butchering horses to preserve their sheep and goat herds.

20. Frank Mitchell said that before 1900, Navajos in his area had no shovels, plows, or harness sets, and used almost no metal tools besides axes (Frisbie and McAllester 1978:30–31).

21. Climatic conditions determined the amount of acreage the Navajos planted in the twentieth century, as well as the late nineteenth. In 1927 the superintendent of Northern Navajo noted, "The acreage cultivated and the number of Indians engaged in agriculture is not regulated by the will or desire of the Indians themselves but rather by the amount of water available" (NN NR 1927:17).

22. Navajos reverted to gathering during economically difficult times. The crop failure of 1880 and the hard winter of 1880–81 forced many families to dig "roots" for food in the spring (Pope to AA Gen'l, Ft. Leavenworth, Apr. 28, 1881, RBIA LR GR). See also Frisbie and McAllester (1978:33–34) for a discussion of wild plants used for food during this period.

23. Amsden's book, originally published in 1934, remains the classic study of late nineteenth-century weaving, but valuable contributions have since been made by J. J. Brody (1976), Kate Peck Kent (1985), H. P. Mera (1947), and Joe Ben Wheat (1977; 1979).

24. Mormon trade grew out of the earlier trade network, and did not involve "trading posts." Navajos and Mormon farmers and ranchers traded mainly for blankets and livestock.

25. Northern Chaco Plateau Navajos reported that in the past, some women from that area had a *hak'is* relationship with women from Jemez Pueblo (Bailey field notes).

26. See Victor Mindeleff (1891:plate XLV) for a photograph of the old Mormon woolen mill at Moencopie.

27. Official correspondence of the period illustrates the extreme distrust and hostility between Mormons and other Anglo-Americans. Government officials shared these attitudes with civilians, exemplified by the agent's "fear" that Mormon missionaries would start working among the Navajos.

28. For photographs of these dwellings, see Shufeldt (1892:plates XLII, XLIII).

29. A Mr. Merritt and a Mr. Mitchell, the son of the head of the gentile settlement in southern Utah (Mitchell letter, Feb. 27, 1880, RBIA LR NMS; Eastman to CIA, Mar. 20, 1880, RBIA LR NMS), were apparently prospecting for carbonate when according

to a Navajo account, they were murdered by Paiutes (Gillmor and Wetherill 1953:95–96). Elizabeth Hegemann (1963:351–52) and Byron Cummings (1952:8–9) knew Hoskinini Begay (a Navajo) in his later years, and identified him as one of the murderers.

30. Sheldon Jackson, superintendent of schools for the Presbyterian Church, was convinced that the Utes and the Mormons were "tampering with the tribe," but that the Navajos had "no intention of going on the war path" because they had "too many sheep" (Jackson to Brooks, Aug. 5, 1880, RBIA LR NMS).

31. While there is no evidence of an alliance between the Navajos and the Utes, some Ute participants in the Meeker "Massacre" fled across the Navajo reservation and traded guns and cartridges taken in the battle to Son of Old Man Hat and Has Done It (Hoskinini Begay?) (Dyk 1967:181–82).

32. It was necessary to grind wheat four times to obtain flour of the proper consistency, a difficult process which may explain why Navajos began to trade for wheat flour at such an early date. Corn had to be ground only three times (F. Bailey 1940:275).

CHAPTER 3

1. See Strickland (1982:130–32) for a discussion of the provisions of this act.

2. For additional information and a Navajo account of the difficulties at Round Rock, see Young and Morgan (1952).

3. This council met solely to ratify oil leases on the reservation.

4. Leo Crane (1972), Keams Canyon superintendent from 1911 to 1919, described the tenuous nature of government control in his autobiographical account.

5. See Kelly (1968) for an excellent discussion of relations between the Navajos and the federal government between 1900 and 1935.

6. A drafting error in this order placed the eastern boundary of the withdrawn area in Range 5 East, well east of the area occupied by off-reservation Navajos. The mistake was quickly discovered, and an executive order of January 28, 1908, placed the boundary in Range 6 West (Kappler 1913:669–70).

7. Because Navajos were strongly opposed to participating in the war, a rumor that they were going to be drafted and sent to fight created fears of armed resistance. Some traders had their families seek refuge off the reservation (Faunce 1981:289–95).

8. Calico jumped from between 10¢ and 12¢ per yard to between 20¢ and 25¢; velvet shirts rose from $1.50 to $3.50 each (Faunce 1981:288).

9. For traders' accounts of the epidemic and its effects on the Navajos, see Newcomb (1964:145–49), Gillmor and Wetherill (1953:224–29), Faunce (1981:297–303), and Schmedding (1974:346).

10. The Department of the Interior disapproved the council's lease to Producers and Refiners in March 1923 (SJ NR 1923:24). We can only guess that Standard Oil was influential in the decision.

11. A republican, Hagerman served as territorial governor in 1906 and 1907 (Kelly 1968:62 n.), and remained active in state politics until the 1930s (Holmes 1967:158, 194). As commissioner to the Navajos, he supported Navajo oil leases and oil company interests in general, but also favored expansion of the Navajo land base. He hailed from

the "little Texas" portion of New Mexico, the six southeastern counties, which may explain his lack of sympathy for northwestern New Mexico sheep ranchers.

12. The government introduced Persian, Cotswold, Merino, and Rambouillet rams in Eastern Navajo (PB NR 1915:10; PB NR 1919:5); Rambouillets and Cotswolds in Leupp (L NR 1913:10; L NR 1917); Lincolns and Rambouillets in Western (WN NR 1913; WN NR 1918:23); Rambouillets in Southern (N NR 1913:9); and between 1910 and 1920, Oxfords, Cotswolds, Dorsets, Cheviots, Lincolns, Persians, Shropshires, Rambouillets, and Tunis rams in Northern (SJ NR 1913:19; SJ NR 1914:29). In addition, many Navajo stockmen acquired rams on their own from neighboring white ranchers, and traders were sometimes known to introduce rams (Bailey field notes; Blunn 1940:104).

13. According to Van Valkenburgh (1937:5), these ditches were repaired in the late 1890s. In the case of the Wheatfields ditch, "the Indians had made use of it for many years before" 1905. The Navajos dug the Hosteen Tah, the Costiano, the Tse-he-ya-be-ya, and the San Juan Ditch No. 3 along the San Juan before 1894, as well as the Carrizo and Two Gray Hills ditches.

14. Some sources claimed that Navajos grew potatoes as a cash crop for sale to trading posts, not for subsistence (Sapir and Hoijer 1942:407).

15. According to John Landgraf (1954:57), by 1941 the Ramah Navajos hunted deer primarily for sport.

16. During the early 1930s, Carpenter and Steggerda (1939:302) found that "very few" wild seeds were used for food. In the course of his ethnobotanical study of the Ramah Navajos in 1940–41, Paul Vestal observed that wild food plants were of minor economic importance (Vestal 1952:60).

17. Piñon nuts were the only wild plant food mentioned by Landgraf (1954:58) in his 1940–41 land use study of Ramah Navajos. Vestal (1952:60) called piñons indisputably the most important wild plant food still collected by the Ramah Navajos, noting that they provided a major source of income.

18. A Navajo named Red Mule and his wife, from the northern Chaco Plateau area, traded saddle blankets at Jemez for turquoise (Bailey field notes).

19. Traders also took considerable risk when buying lambs and wool, and in 1921 an unexpected and sharp decline in wool prices sent some into bankruptcy. One older trader said that his family bought wool at 30¢ per pound and sold it for 8¢ per pound the same year. They had a sales contract with a broker, but the price of wool went so low that the broker chose to pay the penalty fee rather than buy at the contract price. The post went bankrupt (Bailey field notes).

20. In 1918 the superintendent of Eastern Navajo noted that traders were giving Navajo stockmen "advances" on their wool crop (PB NR 1918:5).

21. Wool prices tended to cycle every nine years (Horlacher and Hammonds 1945:14); sheep and lamb prices about every five (Peters and Deyoe 1946:19).

22. Use of the terms "blanket" and "rug" often causes confusion. Intended use, rather than weaving technique, determined what a piece was called. Rugs came in a wider range of sizes than blankets, but in the early twentieth century, the size of most Navajo textiles would have allowed them to serve as either. Woven for trade as well as domestic use, saddle blankets further complicated the issue. Colloquially, traders continued to call all Navajo weavings "blankets" even when marketed as "rugs."

23. As early as 1909, unscrupulous dealers were buying Mexican rugs and selling them

as Navajo—an indication of both the popularity and high price of the genuine item (Lipps 1909:89).

24. For a detailed history of Navajo silversmithing during this period, see Adair (1944) and Bedinger (1973).

25. In 1881 approximately 500 Navajos worked on the construction crews of the Atlantic and Pacific Railroad (Hatch to AAG, May 27, 1881, RBIA LR GR), but the jobs only lasted through the construction phase.

26. For example, see the biographical sketch of Sam Akeah in Johnson and Hoffman (1978:26).

27. Most Navajos who owned small posts probably had trouble securing credit from wholesalers. There were exceptions, however. Bob Martin, a full-blood Navajo born near Gallup and educated at several Indian schools, operated the post at Red Mesa, Arizona, from 1916 to 1933. In 1933 he opened his own post at Nenahnezad, across the river from Fruitland, New Mexico (*Farmington Daily Times*, Aug. 25, 1955).

28. Louisa Wetherill (Gillmor and Wetherill 1953:181) wrote that a bridge was built over the San Juan at Mexican Hat, Utah, in 1909, but did not say who built it or what it was made of.

29. Franc Newcomb (1964:162–63) inferred that the road was paved in 1923, with an oil company furnishing materials and the government doing the work.

30. For additional information on Morgan, see Parman (1976).

31. Originally a day school, Toadlena soon became a boarding school, but kept the name Toadlena Day School for a time (SJ NR 1913:6).

32. In their study of Navajo architecture, Jett and Spencer (1981:213) define four geographical regions on the basis of variations in hogan construction: vertical-post/corbeled-log hogans (west and north); cribbed-log hogans (central); stone hogans (east); and vertical-post/corbeled-log hogans (extreme east). We believe that these four regional preferences evolved during the early part of the twentieth century.

33. In the mid-1880s the Navajos were using "comparatively few tents or tepees" (Parsons to Atkins, Apr. 27, 1886, RBIA LR GR).

34. A wall tent had vertical walls and a gabled roof. A Sibley (officer) tent was conical and had a center pole (Jett and Spencer 1981:47–48, fig. 4.17).

35. Tents were easier to move than shades (Hollister 1972:72) and had the advantage of being waterproof. Shades were cooler. Navajos commonly used both, with the tent serving primarily as a storage area for "food and valuables" (Reichard 1969:7).

36. See Jett and Spencer (1981:20, fig. 2.3) for a photograph of a smoke hood. Some were designed so that pots and pans could be heated on them (Bailey field notes).

37. In the early 1950s, Tremblay, Collier, and Sasaki (1954:195–96, 203) found that there was still a correlation between dwellings and their furnishings. Families with hogans had little Anglo-American furniture except for foot-pedal sewing machines; they slept on sheepskins, and ate while sitting on the ground. People living in houses were more likely to own beds, chairs, cupboards, chests of drawers, and tables.

38. Pottery drums and bowls continued to be used in certain religious ceremonies (W. Hill 1937:7–10).

39. Coiled bowls were used in ceremonies, and survived the general decline in basket making. Although some Navajos continued to make these baskets throughout the period (Tschopik 1940:446, 451, 454–55), production failed to meet demand, and Navajos

resorted to baskets woven by Paiutes and Utes (Stewart 1938:758–59). The production of utilitarian baskets declined sharply, but as late as 1939, Navajos in the Oljeto region were still weaving and using pitched water bottles (Bailey field notes).

CHAPTER 4

1. See Parman (1976) for an excellent study of the political history of Collier and the Navajos.

2. Aberle (1966:52–90) has written the best analysis of livestock reduction and its effects.

3. Officials had been aware of overgrazing on the reservation since the nineteenth century, but considered it the Navajos' problem. The government's position changed in the early 1930s with the completion of Hoover (Boulder) Dam and the creation of Lake Mead on the Colorado River. Studies revealed that 37.5 percent of the silt entering the lake came from the Navajo reservation, a situation attributed in part to overgrazing. Stock reduction was conceived of as a means of correcting the silting problem, as well as halting the deterioration of Navajo rangeland (Spicer and Collier 1965:185).

4. Collier saw the Tribal Council's acceptance in a much different light. As he stated later,

> They did it under no sort of duress and bribery of the Indian Service; duress and bribery were not possible and were not attempted. They did it out of political virtue of a high order, and under no compulsion except that of an overwhelming reality which they acknowledged after they entered on responsibility. (Collier 1962:66)

5. There were actually nineteen of these units, but Land Management Unit 6 was occupied by the Hopis.

6. See Kelly (1968:127–31) and Mosk (1944) for discussions of land problems during this period.

7. Hagerman had been reappointed commissioner to the Navajos in March 1930.

8. According to Burge (1937:21), opposition to the Navajo Boundary Bill developed in New Mexico following the death of Senator Cutting and the appointment of Dennis Chavez in 1935. The opposition consisted of "large non-resident stock owners," who ran livestock in the checkerboard area, and the New Mexico Taxpayers' Association, which opposed any loss of taxable land. Chavez expressed his position succinctly: "I'll let the Indian Bureau know that all people in New Mexico are not Indians" (*Farmington Times Hustler*, June 5, 1936).

9. This consolidation affected the five Navajo jurisdictions and that portion of Hopi occupied by Navajos. The Hopi Agency remained separate (Young 1961:598, 603).

10. Donald Parman (1976:46) wrote,

> Collier did not autocratically force the council to accept his program, [but] his strong tactics produced the same result. . . . Collier was highly persuasive in presenting his case and his subordinates were able to supply him with charts,

facts, and figures. Additional leverage was derived from relief work which supplied jobs to several council members. Finally, there always seemed to be the implied threat that existing benefits would not be continued or new ones added unless the council consented to an unwanted action such as herd reduction.

11. As Indian Service employees, Kimball and Provinse were personally involved in the political maneuvering on the reservation. To his credit, Kimball (1950:23) later admitted that he had been mistaken in his assessment of the chapter system.

12. Little has been written about the involvement of Navajos in World War II. Doris Paul (1973) wrote the longest and most detailed study of the code talkers, a somewhat popularized account. *Navajos and World War II*, edited by Broderick Johnson (1977), contains interviews with nine Navajos who were in the military or doing war-related work; one man also chronicled his experiences in World War I.

13. Since the Indian Service did not pressure Navajos to reduce their herds during the war, the decline probably resulted from relatively high livestock prices (appendix B) and wartime labor shortages, both of which would have encouraged owners to sell; as well as the loss of interest in herding that would have accompanied allotment payments to families of servicemen.

14. The increase in percentage of total income derived from rug weaving between 1936 and 1940 did not reflect any major increase in rug production. Considering that in the same period, weaving income fell from $288,840 to $283,480 on the reservation (table 9), the increase probably resulted from sharp declines in other sources of income and a major overall drop in total income.

15. With the Navajos, it is impossible to express the subsistence value of an animal consumed at home as a numerical market value. As one older Navajo stated, "When we're through with [eating] an animal, the only things left are the hide, the hoofs, and the horns" (Bailey field notes). See Carpenter and Steggerda (1939:302) and Steggerda and Eckardt (1941:223–24) for discussions of Navajo consumption of sheep and goats.

16. Chabot had been employed by the New Mexico Association on Indian Affairs, which became an anti-Collier organization (Parman 1976:254–55).

17. At this time, Collier was the secretary of the American Indian Defense Association, which opposed the policies of the Indian Bureau.

18. See Parman (1976) for a full discussion of the political struggles and intrigues involving Morgan, Collier, and others.

19. Since the Navajos had never taken part in such an election before, it was decided that an X on the ballot would mean "yes" and an O would mean "no" (Parman 1976:76). During the campaign, Morgan and other opponents of the bill allegedly told Navajo voters that the X was really a "cross," the sign of death (Bailey field notes). However, we found no direct evidence to support this accusation, and nothing to indicate that Morgan openly used the stock reduction issue to manipulate the vote. Donald Parman (1976:77) wrote,

> The main reason for the government's defeat was not Morgan but the left-over feeling against the second herd reduction. . . . He had merely to allude to herd reduction and his aroused audiences reached the desired conclusion spontaneously. Neither did Morgan or fellow spokesmen bother to explain that reduction and the referendum were not directly related questions.

20. For a discussion of Navajo visionaries during the 1930s and 1940s, see Bailey and Bailey (1982:473–77).

CHAPTER 5

1. By 1972 there were more than 128,000 Navajos on or near the reservation (U.S. Commission on Civil Rights 1975a:37, n. 57).

2. The Office of Indian Affairs, collectively referred to as the Indian Service, officially became the Bureau of Indian Affairs in 1947 (E. Hill 1981:24).

3. Young (1961:1–5) deals comprehensively with the Navajo-Hopi Long Range Rehabilitation Act and its implementation.

4. See Reno (1981) for a discussion of the development of mineral resources on the reservation.

5. An electric railroad for the transportation of coal from the mine to the power plant was completed in 1974 (Reno 1981:108).

6. For a discussion of termination philosophy and policy, see Taylor (1972:48–65).

7. Iverson (1981) has written a detailed and thoughtful history of Navajo politics after 1950.

8. Permits specified the reservation district they were to be used in, and a stockowner with permits in two districts could not consolidate either permits or herds. This arrangement effectively limited owners to purchasing additional permits in one district, inhibiting consolidation and the market for permits. The creation of "traditional use areas" had much the same effect.

9. In the absence of separate statistics for sheep and goats between 1960 and 1975, they will be treated as a unit here.

10. While most Navajos interviewed said that sheep were more profitable than cattle, Downs (1972:88) said the opposite.

11. There were exceptions. Some weavers earned as much as 10¢ per hour. Daisy Taugelchee, a famous weaver of Two Gray Hills-style rugs, sold one tapestry rug in 1958 for $1,100, and another for $1,600 (*Farmington Daily Times*, Jan. 18, 1959).

12. Silas Clau made unusual female figures. Fay Tso made pots with unusual decorations and one shaped like a chicken (Bailey field notes).

13. "Placement" refers to the number of hirings, rather than the number of people hired. If a man worked for the railroad, quit, and got hired again later that year, two "placements" would be recorded.

14. Increases in hourly wages for railroad workers exceeded the rather modest rate of inflation during this period (appendix B).

15. See Victor Uchendu's (1966) study of seasonal farm labor.

16. The 1970 figure did not include the value of food produced and consumed at home; income subsidies such as clothing and food given to children at school; and food stamps, which by themselves increased Navajo food-buying power by an estimated 70 percent (Navajo Tribe 1974:31).

17. In 1935 Superintendent Faris estimated that the Navajos owned more than 4,000 motor vehicles (Memorandum to Secretary Ickes, Dec. 18, 1935, JCP), apparently a gross exaggeration.

18. One older man said that when snow covered the road in the winter, it was useful to have a wagon and team on hand (Bailey field notes).

19. Uchendu (1966:166) reported that traders who recruited Navajo agricultural laborers had them pledge $15 out of their weekly pay to maintain their family's account at the trading post.

20. Besides persuading Navajos to shop in nearby, off-reservation communities, radio and television reduced their cultural isolation. Vogt (1951:27) noted, "As of 1947 no Navaho in the [Ramah] area subscribed to a newspaper or a magazine (except for *The Farm Journal* which some of the veterans ordered in connection with the agricultural training program). There was only one radio in the group." The area was probably typical of the reservation at the time. However, by the time Tom Sasaki (1960:192) left Fruitland in 1956, Navajos owned radios in sufficient numbers to warrant local, off-reservation stations broadcasts in Navajo. A 1966 survey estimated that 25 percent of Navajo homes had radios and 15 percent had television sets (Mizen 1966:457). In addition, most Navajos also had radios in their cars or trucks. By the late 1970s, even families whose homes had no electrical power could watch television: sets powered through the cigarette lighter of a car or truck were being marketed on the reservation (Bailey field notes).

21. The major off-reservation centers for Navajo shopping are Farmington, Gallup, Cortez, Holbrook, Winslow, and Flagstaff (see maps in Kelley 1977:59–60).

22. While changes in Navajo shopping patterns were primarily responsible for the decline in trading posts, two other factors weakened their position. In about 1960 general-merchandise wholesalers stopped accepting wool in trade and extending credit to the posts (Kelley 1977:37), and in 1971 the Navajo Wool Marketing Industries, a tribal corporation, started purchasing wool directly from Navajo producers (*Farmington Daily Times*, June 2, 1981).

23. See Bailey and Bailey (1982:526–35) for a discussion of the change from trading posts to "Indian stores" in the San Juan Valley.

24. See Robert Roessel (1979) concerning the growth of Navajo education between 1948 and 1978.

25. Referring to the Black Mesa area in 1960 and 1961, Downs (1972:44–45) stated that more than any other factor, the needs of the herd still determined where a family camp was located. Black Mesa was something of an anachronism in the early 1960s, however. Other factors already controlled camp location in other areas, and before the mid-1970s, the needs of the herds ceased to be the most important determinant on Black Mesa as well.

26. Uchendu (1966:274) reaches a similar conclusion regarding the effects of wage labor on camp permanence.

27. By the late 1970s, the Fruitland Navajos had partially modified their beliefs concerning the performance of certain ceremonies in houses, and minor curing ceremonies were being held in multiroom, Anglo-American style houses. One informant stated that a sing had to be held in the southernmost room of a house built on a north-south axis and the westernmost room of a house built on a east-west axis, but another informant stated that it could be held in any room of the house. All informants agreed that major sings could only be held in hogans, because pollen must be placed in the five corners of the hogan during the ceremony; that is, in the old forked-stick hogan, at the two door

posts, the south post, the north post, and the west post; and in stone hogans with windows, the two sides of the door frame, the west side of the north window, the east side of the south window, and the ledge of the west window. With houses, it is impossible to define these five critical points (Bailey field notes). In addition to traditional ceremonies, meetings of the Native American Church take place in hogans and Plains-style tipis. In the Fruitland area, we never observed peyotists using a tipi, perhaps because of the strong opposition to the church that still prevails in the area. A tipi would be too conspicuous (Bailey field notes).

28. The reservation chapters with the highest population density, including Shiprock, Window Rock, and Chinle, also have the most employment opportunities (Goodman 1982:63, map 30).

29. See Kunitz (1976, 1977) for quantitative studies of regional variability using demographic and economic data from 1936 to 1974.

30. Sex differences also need to be taken into account. Vogt (1951:92–93) felt that Navajo men accepted acculturation more readily than Navajo women because of their exposure to the outside world. Downs (1963) noted that men found an acceptable Anglo-American role model in the cowboy, but that women did not have an equivalent model. However, Robert Rapoport (1954:62, 78) reported that Navajo women accepted Christianity more readily than Navajo men.

Key to Abbreviations Used in Citations

A Gen'l	Adjutant General
AA Gen'l	Assistant Adjutant General
AAA Gen'l	Acting Assistant Adjutant General
AR	Annual Report
ARIRA	Annual Report of the Indian Rights Association
AZ	Arizona
BIA	Bureau of Indian Affairs
BINM	Bureau of Immigration, State of New Mexico
CIA	Commissioner of Indian Affairs
EN	Eastern Navajo Agency
FD	Fort Defiance
FL	Fort Lewis
FW	Fort Wingate
GR	General Records
JCP	John Collier Papers
L	Leupp Agency
LB	Letter Book
LR	Letters Received
LS	Letters Sent

N	Navajo Agency
NM	New Mexico
NMS	New Mexico Superintendency
NMSRC	New Mexico State Records Center and Archives
NN	Northern Navajo Agency
NR	Narrative Report
OLO	Office of Land Operations
PB	Pueblo Bonito Agency
RBIA	Records of the Bureau of Indian Affairs
RBIC	Annual Report of the Board of Indian Commissioners
RCIA	Annual Report of the Commissioner of Indian Affairs
RDC	Records of the Department of Commerce
RDI	Annual Report of the Department of the Interior
RNMS	Records New Mexico Superintendency
RGNM	Annual Report of the (Territorial) Governor of New Mexico
RSI	Annual Report of the Secretary of the Interior
RSW	Annual Report of the Secretary of War
RUSAC	Records of the United States Army Commands
RUSACC	Records of the United States Army Continental Command
SD	Selected Documents
SJ	San Juan Agency
SN	Southern Navajo Agency
SR	Statistical Report
SS	Congressional serial set
UT	Utah
WD	War Department
WN	Western Navajo Agency

Archival Materials

ARIZONA HISTORICAL SOCIETY, TUCSON, ARIZONA
Richard Van Valkenburgh Collection

BUREAU OF INDIAN AFFAIRS
Shiprock Agency, Shiprock, Arizona
Land Management Branch Files
Window Rock Agency, Window Rock, Arizona
Office of Land Operations, Range Unit Records

CARSON TRADING POST, FARMINGTON, NEW MEXICO
Post ledger book, 1929–1932

FEDERAL REGIONAL RECORDS DEPOSITORY, LAGUNA NIGUEL, CALIFORNIA
Navajo Agency
Letterpress books, 1880–1884, 1893–1895, and 1902–1904

HISTORICAL SOCIETY OF PENNSYLVANIA
Indian Rights Association Papers
Incoming correspondence, 1894–1908 (microfilm copies at Oklahoma State
University)
Papers 1868–1968 (microfilm copies at the University of Tulsa)

NATIONAL ARCHIVES, WASHINGTON, D.C.
Records of the Bureau of Indian Affairs, Record Group 75
Records of the New Mexico Superintendency of Indian Affairs, 1849–1880
(microfilm copies at the University of Tulsa)
Letters received by the Office of Indian Affairs, New Mexico
Superintendency, 1849–1880 (microfilm copies at the University of
Tulsa)

Superintendents' Annual Narrative and Statistical Reports
(microfilm copies at the University of Tulsa)

Eastern Navajo, 1927–1935	Pueblo Bonito, 1910–1926
Leupp, 1910–1935	San Juan School, 1910–1926
Navajo, 1910–1926, 1936	Southern Navajo, 1927–1935
Northern Navajo, 1927–1935	Western Navajo, 1910–1935

Letters received by the Office of Indian Affairs, General Records,
1881–1907 (microfilm copies of selected documents relating to the
Navajos at Fort Lewis College, Durango, Colorado).

Records of the Department of Commerce, Record Group 29

Population Schedules of the Tenth Census, 1880, Rio Arriba County, New
Mexico (microfilm copies)

Population Schedules of the Twelfth Census, 1900, San Juan County, New
Mexico (microfilm copies)

Records of the War Department

U.S. Army Commands, Record Group 98

Fort Lewis, Colorado, 1880–1886, 1890 (microfilm copies at Fort Lewis
College)

Fort Wingate, New Mexico, 1885–1891 (microfilm copies at Fort Lewis
College)

U.S. Army Continental Commands, Record Group 393, Fort Wingate,
1868–1869, 1885–1898 (microfilm copies at Fort Lewis College)

NEW MEXICO STATE RECORDS CENTER AND ARCHIVES, SANTA FE,
NEW MEXICO

McNitt Collection

NEWSPAPERS AND NEWSLETTERS

Farmington Daily Times	*Navajo Times* (Window Rock, Arizona)
Farmington Enterprise	*Navajo Trails* (Farmington, New Mexico)
Farmington Hustler	*Padres' Trail* (St. Michaels, Arizona)
Farmington Times	*San Juan Times* (Farmington, New Mexico)
Farmington Times Hustler	*Santa Fe New Mexican*
Gallup Independent	

UNITED STATES MILITARY ACADEMY, WESTPOINT, NEW YORK

John Gregory Bourke Diary, 1869–1896, 84 volumes (photoprint copy, Special
Collections, University of New Mexico Library)

UNIVERSITY OF NEW MEXICO LIBRARY, SPECIAL COLLECTIONS,
ALBUQUERQUE, NEW MEXICO

Soil Conservation Service Records

Land Management Survey Reports, 1936–1941

YALE UNIVERSITY LIBRARY, NEW HAVEN, CONNECTICUT

The John Collier Papers, 1922–1968 (microfilm copies at the University of Tulsa)

References

Abel, Annie Heloise, ed.
1915   *The Official Correspondence of James S. Calhoun.* Washington: Government
        Printing Office.

Aberle, David F.
1962   "Navaho." In *Matrilineal Kinship*, edited by David M. Schneider and
        Kathleen Gough. Berkeley and Los Angeles: University of California
        Press.
1963   "Some Sources of Flexibility in Navaho Social Organization." *Southwestern
        Journal of Anthropology* 19:1–8.
1966   *The Peyote Religion Among the Navaho.* Viking Fund Publications in Anthro-
        pology no. 42. New York: Wenner-Gren Foundation for Anthropological
        Research.
1969   "A Plan for Navajo Economic Development." In *Toward Economic Develop-
        ment for Native American Communities.* Vol. 1, pt. 1A, 223–76. Compendium
        of papers submitted to Subcommittee on Economy in Government of the
        Joint Economic Committee, 91st Congress, 1st session. Washington:
        Government Printing Office.
1982a   "The Future of Navajo Religion." In *Navajo Religion and Culture: Selected
        Views*, edited by David M. Brugge and Charlotte J. Frisbie. Museum of
        New Mexico Papers in Anthropology no. 17.
1982b   *The Peyote Religion Among the Navaho.* 2d ed. Chicago: University of
        Chicago Press.
1983   "Peyote Religion Among the Navajo." In *Handbook of North American
        Indians.* Vol. 10, *Southwest.* Washington: Smithsonian Institution.

Adair, John
  1944   *The Navajo and Pueblo Silversmiths.* Norman: University of Oklahoma
          Press.
  1947   "The Navajo and Pueblo Veteran." *The American Indian* 4 (1): 5–11.

Adair, John, and Evon Z. Vogt
  1949   "Navajo and Zuni Veterans: A Study in Contrasting Modes of Culture
          Change." *American Anthropologist* 51:547–61.

Adams, William Y.
  1963   *Shonto: A Study of the Role of the Trader in a Modern Navaho Community.*
          Bureau of American Ethnology, Bulletin 188. Washington: Government
          Printing Office.

Adams, William Y., and Lorraine T. Ruffing
  1977   "Shonto Revisited: Measures of Social and Economic Change in a
          Navajo Community, 1955–1971." *American Anthropologist* 79 (1): 58–83.

Amsden, Charles Avery
  1975   *Navajo Weaving.* Reprint of the 1934 edition. Salt Lake City and Santa
          Barbara: Peregrine Smith.

ARIRA
  1883–   *Annual Reports of the Executive Committee of the Indian Rights Association.*
  1935   Philadelphia: Office of the Indian Rights Association.

Bailey, Flora
  1940   "Navajo Foods and Cooking Methods." *American Anthropologist* 42:270–90.

Bailey, Garrick A.
  1973   *Changes in Osage Social Organization 1673–1906.* University of Oregon
          Anthropological Papers no. 5. Eugene: University of Oregon Press.

Bailey, Garrick A., and Roberta Glenn Bailey
  1980   "Ethnohistory." In *Prehistory and History of the Ojo Amarillo,* edited by David
          Kirkpatrick. Vol. 4. Cultural Resources Management Division, Report
          no. 276. Las Cruces: New Mexico State University.
  1982   *Historic Navajo Occupation of the Northern Chaco Plateau.* Tulsa: Faculty of
          Anthropology, University of Tulsa.

Bailey, Lynn R.
  1964   *The Long Walk, a History of the Navajo Wars, 1846–68.* Great West & Indian
          Series 26. Los Angeles: Westernlore Press.
  1970   *Bosque Redondo: An American Concentration Camp.* Pasadena: Socio-Technical
          Books.

Bailey, Vernon
    1931   *Mammals of New Mexico.* U.S. Department of Agriculture, Bureau of Bio-
            logical Survey, North American Fauna no. 53. Washington: Government
            Printing Office.

Bancroft, Hubert Howe
    1962   *History of Arizona and New Mexico 1530–1888.* Facsimile reprint of 1889
            edition. Albuquerque: Horn & Wallace Co.

Barber, Bernard
    1941   "Acculturation and Messianic Movements." *American Sociological Review*
            6:663–69

Barnes, Will C.
    1935   *Arizona Place Names.* General Bulletin 6 (1). Tucson: University of
            Arizona.

Baydo, Gerald
    1970   "Cattle Ranching in Territorial New Mexico." Ph.D. dissertation, Uni-
            versity of New Mexico.

Beadle, J. B.
    1873   *The Undeveloped West, or Five Years in the Territories.* Cincinnati: National
            Publishing Company.

Bedinger, Margery
    1973   *Indian Silver Navajo and Pueblo Jewelers.* Albuquerque: University of New
            Mexico Press.

Bell, William A.
    1869   *New Tracks in North America.* 2 vols. London: Chapman and Hall.

Benavides, Fray Alfonso de
    1916   *The Memorial of Fray Alfonso de Benavides, 1630.* Translated by Mrs. Edward
            E. Ayer. Annotated by F. W. Hodge and C. F. Lummis. Privately printed.

Benedict, Ruth
    1946   *The Chrysanthemum and the Sword: Patterns of Japanese Culture.* Boston:
            Houghton Mifflin Co.

Benson, Michael
    1976   *The Navajo Nation and Taxation.* Window Rock, Arizona: DNA People's
            Legal Services.

Bieber, Ralph, ed.
    1936   *Marching with the Army of the West, 1846–1848.* Southwest Historical Series
            vol. 4. Glendale, California: Arthur H. Clark.

BINM (Bureau of Immigration of New Mexico)
1908   *San Juan County in New Mexico.* Albuquerque: Albuquerque Morning
        Journal.

Bittle, William E.
1971   "A Brief History of the Kiowa Apache." *Papers in Anthropology* 12 (1): 1-34.

Black, William L.
1900   *A New Industry, or Raising the Angora Goat and Mohair, for Profit.* Black of Texas.

Blanchard, Kendall
1977   *The Economics of Sainthood: Religious Change among the Rimrock Navajos.* Cran-
        bury, New Jersey: Associated University Presses.

Bloom, Lansing B., ed.
1936   "Bourke on the Southwest." *New Mexico Historical Review* 11 (1): 77-122.

Blunn. G T.
1940   "Improvement of the Navajo Sheep. *Journal of Heredity* 31:99-112.
1943   "Characteristics and Production of Old-Type Navajo Sheep." *Journal of
        Heredity* 34:141-52.

Boyce, George A.
1974   *When Navajos Had Too Many Sheep.* San Francisco: Indian Historical Press.

Brody, J. J.
1976   *Between Traditions.* Iowa City: University of Iowa Museum of Art.

Brugge, David M.
1963   *Navajo Pottery and Ethnohistory.* Navajoland Publications, series 2. Window
        Rock: Navajo Tribal Museum.
1968   *Navajos in the Catholic Church Records of New Mexico: 1694-1875.* Research
        Report no. 1. Window Rock: Navajo Tribe.
1980   *A History of the Chaco Navajos.* Reports of the Chaco Center no. 4. Division
        of Chaco Research, National Park Service. Washington: Government
        Printing Office.
1983   "Navajo Prehistory and History to 1850." In *Handbook of North American
        Indians.* Vol. 10, *Southwest.* Washington: Smithsonian Institution.

Brugge, David M., and Curtis E. Schaasfsma
1981   "Comments on Athabaskans and Sumas." In *The Protohistoric Period in the
        North American Southwest, A.D. 1450-1700.* Tempe: Arizona State Univer-
        sity Research Papers no. 24.

Bruner, Edward M.
1961   "Mandan." In *Perspectives in American Indian Culture Change,* edited by
        Edward Spicer. Chicago: University of Chicago Press.

Bryan, Kirk
    1929   "Flood-Water Farming." *Geographical Review* 19 (3): 444–56.

Burge, Moris S.
    1937   *The Navajos and the Land*. American Indian Defense Association and National Association on Indian Affairs, Bulletin 26.
    1949   "Report to Commissioner of Indian Affairs on Navajo Trading." U.S. Department of the Interior. Mimeo.

Calkins, Hugh G.
    1937a   *A Report on the Cuba Valley*. U.S. Dept. of Agriculture, Soil Conservation Service, Regional Bulletin no. 36. Albuquerque: Conservation Economics Series no. 9.
    1937b   *National Significance of the Navajo Problem*. Navajo School Service Bulletin 1, Navajo Service Land Management Conference, Mar. 2–6, Flagstaff.

Carlson, Alvar Ward
    1969   "New Mexico's Sheep Industry, 1850–1900: Its Role in the History of the Territory." *New Mexico Historical Review* 44:25–49.

Carlson, Roy L.
    1965   *Eighteenth Century Navajo Fortresses of the Gobernador District*. Earl Morris Papers 2. Boulder: University of Colorado Studies, Series in Anthropology 10.

Carpenter, Throne M., and Morris Steggerda
    1939   "The Food of the Present-day Navajo Indians of New Mexico and Arizona." *Journal of Nutrition* 18:297–305.

Chabot, Maria
    c. 1941   "Some Aspects of the Navajo Problem." For the New Mexico Association on Indian Affairs. Copy of manuscript at Laboratory of Anthropology, Santa Fe.

Chittenden, George P.
    1877   "Report George P. Chittenden (Topographer) of the San Juan Division, 1875." *U.S. Geological and Geographical Survey of the Territories, 9th Annual Report*. Washington: Government Printing Office.

Clark, Elizabeth P.
    1946   *Report on the Navajo, 1946*. Home Missions Council of North America. Indian Rights Association Papers, Series 3. Microfilm, reel 126.

Clark, Hartsill Lloyd
    1963   "A History of San Juan County, New Mexico." M.A. thesis, University of Tulsa.

Collier, John
    1962   *On the Gleaming Way: Navajos, Eastern Pueblos, Zunis, Hopis, Apaches, and Their Land; and Their Meanings to the World.* Revised edition. Denver: Sage Books.

Correll, J. Lee
    1970   *Bai-a-lil-le: Medicine Man—or Witch?.* Navajo Historical Publications Biographical Series no. 3. Window Rock: Navajo Parks and Recreation.
    1976   *Through White Men's Eyes: A Contribution to Navajo History.* Vol. 1. Window Rock: Navajo Heritage Center, Publication no. 1.
    1979   *Through White Man's Eyes: A Contribution to Navajo History: A Chronological Record of the Navajo People from Earliest Times to the the Treaty of June 1, 1868.* 6 vols. Window Rock: Navajo Heritage Center.

Counselor, Jim, and Ann Counselor
    1954   *Wild, Woolly and Wonderful.* New York: Vantage Press.

Crane, Leo
    1972   *Indians of the Enchanted Desert: An Account of the Navajo and Hopi Indians and the Keams Canyon Agency.* Reprint of the 1925 edition. Glorieta, New Mexico: Rio Grande Press.

Cummings, Byron
    1952   *Indians I Have Known.* Tucson: Arizona Silhouettes.

Cushing, Frank H.
    1920   *Zuni Breadstuff.* New York: Museum of the American Indian, Heye Foundation.

Davis, William Watts Hart
    1938   *El Gringo; or New Mexico and Her People.* Reprint of 1857 edition. Santa Fe: Rydal Press.

Dittert, Alfred E., Jr., James J. Hester, and Frank W. Eddy
    1971   *An Archaeological Survey of the Navajo Reservoir District, Northwestern New Mexico.* Monograph no. 23. Santa Fe: School of American Research and Museum of New Mexico.

Dobyns, Henry F.
    1976   *Native American Historic Demography: A Critical Bibliography.* Bloomington: Indiana University Press.
    1983   *Their Number Became Thinned: Native American Population Dynamics in Eastern North America.* Nashville: University of Tennessee Press.

Dolaghan, Thomas, and David Scates
    1978   *The Navajos Are Coming to Jesus.* South Pasadena, California: William Cary Library.

Dolfin, Reverend J.
   1921   *Bringing the Gospel in Hogan and Pueblo, 1896–1921.* Grand Rapids: Van Noord.

Domenech, Abbé Emmanuel H.
   1860   *Seven Year's Residence in the Great Deserts of North America.* London: Longman, Green, Longman and Roberts.

Downs, James F.
   1963   *The Cowboy and the Lady; Contrasting Modes of Navajo Acculturation.* Kroeber Anthropological Society Papers no. 29.
   1964   *Animal Husbandry in Navajo Society and Culture.* University of California Publications in Anthropology, vol. 1. Berkeley: University of California Press.
   1972   *The Navajo.* New York: Holt, Rinehart and Winston.

Downes, Randolph C., and Elizabeth Clark
   1946   "Navajo Report." Coordinating Committee of the Association on American Indian Affairs. Copy in possession of authors. Mimeo.

Dustin, C. Burton
   1960   *Peyotism and New Mexico.* Santa Fe: Vergara Printing Co.

Dyk, Walter
   1967   *Son of Old Man Hat. A Navaho Autobiography.* Lincoln: University of Nebraska Press.

Eggan, Fred
   1966   *The American Indian: Perspectives for the Study of Social Change.* Chicago: Aldine Publishing Company.

Eickemeyer, Carl
   1900   *Over the Great Navajo Trail.* New York: J. J. Little Co.

Ellis, Florence H.
   1974   *Navajo Indians I, An Anthropological Study of the Navajo Indians* (Indian Claims). New York: Garland Publishing, Inc.

Elmore, Francis
   1943   *Ethnobotany of the Navajo.* Monograph Series, vol. 1, no. 7. University of New Mexico Bulletin with the School of American Research. Albuquerque: University of New Mexico Press.

Faunce, Hilda
   1981   *Desert Wife.* Reprint of the 1928 edition. Lincoln and London: University of Nebraska Press.

Flake, David K.
1965   "A History of Mormon Missionary Work with the Hopi, Navaho and Zuni Indians." M.A. thesis, Brigham Young University.

Forbes, Jack D.
1960   *Apache, Navaho, and Spaniard.* Norman: University of Oklahoma Press.

Forrest, Earle R.
1970   *With a Camera in Old Navaholand.* Norman: University of Oklahoma Press.

Franciscan Fathers
1968   *An Ethnologic Dictionary of the Navajo Language.* Reprint of the 1910 edition. St. Michaels, Arizona: St. Michaels Press.

Frisbie, Charlotte
1980   "Ritual Drama in the Navajo House Blessing Ceremony." In *Southwestern Indian Ritual Drama*, edited by Charlotte Frisbie. Albuquerque: University of New Mexico Press.

Frisbie, Charlotte J., and David P. McAllester, eds.
1978   *Navajo Blessingway Singer: The Autobiography of Frank Mitchell, 1881–1967.* Tucson: University of Arizona Press.

Gilbreath, Kent
1973   *Red Capitalism: An Analysis of the Navajo Economy.* Norman: University of Oklahoma Press.

Gillmor, Frances, and Louisa Wade Wetherill
1953   *Traders to the Navajos.* Albuquerque: University of New Mexico Press.

Goldfrank, Esther S.
1945   "Irrigation Agriculture and Navaho Community Leadership." *American Anthropologist* 47:262–77.

Goodman, James M.
1982   *The Navajo Atlas.* Norman: University of Oklahoma Press.

Goodwin, Grenville
1969   *The Social Organization of the Western Apache.* Tucson: University of Arizona Press.

Granger, Byrd H., rev.
1960   *Will C. Barnes' Arizona Place Names.* Tucson: University of Arizona Press.

Greever, William S.
1954   *Arid Domain: The Santa Fe Railway and its Western Land Grant.* Stanford: Stanford University Press.

1957   "Railway Development in the Southwest." *New Mexico Historical Review* 32:151–203.

Gregg, Josiah
1954   *Commerce of the Prairies*. Norman: University of Oklahoma Press.

Gregory, David A.
1981   "Western Apache Archaeology: Problems and Approaches." In *The Protohistoric Period in the North American Southwest, A.D. 1450–1700*. Tempe: Arizona State University Research Papers no. 24.

Grove, Pearce S., Becky J. Barnett, and Sandra J. Hansen
1975   *New Mexico Newspapers: A Comprehensive Guide to Bibliographical Entries and Locations*. Albuquerque: University of New Mexico Press.

Hagerman, Herbert J.
1924   *A Report by J. H. Hagerman, Commissioner to the Navajo Tribe, for the Fiscal Year Ending June 30, 1924*. Records of the Bureau of Indian Affairs, Superintendent's Annual Statistical and Narrative Reports, Navajo Agency. National Archives.

Haile, Berard
1954   *Property Concepts of the Navaho Indians*. Catholic University of America, Anthropological Series 17. Reprint, 1968.

Hall, Stephen A.
1977   "Late Quarternary Sedimentation and Paleoecologic History of Chaco Canyon, New Mexico." *Geological Society of America Bulletin* 88 (3): 1593–1618.

Hammond, George P., and Agapito Rey, eds. and trans.
1966   *The Rediscovery of New Mexico 1580–1594*. Coronado Historical Series 3. Albuquerque: University of New Mexico Press.

Harper, Allen G.
1952   *Planning in Action on the Navajo-Hopi Reservations*. Report no. 1. Window Rock: United States Department of the Interior.
1953   *Planning in Action on the Navajo-Hopi Reservations*. Report no. 2. Window Rock: United States Department of the Interior.

Haskell, John Loring
1975   "The Navajo in the Eighteenth Century: An Investigation Involving Anthropological Archaeology in the San Juan Basin, Northwestern New Mexico." Ph.D. dissertation, Washington State University.

Haskett, Bert
1936   "History of the Sheep Industry in Arizona." *Arizona Historical Review* 7:3–49.

Hayes, John L.
1882   *The Angora Goat; Its Origin, Culture and Products.* New York: Orange Judd Company.

Hegemann, Elizabeth C.
1963   *Navaho Trading Days.* Albuquerque: University of New Mexico Press.

Henderson, Eric B.
1982   "Kaibeto Plateau Ceremonialists: 1860–1980." In *Navajo Religion and Culture: Selected Views,* edited by David M. Brugge and Charlotte J. Frisbie. Museum of New Mexico Papers in Anthropology no. 17.

Hester, James J.
1962a   *Early Navajo Migrations and Acculturation in the Southwest.* Museum of New Mexico Papers in Anthropology no. 6. Santa Fe: Museum of New Mexico.
1962b   "An Ethnohistoric Reconstruction of Navajo Culture, 1582–1824." *El Palacio* 69 (3): 130–38.

Hill, Edward E., comp.
1981   *Guide to Records in the National Archives of the United States Relating to American Indians.* Washington: Government Printing Office.

Hill, W. W.
1937   "Navajo Pottery Manufacture." *University of New Mexico Bulletin* 2 (3): 5–23.
1938   *The Agricultural and Hunting Methods of the Navaho Indians.* New Haven: Yale University Publications in Anthropology no. 18.
1940a   "Some Navaho Culture Changes During Two Centuries." In *Essays in Historical Anthropology of North America.* Washington: Smithsonian Miscellaneous Collections 100, 395–415.
1940b   "Some Aspects of Navajo Political Structure." *Plateau* 13:23–28.
1940c   "Navajo Salt Gathering." *University of New Mexico Bulletin,* Anthropological Series 3 (4): 5–25.
1948   "Navaho Trading and Trading Ritual." *Southwestern Journal of Anthropology* 4:371–96.

Hodge, William H.
1969   *The Albuquerque Navajos.* Anthropological Papers of the University of Arizona no. 11. Tucson: University of Arizona Press.

Hoffman, Virginia
1974   *Navajo Biographies.* Vol 1. Phoenix: Navajo Curriculum Center Press.

Hollister, U. S.
1972   *The Navajo and his Blanket.* Reprint of the 1903 edition. Glorieta, New Mexico: Rio Grande Press.

Holmes, Jack E.
   1967   *Politics in New Mexico.* Albuquerque: University of New Mexico Press.

Horlacher, L. J., and Carrie Hammonds
   1945   *Sheep.* Danville, Illinois: The Interstate.

Howard, James H.
   1955   "Pan Indian Culture of Oklahoma." *Scientific Monthly* 81:215–20.
   1976   "The Plains Gourd Dance as a Revitalization Movement." *American Ethnologist* 3:243–59.

Hughes, John T.
   1914   *Doniphan's Expedition; Containing an Account of the Conquest of New Mexico.* Reprint of the 1847 edition. 63rd Congress, 2nd sess., Senate Doc. 608. Washington: Government Printing Office.

Indians at Work
   1937   "Coal Stratum Burns at Shiprock, New Mexico." *Indians at Work* 4 (13): 34–37 (Feb. 15, 1937).
   1941a   *Indians at Work* 8 (12) (Aug. 1941).
   1941b   *Indians at Work* 9 (4) (Dec. 1941).

Iverson, Peter
   1981   *The Navajo Nation.* Westport, Connecticut: Greenwood Press.

Jenkins, Myra Ellen, and Ward Allen Minge
   1974   *Navajo Indians.* Vol. 2, *Navajo Activities Affecting the Acoma-Laguna Area, 1746–1910.* New York: Garland Publishing Co.

Jett, Stephen C., and Virgina E. Spencer
   1981   *Navajo Architecture.* Tucson: University of Arizona Press.

Johnson, Broderick H., ed.
   1977   *Navajos and World War II.* Tsaile, Arizona: Navajo Community College Press.

Johnson, Broderick H., and Virginia Hoffman
   1978   *Navajo Biographies.* Vol. 2. Rough Rock, Arizona: Navajo Curriculum Center.

Johnston, Denis Foster
   1966a   "Trends in Navaho Population and Education, 1870–1955." Appendix A in *The Peyote Religion Among the Navaho,* by David F. Aberle. Viking Fund Publications in Anthropology no. 42. New York: Wenner-Gren Foundation for Anthropological Research.
   1966b   *An Analysis of Sources of Information on the Population of the Navaho.* Bureau of American Ethnology, Bulletin 197. Washington: Government Printing Office.

Jones, T. J., Harold B. Allen, Charles T. Loram, and Ella Deloria
1939   *The Navajo Indian Problem.* New York: Phelps-Stokes Fund.

Jorgensen, Joseph G.
1972   *The Sun Dance Religion: Power for the Powerless.* Chicago: University of Chicago Press.

Judd, Neil M.
1968   *Men Met Along the Trail: Adventures in Archaeology.* Norman: University of Oklahoma Press.

Kappler, Charles J., ed.
1904   *Indian Affairs, Laws and Treaties.* Vol. 1 of 5. Washington: Government Printing Office.
1913   *Indian Affairs, Laws and Treaties.* Vol. 3 of 5. Washington: Government Printing Office.

Keleher, William A.
1952   *Turmoil in New Mexico, 1846–1868.* Santa Fe: Rydal Press.

Kelley, Klara B.
1977   "Commercial Networks in the Navajo-Hopi-Zuni Region." Ph.D. dissertation, University of New Mexico.
1980   "Navajo Political Economy before Fort Sumner." In *The Versatility of Kinship,* edited by Linda Cordell and Stephen Beckerman. New York: Academic Press.

Kelly, Lawrence C.
1968   *The Navajo Indians and Federal Indian Policy 1900–1935.* Tucson: University of Arizona Press.
1970   *Navajo Roundup: Selected Correspondence of Kit Carson's Expedition Against the Navajo, 1863–1865.* Boulder: Pruett.

Kent, Kate Peck
1985   *Navajo Weaving: Three Centuries of Change.* Santa Fe: School of American Research Press.

Kimball, Solon T.
1950   "Future Problems in Navajo Administration." *Human Organization* 9 (2): 21–24.

Kimball, Solon T., and John H. Provinse
1942   "Navajo Social Organization in Land Use and Planning." *Human Organization* 1 (4): 18–25.

King, Dale Stuart
1976   *Indian Silverwork of the Southwest.* Vol. 2. Tucson: Dale Stuart King.

Kluckhohn, Clyde
   1962   *Navaho Witchcraft*. Boston: Beacon Press.

Kluckhohn, Clyde, and Dorothea Leighton
   1960   *The Navaho*. Cambridge: Harvard University Press.
   1974   *The Navaho*. Revised edition. Cambridge: Harvard University Press.

Kluckhohn, Clyde, W. W. Hill, and Lucy Wales Kluckhohn
   1971   *Navaho Material Culture*. Cambridge: Harvard University Press.

Kneale, Albert H.
   1950   *Indian Agent*. Caldwell, Idaho: Caxton Printers, Inc.

Krug, Julian
   1948   "Report on the Navaho; Long-Range Program of Navajo Rehabilitation." U.S. Department of the Interior. Mimeo.

Kunitz, Stephen J.
   1976   *The Relationship of Economic Variations to Mortality and Fertility Patterns of the Navajo Reservation*. Lake Powell Research Project Bulletin no. 20. Los Angeles: University of California.
   1977   "Economic Variation on the Navajo Reservation." *Human Organization* 36:186–93.

La Barre, Weston
   1969   *The Peyote Cult*. Enlarged edition. New York: Schocken Books.

Lake Mohonk Conference
   1894–   *Proceedings of the Annual Meetings of the Lake Mohonk Conference of the Friends of*
   1913   *the Indian*. Philadelphia: Indian Rights Association.

Lamphere, Louise
   1977   *To Run after Them: Cultural and Social Bases of Cooperation in a Navajo Community*. Tucson: University of Arizona Press.

Landgraf, John L.
   1954   *Land-use in the Ramah Area of New Mexico*. Peabody Museum of Archaeology and Ethnology Papers 42, no. 1. Cambridge: Harvard University.

Lange, Charles H., and Carroll L. Riley, eds.
   1966   *The Southwestern Journals of Adolph F. Bandelier 1880–1882*. Albuquerque: University of New Mexico Press; Santa Fe: School of American Research, Museum of New Mexico Press.

LaRouche, F. W.
   1943   "War Comes First in Navajo Life." *Indians at Work* 10 (2–6): 17–21 (Winter 1942–1943).

Letherman, Jonathan
   1856   *Sketch of the Navajo Tribe of Indians, Territory of New Mexico.* Tenth Annual
           Report, Smithsonian Institution, 34th Congress, 1st Sess., Senate Misc.
           Doc. 73:283–97. Washington: A. O. P. Nicholson.

Leupp, Francis E.
   1910   *The Indian and his Problem.* New York: Charles Scribner's Sons.

Ligon, J. Stokley
   1927   *Wildlife of New Mexico, its Conservation and Management.* Santa Fe: New
           Mexico State Game Commission.

Link, Martin A.
   1968   *The Second Long Walk.* St. Michaels, Arizona: St. Michaels Press.

Lipps, Oscar H.
   1909   *The Navajos.* Cedar Rapids, Iowa: Torch Press.

Lockett, H. Claiborne
   1952   "Hogans vs. Houses." In *For the Dean: Essays in Anthropology in Honor of
           Byron Cummings.* Tucson: Hohokam Museums Association.

Luomala, Katharine
   1938   *Navaho Life of Yesterday and Today.* Berkeley: United States Department of
           the Interior, National Park Service.

MacDonald, Eleanor D., and John B. Arrington
   1970   *The San Juan Basin: My Kingdom was a Country.* Denver: Green Mountain Press.

Malehorn, Pauline G.
   1948   "The Tender Plant: The History of the Navajo Methodist Mission, Far-
           mington, New Mexico, 1891–1948." Farmington Public Library. Mimeo.

Matthews, Washington
   1883   "Navajo Silversmiths." In *2d Annual Report of the Bureau of American Ethnol-
           ogy for the years 1880–1881.* Washington: Government Printing Office.
   1884   "Navajo Weavers." In *3d Annual Report of the Bureau of American Ethnology
           for the Years 1881–1882.* Washington: Government Printing Office.
   1894   "The Basket Drum." *American Anthropologist* 7:202–8.

Maxwell, Gilbert S.
   1963   *Navajo Rugs—Past, Present & Future.* Palm Desert, California: Desert-
           Southwest, Inc.

McCall, Col. George Archibald
   1968   *New Mexico in 1850: A Military Review.* Edited by Robert W. Frazer. Nor-
           man: University of Oklahoma Press.

McClintock, James H.
1921   *Mormon Settlement in Arizona: A Record of Peaceful Conquest of the Desert.* Phoenix: Manufacturing Stationers, Inc.

McCombe, Leonard, Evon Vogt, and Clyde Kluckhohn
1951   *Navajo Means People.* Cambridge: Harvard University Press.

McIntire, Elliot G.
1967   "Central Place Studies on the Navajo Reservation." *Yearbook of the Association of Pacific Coast Geographers* 29:91–96.

McNitt, Frank
1962   *The Indian Traders.* Norman: University of Oklahoma Press.
1964   *Navajo Expedition: Journal of a Military Reconnaissance from Santa Fe, New Mexico to the Navajo Country Made in 1849 by Lieutenant James H. Simpson.* Norman: University of Oklahoma Press.
1966   *Richard Wetherill: Anasazi.* Revised edition. Albuquerque: University of New Mexico Press.
1972   *Navajo Wars, Military Campaigns, Slave Raids and Reprisals.* Albuquerque: University of New Mexico Press.

Measeles, Evelyn Brach
1981   *Lee's Ferry: A Crossing on the Colorado.* Boulder: Pruett Publishing Co.

Meinig, D. W.
1971   *Southwest: Three Peoples in Geographical Change, 1600–1970.* New York: Oxford University Press.

Mera, Harry P.
1947   *Navaho Textile Arts.* Santa Fe: Laboratory of Anthropology.
1960   *Indian Silverwork of the Southwest.* Globe, Arizona: Dale Stuart King.

Milich, Alicia Ronstadt, trans.
1966   *Relaciones by Zárate Salmerón.* Albuquerque: Horn and Wallace.

Mindeleff, Cosmos
1898   "Navajo Houses." In *17th Annual Report of the Bureau of American Ethnology for the Years 1895–96,* part 2, 475–517. Washington: Government Printing Office.

Mindeleff, Victor
1891   "A Study of Pueblo Architecture, Tusayan and Cibola." In *8th Annual Report of the Bureau of American Ethnology,* 13–228. Washington: Government Printing Office.

Minutes of Navajo Tribal Council
    1940   *Proceedings of the Meeting of the Navajo Tribal Council.* June 3–6, 1940. Window Rock: U.S. Department of the Interior, Navajo Service. Copy in library of School of American Research.
    1941   *Proceedings of the Meeting of the Navajo Tribal Council.* April 8–11, 1941. Window Rock: U.S. Department of the Interior, Navajo Service. Copy in library of School of American Research.

Mizen, Mamie L.
    1966   *Federal Facilities for Indians, 1965–66.* Committee on Appropriations, United States Senate. Washington: Government Printing Office.

Morris, Daisy
    1938   "Navajo Silverware." *The Sunny San Juan Magazine* 1 (1): 29 (July).

Morrisey, Richard J.
    1950   "The Early Range Cattle Industry in Arizona." *Journal of Agricultural History* 24:151–56.

Mosk, Sanford A.
    1944   *Land Tenure Problems in the Santa Fe Railroad Grant Area.* Publications of the Bureau of Business and Economic Research. Berkeley and Los Angeles: University of California.

Muck, Lee
    1948   *Survey of the Range Resources and Livestock Economy of the Navajo Indian Reservation.* Washington: U.S. Department of the Interior, Office of Land Utilization.

Navajo Indian Agency
    1955a   "Notice of Oil and Gas Mining Leases, Allotted Indian Lands, Sept. 27, 1955." Advertisement no. 54. Window Rock: Navajo Agency.
    1955b   "Summary of High Bids Received, Allotted Lands, San Juan County, N.M., Oct. 27, 1955." Advertisement no. 54. Window Rock: Navajo Agency.

Navajo Tribe
    1974   *The Navajo Nation: Overall Economic Development Program.* Window Rock: Office of Program Development.

Newcomb, Franc J.
    1964   *Hosteen Klah: Navaho Medicine Man and Sand Painter.* Norman: University of Oklahoma Press.
    1966   *Navajo Neighbors.* Norman: University of Oklahoma Press.

Opler, Morris E.
    1941   *An Apache Life-Way: The Economic, Social, and Religious Institutions of the Chiricahua Indians.* Chicago: University of Chicago Press.

Ostermann, Leopold
    1917   "Navajo Houses." *Franciscan Missions of the Southwest* 5:20–32

Palmer, Edward
    n.d.   "Notes on the Navajo Indians of New Mexico Made in 1869." Peabody
             Museum Library, Harvard University. Manuscript.

Parezo, Nancy J.
    1982   "Social Interaction and Learning in the Spread of Navajo Commercial
             Sandpaintings." In *Navajo Religion and Culture: Selected Views*, edited by
             David Brugge and Charlotte Frisbie. Museum of New Mexico Papers in
             Anthropology no. 17. Santa Fe: Museum of New Mexico Press.

Parman, Donald L.
    1976   *The Navajos and the New Deal.* New Haven: Yale University Press.

Parsons, Elsie Clews, ed.
    1936   *Hopi Journal of Alexander M. Stephen.* New York: Contributions to Anthro-
             pology, vol. 23, Columbia University.

Paul, Doris
    1973   *The Navajo Codetalkers.* Philadelphia: Dorrance.

Peters, Walter H., and George P. Deyoe
    1946   *Raising Livestock.* New York: McGraw-Hill.

Philp, Kenneth E.
    1977   *John Collier's Crusade for Indian Reform, 1920–24.* Tucson: University of Ari-
             zona Press.

Prewitt, Terry J.
    1981   *Tradition and Change in the Oklahoma Delaware Big House Community: 1867–
             1924.* Tulsa: University of Tulsa Contributions in Archaeology no. 9.

Rapoport, Robert
    1954   *Changing Navaho Religious Values.* Peabody Museum of Archaeology and
             Ethnology Papers 41, no. 2. Cambridge: Harvard University.

RBIC
    1869–   *Annual Report of the Board of Indian Commissioners.* U.S. Department of the
    1932   Interior. Washington: Government Printing Office.

RCIA
    1850–   *Annual Report of the Commissioner of Indian Affairs.* U.S. Department of the
    1931   Interior. Washington: Government Printing Office.

Reagan, Albert B.
   1919   "The Influenza and the Navajo." *Proceedings Indiana Academy of Science*
           29:243–47.

Reed, Erik K.
   1945   "The Dinetxa Tradition and Pre-Spanish Navajo Distribution." *Plateau* 1 (3): 54.

Reeve, Frank D.
   1946   "A Navaho Struggle for Land." *New Mexico Historical Review* 21 (1): 1–21.
   1957   "Seventeenth Century Navaho-Spanish Relations." *New Mexico Historical
           Review* 32 (1): 36–52.
   1958   "Navaho-Spanish Wars: 1680–1720." *New Mexico Historical Review* 33 (3):
           205–31.
   1959   "The Navaho-Spanish Peace: 1720s-1770s." *New Mexico Historical Review*
           34 (1): 9–40.
   1960   "Navaho-Spanish Diplomacy, 1770–1790." *New Mexico Historical Review*
           35 (3): 200–235.
   1971   "Navaho Foreign Affairs, 1795–1846." *New Mexico Historical Review* 46 (2):
           101–32 (part 1, 1795–1815); 46 (3): 323–51 (part 2, 1815–1824).

Reichard, Gladys A.
   1969   *Social Life of the Navajo Indians.* Reprint of 1928 edition. New York: AMS
           Press, Inc.
   1973   *Navajo Shepherd and Weaver.* Reprint of 1936 edition. Glorieta, New Mex-
           ico: Rio Grande Press.

Reno, Philip
   1981   *Mother Earth, Father Sky, and Economic Development: Navajo Resources and Their
           Use.* Albuquerque: University of New Mexico Press.

RGNM
   1903–08 *Report of the Governor of New Mexico.* U.S. Department of the Interior.
           Washington: Government Printing Office.

Ricketts, Orval, and John McPhee
   1941   *The Navajo Indians in a Changing World.* Window Rock: Navajo Service,
           U.S. Department of the Interior.

Rittenhouse, Jack D.
   1965   *Cabezon, A New Mexico Ghost Town.* Santa Fe: The Stagecoach Press.

Roessel, Robert A., Jr.
   1951   "Sheep in Navaho Culture." M.A. thesis, Washington University.
   1979   *Navajo Education 1948–1978, Its Progress and Its Problems.* Rough Rock, Ari-
           zona: Navajo Curriculum Center.
   1980   *Pictorial History of the Navajo from 1860 to 1910.* Rough Rock, Arizona:
           Navajo Curriculum Center.

Roessel, Ruth
    1983   "Navajo Arts and Crafts." In *Handbook of North American Indians*. Vol. 10, *Southwest*. Washington: Smithsonian Institution.

Roessel, Ruth, and Broderick H. Johnson, comps.
    1974   *Navajo Livestock Reduction: A National Disgrace*. Tsaile, Arizona: Navajo Community College Press.

Russell, T. Paul
    1964   *Antelope of New Mexico*. Santa Fe: New Mexico Department of Game and Fish, Bulletin 12.

Sahlins, Marshall
    1981   *Historical Metaphors and Mythical Realities Structure in the Early History of the Sandwich Islands Kingdom*. Association for Social Anthropology in Oceania, Special Publication no. 1. Ann Arbor: University of Michigan Press.

Sanchez, George I.
    1948   *"The People": A Study of the Navajos*. Lawrence, Kansas: U.S. Indian Service.

Sapir, Edward, and Harry Hoijer
    1942   *Navaho Texts*. William Dwight Whitney Linguistic Series. Iowa City: Linguistic Society of America.

Sasaki, Tom
    1960   *Fruitland, New Mexico: A Navaho Community in Transition*. Ithaca: Cornell University Press.

Schmedding, Joseph
    1974   *Cowboy and Indian Trader*. Reprint of 1951 edition. Albuquerque: University of New Mexico Press.

Schroeder, Albert H.
    1965   "A Brief History of the Southern Utes." *Southwestern Lore* 30 (4): 53–78.

Shepardson, Mary
    1963   *Navajo Ways in Government: A Study in Political Process*. American Anthropological Association Memoir 96. Menasha, Wisconsin: American Anthropological Association.

Shepardson, Mary, and Blodwen Hammond
    1970   *The Navajo Mountain Community: Social Organization and Kinship Terminology*. Berkeley: University of California Press.

Shufeldt, R. W.
    1892   "The Evolution of House-Building among the Navajo Indians." *Proceedings of the United States National Museum* 15:279–82.

Shweder, Richard A.
1982   "On Savages and Other Children." *American Anthropologist* 84:354–66.

Simmons, Marc, and Frank Turley
1980   *Southwestern Colonial Ironwork: The Spanish Blacksmithing Tradition from Texas to California.* Santa Fe: Museum of New Mexico Press.

Smith, Anne M.
1966   *New Mexico Indians: Economic, Educational and Social Problems.* Santa Fe: Museum of New Mexico Research Record no. 1.

Spicer, Edward H.
1954   "Spanish-Indian Acculturation in the Southwest." *American Anthropologist* 56:663–78.

Spicer, Edward H., with comments by John Collier
1965   "Sheepmen and Technicians: A Program for Soil Conservation on the Navajo Indian Reservation." In *Human Problems in Technological Change,* edited by Edward H. Spicer. New York: John Wiley & Sons Science Editions.

Stacher, Samuel F.
c. 1940   "Crown Point and Eastern Navajo." Van Valkenburgh Collection, Arizona Historical Society, Tucson. Manuscript.

Steggerda, Morris, and Ruth B. Eckardt
1941   "Navajo Foods and their Preparation." *Journal of the American Dietetic Association* 17:217–25.

Stephen, Alexander M.
1893   "The Navajo." *American Anthropologist* (old series) 6:345–62.

Stewart, Omer C.
1938   "Navaho Basketry as Made by Ute and Paiute." *American Anthropologist* 40:758–59.

Strickland, Rennard, ed.
1982   *Felix S. Cohen's Handbook of Federal Indian Law.* Charlottesville, Virginia: Michie Bobbs-Merrill.

Swanton, J. R.
1911   *Indian Tribes of the Lower Mississippi Valley and Adjacent Coast of the Gulf of Mexico.* Bureau of American Ethnology Bulletin 43. Washington: Government Printing Office.

Taylor, Theodore W.
1972   *The States and Their Indian Citizens.* Washington: Government Printing Office.

Thomas, Alfred Barnaby
1932   *Forgotten Frontiers: A Study of the Spanish Indian Policy of Don Juan Bautista de Anza, Governor of New Mexico 1777–1787.* Norman: University of Oklahoma Press.

Thomas, Robert K.
1961   "The Redbird Smith Movement." In *Symposium on Cherokee and Iroquois Culture,* edited by William Fenton and John Gulick. Bureau of American Ethnology, Bulletin no. 180. Washington: Government Printing Office.

Thompson, Gerald E.
1976   *The Army and the Navajo: The Bosque Redondo Reservation Experiment, 1863–68.* Tucson: University of Arizona Press.

Topper, Martin D.
1972   "The Daily Life of a Traditional Navajo Household: An Ethnographic Study in Human Daily Activities." Ph.D. dissertation, Northwestern University.

Trafzer, Clifford E.
1982   *The Kit Carson Campaign: The Last Great Navajo War.* Norman: University of Oklahoma Press.

Tremblay, Marc-Adélard, John Collier, Jr., and Tom T. Sasaki
1954   "Navaho Housing In Transition." *América Indígena* 14 (3): 187–219.

Trockur, Fr. Emmanuel
1973   "A Brief History of St. Michaels Mission." *Padres Trail* no. 2 (Oct.-Nov. 1973).

Tschopik, Harry, Jr.
1938   "Taboo as a Possible Factor Involved in the Obsolescence of Navaho Pottery and Basketry." *American Anthropologist* 40 (2): 257–62.
1940   "Navaho Basketry: A Study of Culture Change." *American Anthropologist* 42 (3): 444–62.

Uchendu, Victor
1966   "Seasonal Agricultural Labor among the Navaho Indians: A Study in Socio-Economic Transition." Ph.D. dissertation, Northwestern University.

Underhill, Ruth
1953   *Here Come the Navaho!* Lawrence: United States Indian Service, Indian Life and Customs no. 8.
1956   *The Navajos.* Norman: University of Oklahoma Press.

U.S. Bureau of the Census

1894   *Report on Indians Taxed and Indians not Taxed in the United States (excepting Alaska) at the Eleventh Census: 1890. Navajo Reservation.* Washington: Government Printing Office.

1975   *Historical Statistics of the United States. Colonial Times to 1970.* Washington: Government Printing Office.

U.S. Bureau of Indian Affairs

1941   "1940 Statistical Summary: Human Dependency Survey, Navajo Reservation and Grazing District 7." Window Rock. Mimeo.

1949   *You Asked about the Navajo!* Lawrence: Haskell Institute.

1969   *Fiscal Year 1969 Statistics Concerning Indian Education.* Lawrence: Haskell Institute.

U.S. Commission on Civil Rights

1973   "Demographic and Socio-economic Characteristics of the Navajo." Staff report by the Office of General Counsel. Mimeo.

1975a   *The Farmington Report: A Conflict of Cultures.* New Mexico Advisory Committee. Washington: U.S. Commission on Civil Rights.

1975b   *The Navajo Nation: An American Colony.* A Report of the United States Commission on Civil Rights. Washington: The Commission.

U.S. Congress

1854   *Reports of Explorations and Surveys, to Ascertain the Most Practicable and Economical Route for a Railroad from the Mississippi River to the Pacific Ocean.* Vol. 3, pt. 1, "Route Near the 35th Parallel, under the Command of Liet. A. W. Whipple in 1853 and 1854." 33rd Congress, 2nd Sess., H.E.D. 91. Washington: Government Printing Office.

1867   *Condition of the Indian Tribes.* Report of the Joint Special Committee appointed under joint resolution of March 3, 1865. Washington: Government Printing Office.

1886   *Navajo Indian Reservation.* 49th Cong. 1st Sess. House Exec. Doc. 263. Washington: Government Printing Office.

1891   *A Recommendation of the Commissioner of Indian Affairs for an Appropriation to Aid Negotiations with the Navajo Indians.* 51st Cong. 2nd Sess. Senate Exec. Doc. 52. Washington: Government Printing Office.

1893   *Certain Reports upon the Condition of the Navajo Indian Country.* 52nd Cong. 2nd Sess. Senate Exec. Doc. 68. Washington: Government Printing Office.

1907   *Report on Employment of United States Soldiers in Arresting By-a-lil-le and Other Navajo Indians.* 60th Cong. 1st Sess. Senate Exec. Doc. 517. Washington: Government Printing Office.

1912   *Bridges Across San Juan River.* 62nd Cong. 3rd Sess. Senate Exec. Doc. 1015. Washington: Government Printing Office.

1932   *Survey of Conditions of the Indians in the United States.* Part 18, "Navajos in Arizona and New Mexico," and Part 22, "Grazing on Indian Lands." Hearings before a subcommittee of the Senate Committee on Indian

Affairs, 71st Cong. 1st Sess. Washington: Government Printing Office.

1937   *Survey of Conditions of the Indians in the United States.* Part 34, "Navajo Boundary and Pueblos in New Mexico." Hearings before a subcommittee of the Committee on Indian Affairs of the United States Senate, 75th Cong. 1st Sess. Washington: Government Printing Office.

U.S. Department of Agriculture
1937   *Livestock on Farms. Jan. 1, 1937, by States.* Bureau of Agricultural Economics. Washington: Government Printing Office.

U.S. Department of the Interior
1948   "Report on the Navajo Long-Range Program of Navajo Rehabilitation." Department of the Interior. Mimeo.

U.S. Soil Conservation Service
1938   "Statistical Summary Human Dependency Survey Navajo and Hopi Reservations." Section of Conservation Economics. Navajo District Region 8. Mimeo.

Van Valkenburgh, Richard F.
1936   "Navajo Common Law I, Notes on Political Organization, Property and Inheritance." *Museum Notes* (Museum of Northern Arizona) 9 (4): 17–22.
1937   "Historical Notes on Agriculture & Irrigation." Van Valkenburgh Collection (box 5, S-2, f. 117), Arizona Historical Society, Tucson. Manuscript.
1938   "A Short History of the Navajo People." U.S. Department of the Interior, Navajo Service, Window Rock. KTGM radio series. Mimeo.
1945   "The Government of the Navajos." *Arizona Quarterly* 1 (4): 63–73.
n.d.   "Reference Manual for Guide Book to the Navajo Country." Edited and revised by Gerhardt Laves. Laboratory of Anthropology, Santa Fe. Manuscript.

Verplanck, James D.
1934   *A Country of Shepherds.* Boston: Ruth Hill.

Vestal, Paul A.
1952   *Ethnobotany of the Ramah Navajo.* Peabody Museum of American Archaeology and Ethnology Papers 40, no. 4. Cambridge: Harvard University.

Voget, Fred W.
1984   *The Shoshoni-Crow Sun Dance.* Norman: University of Oklahoma Press.

Vogt, Evon Z.
1949   "Between Two Worlds: Case Study of a Navajo Veteran." *The American Indian* 5 (1): 13–21.
1951   *Navaho Veterans: A Study of Changing Values.* Peabody Museum of Archaeology and Ethnology Papers 41, no. 1. Cambridge: Harvard University.

1961   "Navaho." In *Perspectives in American Indian Culture Change*, edited by Edward H. Spicer. Chicago: University of Chicago Press.

Vogt, Evon Z., and Ethel M. Albert, eds.
1970   *People of Rimrock: A Study of Values in Five Cultures*. New York: Atheneum.

Wallace, Anthony F. C.
1972   *The Death and Rebirth of the Seneca*. Originally published 1969. New York: Vintage Books.

Ward, Elizabeth
1951   *No Dudes, Few Women: Life with a Navajo Range Rider*. Albuquerque: University of New Mexico Press.

Warner, Michael J.
1970   "Protestant Missionary Activity among the Navajo, 1890–1912." *New Mexico Historical Review* 45:209–32.

Webb, Walter Prescott
1931   *The Great Plains*. Boston: Ginn and Company.

Wentworth, Edward Norris
1948   *America's Sheep Trails*. Ames: Iowa State College Press.

Wheat, Joe Ben
1977   "Documentary Basis for Material Changes and Design Styles in Navajo Blanket Weaving." In *Proceedings for 1976*, Irene Emery Roundtable on Museum Textiles. Washington: Textile Museum.
1979   "Rio Grande, Pueblo, and Navajo Weavers: Cross Cultural Influence." In *Spanish Textiles of New Mexico and Colorado*. Santa Fe: Museum of New Mexico Press.

White, Eugene E.
1965   *Experiences of a Special Indian Agent*. Norman: University of Oklahoma Press.

White, Richard
1983   *The Roots of Dependency Subsistence, Environment, and Social Change among the Choctaws, Pawnees, and Navajos*. Lincoln: University of Nebraska Press.

Wilcox, David R.
1981   "The Entry of Athapaskans into the American Southwest: The Problem Today." In *The Protohistoric Period in the North American Southwest, A.D. 1450–1750*. Tempe: Arizona State University Anthropological Research Papers no. 24.

Williams, Aubrey W.
1970   *Navajo Political Process*. Smithsonian Contributions to Anthropology, vol. 9. Washington: Smithsonian Institution Press.

Williams, Jerry L., and Paul E. McAllister, eds.
1981   *New Mexico in Maps*. Albuquerque: University of New Mexico Press.

Wilson, John P.
1967   *Military Campaigns in the Navajo Country, Northwestern New Mexico, 1800-1846*. Museum of New Mexico Research Records no. 5. Santa Fe: Museum of New Mexico Press.

Wistisen, Martin J., Robert J. Parsons, and Annette Larson
1975   *A Study to Identify Potentially Feasible Small Businesses for the Navajo Nation. Phase I: An Evaluation of Income and Expenditure Patterns*. Vol. 2. Provo: Brigham Young University Center for Business and Economic Research.

Wood, John J.
1982   "Western Navajo Religious Affiliations." In *Navajo Religion and Culture: Selected Views*, edited by David M. Brugge and Charlotte J. Frisbie. Museum of New Mexico Papers in Anthropology no. 17.

Woodward, Arthur
1971   *Navajo Silver: A Brief History of Navajo Silversmithing*. Flagstaff: Northland Press.

Wooton, E. O.
1908   *The Range Problem in New Mexico*. New Mexico College of Agriculture and Mechanical Arts, Bulletin no. 66. Albuquerque: Albuquerque Morning Journal.

Worcester, Donald E.
1947   "Early History of the Navaho Indians." Ph.D. dissertation, University of California, Berkeley.

Wyman, Leland C.
1983   "Navajo Ceremonial System." In *Handbook of North American Indians*. Vol 10, *Southwest*. Washington: Smithsonian Institution.

Young, Robert W.
1954   *The Navajo Yearbook of Planning in Action* (comp.). Report no. 4. Window Rock: Navajo Agency.
1955   *The Navajo Yearbook of Planning in Action* (comp.). Report no. 5. Window Rock: Navajo Agency.

1957   *The Navajo Yearbook* (comp. and ed.). Report no. 6. Window Rock: Navajo Agency.

1958   *The Navajo Yearbook* (comp. and ed.). Report no. 7. Window Rock: Navajo Agency.

1961   *The Navajo Yearbook 1951–1961, A Decade of Progress* (comp. and ed.). Report no. 8. Window Rock: Navajo Agency.

1968   *The Role of the Navajo in the Southwestern Drama.* Gallup: Gallup Independent.

1978   *A Political History of the Navajo Tribe.* Tsaile, Arizona: Navajo Community College Press.

Young, Robert W., and William Morgan
1952   *The Trouble at Round Rock.* Phoenix: Navajo Historical Series no. 2.

Youngblood, B.
1935   "Navajo Trading." A Report to the Office of Experiment Stations, U.S. Department of Agriculture. Mimeo.

Military expeditions, 15, 17; Navajo War of 1863, 9–10, 21; for murder at Fort Defiance, 18
Mineral resources, 232, 235–37: income from, 237, 261–62
Mining, coal, 161, 235–37
Missionary activity, 62, 66–67, 99, 171–72, 232, 277; of Mormons, 66–67, 278–80; of Navajos, 172
Morgan, J. C., 224–26
Mormons: alleged role in Meeker Massacre, 81; missionary work of, 66–67, 75, 278; relationship with Indians, 74–75; as settlers in Navajo country, 77, 100; trade with, 57, 62

Naat'anii system, 29–36, 98–99
Nabajú, 12
Native American Church, 226–27, 229, 242, 277–79
Natural gas, 120, 235–36
Navajo Agency, 31–36; attempts to increase reservation productivity, 90–94; centralized, 196; inability to "civilize" Navajos, 99–100; land removed from jurisdiction of, 107; paranoia of Anglos at, 81
Navajo Cavalry, 31
Navajo Division of Education, 243
Navajo Extension, 107
Navajo Forest Products Industries, 243
Navajo Health Authority, 243
Navajo-Hopi Long Range Rehabilitation Act, 232–35, 248, 256, 260, 273
Navajo Housing Authority, 243, 283
Navajo Progressive League, 225
Navajo Rights Association, 226
Navajos: administration of, 28–36; agencies, 241; Anglo plans for rehabilitation, 232; attitudes toward Anglos, 80–82, 106, 115, 181, 221, 230; "civilization" of, 62–73; clergy, 278–79; courts, 242; distrust of military service, 222; as entrepreneurs, 161–63; as heterogeneous population, 165–80; institutions of,

293; as missionaries, 172; origin of the name, 12; population growth, 19–20, 28, 73; relocation under Rehabilitation Act, 233–34; social identity, 233, 287, 289–97; as U.S. citizens, 198; U.S. control over, 107–11; villages of, 15
Navajo Times, 243
Navajo Tribal Council, 111, 225, 237, 239–44; allocation of revenues, 240; after depression, 196–97; and livestock reduction, 186–87; against peyote, 226, 242, 278; political offices, 243–44
Navajo Tribal Utility Authority, 243
Navajo War of 1863, 9–10, 21, 74, 76
New Deal, 184–93
New Mexico, 18, 73, 116
Newspaper, tribal, 243
Nomadic lifestyle, 64, 173

Office of Navajo Economic Opportunity, 243–44
Oil, 111–12, 116, 120–23, 235–36
Outfit system, 99

Panic of 1893, 100–104, 105, 163
Paternalism, 181
Pawn system, 54
Peyote, 226–27, 242, 277–79
Police, Navajo: inadequate funding of, 35; jurisdictions of, 242; Navajo Cavalry, 31; range riders, 190; voluntary, 31
Political movements, 221–30
Political systems: centralized, 33, 196; chiefs' council, 29–30, 34–36; community chapters, 111, 237, 239, 240; growth after 1950, 239–44; *naat'anii*, 29–36, 98–99; Navajo autonomy, 244; Navajo Progressive League, 225; Navajo Rights Association, 226; Navajo Tribal Council, 111, 239–44; Navajo vs. Anglo, 29–30, 222; outfit system, 99; tribal self-government, 196; U.S. system, 30–31. *See also* Navajo Tribal Council
Population of Navajos: contributing to

economic depression, 105; after depression, 184; growth through 1850, 19–20; growth through 1890, 28, 73; growth through 1900, 104, 112; by late 1940s, 231; living off reservation, 89–90

Pottery, 15, 51, 54; decline of, 55, 97–98, 176; extinction due to mobility, 21; Puebloan influence, 15; for religious purposes, 177; revival of, 252

Public domain land: allotment applications, 122–24; Anglo opposition to Navajo allotments, 116–17, 122; competition for, 112, 114, 185, 193–96; given to Navajos, 107; for grazing, 77, 78, 84; Navajo economy, importance to, 88–94; Navajo right to settle on, 90, 113, 193; returning reservation land to, 89, 123; Taylor Grazing Act, 193–96; wells found on, 112

Public work projects, 192–93, 217, 218

Pueblo revolt, 13

Pueblo technology, 14–16

Querechos, 11–12

Raiding: chiefs' control over, 30; decline of, 31, 40; after establishment of Fort Defiance, 18; as means of expanding herds, 38–39, 41; of and by other Indians, 15–17, 39; after release from Bosque Redondo, 30, 38; return of goods from, 30–31; of Spanish herds, 17–18, 21, 39; of Spanish settlements, 13, 15, 16–18, 39; after Treaty of Ojo del Oso, 18; U.S. attitude towards, 39

Railroads, Navajos employed by, 253–55

Ranching, 73; Anglo, in San Juan Valley, 76; cattle, 83–85; collapse of, 100–104; commercial, 105, 124; Hispanic encroachment, 76; increase after statehood, 116; migration to Arizona, 78; range utilization, 84; sheep holdings in Arizona, 86; struggle for grazing lands, 77

Rangelands. See Grazing lands and Public domain lands

Rations. See Annuity goods

Rehabilitation Act, 232–35

Religion: Catholicism, 13, 279; changes in, 226–27, 228, 277–80; conversion to Christianity, 62, 66–67, 278; Indian, 63; Mormonism, 66–67, 278–80; Navajo clergy, 278–79; traditional, 280

Relocation of Navajos, 10

Reservation: agency attempts to increase productivity of, 90–94; boundaries of, 26, 113–15; checkerboard area, 116; Dawes Act, 106; establishment of, 10, 25–26; land use, 282–83; petitions for enlargement of, 78–80, 89, 113, 115, 187, 193, 195; private industry on, 258–59; purchase of private land for, 123; wage labor on, 256–60

Rio Grande settlements, 73

Roads, 165–66, 232, 264–68

Roosevelt, Franklin Delano, 184

Round Rock Trading Post, 162

Rugs, 150–54, 164, 179–80; income from, 202–3, 250–52

Sand paintings, 253

San Juan Valley: Navajo-Anglo contact in, 75; resettlement in 45, 77; trading posts in, 62

Santa Fe Railroad, 156

Scabies, 115

Schools. See Education

Seeds, distribution of, 45, 142

Settlement patterns, 15; changes in, 282–86; seasonal camps, 21

Sheep: Anglo, on Navajo rangelands, 112; vs. cattle on range, 93–94; changes in herding and breeding techniques, 127–31; commercial ranching, 137, 201–2; depression, effects of, 182–83; economic importance of, 37, 163; government programs to improve quality of, 90, 92–93, 129–31, 137; herding, 14, 16; herd size by 1860, 19, 21; holdings of, 37–38, 41–42, 44, 78, 85–87, 124–26, 163, 245, 299–303; marketing of, 77–78; market value of, 306–8; pelts, trading in, 60; post-depression holdings, 186, 190, 192, 201; ranching, 73; result on from drought of 1893, 101;

scabies, 115; switch from, to cattle, 83, 248; subsistence ratios of, 20, 94–95, 104, 163, 203

Sherman, General William, 10, 25–26

Shoes, 72, 178

Silversmithing, 51, 53–54, 98; commercialization of, 154–55; income from, 252; trade, 57

Social identity of Navajos, 233, 287, 289–97

Soil Conservation Service, 192

Spanish reconquest, 14–15

Spanish settlements: establishment of, 13; Pueblo revolt against, 13; raiding of, 13, 15–18

Spanish technology, 14

Stock Raising Homestead Act, 122

Stoves, 175

Sumner, Colonel Edwin, 18

Tappan, Samuel, 10

Taylor Grazing Act, 193–96

Teachers, 64

Tents, 174–76

Tools: distribution of, 46; for farming, 141–42; for silversmithing, 53

Trade, 50–51, 95–97; for cloth, 70; customs, 57, 148–50; dangers of, 40; annuity goods used for, 46; for farm produce, 144; in horses, 44; intertribal, 147–48; isolated from Rio Grande settlements, 73; for leather, 48; as means to expand herds, 40; Navajo entrepreneurs, 161, 162–63; in Navajo textiles, 51; networks, 56–62, 73–74, 95–96, 100, 147; railroad effect of, 83; in wool, 56, 59–60

Trading posts, 56, 58–62, 144, 147–50; clothing at, 177–78; credit at, 218; decline after 1960, 268–71; harmful effects of, 78; sales at, 218; stock at, 178

Transportation: bridges, 166, 167; effect on Navajos, 73, 232; motor vehicles, 165, 167, 232; railroad, effect of on trade, 78, 82, 83; road conditions and development, 165–66, 232; wagons, demand for, 166–67

Treaty: creating a reservation, 25–28; to relinquish San Juan area, 31

Treaty of 1868, 10, 29, 79; distributions of, 34, 40, 45, 46, 49–50

Treaty of Ojo del Oso, 18

Tribal council. *See* Navajo Tribal Council

Tribal government: absence of, 109; after depression, 185; establishment of, 11

Trucks, 167–68, 232, 266, 268

Truman, Harry S., 220

Typhoid, 223–24

United States government: assimilation, policy of, 106–11; decreased programs, 197, 200, 218; federal management of tribes, end of, 239; Indian Service, 108–9; Navajo dependence on, 184, 228; Navajo-Hopi Rehabilitation Act, 232–35; public projects, 192, 217; reservation land use defined by, 282–83; relief funds from, 220

Uranium, 236, 237

Urban areas, relocation to, 285–86

Utes, 75, 81; government policy toward, 80; peyote, 226

Vanadium, 236, 237

Villages, 15; permanent, 173; seasonal, 21, 174

Wage labor, 155–60, 163, 179–80, 217, 218, 222; agricultural, 255–56; availability during 1960s, 285; during depression, 183–84; public work projects, 192–93; railroad, 253–55; on-reservation, 256–60; after World War II, 199–201, 203, 230

Wagons, demand for, 166–67; shift to motor vehicles, 266, 268

Wars: during Mexican rule, 18; Navajo War of 1863, 9–10, 21, 74, 76; range, 93–94